Real Work for Real Pay

Real Work for Real Pay

INCLUSIVE EMPLOYMENT FOR PEOPLE WITH DISABILITIES

by

Paul Wehman, Ph.D.
Katherine J. Inge, Ph.D., OTR
W. Grant Revell, Jr., M.S., M.Ed.
and
Valerie A. Brooke, M.Ed.

with invited contributors

PAUL H.
BROOKES
PUBLISHING CO.®

Baltimore • London • Sydney

·P·A·U·L·H·
BROOKES
PUBLISHING C°®

Paul H. Brookes Publishing Co.
Post Office Box 10624
Baltimore, Maryland 21285-0624

www.brookespublishing.com

Typeset by Barton Matheson Willse & Worthington, Baltimore, Maryland.
Manufactured in the United States of America by
Victor Graphics, Inc., Baltimore, Maryland.

Library of Congress Cataloging-in-Publication Data

Real work for real pay : inclusive employment for people with disabilities / by
    Paul Wehman . . . [et al.].
        p.   cm.
    Includes index.
    ISBN-13: 978-1-55766-753-3 (pbk.)
    ISBN-10: 1-55766-753-5 (pbk.)
    1. People with disabilities—Employment.   I. Wehman, Paul.   II. Title.
    HD7255.R415 2007
    331.5'95—dc22
                                                                2006026478

British Library Cataloguing in Publication data are available from the British Library.

Contents

About the Authors

Paul Wehman, Ph.D., Professor, Department of Physical Medicine and Rehabilitation; Chairman, Division of Rehabilitation Research; Director, Virginia Commonwealth University Rehabilitation Research and Training Center (VCU-RRTC) on Workplace Supports and Job Retention; Virginia Commonwealth University, 1314 West Main Street, Post Office Box 842011, Richmond, Virginia 23284

Dr. Wehman is Professor of Physical Rehabilitation, with joint appointments in the Department of Special Education and Disability Policy and the Department of Rehabilitation Counseling at VCU. He pioneered the development of supported employment at VCU in the early 1980s and has been heavily involved in the use of supported employment with people who have severe disabilities, such as those with severe mental retardation, brain injury, spinal cord injury, or autism spectrum disorders. Dr. Wehman has written extensively on issues related to transition from school to adulthood and special education as it relates to young adulthood. He has published more than 180 articles and 30 book chapters, and he has authored or edited 33 books. He is a recipient of the Joseph P. Kennedy, Jr. Foundation International Award in Mental Retardation; was a Mary Switzer Fellow for the National Rehabilitation Association in 1985; and received the Distinguished Service Award from the President's Committee on Employment of People with Disabilities in October 1992. Dr. Wehman was recognized as one of the 50 most influential special educators of the millennium by a national survey coordinated by the *Remedial and Special Education* journal (December 2000), and he received the VCU Distinguished Service Award, 2001 (September 6, 2001). He is also Editor-in-Chief of the *Journal of Vocational Rehabilitation*.

Katherine J. Inge, Ph.D., OTR, Director of Instructional Technology, Virginia Commonwealth University Rehabilitation Research and Training Center (VCU-RRTC) on Workplace Supports and Job Retention, 1314 West Main Street, Post Office Box 842011, Richmond, Virginia 23284

Dr. Inge is Assistant Professor at VCU and has been associated with the university for 24 years. She is currently the Director of the Training and Technical Assistance for Providers, a project funded by the U.S. Department of Labor, Office of Disability Employment Policy, that is charged with providing technical assistance and information to improve the employment outcomes of individuals with significant disabilities and to reduce the use of subminimum wage certificates. Dr. Inge has directed a number of federally funded employment projects for individuals with significant intellectual and physical disabilities. She has co-edited two books and written numerous book chapters, newsletters, and other resource materials for facilitating the competitive employment outcomes of citizens with significant disabilities.

W. Grant Revell, Jr., M.S., M.Ed., Research Associate, Virginia Commonwealth University Rehabilitation Research and Training Center on Workplace Supports and Job Retention, 1314 West Main Street, Post Office Box 842011, Richmond, Virginia 23284

Mr. Revell conducts research in the areas of state systems change and funding of competitive enrollment outcomes. He is Training Manager for the Training and Technical Assistance for Providers, a project funded by the U.S. Department of Labor, Office of Disability Employment Policy, that is charged with providing technical assistance and information to improve the employment outcomes of individuals with significant disabilities and to reduce the use of subminimum wage certificates. He has worked for more than 30 years in the area of building competitive employment opportunities for individuals with disabilities.

Valerie A. Brooke, M.Ed., Director of Training, Virginia Commonwealth University Rehabilitation Research and Training Center (VCU-RRTC) on Workplace Supports and Job Retention, 1314 West Main Street, Post Office Box 842011, Richmond, Virginia 23284

Ms. Brooke is a faculty member at VCU and has been working in the field of employment for people with disabilities since 1979. She is Project Director for the Social Security Administration's Regional Benefits Planning, Assistance, and Outreach Technical Assistance Center. Ms. Brooke is nationally recognized for her personnel training programs and technical assistance work at the local, state, and federal levels. She has authored numerous book chapters, journal articles, newsletters, and fact sheets on transition and employment for people with disabilities. Her areas of interest include creating business partnerships, systems change, and self-advocacy leadership.

CONTRIBUTORS

Amy J. Armstrong, Ph.D., M.A., Assistant Professor, Virginia Commonwealth University (VCU), Department of Rehabilitation Counseling, Post Office Box 980330, Richmond, Virginia 23298. Dr. Armstrong has been involved in advocacy, education, and employment issues related to individuals with disabilities for 23 years. She has experience providing national personnel training on disability-related issues, employment of marginalized populations, and distance education. Dr. Armstrong has held a variety of community agency positions, including both direct service and management at the local, regional, and national levels. She has worked at the United Cerebral Palsy Association and the VCU Rehabilitation Research and Training Center on Supported Employment and Workplace Supports. Her interests include the employment of individuals with significant disabilities, advocacy, welfare and poverty issues, disability policy and systems issues, building community liaisons, and distance education.

Nancy Brooks-Lane, M.S., Director, Developmental Services and Supports, Cobb and Douglas Counties Community Services Boards, 2051 Greenridge Street, Smyrna, Georgia 30080. Ms. Brooks-Lane has spent the last 5 years developing expertise in the area of self-employment with the guidance of Cary Griffin. She has helped individuals with significant disabilities start their own businesses through work on U.S. Department of Labor Customized Employment and WorkFORCE Action Grants. Ms. Brooks-Lane is affiliated with Training and Technical Assistance for Providers through Virginia Commonwealth University and the Institute for Community Inclusion at the University of Massachusetts Boston, providing her the opportunity to train other providers in the processes of self-employment for individuals with disabilities. She serves on the editorial board for the *Journal of Vocational Rehabilitation* and is an associate of Griffin-Hammis Associates, LLC. Ms. Brooks-Lane has presented extensively throughout the country on conversion; system change; and customized employment, including self-employment, resource ownership, and business within a business.

Doug Crandell, Director of Supported Employment, Cobb and Douglas Counties Community Services Boards, 2051 Greenridge Street, Smyrna, Georgia 30080. Mr. Crandell directs Project Exceed, a customized employment grant funded by the U.S. Department of Labor, Office of Disability Employment Policy. He has worked extensively with the Georgia Department of Rehabilitation on developing new strategies to improve customized employment services for people with disabilities.

Carolyn W. Green, Ed.D., School Administrator, J. Iverson Riddle Developmental Center, 300 Enola Road, Morganton, North Carolina 28685. Dr. Green has 25 years of experience in educational settings for children and adults with severe disabilities. Her work tasks have included teacher, manager, staff trainer, and researcher.

J. Howard Green, M.S., Instructor and Business Liaison, Virginia Commonwealth University Rehabilitation Research and Training Center on Workplace Supports and Job Retention, 1314 West Main Street, Post Office Box 842011, Richmond, Virginia 23284. Mr. Green has more than 30 years of experience in the rehabilitation field and tremendous experience in working with business on national, state, and local levels. Over the past several years, Mr. Green has co-authored and contributed to several articles and book chapters relating to the employment of people with disabilities.

Cary Griffin, M.A., Senior Partner, Griffin-Hammis Associates, LLC, 5582 Klements Lane, Florence, Montana 59833. Mr. Griffin is Senior Partner at Griffin-Hammis Associates, LLC, a full-service consultancy specializing in building communities of economic cooperation, creating high performance organizations, and focusing on disability and employment. He maintains a strong relationship with the Rural Institute at the University of Montana, where he served as Director of the Region VII Community Rehabilitation Providers Rehabilitation Continuing Education Program at the Center for Technical Assistance and Training, which he founded at the University of Northern Colorado in 1989. Mr. Griffin provides training to administrative and direct-service–level professionals in the rehabilitation field; consultation to businesses and rehabilitation agencies regarding the employment of individuals with significant disabilities; field-initiated research and demonstration; family and consumer case consultation; resource development; and organizational development.

David G. Hammis, Senior Partner, Griffin-Hammis Associates, LLC, 317 Franklin Street, Middletown, Ohio 45042. Mr. Hammis is Senior Partner at Griffin-Hammis Associates, LLC, a full-service consultancy specializing in building communities of economic cooperation, creating high performance organizations, and focusing on disability and employment. He maintains an ongoing relationship with the Rural Institute at the University of Montana, where he served as Project Director for multiple self-employment, employment, and Social Security outreach training and technical assistance projects, including the Rural Institute's Rural Entrepreneurship and Self-Employment Expansion Design Project. Mr. Hammis works with organizations nationally and internationally on self-employment, benefits analysis, supported employment, and employment engineering.

Suzanne Hutcheson, President and Chief Executive Officer, HPS, Helping People Succeed, Inc., 1650 S. Kanner Highway, Stuart, Florida 34990. Ms. Hutcheson has been President and Chief Executive Officer of HPS, Helping People Succeed, Inc. (formerly Tri-County TEC), since August 1977. She led the association through major organizational change from a sheltered workshop/work activity center to a totally community-based organization specializing in employment options. HPS has assisted more than 1,000 individuals with disabilities to obtain and maintain competitive integrated employment. Ms. Hutcheson believes that all people who have a disability should have the opportunity and right to be participating members of their community.

Patrice A. Londoner, M.Ed., Ph.D. Candidate, Virginia Commonwealth University, 1533 Monmouth Drive, Richmond, Virginia 23238. Ms. Londoner is a doctoral candidate in Adult Education and Human Resource Development at Virginia Commonwealth University in Richmond, Virginia. Her areas of concentration include the social psychology of organizational behaviors. Ms. Londoner has more than 15 years of experience in business and industry and enjoyed the opportunity to apply her knowledge to a chapter in this book. She anticipates a December 2006 Ph.D. completion date.

John W. Luna, Community Affairs Director, Dallas Metrocare Services, 1380 River Bend Drive, Dallas, Texas 75247. Mr. Luna is the Community Affairs Director of Dallas Metrocare Services (formerly Dallas County Mental Health and Mental Retardation Center), Executive Board Member and Ambassador of the Great Irving–Las Colinas Chamber of Commerce, and appointed Chairperson of the Texas Council of Purchasing from People with Disabilities by the governor of Texas. Mr. Luna's expertise in the vocational field has been shared in local, state, and national conference presentations.

Jennifer Todd McDonough, M.S., Training Associate, Virginia Commonwealth University Rehabilitation Research and Training Center (VCU-RRTC) on Workplace Supports and Job Retention, 1314 West Main Street, Post Office Box 842011, Richmond, Virginia 23284. Ms. McDonough has been a faculty member at VCU and working in the field of employment for people with disabilities for more than 10 years. She earned her master of science degree from the Medical College of Virginia at VCU in Rehabilitation Counseling. Ms. McDonough is a training associate at VCU-RRTC, where she provides training and technical assistance on Social Security benefits management and work incentives for the Benefits Assistance Resource Center and the Youth Transition Demonstration Technical Assistance Office. In addition, she provides technical assistance on employment issues for individuals with disabilities for the Region III Community Rehabilitation Program—Regional Continuing Education Program.

Allyson J. Merkle, M.S.S.W., LMSW, Care Manager, MHN Insurance, a subsidiary of Healthnet, Inc., a Managed Healthcare Company, 503 Canal Boulevard, Richmond, California 94804. Ms. Merkle graduated from Loyola University, New Orleans, with a degree in psychology and obtained a master's in social work from the University of Texas at Arlington. She has worked extensively in supported employment as a job consultant assisting adults with mental illness to obtain and maintain employment and also has worked as a consultant with the Dallas Independent School District's Special Education Department assisting in the continuing development of the Transition Program for high school students with disabilities entering the work force.

Daniel E. O'Brien, M.P.A., Administrator, 9624 Basket Ring Road, Columbia, Maryland 21045. Mr. O'Brien has been an innovator in the supported employment and vocational rehabilitation fields for more than 20 years. He is the co-developer of the milestone payment system, which is widely used and one of the most successful systems for results-based funding of employment services. He has consulted extensively in the United States and Australia on results-based funding of employment services for people with disabilities.

Dennis H. Reid, Ph.D., Director, Carolina Behavior Analysis & Support Center, Ltd., Post Office Box 425, Morganton, North Carolina 28680. Dr. Reid is the founder and director of the Carolina Behavior Analysis & Support Center. He has worked in developmental disabilities for more than 30 years and has published more than 100 applied research articles and seven books.

Patricia M. Rogan, M.S., Ph.D., Professor, Indiana University School of Education, 902 West New York Street, Indianapolis, Indiana 46202. Dr. Rogan prepares school and adult service personnel; provides training and technical assistance at the national, state, and local levels; and conducts research related to transition, employment, and organizational change. Dr. Rogan is a past president of National APSE: The Network on Employment and has been active in the National Organizational Change Network and conferences. She has written numerous articles and book chapters and has co-authored several books.

Pamela Sherron Targett, M.Ed., Program Director, Virginia Commonwealth University Rehabilitation Research and Training Center on Workplace Supports and Job Retention, 1314 West Main Street, Post Office Box 842011, Richmond, Virginia 23284. Ms. Targett has been involved in assisting individuals with severe disabilities with employment since 1986. She oversees day-to-day operations of a supported employment program and provides training and technical assistance to others on supported employment and other disability and employment-related topics.

Edmond Turner, Training Associate, Virginia Commonwealth University Rehabilitation Research and Training Center on Workplace Supports and Job Retention, 1314 Main Street, Post Office Box 842011, Richmond, Virginia 23284. Mr. Turner has more than 30 years of experience in the disability service delivery field. He has been a special educator, an independent living peer counselor, and a state board administrator and is currently a training associate in the field of disability rights. Mr. Turner was recently appointed Special Advisor to the Governor of Virginia on disability issues and concerns.

Michael D. West, Ph.D., Research Associate, Virginia Commonwealth University Rehabilitation Research and Training Center (VCU-RRTC) on Workplace Supports and Job Retention, 1314 West Main Street, Post Office Box 842011, Richmond, Virginia 23284. Dr. West is an associate professor at VCU. His research reports have included national surveys of supported employment policies and practices, a study of students with disabilities in higher education in Virginia, and states' use of Medicaid Home and Community-Based Services Waivers to fund employment services. Dr. West is also involved in research and demonstration efforts related to Social Security disability reform at the VCU-RRTC on Workplace Supports and Job Retention.

Foreword

This welcome contribution to our knowledge of work opportunities for individuals with disabilities could have been aptly titled *The Right Stuff from the Right Folk at the Right Time!* Paul Wehman and his colleagues at Virginia Commonwealth University (VCU), together with many of the national leaders in the field of paid work and income generation for individuals with disabilities, not only have set the stage for moving forward, but also have provided the tools, examples, steps, and issues to be addressed as we know them today and defined in the context of events in the field over the past 20 years.

In the early 1980s, a few of "us"—parents, researchers, politicians, human services professionals, individuals with disabilities and their advocates—began to hear about the promise of something called *supported employment*. I remember when I first "got it" after several rather academic presentations that discussed the social, economic, and personal values in somewhat general terms. Our daughter, Dusty, was just entering her teens, but I realized how important something like this could be to the quality of her life experience as an adult, down the road. The ideas of integration, inclusion, responsible citizenship, and social capital were relatively new to the then-current expectations for individuals with significant disabilities, but the thought of "real work for real pay" seemed a quite logical and reachable goal—one worth working toward and one which would assist a lot of people.

Many of those early adopters (some of us!) formed an almost cult-like network of information, inspiration, experience sharing, and at times, evangelical marketing of the process and the potential results. However, as this text points out, the promise has not been fulfilled for many for whom it holds great opportunity—despite the sincere hard work and seemingly tireless efforts of a now very large cadre of support. The publication of *Real Work for Real Pay* is an opportunity to regroup, reflect on our efforts, and look forward.

Building on recent strides in self-determination, self-direction, and self-advocacy, we now have a blueprint of where our past success and knowledge base lies, where we might have been a bit sidetracked, and a clear path to the future. The editors and contributors are very clear about expanding our vision from "let's get a job" to "let's make a meaningful life that includes work and makes money"!

Providing the opportunity to be a true "consumer" through income generation isn't a new or novel idea. But, unfortunately, how to make it a reality in the lives of people with significant disabilities still eludes many of us. Bureaucratic and organizational lethargy are chronicled in these pages, paralleled with many creative examples of individual and organizational success in spite of the natural inertia.

In addition to the highly regarded staff and their work at VCU, experts with hands-on experience in our field, such as Pat Rogan, Cary Griffin, Dave Hammis, Suzanne Hutcheson, and John Luna (to name only a few of the contributors—those with whom I have had the direct experience to back up this accolade), add the realism of what is possible when we think differently. Thinking differently becomes the key or lynchpin to making these things a reality:

- Expectation of paid work for all

- Replacement of time-wasting day programs with meaningful income-generating activities

- Reimbursement of support services for results/outcomes rather than processes

- Utilization of public benefits without becoming dependent on them

- Leveraging of public benefits with private resources

- Adaptation of nondisability strategies such as resource ownership and self-employment

New partnerships, new funding opportunities, new support possibilities, new expectations—they are all here and presented in a form that makes argument very difficult.

Advances in assistive technology, person-centered planning, staff selection and training, workplace assistance (and assistants!), applied behavior analysis, employer acceptance, telecommuting, public benefits planning and management, transition from school programs—they are all here, too, and with abundant references for sources of additional information. The positive effects in the lives of individuals with disabilities—parent, family, and advocate encouragement; community presence and participation; and money to purchase goods and services (and pay taxes!) like every-one else—are vividly displayed in numerous real-world examples of success. System change and organizational development are chronicled as well—by the very people who initiated and participated in the processes. Step-by-step suggestions, pitfalls to avoid, aids to enlist, milestones to celebrate, all add to make this a virtual cookbook for paid work and income generation.

In Chapter 1, Paul Wehman and his colleagues describe who this book is for. We sincerely hope that it finds its way into each and every hand defined in those pages—and that it is read thoroughly and used widely. This contribution to our literature moves the questions from "Why?" and "How?" to "Why not?" and "Why not now?" while it takes away any opportunity to argue "I don't know how" or "That won't work."

There are no excuses left!

Dale L. Dutton (Dusty's Dad)
Larkspur, California

Preface

The ideas for books come in many different ways. At times, there is such an overpowering need that it is obvious that new material must be generated and published. At other times, people gather together to discuss the different possibilities of how a certain book could make a difference. Still another way is through colleague-to-colleague communication, done informally enough at first but then blossoming into a full project.

Real Work for Real Pay came about the last way. In 2001, Nancy Brooks-Lane and Paul Wehman, the lead author of this book, began discussions. "Wouldn't it be nice if there was one employment book that was comprehensive and covered everything employment specialist professionals need to know?" Over a few-day period, several ideas were spawned, with Nancy generating numerous ideas and thoughts. Little by little, over several months, the ideas took the form of book chapters that eventually evolved into *Real Work for Real Pay*. We would like to acknowledge Nancy's creative thinking and push for us to develop this book. We thank her and her wonderful colleagues from Cobb and Douglas Counties, Georgia, for their high quality of dedication and professionalism. The seed was planted by her and then ultimately presented to Rebecca Lazo at Paul H. Brookes Publishing Co.

Our experience as trainers, on-line instructors, mentors, and students has taught us that employment books are most effective when the best of research converges with clear philosophical values. The values come first with the strategies, tools, and techniques based on the quality research evidence. In this book, we have tried to balance philosophical foundations with tools for change and policy implementation.

The employment of individuals with significant disabilities directly into the nation's labor force is not easy. If it were, the unemployment rate of people with disabilities would not continue to be around 60%–65%. Attitudes of professionals and people in business; knowledge of capacity and rights, funding, work preparation and retention strategies; and diversity issues are just a few of the items that have made this societal problem challenging.

Our purpose in writing this book is to take yet another small step in the direction of progress toward resolving these challenges. We think that we have created a constructive and useful resource and hope the professionals and families alike find it useful.

The purpose of *Real Work for Real Pay* is to be *the* comprehensive resource on inclusive employment. This book provides important values, behavioral tools for change, assistive technology for change, and policy directions. Case studies and program tables are used to illuminate the points in each of the 17 chapters.

We believe we have a book that is thorough yet readable. Employment specialists, consultants, rehabilitation counselors, transition specialists, advocates, and families should use this book as the resource they always can go to for assistance. Customized employment, self-employment, and telework join supported employment as inclusive employment models that are presented in detail. We believe this book presents a fair profile of where we are for employment services and knowledge in the early part of the new millennium.

This book is for all of the employment services personnel working in the trenches, looking for ideas, techniques, and guidelines to improve the lives of individuals with disabilities who want to work. We hope it can make a difference.

Acknowledgments

We have had the opportunity to team up with a really strong group of collaborators to make this book an excellent resource for those interested in employment of individuals with disabilities and special needs. Our contributors include Nancy Brooks-Lane, J. Howard Green, Cary Griffin, Suzanne Hutcheson, Jennifer Todd McDonough, Dan O'Brien, Dennis Reid, Pat Rogan, Pam Sherron Targett, Ed Turner, Michael West, and a number of others who have provided valuable time, experiences, and insights that one author could never provide. Each of these individuals is an expert in his or her field and has direct clinical and/or research experience, which has provided for rich case studies, evidence-based findings, and innovative ideas that are not available elsewhere.

We also know what we have written in this book is founded on the heroic and pioneering efforts of a number of outstanding professionals and advocates. We clearly stand on the shoulders of these national disability leaders and have drawn from their wisdom. People such as Lou Brown, Susan Daniels, Judy Heumann, Justin Dart, Christy Lynch, Marc Gold, David Braddock, Madeleine Will, Don Baer, Celane McWhorter, Wayne Sailor, Doug Guess, Janis Chadsey, Norris Haring, Tom Bellamy, Bill Kiernan, David Mank, Sue Swenson, Dennis Mithaug, Jan Nisbet, Christopher Button, Adelle Renzaglia, Michael Callahan, Paul Bates, Frank Rusch, and Michael Wehmeyer have been there from the start with creative and challenging ideas and thoughts about how to enhance employment outcomes for individuals with significant disabilities.

Whenever one starts naming names, it is always dangerous because there are so many others with wonderful ideas and dreams, including those in the trenches of direct service who innovate regularly with new ideas. But we could not have written a book like this, which is laced with ideology and training technology, without acknowledging these pioneers, some retired and some still active, who shape our thinking and philosophies and practices. We are essentially a small group that draws on each other's strength and energies.

We also thank Virginia Commonwealth University (VCU) and colleagues such as Brian McMahon, John Kregel, Jeff Kreutzer, Dave Cifu, Mike West, Liz Getzel, and so many other positive colleagues. Our VCU family provides an uncommonly wonderful place of support. The technical development of the book was handled by Jeanne Dalton, who does a beautiful job of editing, organizing, and administering the multitude of tasks necessary for a book of this magnitude. People such as Tricia Zeh and Jan Hensel-Smith provide critical administrative support for our work activity, and we thank them.

Finally, we would like to thank Steve Peterson and Rebecca Lazo at Paul H. Brookes Publishing Co. for their helpful "assists" along the way. They edited original drafts over and over to make this the excellent book it is today. We are most appreciative of their faith in this project.

*To the thousands of individuals with significant disabilities
who left segregated programs for inclusive employment*

Setting the
Stage for Change

Chapter 1

Inclusive Employment

Rolling Back Segregation of People with Disabilities

Paul Wehman, Valerie A. Brooke, and W. Grant Revell, Jr.

MARK

Mark is a 24-year-old with a diagnosis of severe autism. He lives with his family members, who provide extensive supports across a variety of areas. Mark has many skills, including the ability to dress himself, bathe himself, and brush his hair and teeth. In addition, he performs simple food preparation tasks such as using the toaster and preparing a bowl of cereal. Mark has mastered the operation of the family television, DVD player, and stereo system, which serve as his preferred forms of recreation. Mark is verbal, although he speaks extremely fast and his syntax is unclear. Those who know Mark well can understand what he is saying; however, strangers have a difficult time understanding what he has to say.

When Mark graduated from school, earning a special education diploma, he made the transition to a segregated sheltered workshop. At the workshop, Mark was typically engaged in collating materials, for which he earned wages based on his production rate. His production rate resulted in earnings that averaged $20.00 over a 5-day workweek. In the last year, with the support of a job coach, Mark has found employment as an inventory clerk with the local electric company. After an intensive period of full-time support from a job coach, Mark is able to ride the bus to work each day and complete all areas of work with minimal support from a co-worker.

Recently, Mark has been expressing an interest in getting his own apartment and moving to a data-entry position within the company. He contacted his supervisor and discussed his career goals. Together, Mark and his manager are looking into the possibility of a job transfer within the electric company. Mark's parents are also supportive of his moving out of the family house into his own apartment. Mark's job coach has contacted the local residential services program to learn more about this community service option.

In this case study, Mark changed from being labeled and segregated to becoming a productive tax-paying citizen who is included in the workplace. Mark is in inclusive employment where millions of other Americans work every day, which includes different industries, different jobs, and different work conditions in which all employees receive pay for work that is done in order for the business to be productive. Mark is lucky. He made it.

Mark is part of the evolution that we are currently witnessing in the field where there is a steady and dynamic progression from separate and protective services for people with disabilities to a new level of inclusion within our society. As the evolution continues and the transfer of power and influence moves away from the professional to the individual with disabilities, we will see the chronic unemployment and under-employment of people with disabilities come to an end. It is the act of actually work-ing together that will ultimately make the difference to people with disabilities, to business recruiters, to human service managers, to rehabilitation professionals, and to our nation's economy.

This book is about how to provide inclusive employment for people like Mark and others with significant disabilities. We define *inclusive employment* as work for all peo-ple with disabilities in real or typical work settings at a decent wage with people with-out disabilities. By *people with disabilities*, we mean people with intellectual disabilities (McLaughlin & Wehman, 1996; Rizzolo, Hemp, Braddock, & Pomeranz-Essley, 2004), physical disabilities (Inge, Strobel, Wehman, Todd, & Targett, 2000; Targett, Wehman, & Young, 2004), mental illness disorders (Becker & Drake, 2003; Bond, 2004; Drake, Becker, Bond, & Mueser, 2003; Drake, Mueser, Brunette, & McHugo, 2004), autism (Smith, Belcher, & Juhrs, 1995), and health-related disabilities (Hammond et al., 2004). Many of these individuals are unemployed (Stapleton & Burkhauser, 2003), but others have become successfully employed (McMahon et al., 2004), hence demonstrating the formidable work potential of people with disabilities (Wehman, 2001).

WHY DO WE WORK?

What are the reasons for work and promoting meaningful career development and ca-reer advancement for individuals with intellectual and developmental disabilities? Why should the large number of adult day programs reevaluate their mission and move to supporting competitive employment outcomes as their predominant service? First, work is a way of human life in the United States. Work enhances other skills such as communication, socialization, academics, physical health, and community skills. Most important, work is good because it is a normal feature of what people in our society do and how they are perceived.

Second, many of the laws (e.g., Americans with Disabilities Act of 1990 [PL 101-336]) that have been passed by Congress related to disability services promote mean-ingful employment (Kruse & Hale, 2003). There are no laws that promote protracted day program services and protracted day program institutionalization, and there are no laws that promote not having a defined opportunity to be able to work, even for those individuals with the most severe disabilities.

Third, work is a vehicle to promote the greatest amount of economic well-being. For some individuals with disabilities, going to work may require carefully planned benefits counseling and arrangement of state and federal income programs to go along with Social Security incentives and Medicare/Medicaid rules; however, it is more likely that people who are employed in a competitive job, as compared with sit-ting in a day program day after day, will have the better opportunity to improve their economic situation.

Fourth, regular inclusive employment leads to a greater opportunity for upward mobility and career advancement. Very few people start with high-paying jobs and the best benefits. It is essential to have the "first job." It is essential to have paid work experience in a real work setting to learn how to perform under pressure. Only with paid employment or the establishment of a personally owned small business can an individual hope to expand the business or increase the amount of hours or pay rate received.

Consider another extremely important reason for promoting employment—that of greater self-esteem and perceived self-competence. Knowing that one has a regular job in which work performance is valued and needed has a tremendous influence on one's dignity and on the perception that one has about personal capabilities and capacity. The inability to work regularly contributes to "learned helplessness," or a self-fulfilling prophesy of incompetence. The longer this self-perception occurs, the less likely that one will be able to successfully work. An additional reason for work is the greater likelihood of establishing new social networks and community participation. It is increasingly well known by those who are among the most skilled at job procurement that social networks are some of the best ways to open up possible jobs (Bissonette, 1994). Family members, friends, neighbors, church members, classmates, or people who have been helped by professionals all can play a crucial role in opening the doors for employment possibilities. If one only experiences two environments, the home and the workshop, and sees relatively few other people, thereby creating only one or two networks, then the chances of furthering meaningful employment are greatly reduced.

It is important that all individuals labeled with intellectual and other developmental disabilities have the informed choice to decide whether they want to advantage themselves of these reasons to work. It is unlikely that most people who work competitively or run a business would choose to stop working in order to return to an adult day program, but it is essential that they be informed of their choices. How do we get to the point where the remaining several hundred thousand individuals in day programs, and perhaps many more who have not been counted, do not remain there any longer and instead take their rightful place in the work force? What are the solutions to change? What are the strategies that we must persevere toward to stop this last bastion of segregation and daily institutionalization? And how can we reverse this seemingly locked-in inertia pattern against vocational growth potential and capacity? In this book, we begin to explore the answers.

WHO IS THIS BOOK FOR?

Our intent for this book is to help many people with disabilities, organizations, and businesses understand inclusive employment alternatives and how to implement these options. Through this book we can help the National Organization on Disability set policy statements that are reasonable benchmarks for employment success of people with disabilities as well as help members of organizations, such as the National Down Syndrome Society, understand employment for people with intellectual disabilities. It will also help the Council on State Administrators in Vocational Rehabilitation (VR) evaluate the viability of public–private sector partnerships and their financial investment in extended services. Organizations such as the U.S. Chamber of Commerce will be able to disseminate findings on disability management practice and job retention. The Council on Exceptional Children will be able to assess the relationship between school practice and employment for thousands of students with disabilities.

Rehabilitation service personnel (e.g., counselors, providers, therapists) are a primary target audience who will be able to benefit from the material in this book. They will be provided information on employers' perspectives on disability management and return-to-work, reasonable accommodations, and other workplace supports. They will learn about the workplace supports that customers of their services want and need in order to gain access to and maintain employment.

Communities who support people with disabilities and their *federal and state policy makers and officials* are concerned with the extraordinary costs associated with maintaining people with disabilities on Social Security Disability rolls. This is a highly nonproductive and inefficient use of human potential that is reaching an unacceptable level. This high level of entitlement leads to greater federal deficits and ultimately fosters the incorrect perception among society that people with disabilities are dependent on public support and not capable of active lives that include competitive employment.

Business personnel (e.g., employers, corporate recruiters, human resource managers, supervisors, co-workers) will be affected as they become better equipped to help people with disabilities be productive members of the work force. They will be provided access to state-of-the-art information on disability management, return-to-work, employer incentives, and workplace supports (e.g., job accommodations, assistive technology, rehabilitation supports). Increased knowledge will influence the current attitudes of employers about hiring and maintaining workers with disabilities. They will be better equipped to integrate employees back into the workplace as well as provide employment for individuals who have not had access to competitive employment. The research and training efforts from this Center on Workplace Supports will empower the business community to maximize a human resource that has to date remained untapped or underutilized.

Students in preservice programs are tomorrow's leaders. This book will affect these future leaders through preservice efforts at the master's as well as doctorate levels. This book will generate tremendous amounts of information to other programs nationally that prepare rehabilitation personnel on inclusive employment. In reality, this book may have its greatest impact on students who become the change agents of the service-delivery system that supports people with disabilities.

Guardians, advocates, or authorized representatives of individuals with disabilities are concerned about the futures of the individuals whom they support. They are worried about what will happen when they are no longer available to provide for these individuals. Gaining knowledge that people with disabilities can indeed be productive members of the work force will raise expectations of family members. Parents will have access to information on the supports that their sons or daughters will need to work rather than be maintained by society. They will explore and assist their family members to gain access to these workplace supports rather than worry about maintaining Social Security Disability benefits through Supplemental Security Income (SSI) and/or Social Security Disability Income (SSDI).

Individuals with disabilities will benefit from inclusive employment for many important reasons. First, working in inclusive employment settings provides an opportunity to receive wages and benefits that leads to greater independence, inclusion in the community, and removal from the nation's poverty and disability rolls. Second, being productive on a daily basis in a meaningful vocation is critically important to one's self-esteem and dignity. Third, having a job within a career path almost always facilitates establishing new friends and networks of social support in the community.

In order to become contributing members of society, individuals with disabilities must have access to meaningful information on how to enter or reenter the labor force and maintain employment. They must be knowledgeable of the workplace supports that can maximize their employment outcomes.

This book will also affect public policy, including tax credits and partial support of health benefits, which in turn will empower employers to hire people with disabilities. This will clearly reduce the number of individuals who are maintained on disability rolls. Society will benefit as more people with disabilities enter and reenter the workplace and require less SSI or SSDI cash payments for life. In addition, society will be affected as individuals take on meaningful roles in their communities and are seen as contributors rather than dependents.

Employment for People with Disabilities: Where Are We Now?

Clearly, one of the more frustrating public policy failures in the United States since the mid-1990s has been the inability to substantially decrease the unemployment rate of individuals with disabilities, a rate that seems intransigent at 60%–70% (e.g., Stapleton & Burkhauser, 2003). There are many positive events in place that presumably should expand and maintain employment opportunities, such as empowering legislation, efforts by the Social Security Administration (SSA) to create work incentives, clinical advances in rehabilitation (e.g., assistive technology), and supported employment (Wehman, 2001; Wehman & Kregel, 1998). Also, since 1990, there has been a solid economy and growing labor force. People with disabilities indicate that they want to work. Employers indicate on surveys that they believe individuals with disabilities can work and that they are willing to hire qualified people with disabilities (Unger, 2002).

Furthermore, despite the downturn in past years, *Barrons Financial Magazine* (Epstein, 2004) indicated in the January 5, 2004, issue there should be a renewed upswing in jobs in the years ahead. Labor market forecasters predict growth will be dramatic in many businesses and industries. Where is this huge employment disconnect coming from for individuals with disabilities? Why are so many young people with disabilities coming out of school with no jobs or careers? Why are parents consistently told there are no jobs for their children? Why do businesses seemingly have no concept of where to find qualified workers with disabilities when there are so many programs in place? Why do workers fail to return to work after disability? There are 882,000 youth on SSI in the schools, and if most of them remain unemployed like the generations before them, then costs to the government will continue to spiral out of control for disability-related benefits. Human resources for the economy will be wasted, and individuals with disabilities will continue to experience a loss of personal fulfillment and earning power (Wittenburg & Maag, 2002). Consider the Harris Poll data (2004) summarized next:

- Only 35% of people with disabilities reported being employed full or part time, compared with 78% of those who do not have disabilities.

- Three times as many people with disabilities live in poverty with annual household incomes less than $15,000 (26% versus 9%).

- People with disabilities remain twice as likely to drop out of high school (21% versus 10%).

- People with disabilities are twice as likely to have inadequate transportation (31% versus 13%) and a much higher percentage go without needed health care (18% versus 7%).

- People with disabilities are less likely to socialize, eat out, or attend religious services than their peers without disabilities.

- Not surprisingly, given the persistence of these gaps, life satisfaction for people with disabilities also trails, with only 34% saying they are very satisfied with their lives compared with 61% of those without disabilities.

- The severity of disability makes a significant difference in all of the gap areas, and people with severe disabilities have much greater disadvantages.

These data indicate much work lies ahead to create more economic and employment opportunity for people with disabilities.

The chronic unemployment of people with disabilities places a tremendous strain on our nation's economy. Some 7.5 million unemployed Americans with disabilities will draw $73 billion in Social Security benefits this year, with less than 1% of those receiving benefits becoming self-supporting through employment (Gerry, 2002). Yet, many would suggest that the real economic cost of disability is the loss of production from individuals who are not working. Advances in assistive technology (Carey, Del-Sordo, & Goldman, 2004), health interventions (Roessler & Rumrill, 1998), job coaches, natural supports (Mank, Cioffi, & Yovanoff, 2000), new training techniques, and progressive laws support the entry of people with disabilities into the competitive work force (Wehman, 2001). Unfortunately, these advances have not yet resulted in a significant improvement in the employment rates of people with disabilities.

What makes these disappointing data all the more remarkable is that labor market demands in many industries have created a fierce competition among employers for attracting and retaining a qualified work force. Businesses, large and small, are doing everything in their power to identify ways to address this concern. The U.S. Chamber of Commerce has identified the lack of skilled workers as one of its top issues (Donahue, 2001). In order to stay competitive, businesses must seek ways to tap nontraditional labor pools (Green & Brooke, 2001). The fact that most businesses have not hired people with disabilities should not signal that companies are not willing (Unger, 2002). Businesses are more interested than ever in learning which business models, supports, and policies will promote the economic advantages of hiring, retaining, and advancing the employment of people with disabilities.

Strong businesses recognize the advantages of recruiting a work force that represents their customer base. People with disabilities represent a large customer base for businesses throughout the United States. The U.S. Census Bureau (2000) reported that 53 million people are limited in their activities due to a disability; 73% are head of households; 48% are principal shoppers; 46% are married; and 58% own their own home. Companies leading the charge in the hiring, retention, and advancement of people with disabilities are aware of these numbers and have developed strategies that market their goods and services to these individuals. The key to successful marketing campaigns is aggressively recruiting people with disabilities to join their work force and increasing corporate profit levels, as well as their competitive edge over companies who are slow to see the benefits.

Therefore, the question that is increasingly being asked is "Why is the shortage of qualified labor in business not leading to increased employment of people with disabilities?" (Wehman, 2002a, 2002b). Unfortunately, we do not yet have a definite answer, but a major purpose of this book is to provide some answers. Congress, numerous federal agencies, state policy makers, consumer groups, professionals, and corporations have focused significant attention on why the unemployment rate of people with disabilities remains so high (Harris, 2004). From 1980 through 2000, the unemployment rate for people with disabilities held steady at 60%–70%. This rate has not dropped despite the fact that more than two thirds of those not employed say they would prefer to be working (Harris, 2000).

Unemployment: A Multidimensional Issue

These unemployment issues are complicated, whether viewed from a societal, business, or human service day program perspective. It becomes inherently clear, however, that the problem is multidimensional in nature (Stapleton & Burkhauser, 2003). All of the following must align appropriately for a successful long-term employment experience to occur: 1) the needs and motivation of individuals with disabilities, 2) the willingness of businesses to hire, 3) government policies, and 4) the availability of progressive rehabilitation techniques (McMahon et al., 2004). These four variables make up the workplace supports model. They come from the different perspectives of 1) the individual, 2) business, 3) government policies, and 4) the rehabilitation agency. Since 1999, we have studied corporations that successfully employ people with disabilities (see McMahon et al., 2004). We have also operationalized workplace supports into a taxonomy of different supports and sorted out the different aspects of this multidimensional challenge (Wehman, Bricout, & Kregel, 2000), which include

1. Individual- and family-mediated supports (e.g., personal assistance, control over one's benefits)

2. Business-mediated supports (e.g., mentoring, job restructuring)

3. Government-mediated supports (e.g., job discrimination protection, work incentives, health buy-in)

4. Agency-mediated supports (e.g., customized employment, job coaches, assistive technology)

Individual- and Family-Mediated Supports

In a consumer-driven system of human services, people with disabilities should be serviced as true customers of the rehabilitation system. Brooke, Wehman, Inge, and Parent (1995) outlined a series of steps and strategies for individuals and their families that help them take more power and responsibility for the supports they need. But, as will soon become evident, the amount of literature in this area is very scant. Two areas of supports are family supports and personal assistant services.

Families play an important role in the quality of life, adjustment, and health outcomes of people with disabilities (Kelley & Lambert, 1992). Families can provide informal care that ranges from general psychosocial support to job-related skills training (Prosser & Moss, 1996; Turner & Alston, 1994; Urbain, 1997). The ethnic group and culture to which a person with disabilities belongs may have an impact on how strongly family members influence life choices and decisions, with some groups and cultures emphasizing independence more than others (Parette, 1997; Turner & Alston,

1994). Individual differences may also influence how much independence a person with disabilities has from his or her family (Mowbray, Bybee, Harris, & McCrohan, 1995); however, family continues to be an important mediator of various work supports (Killam, Petranek, & Harding, 1996; Kutty, 1993). For instance, family members have an important role to play in the selection and implementation of assistive technology devices and services.

Personal assistants are another source of individual control for workplace supports and are also seen as vital to successful independent living for many people with disabilities (e.g., Turner, Barcus, West, & Revell, 1999). Personal assistants make it possible for people with disabilities to live in their own residences and to work in the community (Budde & Bachelder, 1986). Attendants help individuals with domestic chores, personal hygiene and dressing, cooking, and other daily living tasks (Asher, Asher, Hobbs, & Kelley, 1991). The services of the attendant can also be modified to include the role of advocate, advisor, or job coach. Personal care decisions are an important domain for individual self-direction.

Business-Mediated Supports

Even though agencies have traditionally initiated the work support process, an ever-increasing number of professionals are concluding that employers should also be initiating work supports (Hanley-Maxwell & Millington, 1992; Harper, 1993; McMahon et al., 2004; Sandow, Olson, & Yan, 1993; Test & Wood, 1996). Businesses are a vital source of in-house work supports including people (i.e., supervisors and co-workers), practices (e.g., flexible scheduling), policies (e.g., early return to work), and environmental supports (e.g., accessible workspaces) (Sowers, Kouwenhoven, Sousa, & Milliken, 1997). Businesses can also lead to collaborations with human service providers (McMahon et al., 2004). A wide variety of programs designed to meet the support needs of workers with disabilities have been sponsored by businesses. Mentoring is also initiated by some businesses. Businesses have entered into partnerships to hire and provide supports for workers with disabilities with public entities, nonprofit organizations, insurance companies, and other businesses (Luecking, Fabian, & Tilson, 2004; Miano, Nalvern, & Hoff, 1996; Taylor, 1994; Tilson, Luecking, & West, 1996). Finally, businesses have also contracted with employment consultants and Employee Assistance Programs to provide work supports. In each of these instances, business is the mediator through which work-support programs, practices, policies, and procedures for workers with disabilities are realized.

Government-Mediated Supports

Government-mediated supports are those policies and practices that enhance the likelihood of people with disabilities gaining or maintaining employment. Examples of government supports include selected Social Security policies, U.S. Department of Treasury tax policies, civil rights legislation, and other laws targeted specifically at the employment of people with disabilities.

The SSA has implemented a number of incentives to help support individuals with disabilities who want to work. For example, referral to state VR services, trial work periods, continuing eligibility for Medicare, deduction of impairment-related work expenses from taxable earnings, and development of a Plan for Achieving Self-Support (PASS) are all major elements of how SSA tries to support employment for individuals with disabilities. Many of these supports have been underutilized because some of these incentives or supports are difficult for many beneficiaries to gain access to or understand (see Fagnoni, 1999).

Agency-Mediated Supports

Because most human services funding for rehabilitation flows through one common agency, an important "starting point" for examining workplace supports is the human service agency (or agencies) that provides supported employment services (Brooks-Lane, Hutcheson, & Revell, 2005). One of the services provided by such agencies may be to coordinate services with other entities, be they employers; the government; or providers of specialized services such as mental health treatment, VR, or education. Additional services include provision of work evaluation, job coaching, customized employment, and assistive technology (Targett & Inge, 2005). These services, which will be discussed in chapters that follow, typically originate or are mediated by local agencies. Historically, state and local rehabilitation agencies mediate the flow of supports.

ADULT DAY PROGRAMS FOR PEOPLE
WITH DEVELOPMENTAL AND OTHER DISABILITIES

When we examine where we are in 2006 related to day services, work, and employment, we must ask two questions: 1) Is competitive employment the first choice readily available to people with significant disabilities? and 2) Why do adult day programs continue as the predominant service for adults with intellectual and developmental disabilities (e.g., Braddock et al., 2005)? The answers to these questions are neither encouraging nor clear. Recent participation and expenditure information reported in the *State of the States in Developmental Disabilities 2005* provided a sobering indicator of where we are and how far we still have to go to truly make the opportunity for competitive employment the first choice for people with significant disabilities. For state fiscal year (FY) 2004, state disability agencies report that approximately 118,391 individuals participated in supported/competitive employment compared with approximately 374,498 individuals who participated in day, work, and sheltered employment programs that did not involve supported/competitive employment. Since 1990, the growth rate in the number of workers in supported employment closely parallels the growth rate in segregated day program participants. For every one person working in competitive employment, three individuals remain in a segregated day program.

Recent expenditure statistics demonstrate the impact of funding on the type of programs available to individuals with significant disabilities. In FY 2004, states spent approximately $496 million in federal Medicaid funding for segregated day programs, compared with $188 million for supported/competitive employment (Braddock et al., 2005). State disability agencies spend approximately $3 for noncompetitive employment outcomes for every $1 spent for competitive employment outcomes. Despite the fact that the Medicaid Home and Community-Based Services (HCBS) Waiver is an excellent potential funding source for ongoing supports in supported employment, only about 15% of the more than 130,000 people receiving day habilitation services in FY 1999 through the Waiver were in supported employment. The rest were in a variety of day habilitation service categories that were not competitive work oriented and frequently not community integrated (West et al., 2002). Clearly, competitive employment is not the first choice available for the majority of individuals with significant disabilities. The continuing growth in segregated day program participation and funding indicates that without a drastic change in the control of funding for day and employment programs, segregated day and work services, not competitive employment, will continue to be the predominant first choice available.

Beginning in the mid-1980s, a number of states initiated formal systemic initiatives directed at expanding the availability of services that support integrated employment outcomes. Federal grants from the Rehabilitation Services Administration, the Administration on Developmental Disabilities, and other agencies helped fuel these initiatives (Mank & Revell, 2001). States have used a variety of strategies to drive their systems-change efforts. These strategies include sustained leadership that supports mission-driven state systems emphasizing integrated employment outcomes, aligning available dollars with this mission, expanding partnerships with business and industry, and supporting self-determination and informed choice in selection of employment programming by individuals with significant disabilities. States such as Alaska, Connecticut, Oklahoma, and Washington successfully support competitive employment outcomes for approximately 50% or more of the individuals in day and work programs (Rizzolo et al., 2004); however, these states are the exception, as clearly documented by the continued dominance of nonintegrated programs cited earlier. In most states, the available funding resources to support integrated employment remain enormously underutilized.

Segregated day activities are clearly inconsistent with independence and community inclusion (Wehman, 2001). Consider the experience of a good friend of ours named Harold. During the late 1970s, Harold's days were spent sitting in an adult day activity center creating simple arts and crafts projects. The story of his move from this center to a position as a utility worker at a medium-size private college is significant and perhaps historic.

Twenty-five years ago, Harold, like many of his peers in the segregated adult day center, had very little muscle tone, limited receptive language, and virtually no expressive language. Typical of the late 1970s, the professionals involved in Harold's life both at school and adult services did not give his parents any hope that he could be productive or achieve competitive employment. Therefore, Harold had very little home-based experience with work and no industrial-based work experiences. He did not seek competitive work because neither he nor his family thought this was an option. When he eventually worked at a competitive job, his employer had no experience supervising an employee with significant disabilities, and there were no business colleagues to turn to for testimonials on the employment potential of people with significant disabilities.

Yet Harold overcame these impressive odds to enjoy the benefits of competitive employment and, currently, the joys of retirement. He, unlike many people with disabilities, was not denied access to the very events that provided him with opportunity to take risks, make decisions, and ultimately achieve the highly prized American values of choice, power, and control through inclusive employment.

The time is long overdue to cease segregated program services and to expand competitive employment opportunities. A drastic change is needed both in the way funding decisions are made and in who controls the dollars currently sustaining segregated day activities. How can this change be accomplished? It can be accomplished by placing the individual with disabilities in control of the decisions around funding a personal choice for an employment outcome.

STRATEGIES FOR CHANGE

Harold, as well as the thousands of other individuals with intellectual and developmental disabilities who have taken their rightful place in the labor market, serve as shining examples of what can happen when people are viewed in terms of their productivity and ability rather than in terms of dependence and disability (Brown, Shiraga, & Kessler, in press). The evolution of services to people with disabilities is moving at a steady and dynamic pace away from separate and protective services to a new level of inclusion within our society. To help guide this change, we propose five major solutions. It is our firm belief that if these solutions are put into place relatively quickly, then a dramatic decline in the number of participants within day programs would occur over the 5 years following these changes.

There are a number of ways to reduce the day program institutionalization and large unemployment issues that affect hundreds of thousands of people with developmental and other disabilities, including those with mental illness (Wehman et al., 2005). If at least several of these strategies, some of which are policy changes and some of which are programmatic changes, were consistently put into place, then we would begin to see rather quickly a steady decrease of people in day program service.

Paid Work Before Exiting School

The first strategy is the inclusion of a pronounced statement in amendments to the Individuals with Disabilities Education Improvement Act of 2004 (PL 108-446), the Developmental Disabilities Assistance and Bill of Rights Act of 1975 (PL 94-103), and the Rehabilitation Act of 1973 (PL 93-112), that *all individuals with significant support needs should have paid employment before they leave school* (Johnson, 2004; Rusch & Braddock, 2004; Wehman et al., in press). This is specifically paid employment, be it part time, full time, or self-employment, but not simply work experiences, tryouts, or prevocational training activity. We know that paid employment while in school directly relates to paid integrated employment in adulthood and, therefore, there must be a more coordinated and pronounced legislative statement about paid employment for students while they are still under special education entitlement in the public schools. The specific outcome associated with this policy change would be the demonstration of vocational competence on the part of individuals with serious support needs and would raise the threshold of expectation for service providers that have typically shuttled these individuals into segregated day programs. Although there can be no guarantee that paid employment in school will automatically lead to employment after school entitlement has ended, the probabilities are significantly higher than if there had not been a real work experience.

Presumption of Employability

A second solution to long-term participation in day programs is the placement of stringent time limits or annual reviews that would prevent protracted participation and funding for these individuals in day programs. There needs to be a presumption of employability that all funders must come to expect for anybody who receives funding in a day program. The same model of time-limited services has been used repeatedly in the Rehabilitation Act and has also been modeled in efforts to deinstitutionalize state residential facilities. There is absolutely no reason why funding agencies at the state and federal level could not set a time limit that would require a full review before continued enrollment in a day program. The simple presence of time limits would serve to communicate to all involved—funding agency, parents, individuals with disabilities, or professionals—that the day program service is a second choice and there must be stringent reasons why an individual needs to stay in this type of situation. A presumption of employability is consistent with the concept that competitive employment should be the first choice, not the last choice (Wehman, Revell, & Brooke, 2003).

Real Work Vouchers

A third solution would be the issuance of Real Work Vouchers to all clients who are currently in day programs. A Real Work Voucher would give an individual the option to petition the funding agency and the professionals who are directing his or her program to have an integrated employment program available. This program may be competitive employment, customized employment, self-employment, or part-time employment. No matter which program option is chosen, the result will be pay, benefits coordination, and advice for how to maximize personal economic development and career advancement. Real Work Vouchers would be issued by state mental retardation and/or mental health agencies to every individual with an understanding that there needs to be a response by the local program as to what the plan will be to help that person implement his or her Real Work Voucher. The Real Work Voucher should have the amount of time that it will take to find employment, which resources are going to be utilized to help implement the employment plan, and a program design for what to do if initial plans fail.

Self-Determination Training

A fourth strategy would be to provide nationally funded Self-Determination Institutes that every state will be encouraged to offer to those individuals who are in existing day programs. By taking the full spirit of the *Olmstead* court decision and the Developmental Disabilities Rehabilitation and Bill of Rights Act, as well as position statements by The Arc of the United States, it would appear that individuals with intellectual disabilities and other serious support needs should have the opportunity to determine their own vocational destiny (Wehman et al., in press). Clearly, with the impact of the Robert Wood Johnson Self-Determination Demonstration Projects, there is a precedent for this type of national training model to be further extended into localities. State and federal dollars would be utilized to enroll all clients into Self-Determination Institutes similar to the Partners and Policy Making Projects that developmental disabilities councils have funded for years. These activities have been grossly underutilized and underfunded.

Without sufficient training and knowledge, it is extremely difficult for individuals with significant support needs who are segregated into adult day programs to even be aware of what their choices are and what options they have in front of them. Mandatory participation in self-determination training will go a long way to help implement these other strategies. Knowledge is clearly power. Individuals with disabilities need ready access to knowledge about possible employment options and the technical assistance available to help with benefits coordination and employment planning.

Medicaid Home and Community-Based Services Waiver Dollars

A fifth strategy is accelerated and expanded utilization of Medicaid Waiver dollars for inclusive employment. Increased participation in competitive employment could help prevent long-term residential institutionalization and prevent nursing home costs that are completely unnecessary, as well as the other secondary problems associated with the daily boredom and depression that result from being in segregated adult day programs. As discussed previously, the Medicaid HCBS Waiver dollars and other Medicaid funds are currently being used predominantly to support participation in segregated day and work programs. Developing strategies to make these funds available as a resource within individual-directed funding accounts, such as the Real Work Vouchers described previously, will help provide a strong funding base for a person-centered employment initiative.

CONCLUSION

In this book, we take the position that for inclusive employment outcomes to become the true first choice readily available for individuals with significant disabilities, the power to control funds must move into the hands of the person using the needed supports. Despite repeated systems change efforts that began in the 1980s with the intent of redirecting dollars away from segregated programs to supporting integrated employment, approximately 75% of the people served in day and work programs continue in activities that do not include competitive employment. Segregated day and work programs continue to grow.

A change in direction is strongly needed. It is important to note that the five change strategies presented here all focus on individuals who are in or are targeted for day programs. There are no calls for more training of professionals. There are no calls for more seminars, conferences, or meetings of staff. Instead, each change strategy is focused on the individual. The key to self-determination is informed choice that will provide youth with disabilities individual paid work experiences starting at the secondary education level that will expand their personal awareness of employment opportunities in the community. Self-determination training helps build the skills needed for an individual to make a considered choice and exercise control. Policies built around a presumption of employability prevent that individual from having to stay for extended time in a day program without a real opportunity. Flexible funding accounts such as the Real Work Voucher truly allow the money to follow the individual's self-determined employment path. Redirecting Medicaid HCBS Waiver and other dollars away from segregated day and work programs to supporting individual competitive employment outcomes is an effective illustration of money following an individual's job interests instead of being locked into funding a day program.

A few states are setting an example on how to align the use of HCBS Waiver and other funds with a primary focus on person-centered plans of support for achieving competitive employment outcomes (Wehman & Revell, 2005). For competitive employment to truly become the first choice available for individuals with significant disabilities, however, we must move from a state- and program-centered funding process to a set of strategies that focus on individual choice and control. The day and work programs of our future must emphasize community-integrated employment experiences through our schools, build work programs around supports needed for a person with disabilities to work competitively, provide training on how to make informed choices, place funding control in the hands of the individual, and align funds to support competitive employment outcomes. These changes will move the evolution forward, and as the transfer of power and influence actually occurs, the chronic unemployment and underemployment of people with disabilities will come to an end.

REFERENCES

Americans with Disabilities Act of 1990, PL 101-336, 42 U.S.C. §§ 12101 *et seq.*

Asher, C.C., Asher, M.A., Hobbs, W.E., & Kelley, J.M. (1991). On consumer self-direction of attendant care services: An empirical analysis of survey responses. *Evaluation and Program Planning, 14*(3), 131–139.

Becker, D.R., & Drake, R.E. (2003). *A working life for people with severe mental illness.* New York: Oxford Press.

Bissonette, D. (1994). *Beyond traditional job development: The art of creating opportunity.* Chatsworth, CA: Milt Wright & Associates.

Bond, G.R. (2004). Supported employment: Evidence for an evidence-based practice. *Psychiatric Rehabilitation Journal, 27*(4), 345–359.

Braddock, D., Hemp, R., Rizzolo, M., Coulter, D., Haffer, L., & Thompson, M. (2005). *The state of the states in developmental disabilities 2005.* Boulder: University of Colorado at Boulder, Coleman Institute for Cognitive Disabilities.

Brooke, V., Wehman, P., Inge, K., & Parent, W. (1995). Toward a customer-driven approach of supported employment. *Education and Training in Mental Retardation and Developmental Disability, 30*(4), 308–319.

Brooks-Lane, N., Hutcheson, S., & Revell, W.G., Jr. (2005). Supporting consumer-directed employment outcomes. *Journal of Disability Policy Studies, 23*(2), 123–124.

Brown, L., Shiraga, B., & Kessler, K. (in press). The quest for ordinary lives: The integrated post-school vocational functioning of fifty workers with significant disabilities. *Research and Practice for Persons with Severe Disabilities.*

Budde, J.F., & Bachelder, J.L. (1986). Independent living: The concept, model and methodology. *Journal of The Association for Persons with Severe Handicaps, 11*(4), 240–245.

Carey, A.C., DelSordo, V., & Goldman, A. (2004). Assistive technology for all: Access to alternative financing for minority populations. *Journal of Disability Policy Studies, 14,* 194–203.

Developmental Disabilities Assistance and Bill of Rights Act of 1975 PL 94-103, 100 Stat. 840, 42 U.S.C. §§ 6000 *et seq.*

Donahue, T. (2001). *National workplace forum: Setting a national agenda for increasing the employment of individuals with disabilities.* Forum hosted by Virginia Commonwealth University Rehabilitation Research and Training Center on Workplace Supports and Job Retention and Center for Workforce Preparation, U.S. Chamber of Commerce, Washington, DC.

Drake, R.E., Becker, D.R., Bond, G.R., & Mueser, K.T. (2003). A process analysis of integrated and non-integrated approaches to supported employment. *Journal of Vocational Rehabilitation, 18,* 51–58.

Drake, R.E., Mueser, K.T., Brunette, M.F., & McHugo, G.J. (2004). A review of treatments for people with severe mental illnesses and co-occurring substance use disorders. *Psychiatric Rehabilitation Journal, 27*(4), 360–374.

Epstein, G. (2004, January 5). Tomorrow's jobs. *Barrons Financial Magazine, 17.*

Fagnoni, C.M. (1999). *Social Security Disability: Multiple factors affect return to work.* Washington, DC: U.S. General Accounting Office.

Gerry, M. (March, 2002). *Keynote address.* Presented at the State Partnership Systems Change Initiative's Topical Conference, Albuquerque, NM.

Green, J.H., & Brooke, V. (2001). Recruiting and retaining the best from America's largest untapped pool. *Journal of Vocational Rehabilitation, 16*(2), 83–88.

Hammond, F.M., Grattan, K.D., Sasser, H., Corrigan, J.D., Rosenthal, M., Bushnik, T., et al. (2004). Five years after traumatic brain injury: A study of individual outcomes and predictors of change in function. *NeuroRehabilitation, 19,* 25–35.

Hanley-Maxwell, C., & Millington, M. (1992). Enhancing independence in supported employment: Natural supports in business and industry. *Journal of Vocational Rehabilitation, 2*(4), 51–58.

Harper, J. (1993). Securing a role for people with disabilities in the work force. *Journal of Vocational Rehabilitation, 3*(4), 70–73.

Harris, L. (2000). *2000 National Organization on Disability/Harris survey of Americans with disabilities.* New York: Author.

Harris, L. (2004). *Harris survey documents trends impacting 54 million Americans.* Washington, DC: National Organization on Disability.

Individuals with Disabilities Education Improvement Act of 2004, PL 108-446, 20 U.S.C. §§ 1400 *et seq.*

Inge, K.J., Strobel, W., Wehman, P., Todd, J., & Targett, P. (2000). Vocational outcomes for persons with severe physical disabilities: Design and implementation of workplace supports. *NeuroRehabilitation, 15,* 175–187.

Johnson, D.R. (2004). Supported employment trends: Implications for transition-age youth. *Research and Practice for Persons with Severe Disabilities, 29*(4), 243–247.

Kelley, S.D.M., & Lambert, S.S. (1992). Family support in rehabilitation: A review of research, 1980–1990. *Rehabilitation Counseling Bulletin, 36*(2), 98–119.

Killam, S.G., Petranek, I., & Harding, G. (1996). Parents in charge of the system: Strategies for increasing supported employment opportunities for individuals with severe disabilities. *Journal of Vocational Rehabilitation, 6*(1), 41–45.

Kruse, D., & Hale, T. (2003). Disability and employment: Symposium introduction. *Industrial Relations, 42*(1), 1–10.

Kutty, A.T.T. (1993). Parent associations for vocational training and employment of persons with mental retardation. *Indian Journal of Disability and Rehabilitation, 7*(1), 53–58.

Luecking, R.G., Fabian, E.S., & Tilson, G.P. (2004). *Working relationships: Creating career opportunities for job seekers with disabilities through employer partnerships.* Baltimore: Paul H. Brookes Publishing Co.

Mank, D., Cioffi, A., & Yovanoff, P. (2000). Direct support in supported employment and its relation to job typicalness, coworker involvement, and employment outcomes. *Mental Retardation, 38*(6), 506–516.

Mank, D., & Revell, G. (2001). Systemic change for supported employment: Old lessons and new possibilities. In P. Wehman (Ed.), *Supported employment in business: Expanding the capacity of workers with disabilities* (pp. 215–226). St. Augustine, FL: Training Resource Network.

McLaughlin, P.J., & Wehman, P. (1996). *Mental retardation and developmental disabilities* (2nd ed.). Austin, TX: PRO-ED.

McMahon, B., Wehman, P., Brooke, P., Habeck, R., Green, H., & Fraser, R. (2004). *Business, disability and employment: Corporate models of success. A collection of successful approaches reported from 20 employers.* Richmond: Virginia Commonwealth University Rehabilitation Research and Training Center on Workplace Supports and Job Retention.

Miano, M.N., Nalvern, E.B., & Hoff, D. (1996). The Pachysandra Project: A public-private initiative in supported employment at the Prudential Insurance Company of America. *Journal of Vocational Rehabilitation, 6*(1), 107–118.

Mowbray, C.T., Bybee, D., Harris, S.N., & McCrohan, N. (1995). Predictors of work status and future work orientation in people with a psychiatric disability. *Psychiatric Rehabilitation Journal, 19*(2), 17–28.

Olmstead v. L.C., 527 U.S. 581; 119 S.Ct. 2176 (1999).

Parette, H.P. (1997). Assistive technology devices and services. *Education and Training in Mental Retardation and Developmental Disabilities, 32*(4), 267–280.

Prosser, H., & Moss, S. (1996). Informal care networks of older workers with an intellectual disability. *Journal of Applied Research in Intellectual Disabilities, 9*(1), 17–30.

Rehabilitation Act of 1973, PL 93-112, 29 U.S.C. §§ 701 *et seq.*

Rizzolo, M.C., Hemp, R., Braddock, D., & Pomeranz-Essley, A. (2004). *The state of the states in developmental disabilities* [Electronic version]. Washington, DC: American Association on Mental Retardation. Retrieved March 24, 2006, from http://www.cu.edu/ColemanInstitute/stateofthestates/

Roessler, R., & Rumrill, P. (1998). Reducing workplace barriers to enhance job satisfaction: An important post-employment service for employees with chronic illnesses. *Journal of Vocational Rehabilitation, 10,* 219–229.

Rusch, F.R., & Braddock, D. (2004). Adult day programs versus supported employment (1988–2002): Spending and service practices of mental retardation and developmental disabilities state agencies. *Research and Practice for Persons with Severe Disabilities, 29*(4), 237–242.

Sandow, D., Olson, D., & Yan, X.Y. (1993). The evolution of support in the workplace. *Journal of Vocational Rehabilitation, 3*(4), 30–37.

Smith, M.D., Belcher, R.G., & Juhrs, P.D. (1995). *A guide to successful employment for individuals with autism.* Baltimore: Paul H. Brookes Publishing Co.

Sowers, P.C., Kouwenhoven, K., Sousa, F., & Milliken, K. (1997). *Community-based employment for people with the most severe disabilities: New perspectives and strategies.* Durham: University of New Hampshire, Institute on Disability.

Stapleton, D.C., & Burkhauser, R.V. (2003). *The decline in employment of people with disabilities: A policy puzzle.* Kalamazoo, MI: W.E. Upjohn Institute for Employment Research.

Targett, P., Wehman, P., & Young, C. (2004). Return to work for persons with spinal cord injury: Designing work supports. *NeuroRehabilitation, 19* (2), 131–139.

Taylor, M.C. (1994). *Managing disability, recovery and reemployment.* Paper presented at the eighth annual National Disability Management Conference, October, 17, 1994, Northwestern National Life, Minneapolis, MN.

Test, D.W., & Wood, W.M. (1996). Natural supports in the workplace: The jury is still out. *Journal of The Association for Persons with Severe Handicaps, 21*(4), 155–173.

Tilson, G.P., Luecking, R., & West, L.L. (1996). The employer partnership in transition for youth with disabilities. *Journal for Vocational Special Needs Education, 18*(3), 88–92.

Turner, E., Barcus, M., West, M., & Revell, G. (1999). Personal assistance services: A vital workplace support. In G. Revell, K.J. Inge, D. Mank, & P. Wehman (Eds.), *The impact of supported employment for people with significant disabilities* (pp. 151–160). Richmond: Virginia Commonwealth University Rehabilitation Research and Training Center on Workplace Supports and Job Retention.

Turner, W.L., & Alston, R.J. (1994). The role of the family in psychosocial adaptation to physical disabilities for African Americans. *Journal of the National Medical Association, 86*(12), 915–921.

Unger, D. (2002) Employer's attitudes toward persons with disabilities in the workplace: Myths or realities? In D. Unger, J. Kregel, P. Wehman, & V. Brooke (Eds.), *Employers' views of workplace supports* (pp. 1–11). Richmond: Virginia Commonwealth University Rehabilitation Research and Training Center on Workplace Supports and Job Retention.

Urbain, C. (1997). *Supported employment using a natural supports approach: A handbook for parents.* Minneapolis, MN: PACER Center.

U.S. Census Bureau. (2000). *Meeting the challenge: Americans with disabilities, 1997.* Retrieved March 24, 2006, from http://www.census.gov/population/pop-profile/2000/chap19.pdf

Wehman, P. (2001). *Supported employment in business: Expanding the capacity of workers with disabilities.* St. Augustine, FL: Training Resource Network.

Wehman, P. (2002a). Testimony to the United States General Accounting Office on Business Tax Credits, Washington, DC.

Wehman, P. (2002b). Testimony to the White House Commission on Excellence in Special Education, Washington, DC.

Wehman, P., Bricout, J., & Kregel, J. (2000). Supported employment in 2000: Changing the locus of control from agency to consumer. In M. Wehmeyer & J.R. Patton (Eds.), *Mental retardation in the 21st century* (pp. 115–150). Austin, TX: PRO-ED.

Wehman, P., & Kregel, J. (1998). *More than a job: Securing satisfying careers for people with disabilities.* Baltimore: Paul H. Brookes Publishing Co.

Wehman, P., Mank, D., Rogan, P., Luna, J., Kregel, J., et al. (2005). Employment and productive life roles. In K.C. Lakin & A.P. Turnbull (Eds.), *National goals and research for persons with intellectual and developmental disabilities.* Washington, DC: American Association on Mental Retardation.

Wehman, P., & Revell, W.G. (2005). Lessons learned from the provision and funding of employment services for the MD/DD population: Implications for assessing the adequacy of the SSA Ticket to Work. *Journal of Disability Policy Studies, 16*(2), 84–101.

Wehman, P., Revell, W.G., & Brooke, V. (2003). Competitive employment: Has it become the "first choice" yet? *Journal of Disability Policy Studies, 14*(3), 163–173.

West, M., Hill, J., Revell, G., Smith, G., Kregel, J., & Campbell, L. (2002). Medicaid HCB Waivers and supported employment: Pre- and post–Balanced Budget Act of 1997. *Mental Retardation, 40*(2), 8.

Wittenburg, D.C., & Maag, E. (2002). School to where? A literature review on economic outcomes of youth with disabilities. *Journal of Vocational Rehabilitation, 17,* 265–280.

Chapter 2

Community Rehabilitation Programs and Human Services

Their Evolution and Role

Nancy Brooks-Lane, Suzanne Hutcheson, and W. Grant Revell, Jr.

Community rehabilitation programs are a primary source of employment supports used by individuals with significant disabilities. Historically, many community rehabilitation programs were primarily providers of day programs offered within settings segregated from the mainstream of the community and outside of the competitive labor market (Wehman, 1981). In recent years, many of these programs have gone through an evolutionary process involving a comprehensive redirection of their mission, goals, and services to reflect a prevailing emphasis on supporting program participants in achieving inclusive employment outcomes (Rogan, Held, & Rinne, 2001).

This chapter describes this evolution of community rehabilitation programs and the role these programs serve in providing employment supports to people with disabilities. After briefly reviewing factors that are influencing the evolution of community rehabilitation programs, detailed examples of this evolutionary process are used with two specific community rehabilitation programs. The core mission of both programs is to support individual-directed employment outcomes. The organizational change descriptions for the two programs are accompanied by stories about individuals who are now working in inclusive employment opportunities after receiving supports through these programs.

BACKGROUND

Prior to the Rehabilitation Act Amendments of 1986 (PL 99-506), funding for community rehabilitation programs serving individuals with significant disabilities focused mainly on services in work activity and/or sheltered work programs (Wehman, Revell, & Kregel, 1998). Examples of these programs included sheltered work settings that performed a variety of short-term sorting, collating, assembly, and disassembly tasks drawn from contracts with local employers. Whitehead (1979) found that the average wage paid to workers within a sheltered workshop facility was $.81

per hour in 1976, at a time when the minimum wage was $2.30 per hour. The 1986 Amendments to the Rehabilitation Act, in Title VI Part C, established the Supported Employment Formula Grants to all state vocational rehabilitation (VR) agencies. These funds could only be used to provide supported employment services that involved providing ongoing support to a person with significant disabilities for as long as required to maintain job stability, including training and other supports at the jobsite itself as needed.

Supported employment targeted supports to individuals with significant disabilities who had not been successful or had been limited to intermittent success in the competitive labor market. With supported employment, VR agencies had a new resource that focused on employment in integrated community work settings where individuals with significant disabilities would work side by side with co-workers without disabilities as peers and earn wages at minimum wage or above consistent with the Fair Labor Standards Act of 1938 (PL 75-718) (Wehman et al., 1998). Detailed discussions regarding supported employment and the provision of workplace and related supports are found in Chapters 6 and 7.

Since the passage of the Rehabilitation Act Amendments of 1986, the number of individuals with significant disabilities working in competitive employment has increased steadily, and the funding for supported employment has grown substantially; however, growth has also occurred in the number of people in day and work programs in sheltered/segregated settings. Table 2.1 tracks growth in participation in supported employment and day programs from 1988 to 2002 (Braddock, Rizzolo, & Hemp, 2004). In fiscal year (FY) 1988, only 23,000 individuals served by state disability agencies were in supported employment; by comparison, 237,000 individuals were in sheltered day or work programs. By FY 1992, the people in supported employment had grown more than 200% to 75,000. From FY 1992 through FY 2002, supported employment participation continued to grow but at a much slower rate than experienced from 1988 through 1992. In FY 2002, 118,00 individuals were in supported employment compared with almost 365,000 in a sheltered day or work program. The percent of individuals in supported employment of the total number in day or work programs leveled off at 24% in FY 2002 (Braddock, Hemp, Parish, & Rizzolo, 2002). For every one person working in an integrated job setting earning competitive wages, three individuals continued in sheltered settings. Earnings for those in sheltered employment were, on average, substantially below minimum wage (Wehman, Revell, & Brooke, 2003).

Table 2.1.   Individuals with intellectual and developmental disabilities in supported employment as a percentage of all people with intellectual and developmental disabilities in work-related programs

Fiscal year	Percent in supported employment as a percentage of total in day/work programs	Number of people in supported employment	Number of people in day or sheltered programs
1988	9%	23,000	237,000
1992	18%	75,000	300,000
1996	20%	92,000	328,000
2000	24%	108,000	357,000
2002	24%	118,000	365,000

Source: Braddock, Rizzolo, and Hemp (2004).

Table 2.2.   Federal Medicaid funding for day programs and supported employment

Fiscal year	Funding for supported employment (in millions)	Funding for day programs (in millions)
1997	$0	$514
1998	$35	$517
1999	$69	$514
2000	$104	$501
2001	$106	$488
2002	$108	$488

Source: Braddock, Rizzolo, and Hemp (2004).

The growth in funding of supported employment paralleled closely the growth in participation. Table 2.2 presents federal funding of Medicaid for day programs and supported employment from FY 1997 through 2002. The Balanced Budget Act of 1997 (PL 105-33) opened up funding for supported employment through the Home and Community-Based Medicaid Waiver (West et al., 2002). In FY 1998, federal Medicaid funding for supported employment totaled $35 million, compared with $517 million for day program services that did not include supports to people in competitive employment. From 1998 to 2002, the funding for supported employment grew to $108 million, and the funding for day programs dropped slightly to $488 million; however, for every $1 spent on supported employment services that encourage competitive employment outcomes, $4 continued to be spent for services that did not support competitive employment outcomes (Braddock et al., 2002; Braddock et al., 2004).

FACTORS INFLUENCING COMMUNITY REHABILITATION PROGRAMS

It is clear from the participation and funding data that community rehabilitation programs continue to operate in environments where the higher percentage of funds are used toward supporting noncompetitive work outcomes; however, in states such as Connecticut, Alaska, and Oklahoma, the number of people in competitive employment stands at approximately 50% or higher of day or work program participants (Braddock et al., 2004). These states provide excellent examples of effective systems-change strategies that support community rehabilitation programs evolving their services and supports to a primary emphasis on competitive employment. These strategies can be cataloged under the following headings (Mank & Revell, 2001):

1.   Focus on job outcomes

2.   Create mission-driven systems

3.   Align dollars with the mission

4.   Expand relations with business

5.   Support self-determination among program participants

These five state-level strategies parallel closely the key points emphasized by the community rehabilitation program case studies detailed later in this chapter.

A clear example of these five strategies forming a national systemic change effort follows. The passage of the Rehabilitation Act Amendments of 1986 created a mission-driven national system emphasizing provisions of supported employment by state VR agencies. As a result, VR agencies have made supporting individuals in competitive employment outcomes their primary mission (Wehman et al., 1998). Implementation of this new mission required that VR systems focus specifically on services directed at achieving job outcomes in the competitive labor market, and VR agencies realigned their available monetary resources to accomplish their redirected mission.

On January 22, 2001, the Rehabilitation Services Administration of the U.S. Department of Education amended the regulations governing the state VR programs to redefine the term *employment outcome* to mean "an individual with a disability working in an integrated setting" (Federal Register, January 22, 2001). For decades with state VR agencies, extended employment (sometimes referred to as *nonintegrated* or *sheltered employment*) was an approved potential employment outcome for individuals with disabilities who received VR services. Because extended/sheltered employment utilizes nonintegrated work settings, the redefining of an employment outcome for a VR participant to mean "work in an integrated setting" removed extended/sheltered employment as an approved potential employment outcome for VR services.

Emphasis on developing relationships with business became a priority with the passage of the Workforce Investment Act of 1998 (PL 105-220) and the alignment of the VR system with business through the Business Leadership Networks and the One Stop Career Centers. Finally, the Rehabilitation Act Amendments of 1986, sharpened further by its subsequent amendments (i.e., Rehabilitation Act Amendments of 1998 [PL 105-220]), emphasized choice and self-determination as the driving forces in the development of the individualized plan for employment (IPE) by individuals receiving services from the VR system. These five systems-level strategies set the standard for national- and state-level systems change. Community rehabilitation programs should focus on the same five key factors to successfully initiate and carry out plans for organizational redesign and development leading to an increased focus on supporting individual-driven employment outcomes.

For example, a first step in the evolutionary process for a community rehabilitation program is to develop an organizational focus on achieving competitive employment outcomes (i.e., focus on job outcomes) (Butterworth & Fesko, 2004). This focus sets in place an organizational change process that is driven by a clear mission that focuses attention and resources on program participants achieving competitive employment outcomes (Hutchinson & Revell, 2005). This mission-driven effort involves the program's board, administration, staff, and participants with disabilities. Staff and programs are then realigned to support this mission (i.e., create mission-driven systems) (Inge & Targett, 2004). A diversified funding base is developed, and funding is realigned to support the mission and focus on job outcomes (i.e., align dollars with mission) (Butterworth, Ghiloni, Revell, & Brooks-Lane, 2004). Business and industry become a partner and a customer (i.e., expand relations with business) (Targett & Inge, 2005). Finally, the consistent thread that runs through these efforts is the self-determined, informed goal of each individual served, including addressing the questions and concerns of family members (i.e., support self-determination among program participants). National and state-level systems change strategies and organizational-level change strategies must be linked and fully complement each other if the desired goal is to be achieved—inclusive employment that reflects the personal goals and dreams of the individuals supported by community rehabilitation programs.

TWO EXAMPLES OF THE EVOLUTION
OF COMMUNITY REHABILITATION PROGRAMS

Participation in sheltered/segregated programs continues to exceed participation in supported employment by individuals with significant disabilities; however, it is very important to emphasize that *a number of community rehabilitation programs have moved from providing services and supports that maintain individuals in segregated settings to a focus on providing supports to individuals in community-integrated, inclusive employment settings.* The Cobb and Douglas Counties Community Services Boards in Georgia and Helping People Succeed, Inc. (HPS; formerly Tri County TEC) in Florida are two excellent examples of community rehabilitation programs that are moving through an extended organizational redesign process that has resulted in the elimination of their sheltered work programs. Both programs now provide individual-directed supports to people working in a variety of integrated job settings in the community. The remainder of this chapter provides a description of the organizational redesign steps taken by each program and also contains the stories of a variety of individual program participants who are now working successfully in competitive employment.

Cobb and Douglas Counties Community Services Boards

During the summer of 2002, a business plan was sent to the local funding board from the leadership of the Cobb and Douglas Counties Community Services Boards, two boards that work together under the same administrative umbrella. This document contained the following value statement:

> We will concentrate efforts on service/support delivery that maximizes each individual's opportunity for inclusion, both socially and professionally. Consumers will be provided with the tools to compete for employment, including white collar jobs, in their respective communities.

The boards had been done with sheltered employment for about 3 years and were forging a culture focused on assisting individuals with disabilities in the development of career paths. Although change had come rapidly in those years, it had not been without pain.

The Cobb and Douglas Counties Community Services Boards are public agencies in the state of Georgia created by law to provide mental health, developmental disability, and substance abuse services/supports. The organization provided supports to more than 13,000 individuals in 2003. The majority of funds utilized to provide services are generated through a contract with the state of Georgia, Medicaid and Medicare revenue, funding from Cobb County and Douglas County, VR agency, grants, and private pay. The organizational goals include individual choice, community inclusion, work initiatives, and the expansion of the availability and access to natural community supports through the reduction of stigma.

In 1999, the Developmental Disabilities Services of the Cobb and Douglas Counties Community Services Boards operated four sheltered workshop programs. The state funding streams reinforced facility-based services, meaning that funds were used to maintain individuals in day activity and sheltered work programs. The majority of parents of the individuals attending the workshops were elderly and did not want changes to be made in the service system. In addition, several of the staff had worked in the programs for many years and were more comfortable with the facility-based model. At that time, shifting from a sheltered workshop to community-based supports was not a priority for the boards. As a result, previous attempts at change were minimally successful.

In 1999, the Community Services Boards hired a new chief executive officer who supported innovation involving moving the program to a more community-integrated approach to services. At this point, the change process began in earnest, underlining the importance of leadership support to implement system change. Subminimum wage contracts were phased out. Individual or small-group meetings were held to involve families and advocates in the change process. Many families were not in favor of the plans and struggled with the idea for about 6 months. These struggles presented themselves through a range of behaviors from productive discussion to personal attacks. This system-change effort was driven by the values of community integration and self-determination for individuals with significant disabilities. Those same ideals were returned to frequently as a guide for problem solving, decision making, and moral support during those first difficult months.

Complicating this situation was sabotage from a small number of staff members who felt threatened by the dissolution of the facility-based program. Through discussion, planning meetings, and training, most of these staff members became resigned and even committed to community-based supports. The few remaining saboteurs finally recognized they were not a good match for the new direction the organization was taking and left, but unfortunately not soon enough. In a last attempt to thwart the plans, they effectively created myths that fueled families' fears, so extensive energy had to be devoted to damage control.

If the program leaders expected staff members to support individuals differently, then it was their responsibility to give them the tools to succeed. In 2000, weekly on-site training began using best practice resources such as *A Customer Driven Approach for Persons with Significant Disabilities* (Brooke, Inge, Armstrong, & Wehman, 1997) and *Closing the Shop* (Murphy & Rogan, 1995). This inexpensive training method of purchasing the resources and utilizing them in roundtable, open discussions fit the very meager training budget. These weekly sessions laid the foundation for providing community-based supports.

Concurrently, the organizational structure was flattened. Staff members were offered opportunities to assume different support roles based on their interests and skills. Self-directed work teams were formed with staff members assuming more generic roles. Employment and the principles of community inclusion were the guiding light. Goal development was participant driven and determined by the individual's passions. Person-centered planning determined how staff turned these passions into customized employment outcomes.

The importance of pursuing diverse funding was critical for the programs to continue the innovations begun without the aid of additional dollars. By this time, staff and participants had achieved notable outcomes, demonstrating that the organization was worthy of grant dollars. In October 2001, the Cobb County Community Services Board was awarded a Customized Employment Grant through the Department of Labor/Office of Disability Employment Policy (DOL/ODEP). Training funded by the grant enabled staff to achieve competencies in 1) utilizing nontraditional assessments that are community based, decision-support software, vocational profiling, systematic instruction, and Social Security work incentives; 2) writing business plans; 3) using one-stop generic supports to job develop; and 4) assisting individuals with disabilities in such business enterprises as self-employment, resource ownership, and business within a business.

The Cobb and Douglas Counties Community Services Boards also invested funds in staff by purchasing on-line job coach certification training. To increase the efficiency of obtaining quality community-based outcomes, networks with the business community were developed to create coalitions that assisted with linking customers to businesses in their community pertinent to each individual's desires for employment. In 2003, open roundtable discussions using film, creative writing, civil rights, social justice, creativity, and economic development activities were begun to take the participants to the next level of skill acquisition involving undertaking new forms of social connections, community building, and civic renewal.

Staff members have been privileged to witness the creation of a person-centered system and the unfolding of lives in which competent individuals with disabilities have valued roles in their community and satisfaction from achieving their dreams. This experience points to the following five key characteristics of a program that builds supports around the specific interests/needs of an individual with a disability.

1. The program is flexible/creative.

2. The program is participant focused/driven and dedicated to choice.

3. The program uses a strengths model as opposed to a deficit model.

4. Program staff respectfully use people-first language.

5. The program is outcome based, with a focus on employment and inclusion.

In the following case studies, the "diagnosis" or "label" is indicated merely to dispel stereotypes. Each story describes a real person and events surrounding his or her moving into employment, although names and identifying details are changed to protect confidentiality. Each story bears witness to the people supported by the staff of the Cobb and Douglas Counties Community Services Boards. The methodology of customized employment described in these examples has provided the tools to tailor systems to free people from segregation (Buxton, 2004).

MARIE

Marie grew up in one of Georgia's institutions. Her records note her "diagnosis" as mild mental retardation, epilepsy, and "difficulty relating to community due to her institutionalization." Marie loves to work. She loves to clean and organize and keep busy. Her employment history consists of two or three service industry jobs and sheltered employment. As a Customized Employment Grant participant, she has financial resources that have allowed her an aspect of choice she has not previously had. The choices include control over funds, the job development process, and the provision of job supports.

Marie enjoys sweeping. She finds it soothing and likes the satisfaction of watching the dirt, crumbs, or other debris disappear from the floor under her skilled hands, so it was important to ensure times during her workday when she could sweep. She also loves to be around people, despite the traditional assessment notation of "difficulty relating to community," so it was important that Marie's work environment offered opportunities to interact and connect with others. She also needed a certain income to meet her expenses and needs and to have money to do those things she enjoys, as well as saving for unplanned expenses.

As a result of creative planning, Marie and her support team determined that a wage job with resource ownership would possibly result in a customized employment outcome that would meet her requirements. Resource ownership involves an individual bringing a resource of value, such as a piece of equipment, to an employer and establishing an agreement with the employer that potentially pays the individual for use of the equipment. The path leading to this decision involved

- Matching Marie's passion with job choices through a nontraditional, community-based vocational profile assessment
- Planning person-centered employment
- Analyzing the financial benefits and potential income
- Including VR services in this process

As a result, Marie is employed in a hair salon in her community, and co-workers assist with job support. Marie has created an environment that is pleasant and that has never been cleaner. As she wished, her day includes cleaning, organizing, and sweeping. She purchased a washer and dryer, as well as a hair dryer chair, with funds from her Individual Training Account through the grant. Marie is responsible for washing, drying, and folding the salon towels and retuning these clean towels to the cabinets for the stylists' use. With her hair dryer chair, she assists customers with the correct setting and positioning of the dryer head. She owns these resources that she brought to the job with her and which she used to negotiate specific conditions for her employment that were important to her. Marie now has choices she never had before, including remaining with this business; choosing another salon at some future point, should that be to her advantage; or exploring self-employment. Whatever Marie's choice, the resources remain with her.

TANYA

Tanya attended a segregated day program for individuals diagnosed with both intellectual disabilities and mental illness. Her disability descriptions were recorded as moderate mental retardation and schizophrenia. As a result of her involvement in traditional segregated programs that lacked choice and options, she became further depressed, which resulted in assistance for bathing, dressing, and eating.

She was identified as a candidate for supported employment early in a systems-change process and before the award of the Customized Employment Grant previously referenced. The strategy was to begin with willing individuals and their families in hopes that their successes would encourage those who were more resistant to the changes to loosen their grip on the status quo. With Tanya's permission and input, staff developed a circle of support involving her family, key friends, and others chosen by Tanya to help learn about her unique skills, talents, and strengths and to begin envisioning a job for her in her community. The support staff spent time with Tanya away from the day program doing what she enjoyed so the staff members could learn about her in diverse environments. A vocational profile emerged that took into account Tanya's desire to dress professionally, have a computer, and work in a business environment.

Time was spent in several companies simply observing the social climate of the business. It became clear during the planning process that a calm and flexible work environment was key. A Fortune 500 company was identified that met these specifications. Although Tanya could not meet all the duties required in the company's various job descriptions, she could meet some of them with job coach and co-worker supports. A customized position was negotiated with input from the company's human resources, administration, and senior management staff.

The company is located in a corporate office in the business district of Atlanta. A facilities clerk position was carved out for Tanya, and her job duties consist of simple data entry, office supply distribution, and conference room scheduling. Tanya has been successfully employed in the position for more than 2 years. As a result of her success, the director of human resources asked if Tanya would be interested in job sharing. Her employment consultant, who was interested in such a position, identified a second person who also has the label of moderate mental retardation. Tanya works from 7 A.M. to 11 A.M., Monday through Thursday, and Lori, her job-share partner, works from 11 A.M. to 3 P.M., Tuesday through Friday.

The work that Tanya and Lori provide for this company has resulted in greater productivity in their co-workers, and neither have been victims of the corporate layoffs that less fortunate co-workers have had to endure. The human resources director told Tanya and Lori that as long as she is employed in the company, they will have jobs.

CHARLES

Charles has a passion for cars and dreams of becoming a mechanic. He and his employment consultant went to various auto-parts companies close to his home to submit applications. He had his sights set on a particular dealership. It was about 2½ miles from his home, brand new, and just the place he wanted to work. There is a story behind Charles and his job search. Every day for 3 months, he walked the 5 miles to this business, showing them his employment consultant's card and letting them know he wanted to work for their company. Even though Charles has the label of mental retardation and has no verbal language, there is no doubt what he is indicating through his facial expressions. Although he has limited use of his right arm and leg, he has learned to adapt and effectively uses his left side in compensation.

His support staff finally received the call they had been hoping for. The car dealership's manager said, "Okay, we are convinced. We will hire him." The CEO was moved by Charles' commitment and determination to work at his business. His job title is mechanic assistant, and his carved-out duties include pressure washing, spray-painting the tire rims of vehicles, stocking, and cleaning up. Charles, who is in his 20s, went from high school into a residential VR agency-funded vocational program. Other than this assessment period, he has not attended segregated programs.

He definitely thinks of his current employment choices as a part of a long-term career path, which he is determined will always involve cars. As support staff explored options with Charles and worked with others on self-employment ideas, the notion of being certified in emissions testing and owning his own emissions equipment became a goal. The team met with the CEO where Charles works. In investigating the certification training, it was discovered that the regulations in Georgia require one to speak and understand English to be certified as an emissions tester. Charles will be the first person in Georgia certified in emissions testing who does not speak English. An assistive technology device was purchased with funds from his Individual Training Account and will enable Charles to utilize preprogrammed verbal commands with his customers as he tests their vehicles. The CEO personally advocated for Charles with the certifying board for emissions testing. With his sense of purpose and persistence, there is no doubt that Charles has taken the first step down his career path.

JOSÉ

José was successfully working as a machinist, manufacturing equipment used in the poultry industry. The depression and alcoholism he struggled with daily had not spilled over into his work—the one area of his life in which he felt competent and in control. This all ended the same year when he injured his back lifting a 20-foot steel I-beam onto the table of a reciprocating saw. José's personal and employment life suffered as his daily routine became driven by surgery, physical therapy, and work restrictions. José stated, "My alcoholism and depression intensified."

There is a humble undercurrent to José as he speaks of his history, not as a victim, but as the difficult road he has traveled. This roller coaster of frustrating attempts at employment, depression, and alcoholism ended in his being arrested after being found in an alcohol blackout. José knew he had hit rock bottom. At this point, he describes a spiritual awakening. This spirituality is most important to José and manifests itself in his gentle nature, kindness, and desire to give back. He sincerely hopes his story is beneficial to others.

After compensating the legal system, José was sent to a homeless shelter with the mandate that he get a job.

"I walked 3 blocks, found a job using a fork lift, and went back to let the staff at the shelter know," José said. "Something about the job did not fit with their policies and procedures, so I was sent to another shelter. I found a job in the newspaper at a machinery shop. The boss there was very supportive. He had a son with some problems, and he thought I might be able to talk to the son about what I'd been through and help him. I began going to a technical school at night and got my certification as a computer tech."

This accomplishment positioned him to fulfill a dream he had for awhile— obtaining employment in the computer industry. He became involved with the VR agency and the local One Stop Career Center, where he received assistance in obtaining employment in the computer industry. Over the next several years, he worked in various positions installing digital prescriber lines (DSL) and as a field service technician. Due to the changes in the company, closings, and layoffs, José began thinking about self-employment as a way to have more control over his work. He continued to pursue his dream with the assistance of the VR agency, Cobb Works (the local One Stop Career Center), and the Cobb County Community Services Board, where with the flexible funding of the U.S. Department of Labor (DOL)/Office of Disability Employment Policy (ODEP) Customized Employment Grant, he was able to start his own business.

VR services provided funds for training, transportation, medical needs, computer equipment, office supplies, and books/manuals. The Customized Employment Grant funding was used by José to supplement the VR resources. He purchased business training through the local microenterprise center. He received assistance with personal supports, transportation, certification training, equipment, advertising, and short-term help with office rent. The One-Stop provided on-site resources for information and searches.

José has found his niche. He has one employee and offers the following services: custom-built PCs, printer repair service, sales and supplies, vendor links, and data backup.

As José enters his eighth year of recovery, ongoing successful management of his depression, and second year of self-employment, he explains what was effective and what was a barrier in the service systems that offered him support and resources.

"The flexible funding of the grant was very helpful and efficient, and clear communication was important. The policies and procedures of the different systems were barriers in that they were not clear, were rigid, or were in conflict."

José has effectively summarized the essence of who he is and his business culture in the name he has chosen. There is a nobility about him and how he has maneuvered the hard knocks of his life and found the path of his dreams. He has gained an understanding of how to move through life.

He says, "Go to any length . . . do whatever it takes to change your life in the areas that are not working. Don't worry about the whys and hows. Do not get caught up in planning only. Make things happen. If you are interested in self-employment, know your motives. Not everyone is meant to be an entrepreneur. It takes a certain quality. If you get easily discouraged, self-employment is not for you."

José, in talking about himself now, says, "I am not supposed to regret the past nor wish to shut the door on it. Resentments are the number one offender regarding happiness. There was always someone there for me along the way once I arrived in Cobb County. I am so very grateful for my new life."

DIONTE

By age 5, Dionte had experienced more in his short life than many people do in a lifetime. His father had been murdered, his mother was struggling with an addiction, and he was in the hospital with life-threatening injuries as a result of a car accident.

He says, "I was not expected to live. I was in the hospital about a year. I still suffer from the accident. I have a limp and some pain I have to live with." But Dionte is a survivor. Seizures began soon after the accident. "My family thought I was being bad so they beat me every time I passed out."

Dionte describes a very difficult time in his life. "I tried to commit suicide when I was 18; I have paranoid schizophrenia. I felt I had nothing to live for. I questioned my mama's love of me. My family was all broken up. I just wanted to take myself out."

He has worked in various service-industry positions and found his passion when he was hired to do painting and maintenance for a hotel chain. "I love to paint," he reports. At times, medications that Dionte takes for epilepsy and mental illness affect his ability to function. He is a perfectionist and "expects more than 100%" from himself, so this is frustrating for him. Dionte is also very organized, well spoken, and takes great pride in his skills as a "top-notch painter." For these and many more reasons, owning his own business appealed to him.

He used the One-Stop Career Center in his community to research the painting business. His employment specialist through the Cobb County Community Services Board assisted him with gaining access to VR services and resources available through the DOL/ODEP Customized Employment Grant. The grant funded a 12-week business skill development course.

"I finished the classes through Cobb Microenterprise and wrote my business plan. I was insecure at first, but now I feel more confident after completing the course."

With his approved business plan, Dionte requested financial support through the VR agency to purchase office equipment and office supplies. The Individual Training Account from the Customized Employment Grant allowed him to purchase painting equipment, painting supplies, advertising, a computer, transportation, and a business license.

Dionte is now proudly self-employed with one employee in a business that provides residential and commercial painting and stenciling of parking areas. He has an impressive portfolio with stellar references and photographs of his expert work. He has lived through the hopelessness of a life lost, the stabilizing force of recovery, and the grounding effects of finding one's passion through employment and then taking the leap to self-employment. He describes his approach to his business as follows: "You have to make your customers happy. You can never stop researching to improve your business, and you have to know your competitors."

"Going into my own business, I have struggled and I know there will be days that will be stormy." With a laugh he adds, "I have stormed, but there have been good people helping me and I have got to give them credit."

Dionte learned at 5 years of age that he is a survivor. His business—the business that he started—reminds him of this every day.

Helping People Succeed, Inc.

Tri-County Training Employment Community (TEC) in Stuart, Florida, recently changed its name to Helping People Succeed, Inc. (HPS). The new name reflects the mission of this community rehabilitation program. Since 1964, HPS has been committed to providing the support that individuals with disabilities need to live everyday lives just like other members of society. The organization has survived and grown through a willingness to change to better fulfill its mission. HPS has moved from an arts and crafts program serving approximately 30 adults with disabilities (1964–1974), to a work activities/sheltered workshop serving approximately 175 people with disabilities (1974–1984), to a totally community-based approach (1984–present) with four distinct divisions (Baby Steps, Behavioral Services, Community Living, and Employment Services). Currently, HPS serves approximately 3,000 children and adults who have a diagnosed condition, are at risk of abuse or neglect, or are part of the typical population of adults who either have a disability or are welfare recipients.

HPS was founded in 1964 as Pioneer Occupational Center for the Handicapped, Inc., by a group of parents who felt that their sons and daughters deserved more in life than sitting at home watching television. In 1974, the organization became the Tri-County Rehabilitation Center, Inc., and, as the board comprised more business people, the focus became subcontract work and training programs such as participant home economics, adult basic education, food service, and carpentry. The organization grew to serve approximately 150–175 individuals with developmental disabilities from the surrounding counties of Martin, St. Lucie, and Indian River. In some cases, individuals had a 3-hour round trip bus ride to receive services.

In 1984, several important events occurred. First, senior management became disenchanted because, despite all the training programs at the facility, individuals were not exiting the programs for employment and, in many cases, were not demonstrating any real skill acquisition. Second, the types of subcontract work offered did not fit the skills or abilities of the individuals served. Wages were minimal, and no jobs were being found. Third, supported employment opened a new way of thinking and opportunities for individuals with severe disabilities.

The Tri-County Rehabilitation Center, Inc., became Tri-County TEC. The senior management staff (executive director, production manager, and rehabilitation manager) determined that supported employment strategies offered the means for the participants to achieve employment outcomes that had been missing from the existing program services. The beginning of a long road to employment and community-based services began. The following were and continue to be the components of change.

Mission and Vision

Moving from a facility-based organization that was proud of its programs and services to one that was community based and proud of its outcomes began with a redefinition of the mission and vision. Although management was convinced that supported employment represented the future, staff had to own the concept. They would have to actually perform the work to make supported employment happen successfully.

The first step was to hold staff in-service training sessions that questioned those values and concepts. A values-clarification session was held with questions that started out global, probing the belief system that all people should have the right and opportunity to work. Then, the values clarification session moved closer and closer to each staff member's commitment and responsibility to helping achieve employment outcomes for the individuals served.

Following the values clarification exercise, all staff members except senior management were asked to determine how many of the 150–175 individuals with developmental disabilities served by the program could work. They were directed to ignore barriers such as behavior, parental concerns, and transportation and to just look at whether the person could work. Senior management expected that approximately 10% of the current population would be identified. Staff identified that 95% of individuals served *could work*, given proper support.

Tri-County TEC's mission evolved from the complicated *Tri-County TEC serves individuals (infants and adults) who need special training, education, employment, and living arrangements to improve their quality of life and become active members in their community* to the very simple *helping people succeed!* The new mission was to the point—it described what would be done as opposed to the population(s) served. It was easy to understand and explain.

Planning and Implementation

Tri-County TEC decided to base its planning on senior staff developing goals to compare and align with goals developed by direct-services staff. Direct-services staff, with senior management staff available for input and advice, developed implementation strategies. The planning process was conducted by an outside facilitator, allowing for questioning and input that otherwise might have been uncomfortable for staff. Presentations and training were conducted by experts in the field, including Dr. Paul Wehman and Michael Barcus from the Virginia Commonwealth University Rehabilitation Research and Training Center on Workplace Supports and Job Retention and Dale DiLeo from the Training Resource Network.

When conversion efforts were being planned, the assumption was that individuals with disabilities and their families would want this option. Management and staff assumed that they were fed-up that the programs were circular—year after year, individuals were performing the same tasks, going through the same training programs, and never leaving the workshop.

The assumption about their preferences was incorrect. In most cases, the families had never considered the fact that their sons or daughters might work in the community; they were satisfied with the current system. Parents felt their sons or daughters were safe and secure in "the workshop." Community-based options threatened that illusion of safety.

A series of parent meetings were held. The approach taken by staff with the parents was, "What kind of employment do you see as most appropriate for your son or daughter?" The answers ranged from "what do you think?" to "over my dead and mangled body will my son or daughter work."

Without family support, any individual with disabilities attempting a community-based placement would very likely fail. Tri-County TEC's conversion effort began with individuals with disabilities and their families who indicated they wanted to work. During the first 3–5 years of conversion efforts, individuals with disabilities were part of the process, and the outcome was the central focus.

As the conversion effort became more solid, community-based employment outcomes became the norm for the organization. Individuals and families began to push for employment as their outcome. As the person-centered approach evolved, families became more comfortable with the idea and actuality of employment—they are now a part and feel included as part of the team. Again, this involvement by families is *critical* to success.

The desire of individuals with disabilities for employment was never an issue. Employment is the natural next step to give individuals the opportunity to experience their community in a positive way. HPS experiences the same issues as every other organization—transportation, benefits, economic changes, and uncertainty in funding. The difference with the program is that each of the issues is approached simply as a cog in the wheel that has to be solved in order to achieve success.

Tri-County TEC's first plan, completed in 1984, was a 3-year plan that attempted to convert all 150–175 individuals served to competitive employment. Staff quickly realized that this goal was impossible to accomplish in a 3-year period. Planning and implementation continued until Tri-County TEC achieved total community-based services in 1991. Tri-County TEC's conversion was a true one—existing funding was converted from training dollars to funding for employment supports; the 19,000 square-foot building was sold; the organization relocated to the Chamber of Commerce building, where no services were provided on site; and success was measured by the employment outcomes achieved. Since 1991, the organization has continued to grow and expand. Tri-County TEC moved from being a totally facility-based program in 1984, to having one job coach (a former bookkeeper) in 1985, to having a staff of 18 employment specialists (job coaches, follow along, and supported living personnel) in 2004.

Present Situation

When the journey to community-based employment services began, HPS did not have a clear picture of where it would end up; however, management and staff knew that providing support for people with disabilities to become a part of their community was the right thing. The changes and results have been dramatic.

Once it was committed to community-based services, the organization expanded significantly in all areas. HPS continues to be defined by its outcomes—services that assist in obtaining and retaining employment. Major changes have included:

- Growing from serving 3 counties (Martin, St. Lucie, and Indian River) to 11 counties (Martin, St. Lucie, Indian River, Okeechobee, Highlands, Hendry, Polk, Hardy, Glades, Broward, and Palm Beach)

- Changing from process-based services to outcome-based options

- Using a funding-sources approach to offer or expand services

- Moving from single-stream funding to 19 funding sources

- Adding the Welfare to Work population funded through Temporary Assistance for Needy Families

- Growing from 25 to 142 staff members

- Moving from 175 participants in a long-term sheltered workshop setting to 225–250 entering employment on an annual basis

- Receiving a 98% satisfaction rating from individuals with disabilities, their families, employers, and funders

HPS successfully converted to a totally community-based series of options, not only for people with disabilities, but also for a variety of populations. Approximately 30 participants work in community jobs being paid under the Section 14c Minimum Wage Certificate; all of the remaining participants work in competitive jobs at minimum wage or higher. HPS is successful because of a complete commitment to helping people succeed through employment and community-based options.

In today's world, for an organization to be successful in making the transition to services in the community, a commitment must be present and must be guided by a person-centered approach that focuses on the wants, desires, and needs of each person served. Helping people who have been invisible in society live everyday lives as taxpayers, not welfare recipients, is the key to long-term success. Here are the stories of three individuals who receive employment support through HPS.

SUE

Sue is a 57-year-old woman who has developmental disabilities and who was institutionalized as an infant and spent the first few years of her life in a crib with two other infants. Her growth was stunted and mobility impaired by this experience. Although her history at the institution is not clear, upon release she was referred to HPS for services. Sue became quite angry working in the sheltered workshop, as her daily tasks were minimal, and she felt she was capable of doing tasks that were meaningful. She became frustrated and actually had screaming outbursts indicating that she wanted a "real" job.

Sue got her wish. With the assistance of a job coach, she was employed in a prestigious multiattorney firm. Her job is to microfilm all of the confidential documents for the firm. Workplace modifications included the strategic placement of mirrors so that she could see the counter to know when she was finished with a task, a "back scratcher" to turn the lights on and off, and a motorized scooter (acquired through VR funding) so that she could move more quickly throughout the office. Due to the shortness of her legs, a footrest was placed on her scooter so that she would be comfortable.

Although extensive job coaching was necessary to help her acquire all of the skills necessary to perform her job, today she requires only minimal follow-up support with very few interventions. She is a full-time employee with full benefits, including profit sharing. She has made many friends who help her with grocery shopping and lawn work and are available just to talk. Sue purchased her own home and has a roommate who pays rent. Sue is included in all of the different activities at the firm, including luncheons and firm parties, and she receives invitations to many birthday parties and other events.

Sue has changed very much during the past years. Once shy and quiet, she now demonstrates a great sense of humor, a wonderful attitude, and no angry outbursts. Sue allows HPS to use her success to let the community know what the organization is about. Sue has won many awards, including the Governor's Employee of the Year Award. Although Sue still has developmental disabilities, she has her job, a home, and a community. Most of all, Sue has her independence.

JOEL

Joel graduated from Martin County High School with a regular diploma, high honors, and a ranking of twelfth in his graduating class, despite the fact he has autism. Following graduation, he attended a business school, where he learned how to use the computer and practiced his typing skills. Although Joel has a very high intellect, his social and work behavior skills were his major barriers to employment.

With the assistance of the Martin County School System job coach, he began working at a Braille institute. He was placed in an office by himself and taught data entry with consistent supervision. After 6 months, he was placed in the regular office with his co-workers. This was a giant step for Joel. Because of his history of struggles with interpersonal interactions, socialization with his co-workers was something no one was sure he could handle. But, he did. And Joel grew.

After 16 years working full time with full benefits, Joel is typing 100 words per minute, scanning in books, and working in the bindery and book cover department. He enjoys full medical benefits and a 401K plan. He has wonderful supports from HPS staff that help him over the rough spots that he encounters. With the ongoing support of HPS, he is able to succeed at his job and life.

Joel will tell you he is proud of his job and his longevity at the Braille institute. He will also tell you that even though he has a disability, he isn't going to let that stop him from trying his best. He is now living in his own apartment and trying hard to work on his judgment skills.

DAN

Dan has developmental disabilities and a history of aggressive behavior issues that have not only been barriers to employment but also to maintaining a place in an adult day training/sheltered workshop. Dan bores easily and needs to keep busy and moving to be successful.

Staff at HPS worked hard with Dan to determine what kind of job might give him his freedom to move around but also offer enough of a challenge to keep him motivated. Dan became employed at Wal-Mart as a shelf stocker, with other duties as needed. This was a challenge as Dan does not read. The on-the-job training that Dan needed had to be very carefully constructed as he did not want to be "different." Dan's supervisor was very clear with him as to the expectations of his job performance, duties, and attitude. Dan responded well to his supervisor's instructions, and HPS staff began to coach the supervisor rather than Dan.

Wal-Mart has found Dan to be a valuable employee who has actually been named the store's Employee of the Month more than once. Dan has found a place that satisfies his needs—he has what he considers a "responsible" job, he can keep moving, and he is quite proud of the fact that he no longer needs "that behavior person."

Dan lives with his mother, who at one time was considering asking the state to place him in a group setting as she was afraid of him. Luckily, there was no such placement available at that time. She has indicated that he is now a "delight" to have around—he's proud of his contributions to the household, helps out some, and does not exhibit the anger that he carried around for many years.

Dan would like to live in his own apartment—a challenge that he will be tackling with the assistance of HPS.

CONCLUSION

The examples provided by Cobb County and Douglas County Community Services Boards and by HPS clearly point out the real challenges and potential rewards involved in evolving a community rehabilitation program from a sheltered service setting to a vibrant, diversified source of supports for people with disabilities working in competitive employment. This evolution is a process that grows slowly but steadily over an extended period of time. It usually involves a one-person-at-a-time focus because time needs to be taken to truly support an individual in pursuing his or her employment dream. Chapter 13 of this book provides a detailed discussion of organizational change strategies for community rehabilitation programs. The rewards for embarking on a mission-driven, person-centered organizational change process are found in the chapter's case studies.

REFERENCES

Balanced Budget Act of 1997, PL 105-33, 111 Stat. 251.

Braddock, D., Hemp, R., Parish, S., & Rizzolo, M. (2002). *The state of the states in developmental disabilities: 2002 study summary.* Boulder: University of Colorado at Boulder, Coleman Institute for Cognitive Disabilities.

Braddock, D., Rizzolo, M., & Hemp, R. (2004). Most employment services growth in developmental disabilities during 1988–2002 was in segregated settings. *Mental Retardation, 42*(4), 317–320.

Brooke, V., Inge, K., Armstrong, A., & Wehman, P. (1997). *Supported employment handbook: A customer driven approach for persons with significant disabilities.* Richmond: Virginia Commonwealth University Rehabilitation Research and Training Center on Workplace Supports and Job Retention.

Butterworth, J., & Fesko, S. (2004). *Successful organizational change.* Richmond: Virginia Commonwealth University Rehabilitation Research and Training Center on Workplace Supports and Job Retention. Available on-line at http://www.t-tap.org/strategies/factsheet/successchange.htm

Butterworth, J., Ghiloni, C., Revell, G., & Brooks-Lane, N. (2004). *Creating a diversified funding base.* Richmond: Virginia Commonwealth University Rehabilitation Research and Training Center on Workplace Supports and Job Retention. Available on-line at http://www.t-tap.org/strategies/factsheet/diversifiedfunding.html

Buxton, V. (2004). Customized employment makes dreams come true. *Making a Difference, 4*(5), 18–21.

Fair Labor Standards Act of 1938, PL 75-718, 29 U.S.C. 201 *et seq.*

Hutchinson, S., & Revell, G. (2005). *Developing a business plan for organizational change*. Richmond: Virginia Commonwealth University Rehabilitation Research and Training Center on Workplace Supports and Job Retention. Available on-line at http://www.t-tap.org/strategies/factsheet/developingbusplan.htm

Inge, K., & Targett, P. (2004). *Changing staff roles*. Richmond: Virginia Commonwealth University Rehabilitation Research and Training Center on Workplace Supports and Job Retention. Available on-line at http://www.t-tap.org/strategies/factsheet/changingstaffroles.html

Mank, D., & Revell, G. (2001). Systemic change for supported employment: Old lessons and new possibilities. In P. Wehman (Ed.), *Supported employment in business: Expanding the capacity of workers with disabilities*. St. Augustine, FL: Training Resource Network.

Murphy, S.T., & Rogan, P.M. (1995). *Closing the shop: Conversion from sheltered to integrated work*. Baltimore: Paul H. Brookes Publishing Co.

Rehabilitation Act Amendments of 1986, PL 99-506, 29 U.S.C. §§ 701 *et seq.*

Rehabilitation Act Amendments of 1998, PL 105-202, 29 U.S.C. §§ 701 *et seq.*

Rogan, P., Held, M., & Rinne, S. (2001). Organizational change from sheltered to integrated employment for adults with disabilities. In P. Wehman (Ed.), *Supported employment in business: Expanding the capacity of workers with disabilities*. St. Augustine, FL: Training Resource Network.

Targett, P., & Inge, K. (2005). *Employment negotiations*. Richmond: Virginia Commonwealth University Rehabilitation Research and Training Center on Workplace Supports and Job Retention. Available on-line at http://www.t-tap.org/strategies/factsheet/employnegotiation.htm

Wehman, P. (1981). *Competitive employment: New horizons for severely disabled individuals*. Baltimore: Paul H. Brookes Publishing Co.

Wehman, P., Revell, G., & Brooke, V. (2003). Competitive employment: Has it become the first choice yet? *Journal of Disability Policy Studies, 14*(3), 163–173.

Wehman, P., Revell, G., & Kregel, J. (1998). Supported employment: A decade of rapid growth and impact. *American Rehabilitation, 24*(1), 31–43.

West, M., Hill, J., Revell, G., Smith, G., Kregel, J., & Campbell, L. (2002). Medicaid HCB waivers and supported employment: Pre- and post-Balanced Budget Act of 1997. *Mental Retardation, 40*(2), 8.

Whitehead, C. (1979). Sheltered workshops in the decade ahead: Work and wages, or welfare. In T. Bellamy, G. O'Connor, & O. Karan (Eds.), *Vocational rehabilitation of severely handicapped persons: Contemporary service strategies*. Baltimore: University Park Press.

Workforce Investment Act (WIA) of 1998, PL 105-220, 29 U.S.C. §§ 2801 *et seq.*

Chapter 3

Self-Advocacy for Supported Employment and Resource Ownership

Listening to the Voices of People with Disabilities

PAUL WEHMAN, NANCY BROOKS-LANE, VALERIE A. BROOKE, AND EDMOND TURNER

In recent years, there has been a rekindling of interests in expanding services and improving access to a full range of activities in the community for people with physical, emotional, intellectual, and sensory disabilities. A variety of legislative programs have helped fuel this initiative. For example, the Technology-Related Assistance for Individuals with Disabilities Act of 1988 (PL 100-407), along with its 1994 amendments (PL 103-218), support the full participation of individuals with disabilities in society and movement toward automation and application of technology in workplaces and homes. The Americans with Disabilities Act (ADA) of 1990 (PL 101-336), signed into law by President George Bush, and the accompanying regulations published on July 26, 1991, in the Federal Register, have served as the driving force in assisting people with all types of disabilities to participate more fully in the labor force and to increase their community involvement and representation.

Specifically, there are hundreds of thousands of people with a variety of disabilities who are speaking for themselves. They are voicing their concerns, needs, and frustrations to a society that sometimes seems to have forgotten them. Although it is always difficult to trace the beginning of new directions in service priorities, a major impetus for greater consumerism, technology, and family involvement has come directly from legislation such as the ADA. Legislation such as the ADA that so clearly establishes a new direction for society does so partly because of an existing vacuum in the law and accompanying practices.

For example, millions of people with disabilities now have a legal mandate for full access when, prior to the ADA, they frequently could not get into movie theaters, grocery stores, shopping malls, restaurants, and other public places. Still, thousands of highly capable individuals who could work are either passively or actively discriminated against by businesses still unwilling to make often very inexpensive accommodations. The ADA prohibits these practices. In addition, the Supreme Court through the *Olmstead* (1999) decision upheld the right of individuals with disabilities to live in the community and not be institutionalized. This further thrust many people with significant disabilities into a movement of consumerism as they began to shop for services to function independently and not depend on a paternalistic professional service-delivery system that has historically ignored them.

In this chapter, we look at several forms of integrated employment from the perspective of an individual with disabilities and describe examples of models such as supported employment, self-employment, and resource ownership. The latter half of the chapter presents numerous stories of success in self-employment.

ORIGIN OF SUPPORTED EMPLOYMENT

It will be beneficial to examine the origin of supported employment. That is, we need to take a look at how and why supported employment emerged as an attractive alternative for people with disabilities because new concepts do not arise unless there is a need for them. Supported employment became a highly viable option because there were thousands of people with severe mental disabilities who were viewed as incapable and unemployable by most service providers, many parents, and scores of advocates. Their options in life were to be in day programs, adult activity centers, or sheltered workshops; to stay at home; or to live in institutions. In the mid- to late 1970s, a number of professionals began to experiment with different ways of providing services. The reason for this experimentation was primarily to meet one need: for people to obtain competitive employment, earn a decent wage, develop a real work history, and realize community inclusiveness.

In the 1986 reauthorization (PL 99-506) of the Rehabilitation Act of 1973 (PL 93-112) the term *supported employment* was defined, and, for purposes of this act, it means:

> Competitive work in integrated settings (A) for individuals with severe handicaps for whom competitive employment has not traditionally occurred, or (B) for individuals for whom competitive employment has been interrupted or intermittent as a result of a severe disability, and who, because of their handicap, need ongoing support services to perform such work.

This legislation called for a new definition of *employability* that implied that everyone possesses the potential to work. With this added feature and emphasis on ongoing or long-term support, it was acknowledged that people with severe disabilities could enter regular jobs in the labor force. Therefore, supported employment was developed to give individuals with disabilities a choice in the labor force. This service model focuses on the interests of individuals with disabilities and provides an opportunity for individuals to identify a job, specify the working conditions, determine the wage level, select the job location, and decide the hours that they will work with support. With 140,000 people currently working in supported employment and the number growing each year, it is clear that more and more individuals with severe disabilities are asserting their rights and going to work for the first time (Rizzolo, Hemp, Braddock, & Pomeranz-Essley, 2004; Wehman, Revell, & Kregel, 1998).

Supported employment will not succeed without the active involvement of individuals with significant disabilities. Supported employment programs cannot be effective and will not flourish without full individual and family participation, support, and contribution, along with a willingness to take the necessary risks that are inherent in competitive employment. Those individuals with disabilities who entered the work force in the late 1970s and early 1980s were pioneers. They were willing to take the risks of losing Social Security disability benefits and their safe spot in an adult day program by entering competitive employment. In most states, there were limited support systems to help replace them if their employment efforts were not successful the first time.

We think that the parallels between this type of risk taking and the pioneering spirit by people with severe intellectual disabilities dramatically parallels visionary thinking and activities on the part of many people. The roots of supported employment are deeply entwined in customer interest, choice, and inclusion. These roots are what has made supported employment one of the most popular and sustainable programs in the United States, even in the face of two significant recessions in this country, one from 1990 to 1992 and the other from 2001 to 2002.

PARALLELS BETWEEN INDIVIDUAL ADVOCACY AND SUPPORTED EMPLOYMENT

There are numerous overlaps in philosophies and a significant number of parallels between the recent emphasis on consumerism and the supported employment programs that have rapidly emerged across the country. To be effective and a valuable support, all people who are working in the field of disability, especially those who are service providers, should be aware of these philosophies and parallels.

The focal point of consumer advocacy and supported employment is the person with disabilities. Traditionally, programs that provide services to people with disabilities have been delivered in large groups and in an aggregate format (i.e., sheltered workshops, large institutional settings). Supported employment does just the opposite. Highly effective supported employment programs, for the most part, provide individualized services designed to support the individual worker based on what he or she wants and needs. For example, if the individual in question has a brain injury and does not want or need frequent visits to the work site from an employment specialist, then it is the responsibility of the employment specialist to do everything in his or her power to respect that wish; however, if a person with a long-term mental illness and his or her family are extremely nervous and anxious about employment, then the employment specialist will be available on a more frequent basis.

Real work is the outcome that individual advocacy and supported employment programs both promote. In many programs that serve individuals with disabilities, the outcomes and goals are very unclear. The bureaucracy of service delivery seems to obscure the intent of the program, and the individual is classically "lost in the shuffle." A major strength of both the individual advocacy and the supported employment movements is that the goals and outcomes are very clear in terms of what all involved wish to see happen—a competitive job in good working conditions earning a decent wage. This type of singular focus empowers professionals, advocates, and individuals who work to promote both of these programs. All involved know what they are there for. Employment is the measure of their success or lack of progress.

Individuals with disabilities participating in individual advocacy and/or supported employment programs have had their potential grossly underutilized. Many individuals with significant disabilities have been "wasted" in terms of their human potential, whether it was when employment service programs focused on people with severe intellectual disabilities, severe autism, and other severe cognitive disabilities in the 1980s or when there were increased employment services reaching people with severe spinal cord injuries or severe cerebral palsy in the 1990s. Many professionals, as well as the business and industry community, have considered these individuals to have little to offer, to be too expensive to work with, and generally to be poor investments for vocational rehabilitation (VR). What could be more devastating to one's self-esteem than to be written off in this fashion? Yet, in fact, that is exactly what has happened, resulting in perhaps the most striking parallel between the supported employment and individual advocacy movements. The motivations held by those who crafted the ADA to emphasize ability and full participation were shared by those who pushed and promoted supported employment opportunities for thousands of people with mental disabilities.

Supported employment and individual advocacy programs have proven themselves to be sustainable. A fourth parallel is that weak programs, weak concepts, and "flash-in-the-pan" fads do not last, and both of these programs have proven to be sustainable innovations. Agency heads will not fund such programs that do not generate the type of outcome data that warrants funding in tight times. Supported employment began in the late 1980s and has endured. Supported employment has withstood the criticism of detractors who are only satisfied with the status quo of service-delivery programs. Individual advocacy programs and other advocates of the ADA have fought for more than 15 years (and in some cases even longer) to get critical federal legislation in place that will begin to promote positive societal attitudes toward people with disabilities.

Individual advocacy has staying power because, like supported employment, it is the principled thing to do. The best concepts are not only those that work, but also those that are logical to people in terms of fairness and common sense. After all, it makes sense to seek input from the very people who are being served in disability programs. Individuals participating in services should assist in the operation of those programs and take leadership roles in them to ensure quality outcomes. Users of services should be solicited for their feedback on how to change and improve those programs. It is only a matter of time before this type of individual advocacy and involvement spreads like wildfire.

CHALLENGES TO INDIVIDUAL
ADVOCACY AND SUPPORTED EMPLOYMENT

A number of issues must be resolved and taken into account as people consider the linkage of individual advocacy and supported employment concepts. The first issue is that each of these major concepts has different constituencies among people with disabilities. For example, the individual advocacy movement in recent years has been most closely identified with people with physical disabilities and other groups of people with disabilities who are able to articulate for themselves. They are able to express their needs, wishes, and hopes in terms of how they want society to respond. Yet, supported employment has been and continues to be most clearly aligned with people who have intellectual disabilities or mental illness as a primary disability (Drake Becker, Clark, & Mueser, 1999; Wehman, Bricout, & Kregel, 2001).

These two groups can often have difficulties in clearly articulating their desires and needs. As a result, the idea of an employment specialist or a job coach arose to assist these individuals in gaining entry into the labor force. In fact, in the late 1970s, when supported employment began, the term used to identify the supported employment service provider was *trainer-advocate* in order to recognize the dual role of the employment specialist on behalf of the person with disabilities. Hence, the first issue that must be resolved in merging these concepts is for people with physical and intellectual disabilities to communicate more frequently and understand the differing points of view that each holds in wanting to make changes in the systems that provide services for people with disabilities.

A second very powerful issue is that those who are identified most closely with individual advocacy generally have a number of goals that they wish to achieve in systems change. That is, transportation, personal care attendants, and improvements in quality of residential choices become paramount and overriding factors for thousands of people who are promoting greater individual advocacy. Specifically, as important as a positive vocational outcome is, there are other factors that are sometimes of equal or even more importance. Those people who are identified as primarily supporters of integrated and supported employment programs tend to have a somewhat more limited agenda. They are advocating for gainful employment as the main change that they want to see occur in the system. In this sense, both groups have much to offer each other because there are many people with physical disabilities who could greatly benefit from supported employment. In similar fashion, many supported employment participants and staff need to be more vocal in taking an activist role in other important life areas (e.g., transportation, independence in community living).

A third issue that needs to be resolved between the two groups is that individual advocacy proponents do not always understand the philosophies or practices that are associated with supported employment. At the same time, those individuals who are narrowly focused on supported employment as the only type of service issue do not recognize many of the individual satisfaction, independence, and nonwork disability incentive issues that are important to people who are associated with individual advocacy programs. There needs to be greater professional communication and dialogue and a far greater integration and merging of mutual goals. A good first step is to have both groups begin to join each other's member organizations, attend collaborative conferences, and perform committed work together. The firepower of both groups working together as a cohesive lobbying force would have a tremendous impact on changing attitudes, values, and practices in society, as well as influencing state and federal legislative action.

INDIVIDUAL-INITIATED SUPPORTED EMPLOYMENT

All too often, the human service system makes decisions for people with disabilities without involving them in the process. Fortunately, this way of doing business is beginning to change. People with disabilities are speaking out, taking control of their lives, and seeking to direct the services they need. Per the Rehabilitation Act Amendments of 1998 (PL 105-220), if an individual chooses to participate in supported employment services, then he or she should expect to receive assistance focused on an employment outcome of competitive work in an integrated setting, with ongoing support services as needed to remain successful in an employment position. One person with disabilities who received supported employment services shared:

> Let me begin by telling you how I discovered supported employment. A friend of mine
> asked me to go with her to an appointment at a local supported employment program

because she was nervous. I had heard about supported employment from another friend who was using it, but I really did not know much about it. Anyway, I agreed to accompany my friend. During the meeting, I thought this sounded like an interesting idea.

So, soon afterwards I went to see my rehabilitation counselor to request supported employment and that is when things began to change for me. I knew which service provider I wanted, the same one my friend had chosen. During the first meeting, we completed some paperwork. Then I was given the opportunity to either choose my employment specialist or have one assigned to me. I chose someone for myself, someone interesting and willing to assist me.

In order to look for jobs, the employment specialist needed to get to know what I wanted. She came to my house and asked me where I would like to work. I was interested in a job that would allow me to transport myself to work. Next, we discussed how I wanted to find a job. I decided to contact businesses near my house. Also, my wife, my employment specialist, and myself brainstormed a list of businesses to contact. Eventually the employment specialist discovered an opportunity at a restaurant. The employer wanted someone to clean the dining area prior to opening. I had cleaned house and enjoyed this type of work, so I decided to check it out. During the interview, I told the employer I was a hard worker and dependable. I got the job.

The employment specialist went to work with me and provided recommendations on how to do the job. Today, the employment specialist visits me on occasion to see how things are going. I've been successful because I worked hard. I have come a long way; a year ago I had no job, and look where I am now! (Anonymous, October 17, 2000)

How to Decide if Supported Employment Is the Right Choice

The question of whether supported employment is the right choice may be somewhat difficult to answer for individuals who have not had any type of work experience. In order to assist potential supported employment candidates to become better acquainted with supported employment services, they will need to visit a supported employment service provider in action and talk with individuals receiving supported employment services. The following points may be useful when assisting an individual with disabilities as he or she considers the type of work supports that may be appropriate for him or her.

- Have you always wanted to work but never been able to obtain your work goals?

- Have you ever been told that you cannot work because of the severity of your disability?

- Have employers said or implied that you might not be able to perform the job to their standards?

If individuals with significant disabilities answer yes to any of these questions, then supported employment may be the work support that they need to achieve their goal of competitive employment.

How to Choose a Service Provider

Once an individual has decided to use supported employment services, then he or she may need assistance in selecting or securing an employment service provider. Prior to this process, it will be important for the potential supported employment candi-

Table 3.1. Supported employment components

Service provider selection

Employment selection

Customer profile

Jobsite training and supports

Job/career development

Ongoing long-term support

---

date to clearly understand the range of supports that are offered from a supported employment service provider. The major work supports or components offered through an individual-driven approach to supported employment services are shown in Table 3.1.

Noteworthy among these six supported employment components is the selection of a service provider. Today, most communities have multiple supported employment service providers, and potential supported employment candidates may want to interview different programs to determine which organization will best match their individual needs. If a state VR counselor is involved in this process, then he or she should be able to provide a list of supported employment providers in that community and assist in setting up interviews. A list of interview questions should be created to help guide this process. For example, Brooke, Wehman, Inge, and Parent (1995) offered a series of questions that individuals with disabilities may use when preparing to interview supported employment service providers and to make subsequent decisions regarding employment supports.

1. Does your program have a written mission statement?

2. What types of services does your agency offer?

3. Do you have experience serving customers with different disabilities?

4. How would you describe the role of the customer in supported employment?

5. Have you excluded people with disabilities from your program? Why?

6. Describe how you present your program to a prospective employer?

7. May I see a copy of your marketing material?

8. How many employment specialists does your agency employ?

9. What is the average length of employment for your employment specialists?

10. Do the majority of your customers have part-time or full-time employment?

11. What is the average weekly earning of your customers?

12. What types of jobs have you assisted customers in finding?

13. Does your program assist customers with Social Security issues?

14. Do customers choose their employment specialists?

15. How do you fund extended services?

16. What is the average length of employment for customers of your services? Do you have any reports?

17. Do you have any references from customers, employers, and family members?

18. How do you involve your customers?

19. Does your program assist customers in accessing Social Security Work Incentives?

20. Does your agency believe that all individuals can be competitively employed?

21. What will you do for me?

22. How do you assess customer satisfaction? Do you have any reports?

Individuals with disabilities interviewing local supported employment service providers may wish to invite a support person or notetaker to accompany them on the interview. As part of the interview process, written documentation should be requested to include employer references and customer satisfaction data results. Results from each interview should be organized in a manner to facilitate easy comparison of results. Once a provider selection has been made, a personal call should be placed to the supported employment program letting the manager know why the program was selected. In addition, a note may be written to the programs that were not selected providing specific feedback on why they lost business. This type of follow-up may go a long way in improving the overall quality of local supported employment services.

How to Choose an Employment Specialist

After selecting a service provider, the next step is to interview staff and choose an employment specialist. Although a top-notch supported employment program will have no problem complying with this request, it can be an intimidating process for the individual with disabilities conducting the interview. Supported employment candidates may request assistance from a rehabilitation counselor, family member, or a self-advocacy mentor.

When interviewing an employment specialist, the supported employment candidate needs to keep in mind the type of person with whom he or she wants to work. Possible interview questions might include

1. Tell me about yourself.

2. How long have you been employed?

3. What types of jobs have you assisted people in obtaining?

4. How will you involve me in the job search?

5. How will you involve me throughout the process?

6. Have you ever worked with a person who has a similar disability to mine?

7. What will you do for me?

8. Why should I choose you?

One of the key factors related to employment retention is the rapport that is established between the job coach and the person with disabilities. The coach or employment specialist will play a key role in facilitating the individual work supports that will ultimately lead to competitive employment success.

How to Get a Job

Some participants will enter into supported employment service efforts to locate a job with a clear understanding of their current interests and their preferences already defined. If an individual is unclear about his or her goals, then the employment specialist should present a variety of options and assist with creating a personal employment profile by getting to know the supported employment participant. The employment specialist should learn what the person likes to do for fun, the experiences and skills he or she possesses, the type of career he or she would like to have, and specific working conditions and social environments that would lead to work productivity. The employment profile put together from this information will be critical in helping to shape the job search. Table 3.2 presents a series of probe questions that can be used to assist the individual seeking employment in putting together his or her personal employment profile.

How to Do a Job Search

Once a clear employment profile is established, the active job search must begin. Together, the employment specialist and the individual with disabilities will determine the roles and responsibilities of each person involved in the marketing and job search process. An organized strategy for locating employment opportunities will be critical. Some examples of the various methods that can be used to help involve individuals looking for supported employment in the job search process are listed next.

1. Develop a job plan of action that specifies roles and responsibilities of all involved in the job search process.

2. Design and select marketing tools.

3. Contact a prospective business and talk with employers.

4. Participate in analysis of available jobs (e.g., reading employment ads, searching web sites, contacting a government employment agency).

5. Participate in interviews with employers.

6. Review the pros and cons of each job.

7. Receive a written progress report from the employment specialist.

8. Select the job that best meets predefined demands.

Analysis of the job market requires that the supported employment participant and employment specialist become familiar with the local economy and the availability of jobs within the community. A general analysis of the types of jobs currently available in a community is a critical first step in the process of a job search. The intent of this analysis is to identify all potential job types and to determine what, if any, new forms of employment are emerging. Developing a comprehensive understanding of the local

Table 3.2.   Questions used to assist an individual seeking employment in putting together his or her personal employment profile

What do you like to do?
   Interests
   Preferences
   Desires

What kind of social environment would you like?
   Co-workers
   Opportunities for socialization
   Lunch/breaks

What skills do you have?
   Talents
   Abilities
   Education

What type of job would you like?
   Type of work
   Location and size of company
   Advancement

What experiences have you had?
   Employment
   Volunteer/training
   Personal development

What work conditions would you like to have?
   Hours/schedule
   Job duties
   Work environment
   Supervision

What kinds of supports do you need?
   Personal
   Workplace
   Community

What financial/nonmonetary benefits do you need or want?
   Wages
   Health insurance
   Vacation, holidays, personal/sick time

community's job market initially may require a considerable amount of effort and time but is necessary in order to develop jobs that are economically stable.

Once a clear picture of the local job market is acquired, it is time to screen the available market for a potential job. The purpose of this screening is to develop a working list of potential employment sites and contacts at these sites. The list should represent all jobs that are available in the community and should not be arbitrarily limited to entry-level positions. This list is the tool from which one can embark on the task of contacting individual employers.

How to Select Employment

As soon as the employment specialist is selected, the employment selection process begins. This new team is led by the job candidate and supported by the employment specialist and others identified by the candidate. Together, they will:

- Identify job openings where the supported employment candidate's skills and knowledge meet the needs of the employer
- Schedule interviews with employers for desired positions
- Negotiate acceptable employment terms

Preparation for the Interview

The supported employment candidate may want to participate in the interview alone or may request that the employment specialist actually sit in on the formal interview. Either way, interviewing should be considered an opportunity for the employer to determine if he or she wants to hire the job candidate and also an opportunity for the job candidate to determine if he or she wants to work at this particular business.

To prepare for an interview, the supported employment candidate and the employment specialist will need to review and determine:

1. The purpose of the interview
2. Who will attend
3. Transportation to and from the interview
4. What the employer will want to know
5. How to present relevant work experience and qualifications
6. Questions regarding employment terms and conditions
7. Dos and don'ts of appropriate businesslike approach to the interview (e.g., appearance, response to interview questions, questions for the employer)

During the Interview

The job interview should be viewed as a chance to gather information about the organization, the employer/supervisor, and the work environment. In some situations, the individual with disabilities and/or the employer may prefer that the applicant attend the interview alone. In other situations, the applicant and/or the employer may want the employment specialist to participate.

Follow-Up After the Interview

The supported employment candidate will want to set him- or herself apart from other job applicants. A good way of accomplishing this goal is to write a brief note to the employer (the person who conducted the interview) thanking him or her for his or her time and commenting on the employer's outstanding business. Also, candidates should use the note as an opportunity to add anything that may have been forgotten during the formal interview.

Negotiating Acceptable Employment Terms

At the point in time when an employer makes an offer of employment, a decision of whether to accept the employment opportunity must be made. The employment specialist may assist with this process; however, it is the decision of the individual with disabilities, based on analysis of the facts, knowledge, and data that have been collected regarding the business and the specific job goal. In essence, the task is to identify the consequences related to accepting or rejecting the position. The employment specialist can assist the individual with disabilities in coming to a decision by securing answers to the following questions:

1. Do you want to work for this employer?

2. Do you want to be employed in this particular work environment?

3. Do you want to work full time or part time?

4. Will the employee wages and benefits package be sufficient?

5. Have you carefully reviewed your benefit analysis to determine how work will affect the current status of benefits?

6. Do you have reliable transportation to and from the job?

Jobsite Training and Support

The employment specialist is hired to provide support services that should enhance the new employee's independence and success on the job. He or she may take on a variety of roles, including facilitator, negotiator, job skills training specialist, and anything in between in order to honor the new employee's preferences. The new employee should lead the service implementation process and guide the employment specialist by sharing information on

- Personal learning style and preferences

- Selection of instructional support techniques

- Recommendations on ways to enhance job performance

- Feedback on learning the job

- Feedback on overall job satisfaction and level of support

- Need for job accommodations

Ongoing Long-Term Supports

It is the employment specialist's responsibility to establish a regular ongoing schedule for review that is suitable to the supported employment customer and the employer. This structured process focuses on gaining an accurate picture of the overall employment situation and identifying activities necessary to maintain a high-quality work experience. Over the years, some individuals with disabilities using supported employment services have voiced their concerns about the follow-along visits from the employment specialist. Typically, these issues centered on the intrusive practices used by some employment specialists to monitor employment progress. Some of these practices were viewed as potentially stigmatizing within the business setting. The intended goal of ongoing supports is to assist the employee in the identification and pro-vision of the assistance and extended services necessary to maintain employment and to enhance career advancement. To facilitate a positive standing of the employee as a valued member of the work force, the employment specialist should secure an indi-vidual's preference in the following areas that will guide the implementation of long-term supports:

- When and where the employment specialist should meet with the employee

- Methods for determining how performance information will be collected

- Processes for assessing employer satisfaction

- Procedures for requesting additional supports or services deemed necessary

- Schedules and methods for assessing the overall job performance of the employ-ment specialist based on the employee's satisfaction with the services

When the Employment Specialist Is Not Listening

All supported employment participants and their advocates should know the grievance procedure to express concerns that will likely be unique to each provider. At any time during the process that participants believe that they are not being listened to by their employment specialists, they should know when and how to contact supported em-ployment program managers. If this strategy is implemented and the individual still feels that he or she is not being heard, then a meeting should be scheduled with the rehabilitation counselor who authorized supported employment services. Individuals participating in supported employment who have their case closed by state VR ser-vices can still gain access to the support of the VR Client Assistance Program (CAP). The CAP was established as a mandatory program in the 1984 Amendments to the Rehabilitation Act (PL 98-221) and can be found in every state and territory, admin-istered by the Rehabilitation Services Administration. CAP services include assistance in pursuing administrative, legal, and other appropriate remedies to ensure the pro-tection of people receiving or seeking services under the act. Most state VR programs should have the telephone number for direct and confidential access to the CAP of-fice, a resource that should be able to investigate problems and help solve a variety of complaint issues.

SELF-EMPLOYMENT

Self-employment, including resource ownership, is another employment model that fits well for many individuals with significant disabilities. Some people do not want to work in competitive employment using a job coach at the workplace. The opportu-nity to create a business and have "part of the American dream" is their vision. Grif-fin and Hammis (2003) have worked very closely with many people and professionals to help them develop skills on how to create self-employment. Resource ownership allows an individual with disabilities to bring his or her own property, equipment, or other resource to the job. If the person is unhappy in that particular situation, then he or she can take the resource and look at other options that might be a better match. It's a very self-reliant option that empowers the individual in negotiating his or her particular employment circumstances.

For example, consider John (Griffin & Hammis, 2003). He was very interested in working with animals. It so happened that there was a veterinary clinic that did pet grooming a few blocks from his house. John, along with his employment specialist, met with the clinic staff and negotiated an employment option. They talked about what this small veterinarian business needed, knowing that many self-employment situations are undercapitalized businesses, with insufficient capital to carry routine functions, and therefore offer a fertile ground for negotiating options that would work well for all parties involved.

John expressed a strong interest in household pet grooming in his employment profile. John used his Individual Training Account (ITA), which is funding potentially available through One Stop Career Centers to help an individual to purchase resources needed for employment, to purchase a hydraulic table that an animal can be put on and raised to a height where John can groom it. The hydraulic table also has a washing table with it. John is now a wage employee of the veterinarian and could not be any happier. He has a career path. He and his father are very active in John's employment support team and are looking into John starting his own dog grooming business.

The following section presents six individuals who have successfully developed small companies through identifying market demand, establishing resource ownership, and using specialized employment and business technical assistance. The voices of these six individuals speak volumes about how this exciting business development process can occur. The employment support teams who assisted them also tell their stories. Listen closely for the lessons these professionals learned in moving away from building employment profiles based on assessment results and instead focusing on achieving the desired employment outcome identified by the individual.

KALEB

Kaleb has a lot to offer an employer, which became clear during his planning process. A set of resources to support his employment plan was obtained by blending funds through the traditional Medicaid Waiver funding system, a typical funding stream for community-based services, with funds from Kaleb's ITA. As staff got to know Kaleb better, they learned that despite his very traditional diagnostic label of having mild or moderate intellectual disabilities, he had tremendous potential. The staff found that traditional assessments really didn't provide information that they could use to help make someone's dreams come true and improve the quality of his or her life and often disregarded that assessment information. Instead, the staff focused on gaining an understanding of the background of an individual with disabilities and recognizing that his or her interests are still evolving and being defined.

Kaleb loved children, and he also had an interest in learning more about computers. Kaleb was able to get computer training, and the staff found a position for Kaleb in a small private school. The owner of the school did not have the means to provide computer training to students. Kaleb was able to purchase a computer and all the software, a computer table, and a chair. He set up a computer lab in the school and began providing lessons to the students. Families loved the new service, and Kaleb became a very valuable member of the school staff. In the future, Kaleb may be interested in a self-employment opportunity in which he has more control.

MARTHA

Martha worked in the laundry room of a hotel. Although she did a very good job and was content with her daily schedule, she would continually talk about wanting to have a job working with athletes, like her father, who was a runner. Martha's employment support team decided to meet with her to learn more about her array of interests.

The team went with Martha to some stores that sell exercise equipment as well as to athletic environments to see how she reacted to these settings. It became very clear that she wanted to work in a gym. The support team contacted the owner of the gym in their office complex. He was open to talking with the team. He happened to have a cousin who had disabilities, and he was sensitive to what work could mean in terms of quality of life for people with disabilities. The owner started out saying, "Okay, we'll try Martha working for us for a week." The week turned into 2 weeks, then 3 weeks, and before long, the employer was saying, "Where's Martha? She didn't come in today."

The support team knew Martha had her eye on some of the equipment that gym members were using. The support team met with the owner and asked him to identify the one piece of equipment that he needed and that would be in pretty continual use. The unequivocal answer was a weight machine.

Martha then actively pursued a weight machine that she could operate. She found the machine and purchased it with funds from her ITA. After that, she attended training to learn how to operate the machine and teach gym members simple exercises to do on the machine. Now, Martha is happy that she works in a fitness environment and enjoys helping others to stay in shape. She has even invited her father a few times and has shown him some exercises to do on her weight machine.

EVERT

Evert, who has a developmental disability and requires psychiatric supports, has a passion about washing cars, which he would practice given any opportunity. He came to his employment support team knowing exactly what he wanted to do. Again, networking connections were used to identify a high-end car wash business called a car spa. The team met with the car spa owner to see what could be worked out.

Because the car spa was a new business and capital was an issue at times, the spa owner wanted access to a piece of equipment called an extractor that cleans the carpet very thoroughly. Fortunately, over time, the team was able to negotiate wage employment for Evert. Evert would purchase the extractor as a resource ownership by blending his wages with funds from VR, his ITA, and some traditional funding through the mental retardation agency. The employment team was able to pull all these funding sources together as part of his funding package.

Evert is an apprentice right now and has just completed his first training session about how to use his extractor. There are probably three or more trainings that he'll go through as an apprentice. Evert's goal is to open his own car wash, and the car spa owner has made a commitment to Evert. He already knows where there is a car wash that Evert could potentially operate. Within 9–12 months they're going to look at branching out so that Evert can open his own business with the support of this owner.

ALICE

Alice came to the community from an institution many years ago. She cannot interact with her employment team verbally in conventional ways. She can, however, let people know her preferences, the things she likes, and the things that are important and not important to her. In working to get to know Alice, the team tried to pick up on cues where they could start, knowing that they may read the cues wrong and have to go back and start again.

The team noticed Alice always kept her fingernails polished and very pretty. Sometimes each one was a different color. Many people today color their fingernails this way as an aesthetic demonstration of what's interesting to them. In meeting with Alice, the support team found out that her personal expression through her nail work was important to her. Alice went with one of the staff to convention halls where they sell products that are related to beauty salons. She found fingernail polishes that were in a cache, with clippers and everything needed to keep fingernails and toenails in well-groomed shape. She purchased all of her necessary grooming materials, and the team had a beautiful cabinet made where they could be displayed. The employment team assisted Alice in developing a business within a business at a local hair salon.

Over time, Alice was hired into a wage job at the hair salon. The team conducted a financial analysis for her business. This was a learning and growth process for the team because they did not have a business background, but in a matter of 6 months, they were talking business plans, market analysis, and other sophisticated business tools. As the team looked at Alice's income, they realized that she wasn't yet at a living wage. The team worked with Alice on a plan to put her nail-grooming kiosk in several beauty salons.

The staff has done marketing research on what related business opportunities are available in Alice's home community. The team has a portfolio on Alice, and the plan is to meet with different companies to see if they would be interested in Alice's skills and services. She is now talking about branching out into costume jewelry, such as rings and hairpieces.

GREG

Greg was diagnosed as having intellectual disabilities and mental illness at a very early age. He spent his childhood and adolescence within the grounds of a state institution and his early and middle adult years in personal care homes, group homes, and segregated day programs. He considered his "family" to be the paid staff who supported him and his state-appointed guardian. Now, Greg lives in the community with support staff of his choosing and is self-employed. As a result of his business, he made friends who are not paid staff and has expanded his community connections.

Independence is greatly valued by Greg and is the driving force behind his decision to start his own business. He had experienced layoffs and firings in various service industry positions during his years of employment, which exacerbated the symptoms of his mental illness. He expressed his fears regarding working in a situation that did not afford stable and long-term earning potential.

"I worked at Pizza Hut and lost good friends. It hurt me to see them go. They lost their jobs," he said.

Therefore, during his person-centered planning meeting, the idea of self-employment was discussed. Greg liked the flexibility of determining his work schedule, the opportunity to meet new people, and the idea of being his own boss.

"When my friends were fired, I wanted to go out on my own," he said. "I talked to my job coach so I could do my own thing like I wanted for a long time."

He explored various options for self-employment through a community-based discovery process and settled on a vending business. Greg wanted to work in an environment that offered him opportunities to meet and talk with people and where he did not have to dress up. He also liked keeping the keys to the machines that he was responsible for maintaining in his possession. He felt this job gave him an identity in the work world that he respected and found comfortable. He and his employment consultant explored the Internet and attended trade shows to learn more about this enterprise and to price the equipment such a business would require. Market analysis was completed to determine businesses within the area that might be interested in purchasing vending services from Greg. A business plan was begun that included the locations of the potential sites.

Greg selected a sleek, black snack and soft-drink machine combination. He specifically chose this model because it was not tied to a contract with a particular company; therefore, he could purchase a variety of brands based on customer preference and also look for product sales that would help him maximize profits.

Funding was blended from Greg's supported employment provider and VR services. He needed assistance from his employment consultant in setting up his business and for transportation. The state VR regulations did not pay for job coaching for self-employment. The state VR services staff met to explore alternatives. As a result of this meeting, the state policy was changed to include the provision of job coach funding for self-employment.

In the past, traditional systems would have excluded Greg from pursuing self-employment due to his lack of accounting skills. Greg overcame this barrier by outsourcing, a general business practice in which small business owners do not perform all the operations of their business but instead contract out specific functions. Greg purchased the services of an accountant for his bookkeeping.

As Greg's business revenue was tracked, it quickly became apparent that he would need to expand his business for it to be profitable. A second location was identified that ensured good customer traffic. Greg and his employment consultant arranged a meeting with his VR counselor to discuss his plans for expansion and to request funding from VR for the purchase of the second piece of vending equipment. His business plan was reviewed and approved, and VR committed funds to purchase the needed machine. As Greg enters his second year of self-employment, his profits show a steady increase. Two additional companies have requested to purchase his vending services. Greg has concluded proudly, "It's a nice job to have."

VAL

Val's employment consultant first met her in the office of a VR counselor at a point when her case with VR was in the process of being closed. The counselor told the employment consultant that Val is a "very difficult case, but I want to give her one more chance." Val has some limitations in the use of her left arm. In addition, her labels include mental retardation, behavior disorder, defiant, and other equally disrespectful terms. Such diagnoses found in traditional assessments only focus on deficits rather than gifts and strengths; these diagnostic labels do not provide the type of information necessary to help people achieve their dreams and improve the quality of their life.

Val's mom is very supportive and wants her daughter to have a "good life." She also wants to make sure her daughter is safe, and she worries about her being taken advantage of, so work options have to be in environments that take these concerns into consideration.

The employment consultant spent time with Val in various places and environments to get to know her. Previous job settings for Val had not worked out for a variety of reasons; however, the thing that consistently made all of the previous placements bad job matches for Val is that none of the jobs took into consideration her passions, desires, and dreams. A new approach was used with Val—a person-centered planning process that involved the people important to her life. The planning process included a community-based vocational profile that helped define choices for Val. Those involved learned that Val wanted to work in an office in a secretarial role and that she loves children.

After extensive creative planning, a starting point for a job search was identified. Val's employment specialist/job consultant knew of an auto detailing company, and she was able to negotiate a carved-out position. As the secretarial manager, Val would be responsible for writing down the VIN numbers of the cars that were being serviced, answering the telephone, and greeting customers. She was readily accepted as one of the team and quickly fell into the good-humored bantering that bonded the employees and defined the office culture as professional, focused on quality, and appreciative of humor in the workplace.

Soon after hiring Val, the owner contacted her employment consultant to let her know Val was not working out in the job. The concerns that had resulted in low productivity in her other jobs were not the issue. Val loved her job and worked hard. The problem was that Val made continual mistakes when copying down the VIN numbers. In a more traditional system, this difficulty might have been the point in which the job was terminated and Val was again viewed as unemployable. But because the focus was on Val's passion, and she had already proven wrong the notion that she was unemployable by her hard work and interest in her duties, the employment consultant convinced the owner to not fire Val and to allow the support team time to determine what could be done to assist her.

State-of-the-art equipment that utilizes a computer program and stick or wand to register the VIN number so that the registering of the vehicles is not subject to human error was identified through an Internet search. This adaptation enabled Val to maintain her job. For once, her employment situation did not end with her being labeled as unsuccessful. The competence she feels as she utilizes the wand that registers the VIN numbers and relays them into the computer gives her a valued role in this business. Val's mom feels secure in the knowledge that Val is doing something she loves and is in a work environment that is accepting of and values Val.

The supported education model was also used to address Val's interest in working with children. Because the customized position at the auto detailing company is part time, Val and her employment consultant were able to explore options in child care. Val and her employment consultant attended specialized training to certify Val as a child care worker. On the days she is not working in her other job, Val is now on-call with a supplemental staffing company that provides a work force to child care centers. Through the discovery process and the tools of customized employment, Val's passions have resulted in economic opportunities of her choosing.

CONCLUSION

The preceding case studies represent clear examples of individual-directed employment outcomes. The employment support team posed the question: "What is your dream and how can we help you accomplish it?" Funds from multiple sources are molded together to support the needs and to achieve the dreams of each individual. These funds are not locked into maintaining programs but instead support accomplishing the employment outcome chosen by each individual with disabilities. The ongoing support assistance focuses on long-term career goals. For example, Evert's success at the car wash is a pathway to his having his own business, and the support team will continue to work with him to fully accomplish his dream. Kaleb, Martha, and the other voices heard in this chapter now have jobs with career potential and a set of ongoing supports that represent a true marriage of individual advocacy and supported employment. The person-centered model of supported employment used with them helped change their lives. It also gave the staff that supports them a totally new focus and provided a source of energy and satisfaction. Staff members know that they are a part of the positive changes that have taken place in the lives of the people they support.

Supported employment and resource ownership are proven employment models that assist large numbers of people with disabilities to gain access to the workplace. It becomes apparent that the individual success stories presented in the case studies should be replicated in small and large communities across the country. The key ingredient to each of these positive employment stories is that the individual did not view his or her disability as a barrier but rather believed in the potential of employment. Professionals supporting individuals with disabilities must also see this potential and be willing and interested in spending time with them to truly listen and thereby discover the career aspirations of the people they support. A quality employment service requires all involved to maintain this vision and work to assemble the right combination of supports and resources to ensure success.

REFERENCES

Americans with Disabilities Act (ADA) of 1990, PL 101-336, 42 U.S.C. §§ 12101 et seq.

Brooke, V., Wehman, P., Inge, K., & Parent, W. (December, 1995). Toward a customer-driven approach of supported employment. *Education and Training in Mental Retardation and Developmental Disabilities, 40,* 308–320.

Drake, R.E., Becker, D.R., Clark, R.E., & Mueser, K.T. (1999). Research on the individual placement and support model of supported employment. *Psychiatric Quarterly, 70,* 289–301.

Griffin, C., & Hammis, D. (2003). *Making self-employment work for people with disabilities.* Baltimore: Paul H. Brookes Publishing Co.

Olmstead v. L.C., 527 U.S. 581; 119 S.Ct. 2176 (1999).

Rehabilitation Act Amendments of 1984, PL 98-221, 29 U.S.C. §§ 701 et seq.

Rehabilitation Act Amendments of 1986, PL 99-506, 29 U.S.C. §§ 701 et seq.

Rehabilitation Act Amendments of 1998, PL 105-22, 29 U.S.C. §§ 701 et seq.

Rehabilitation Act of 1973, PL 93-112, 29 U.S.C. §§ 701 et seq.

Rizzolo, M.C., Hemp, R., Braddock, D., & Pomeranz-Essley, A. (2004). *The state of the states in developmental disabilities.* Washington, DC: American Association on Mental Retardation.

Technology-Related Assistance for Individuals with Disabilities Act Amendments of 1994, PL 103-218, 29 U.S.C. §§ 2201 et seq.

Technology-Related Assistance for Individuals with Disabilities Act of 1988, PL 100-407, 29 U.S.C. §§ 2201 et seq.

Wehman, P., Bricout, J., & Kregel, J. (2001). Supported employment in 2000: Changing the locus of control from agency to consumer. In M.L. Wehmeyer & J.R. Patton (Eds.), *Mental retardation in the 21st century* (pp. 115–150). Austin, TX: PRO-ED.

Wehman, P., Revell, G., & Kregel, J. (1998). Supported employment: A decade of rapid growth and impact. *American Rehabilitation, 24*(1), 31–43.

Chapter 4

Person-Centered Planning

Facilitating Inclusive Employment Outcomes

KATHERINE J. INGE, PAMELA SHERRON TARGETT, AND AMY J. ARMSTRONG

Despite its significance, getting to know an individual with disabilities prior to job development and placement is often shortchanged when more traditional approaches to vocational assessment and job placement are implemented (Parent, Unger, & Inge, 1997). Individualized plans for employment (IPEs) regarding the type and delivery of services are developed using evaluation information and preconceived expectations for the possible vocational outcomes of people with significant disabilities. Decisions are made for or without input from the person, and services are delivered based on disability label, severity of disability, the number of staff available to provide services, and the agency's operating budget.

The purpose of a vocational assessment is to generate information on a person's social, educational, psychological, and physiological functioning and to identify potentially feasible jobs for an individual (Bolton, 2001). This usually includes the use of occupational interest inventories, vocational aptitude batteries, and tests of manual dexterity such as the Minnesota Manual Dexterity Test or the Purdue Pegboard Test. These tests may limit employment outcomes for individuals with significant disabilities by concluding that the individuals are not "ready" or able to work in a competitive job. One obvious concern is that paper-and-pencil tests do not fairly evaluate an individual's work potential if the person has significant disabilities. Also, the individual's language proficiency and comprehension can affect his or her ability to perform on more traditional vocational assessments. The recommended placement using this evaluation approach for individuals with significant disabilities is typically a facility-based program for prevocational skill training; however, participation in prevocational preparation, extended career counseling, or other work readiness activities have not been found to be a predictor of success in competitive employment.

What does this mean for agencies that are supporting individuals with disabilities to achieve inclusive employment outcomes? The answer is fairly straightforward. A person-centered philosophy can set the framework for services to produce inclusive employment outcomes.

PERSON-CENTERED PHILOSOPHY

Everyone, with or without disabilities, has goals that are central to having a satisfying life. Personal goals stem from what is important to each individual and are part of what makes everyone unique. For vocational planning to be successful, each person's individuality must be recognized. The individual's career and "best job match" will be the one that is identified by first learning about the person's uniqueness, interests, preferences, and abilities.

In person-centered services, all major decisions about what is offered or needed are based on information about a specific individual's goals in life. This approach requires direct input from the person being served, those who know him or her best, and observations in community settings to recognize functional abilities and to identify possible support needs. No significant decisions are made without the person being involved, and he or she plays a significant role in determining the services and supports received, as well as who provides them. This involves a shift in decision making from the service provider to the service user and an increase in the involvement of individuals with disabilities in the service-delivery process. The focus is on what is needed to enable the person to meet his or her goals, concentrating on his or her quality of life and community inclusion.

The foundation for person-centered planning stems from visionary thinkers such as John O'Brien and Beth Mount in the United States and Marsha Forest, Jack Pearpoint, and Judith Snow in Canada. According to O'Brien (1987) and Mount (1994), there are three components of person-centered planning. First, everyday activities are the focus of planning efforts. Second, services are less important than family and community connections. Third, no single person can or should do everything. Person-centered planning offers a unique way of thinking about the roles and responsibilities for individuals with disabilities and the roles and responsibilities for service providers, families, and friends (Mount & Zwernik, 1988). In addition, it changes how information is collected, organized, and interpreted about people with disabilities and the contributions that they can make to their communities.

There are a number of approaches to person-centered planning that have evolved over the years (Ducharme, Beeman, DeMarasse, & Ludlum, 1994; Falvey, Forest, Pearpoint, & Rosenberg, 1994; Mount, 1994; Mount & Zwernik, 1988; Pearpoint, O'Brien, & Forest, 1993). These powerful strategies assist individuals with disabilities, their loved ones, and service providers in focusing on what is positive and possible for a person with disabilities. Each approach offers a creative way to uncover an individual's talents, capacities, and support needs. Individual Service Design, Lifestyle Planning, Personal Futures Planning, Making Action Plans (MAPs), Planning Alternative Tomorrows with Hope (PATH), and Essential Lifestyle Planning are included in this family of approaches.

The belief that people with disabilities can have a vision of a desirable future is at the heart of person-centered planning. The individual, rather than existing systems or services, is the "focus" that drives the planning process. This person is often referred to as the *focus person*. Person-centered planning values and respects the input of the person with disabilities and recognizes the meaningful roles of family and significant others in the planning process.

Several authors have suggested that person-centered planning can be an effective way to facilitate inclusive employment outcomes (Everson & Reid, 1997; Inge, Stro-

Table 4.1.   Key principles of person-centered planning

All people, regardless of the type or severity of their disabilities, have unique talents and gifts to offer to their communities.

Person-centered planning leads to action plans that focus on interests, talents, and dreams, not limitations.

All people should live in their communities and make a contribution to society.

When natural or informal supports and customized services are interwoven, individuals can obtain what they need to reach personal life goals.

The service recipient or customer defines the service along with those who love and know him or her best, if needed.

Planning and working with the person along with those who love and know him or her best will result in shared action and positive results.

Person-centered planning is an ongoing process that promotes new learning and understanding about a person's abilities, gifts, and support needs and creates a vision to work toward a positive future.

Sources: Butterworth et al. (1993); Mount (1991); O'Brien (1987).

bel, Wehman, Todd, & Targett, 2000). Despite which person-centered approach is used, each shares a common premise and key principles that are consistent with career planning that is responsive to the support needs of the individual with disabilities and his or her diverse cultural background (see Table 4.1).

Individual Choice

The focus in person-centered planning is on capacity, not on deficits or the individual's disability. In other words, what are the person's strengths? What are his or her interests? Essentially, what are the individual's dreams, hopes, and preferences for employment, and what supports are necessary to make these happen? Individual choice and control are central to the concept. Williams stated,

> Every person, regardless of the severity of his or her disabilities, has the right to communicate with others, express everyday preferences, and exercise at least some control over his or her daily life. Each individual, therefore, should be given the choice, training, technology, respect and encouragement to do so. (1991, p. 543)

Agencies who wish to shift from agency-centered to person-centered services to facilitate inclusive employment outcomes must self-evaluate to determine how much choice and control individuals with disabilities truly have within their organizations. Many programs, when asked if they provide person-centered services, will say, "Yes, our participants have choices!" Unfortunately, some individuals with disabilities are still not offered the choice of inclusive employment. Others have jobs selected for them. Still others have their vocational goals redirected based on what staff members perceive as realistic work outcomes.

Smull said, "Choice is the most powerful word and the most abused word in the current lexicon of the disabilities service system" (1998, p. 6). He went on to say that choice involves three interrelated concepts of preferences, opportunities, and control. These are key concepts to consider when working with individuals who have only been supported in facility-based programs such as sheltered workshops. For instance, it is not uncommon to hear that an individual "chooses" to stay at the facility-based program. Or, the person who is unsuccessful in a job "chooses" to return to the segregated program.

Many people with disabilities lack the life experiences to know what they like or dislike (Smull, 1998). The important question to ask is whether the person is making an informed choice regarding employment (Inge & Targett, 2004). Has the individual had opportunities to participate in community experiences to develop preferences? If the person's only work experience has been within the community rehabilitation program, then perhaps the decision is based on limited experiences and where he or she is comfortable. Or, does the person actually have any control over service and support decisions? Are professionals controlling the supports, services, and choices that the person is offered? Being given the "choice" between a job that someone else has identified without the individual's input and a job in the facility-based program should not be considered "individual choice." Other questions that should be considered when a person does not show interest in moving toward inclusive employment are the following:

- Is "fear" of the unknown preventing the person from taking a chance and seeking a competitive employment position?

- Does the person associate attending the workshop with having friends and finding employment with fear of losing those friends?

- Has the person tried a job and had a bad experience? Was the failure based on the provider's inability to successfully customize a job that reflected the person's interests and abilities?

- Were the workplace supports identified as successful, and, if not, what plans have been put into place to support the individual?

- Can person-centered planning be used to support the person in selecting a career or job of choice?

Programs cannot successfully support a person's choices if they do not actively listen to what individuals with disabilities want and are saying. O'Brien and O'Brien (1998) suggested that listening is paying attention to the details and dreams that disclose a person's identity and desires. Listening is attending to the meaning that emerges as service providers get to know the person and his or her life history, interests, concerns, and passions. Listening to individuals with disabilities regarding their goals and desires for inclusive employment will significantly affect the way that programs identify potential careers *with* their participants as opposed to *for* them. Instead of canvassing businesses within the community for any job opening, employment specialists will negotiate positions based on specific participant choices, gifts, and contributions. Choice making leads to increased independence, greater motivation to participate and succeed, and greater dignity for the individual. There are ample opportunities to promote choice for inclusive employment outcomes, as listed in Table 4.2.

Table 4.2.   Facilitating choice for inclusive employment

The individual decides:

- Where to work (home or community)
- What supports are needed to locate a job or start a business
- How to show a prospective employer personal strengths and talents
- How to present personal attributes and support needs to prospective employers
- The direction of the career search
- Whether to accept a particular job opportunity
- What supports are needed to perform the job
- What supports are needed to communicate with others on the job
- What supports are needed to make new friends on the job
- Who will facilitate or provide the supports needed on the job
- What supports are needed to maintain employment
- Who will provide ongoing support
- Whether to keep or resign a job

Important Considerations for Person-Centered Planning

There are several important things that agencies need to consider before undertaking a person-centered planning process. First, do not engage in person-centered planning if there is no commitment or time for follow through or no belief in the gifts of individuals with disabilities. Simply put, the employment specialist and other members of the support team must respect the individual and support his or her goals for employment. The team must be committed to the belief that people with disabilities are competent and have the right to be competitively employed. If the employment specialist and the person's support team do not believe in the person's competence and abilities to contribute to a business, then how will the individual believe it or, for that matter, how will an employer see the possible contributions?

Next, planning alone does not assist people in achieving their goals. Many groups have met and completed a PATH or held other person-centered meetings only to have no employment outcomes. Long-range dedication is necessary for success as the individual achieves and maintains inclusive competitive employment.

A common question from staff when beginning to implement person-centered planning is, "What if the person has an unrealistic employment dream?" Perceiving a goal as unrealistic usually is related to placing a focus on the disability and a lack of knowledge on how supports and accommodations might assist the individual. All people have dreams and plans that others may label as "unrealistic" or impossible to achieve. No one really knows what the future holds or what may be accomplished with supports. Anyone may achieve a personal goal that at one time was thought to be impossible. This is true as agencies and employment specialists develop the skills to identify the supports and services that maximize an individual's strengths and abilities rather than focusing on his or her disabilities.

As an example, when asked about an employment dream, a person might reply, "I want to be a lawyer." Perhaps the individual does not have a high school degree and has significant disabilities. Rather than telling the person that the dream of becoming a lawyer is unrealistic, the employment specialist must listen to the person to identify what characteristics of being a lawyer are important. Is it the perceived status of the position? Does the person have a perception of the law profession based on what he or she has experienced? Perhaps the person knows someone who is a lawyer but knows little of the requirements for practicing law. Much of the day-to-day work, for instance, may not be quite as glamorous as the person's understanding of the profession. Has he or she had an opportunity to visit a law firm and spent a day seeing what this really involves or to complete a situational assessment to determine preferences and interests (Targett, 2001)?

By providing information to the individual on what the position requires, including education, years of training, and the various skills, the individual can be supported in making decisions regarding future goals and career directions. He or she might decide that the time and commitment necessary does not fit into the long-range plan for employment. Or, the person can be assisted in identifying short-term goals for work based on long-range dreams and passions.

In the previous example, the individual may decide that being a law clerk or assistant who does legal research may be a good first step toward his or her long-range dream of being a lawyer. Or, after gathering information, the individual may realize that the dream is really to work at the local courthouse. Then, the person could begin to identify jobs or a self-employment opportunity that puts him or her in the environment of choice and gets at what is meaningful to that individual.

When assisting individuals with disabilities to identify career plans, the employment specialist also needs to acknowledge that some individuals may have held jobs or had careers prior to the onset of their disabilities. This may be true for individuals with disabilities such as mental illness, traumatic brain injury, or disabilities resulting from traumatic events later in life. Some will have attended college, have career dreams, and will want to return to work in similar positions. Again, the employment specialist and members of the individual's team need to be cautious about deciding for the person that he or she cannot realize those career aspirations because of a disability. The person who wants to return to a career may be able to do so if the characteristics of the workplace can accommodate his or her support needs. The basic point is to help the person identify the characteristics of the desired career. The next step is to develop goals and objectives to guide the job-seeking process with the person rather than making decisions for him or her. The final step is to identify the supports necessary for the individual to achieve the career or job of choice.

Developing Relationships to Identify Goals and Interests

The only way an employment specialist can represent an individual with disabilities is to believe in and know the individual's abilities and interests. Reading clinical records, test results, or case notes written by another professional does not allow the employment specialist to get to know the real person. In addition, people with disabilities are as diverse a group as the general population. Simply reading in a person's chart that he or she has a particular disability may not really provide much information that is important for employment. One professional's perception of an individual's employment barrier may actually be a strength that could be matched to a job. An employment specialist may want to consider delaying the review of formal records until he or she gets to know the individual informally through personal experiences.

It is important to find out what the individual enjoys. Determine what a day in his or her life is like. What are his or her personal interests? What are stressful concerns? Along those lines, it is important to determine what the person really does not like or has no interest in doing. MAPs, one person-centered planning process that is discussed later in this chapter, includes finding out what the person considers as his or her nightmares, in other words, those things that should be avoided when finding a job or pursuing a career. These factors also contribute to decisions regarding the kind of work and characteristics of the job. For any employee, with or without disabilities, satisfaction results when the characteristics of the job are compatible with the person's experiences, interests, and real-life circumstances.

One place to begin to develop relationships is to consider personal experiences. The first step may be to arrange a time to get to know the person in a location of his or her choice. Individuals with disabilities should be provided an opportunity to meet in locations other than the organization's office. This may include meeting informally at a restaurant, at the person's home, or at another nonwork environment. Allowing the individual to select this location will allow him or her to be more comfortable and relaxed during the initial meetings. Characteristics about the selected meeting place can also provide clues that may be useful in identifying a job of choice for the individual. For example, the employment specialist may find out if this is a favorite place for the individual and why. This type of information may go unnoticed in a meeting at an office because the right questions may not be asked or the individual may feel the information is not important. Other questions about interests, friends, and potential job choices may naturally evolve in less formal settings.

Consider ways to reduce the individual's anxiety during these initial meetings and encourage conversation (Targett, 2001). Maintain eye contact, and refrain from staring at the person. Don't look away or around the room because the person may think you are being inattentive. Speak in a normal voice. Be respectful, and ask people how they would like to be addressed. Another way to make the person feel comfortable during an initial interview is to offer personal information. For instance, if the person is asked what he or she likes to do, begin by giving the person an example. Demonstrate an interest in what the individual is saying by nodding and by making comments that would encourage the person to talk. Associated with this is encouraging the person to elaborate on responses to questions. Give the person a chance to also ask questions. Provide the person feedback by paraphrasing what is said and making comments to show the person that he or she has been understood.

The purpose of any initial interview with the person is two-fold. The employment specialist should be getting to know the individual as well as establishing a rapport. This can set the stage for person-centered planning and identifying the support people in the individual's life that he or she would like to invite for charting the career path.

MAPS AS A PLANNING TOOL

MAPs originally was developed from efforts to assist families and school systems to include children with disabilities in inclusive classrooms (Falvey et al., 1994). The process is based on circles of support that include people who are instrumental in supporting the individual with disabilities in his or her everyday life. This could be family members, neighbors, or professionals such as service coordinators, educators, and other community members. The premise behind MAPs is that people are connected to their communities, and they can provide support to the person with disabilities. The circle of support assists the person in forming a network of support and connections for inclusive community living.

One of the first steps is for the person's circle to meet and to explore what the individual wants his or her future to be like. Planning sessions provide a forum for everyone to brainstorm and share ideas and expertise to formulate a blueprint for making the individual's dreams a reality. Essentially, the tool is used to assist an individual with planning his or her future. During this process, a facilitator and recorder guide the individual and his or her personally chosen circle of support through a series of questions designed to identify the person's gifts, talents, and strengths. The eight key questions include the following:

1. What is a MAP?

2. What is the person's history or story?

3. What are the person's dreams?

4. What are the person's nightmares?

5. Who is the person?

6. What are the person's strengths, gifts, and talents?

7. What does the person need?

8. What is the plan of action?

The meeting can take place anywhere, but as previously mentioned, the location should be guided by the individual's preferences and provide a relaxed atmosphere. Meeting in the agency may not be the optimum choice unless it is selected by the individual. The key to successfully completing a MAP is to have a positive approach to the process. The individual's gifts and talents should be highlighted, and he or she should never be described in terms of a disability or problem. Throughout the process, the person's challenges are stated in terms of support needs. Specifically, the outcome should be a better understanding of the person's gifts and talents and the next steps that are needed in order to put a plan for employment into action.

The "nightmare" question allows the group to think about negative events that may happen. These nightmares also can provide some valuable insight into job characteristics or features that should be avoided. For instance, if an individual describes his or her nightmare in terms of never having any friends, this is a "red flag" to avoid jobs with limited social interaction. In addition, plans need to be made to support opportunities for meeting old friends outside of the new employment situation.

Question 7 asks the individual and his or her circle of support to consider what the person will need in terms of people and resources to make the dream a reality.

Table 4.3.   MAPs plan of action

Janice, a family friend, will assist Susan in getting a new hairstyle for work that she can take care of independently before June 30.

Susan and Bill, her employment specialist, will meet with residential support staff by June 15 to discuss how work will affect her personal care needs and how to prepare for work.

Susan and Bill will look through the classified section of the paper weekly as well as meet to discuss job possibilities.

Bill and Susan will use Susan's circle of support to identify job leads and update the team members on progress twice per month.

Susan, with the support of her sister, will schedule an appointment with her physician to discuss the need for a new motorized wheelchair by June 11.

Susan and her father will meet with a benefits specialist by July 1 to discuss how work will affect her benefits and how work incentives can be used to pursue her dreams for employment.

Susan's circle of support will meet a minimum of once per month at her home to review Susan's plan of action and to brainstorm as needed.

During the discussion, the individual may begin to identify specific people who have not been invited to the meeting as key implementers in the plan. Question 7 leads nicely into Question 8, which asks the focus person and the circle members to identify a plan of action and includes who will do what and when. Table 4.3 provides a list of sample items from one individual's plan of action.

PATH AS A PLANNING TOOL

Another person-centered planning tool that has been used successfully for career planning is PATH (Inge et al., 2000; Inge, Wehman, Kregel, & Targett, 1996: Inge, Wehman, Strobel, Powell, & Todd, 1998). PATH was designed to develop a plan of action for the person's future (Falvey et al., 1994). Literally, the process can be used to identify an employment "path" for the focus person to pursue.

The first step is for the individual to identify people in his or her life who will be important in supporting the person's goals. Typically, the group will be made up of friends, family, professionals, and any other people involved in the individual's life. If planning for employment, the employment specialist, the vocational rehabilitation (VR) counselor, and the service coordinator may also be included. Because the people invited to the PATH meeting should be selected by the individual with disabilities, no one should be included without the focus person's consent, even though staff may feel that a particular person should participate. In some cases, the person may come to realize the importance of asking for help during the PATH meeting. For instance, one young woman did not want her VR counselor to attend her PATH meeting; however, during the meeting, she came to realize that the support of the counselor would be needed to fund some of the activities in her career plan. She then made the decision to talk with the counselor as one of her first steps toward her goals.

There are eight steps to the PATH process that take approximately 2 hours to complete. The *facilitator* assists the focus person in brainstorming with the group while the *recorder* produces a graphic representation of the meeting. The facilitator's responsibility is to assist the team in the following: 1) determining the dream, 2) sensing the goal, 3) grounding in the now, 4) deciding who to enroll, 5) building strength, 6) charting actions for 3 months, 7) planning next month, and 8) establishing first steps. The members of the team are there to support the person and not to place limits or censure what is said or the goals that the person wants to set. If this begins to happen, then the facilitator is responsible for redirecting the group back to the intended purpose of the meeting.

Inclusion Press has produced a number of excellent resources on the PATH process that are available on-line at http://www.inclusion.com. Employment programs should review these resources to learn more about person-centered planning. The originators of PATH recommend that professionals should never complete the process with a person who has disabilities unless they have participated in the process and received training. The information provided in this chapter is an overview and does not include sufficient detail to teach staff how to implement the process. One strategy may be to identify another mentor program or agency that has been successful in using person-centered planning to work with staff who wish to learn. Before facilitating an individual's planning meeting, watch the Inclusion Press videotapes, attend training, and read the PATH manual and other training materials (Pearpoint & Forest, 1994).

Step 1: Determining the Dream

The first step in the PATH process is to encourage the focus person to talk about his or her future dreams. When this is being completed as a career planning strategy, the person should focus on those events or supports that would affect inclusive employment. The facilitator asks the individual to imagine what the future would be like as if he or she were describing events that have already happened. Talking about events in the past or present tense helps the group think positively about the future. For instance, the person might say, "I am a veterinarian. I own a car. I have friends. I bought new clothes. I have money!"

The circle of support or planning team can gain insight into what people want to accomplish if individuals are encouraged to fully elaborate on their dreams. In this example, the facilitator might want to follow up with probing questions such as, "What are you doing with the animals? What kind of animals do you see? What does the room/office look like? Who are you working for? Are you working for yourself? Do you see any people there? What are they doing? How many hours are you working? Can you tell us what your car looks like? Tell us about the clothes that you bought. How much money do you have? Do you have a checking or savings account?"

The recorder works to pictorially represent the information provided by the focus person. Other members of the support group or circle who know the person are also asked to contribute their ideas; however, the facilitator needs to make sure that what is added reflects the person's dreams. This can be done by confirming with the individual what is put on the graphic when others contribute their thoughts and suggestions.

The team should not place any restrictions on the person's description of the future. In other words, members should not interrupt or suggest that what the person is saying is impossible to accomplish. If someone continues to interrupt with negative comments, then the facilitator should acknowledge those concerns and then encourage the group to actively listen to what the person is saying.

Some employment specialists or support staff may wonder what the difference is between a person describing dreams during the PATH process and answering questions about what he or she wants to do. The graphic display can assist both the person with disabilities and his or her circle of support to visualize things that may not have been discussed during a question-and-answer session. It can facilitate further discussion and elaboration. It also serves as a permanent product that the individual can have to refer to later as the work toward inclusive employment begins.

Step 2: Sensing the Goal

The second step in the PATH process is to look forward in time to 1 year from the day of the meeting. The person and group are asked to talk about the events of the next year as if they have already happened. Goals identified in this step should be positive and possible (Pearpoint et al., 1993). The individuals supporting the focus person should be careful not to place their own value judgments on what is positive and possible and thereby limit the creativeness of the process during this step.

So, how does the facilitator assist in identifying possible outcomes for the next year without censoring the person's comments? Sometimes, a person will describe events that would be extremely difficult to accomplish within a 1-year time period. For instance, the person says that he or she graduated from college during the year. If the person has never attended college, then this would be impossible within the time frame of the planning. One way to address this would be to place this in the individual's dream. The group then can assist him or her in initiating steps toward this dream.

During this step, a person might say, "I got a job at the Pet Barn. I have money, and bought a new TV! I have new friends! I go to the movies every weekend." Again, the facilitator's role would be to probe the individual for additional information. "What are you doing at the Pet Barn? Tell us about your friends. Where did you buy your TV? How long did it take you to save the money?" If the individual has difficulty or is unable to think of events in the future, then the facilitator should encourage the team members to assist by describing events that "have happened." Again, these outcomes should be verified or confirmed by the focus person before they are placed on the PATH diagram.

Step 3: Grounding in the Now

The third step of the PATH requires the individual to think about how he or she feels now. This step is usually the shortest in the PATH process and can bring up different emotions. Ask the person to quickly express how he or she feels using descriptive words that get at the emotions. For instance, the person may say, "I feel hopeless, lost, confused." Or, of course, the person could say, "I feel excited about beginning work again! I am energized! I finally feel hopeful!" The facilitator can ask why the person feels hopeless, lost, or confused, and these things should be documented on the PATH. The same is true for positive emotions; however, the originators of the process suggest that the facilitator quickly get the feelings expressed and move on to the planning steps. In other words, do not fall into the trap of laboring over negative feelings or perceived barriers to employment rather than planning steps for positive outcomes.

Step 4: Deciding Who to Enroll

The fourth step requires the individual to think about who needs to assist in achieving the goals for employment. People with disabilities are unlikely to be successful in employment unless they have support that they need in other areas of their lives. The person has already identified some of the individuals who will support him or her based on who was invited to the PATH meeting; however, during the process, the person may begin to realize that others will be needed if the goal for competitive employment is to be achieved. During this step, these individuals should be identified and the focus person assisted in inviting these needed people to participate in subsequent planning and implementation activities.

Step 5: Building Strength

The fifth step focuses on ways for the person to build strength. The term *strength* refers to the supports or strategies that will assist or facilitate the person's employment success, including simple daily supports that will make going to work easier. For instance, a person might say, "I can't be rushed when I get dressed in the morning. I have to be able to stay in bed until 8:00 A.M. I need to go to bed no later than 10:30 P.M. I have to see my service coordinator each week on Wednesday afternoon." This information will be useful when assisting the person in finding employment. The person who does not like to rush when getting dressed and likes to stay in bed until 8:00 A.M. most likely will not do well in a job that begins at 8:00 A.M. Although this is a simple example, much insight can be gained from the person during this step of the PATH if he or she is encouraged to describe ways that he or she can successfully face a typical day.

Steps 6–8

The final three steps in the PATH process ask the individual and the support team to set action steps for the next few months. Typically, the sixth step covers outcomes for the next 3 months. The seventh step plans for the next month, whereas the last step covers what will be done the next day and following week. These are called the *action steps* of the PATH and may be the most important. The facilitator again asks the person to talk in the past or present tense. "I opened a checking account. I have been on three interviews. I typed my résumé. I visited the One Stop Career Center to look into job openings." The developers of PATH believe that talking in the past or present tense assists the individual in seeing these activities as possible to achieve.

These are examples of statements that might come up while planning for the next months. Each of the final three steps is completed individually, and the PATH meeting should end with objectives for the person to complete over the course of the next year. Once these things are identified, the person and the support team need to be specific about who does what and when it will be accomplished. In other words, put dates on the accomplishments and revisit them in future discussions and meetings. The person should be given the PATH graphic, which can be used to record success and progress toward the employment goal. Please refer to Table 4.4 for information generated from one individual's PATH meeting.

Table 4.4. Overview of one individual's PATH meeting

Career dreams for the future:
A job where I . . .
- Can help others.
- Can work around people.
- Work with animals (e.g., pet store, veterinarian's office, boarding facility, park).
- Work with flowers (e.g., florist).
- Work in a department store.

One-year goals:
I have . . .
- Selected a job, and I am working!
- Opened a checking and savings account
- Bought new clothes with earnings
- Joined a woman's group (e.g., garden club)

I am . . .
- Earning enough money to pay my own bills (e.g., long-distance telephone bill)
- Making new friends
- Going out into the community independently (e.g., attending concerts on own, going shopping, going out to dinner)

Three-month goals:
I have . . .
- Completed a situational assessment at three different worksites based on my specific interests (e.g., pet store, florist, department store)
- Narrowed my job interests and choices (hopefully identified a job!)
- Gone on three to four job interviews
- Identified where I want to go and used the accessible bus system at least three times by myself
- Gone to a concert with friends at least once without assistance
- Gone out to dinner with a friend at least once without assistance

One-month goals and objectives:
I have . . .
- Picked out my interview outfit
- Identified the sites for my situational assessments
- Ridden the bus system with my mentor at least once per week
- Attended regularly scheduled support group meetings

Next week's activities:
I will . . .
- Buy a day planner to keep up with my new schedule
- Talk with my personal care attendant about my job goals
- Visit at least one jobsite to begin narrowing my choices for situational assessment
- Review the want ads to get an idea about available jobs

JOB CHOICE

Person-centered planning tools such as the ones in this chapter are only tools. Completing a PATH or MAP is only the first step in assisting an individual in pursuing a desirable job of choice. As previously stated, the network of individuals or circle of support must be committed to putting a plan of action into place. Marsha Forest, one of the originators of the tools of person-centered planning, often said in her workshops, "You can't do it alone." So, what happens once the meeting has ended and the graphic has been rolled up and given to the person?

If the meeting has been held to facilitate employment, then the person who will take a primary lead in assisting the person in finding a job must become actively involved. The more time spent getting to know the person, the more likely the job opportunities located will meet the individual's desires and support needs. There are a number of ways to build a positive relationship and gain an even better understanding of the person's abilities and gifts. Spending time with the individual in a number of settings will give the employment specialist a chance to learn more about the person and develop ideas about potential employment opportunities. Investing the time to get to know the person will pay off as the job search is conducted. Consider some of the following:

- Support the person in visiting different types of work settings to observe what employees do there.

- Visit the individual and his or her family in their home.

- Talk about their daily activities.

- Go to the local One Stop Career Center and learn more about the area employers and businesses.

- Go on community outings to places the individual likes.

Once the employment specialist has gotten to know the individual job seeker, either through interviews or person-centered planning activities, there still may be a need for assessment activities. This may be particularly true for the person who has no work history or a very limited one. It is important to note that the assessment is not designed to "screen out" the individual or deny access to competitive employment. An assessment should be conducted to determine the level and intensity of support and the characteristics of the job that the individual needs in order to be successful.

A functional or situational assessment, however, does not include "prevocational" training. A functional assessment focuses on actual performance in inclusive work environments and documents the information in terms of support needs without value judgments. A functional or situational assessment is used to determine the individual's skills, characteristics, and support needs so that the person can identify a career of choice. Often, this type of assessment is a natural result of the first person-centered planning meeting. For instance, the individual may identify several areas of interest but, because of limited or no work experience, does not have a concept of what working in that job entails.

A number of authors have described how to complete a functional assessment (Brooke, Inge, Armstrong, & Wehman, 1997; Targett, 2001). An important point to remember is that this is not a job trial or extended work experience. In other words, the individual is not being asked to demonstrate that he or she is ready to work through a temporary employment situation or participate in assessments over a long period of time such as weeks or months. Multiple assessments must be balanced with the person's ability to gain access to inclusive employment in a timely manner.

One recommendation is to complete a brief assessment in several jobsites that reflect the person's dreams, interests, and goals identified during the person-centered planning process. The time factor should reflect the number of hours that an individual wants to work once employed. So, if the goal is a 4-hour workday, then each assessment should provide an opportunity to experience the work tasks for 4 hours. There are many requirements related to nonpaid work assessments that must be considered and that are not within the scope of this chapter (U.S. Department of Labor, 2006). Any agency assisting individuals through this type of process to further identify their dream jobs must comply with these standards because fines to employers can result.

Functional assessments should be conducted under the natural circumstances and cues of the workplace where the person would perform the type of work identified as the "dream" job. If the assessment and observations occur across different workplaces, then information about vocational preferences, characteristics of the work environment, skills exhibited in response to different demands, and responses to different environmental stimuli can help in making decisions regarding job choices. The assessment should also be used to consider the types of supports that any potential jobsite must provide in order for the person to be successfully employed. Any gaps between what is required in a job and what the individual is able to accomplish are minimized or eliminated by individualized supports. Looking at the functional abilities and interests of the individual in the context of what is required by the environment where the skill is to be performed allows the individual to have a more accurate idea and a foundation on which to make job choices. Any concerns or support needs can also be resolved through customizing or job negotiations with employers during job development.

Summary notes from the assessment listing observed functional behaviors without negative value judgments will be useful when assisting the person in selecting a specific job. The notes should be limited to information that would be useful for identifying and providing supports, not information that would exclude the person from employment. For instance, assume that the person is completing an assessment as a customer service representative at a local department store. The person does fine answering customer questions as long as there are only two people waiting in line. But, when this number increases, the individual seems to become nervous and turns to the employment specialist repeatedly, asking for assistance. This may provide information that the person does well if the environment requires a slow pace or limited demands but becomes stressed if the work pace increases. A job with fewer demands during less busy times of the day might be the best job match initially for this individual.

This is the type of information that will be useful when actually identifying the work environment that will meet the individual's support needs and preferences. For instance, does the person work better at specific times of the day? How long can the person work without taking a break? Are there variables in the workplace that affect the person's performance, such as physical space, noise, odors, interaction with co-workers, supervisors, customers, the physical demands or pace of the workplace, and so forth?

But what about people who cannot express preferences using speech or words? Because the absence of choice is undignified and leads to learned helplessness, as well as dependence on others, providers must be creative in their efforts to allow individuals to speak for themselves. It is very likely that some individuals will require additional assistance, support, or time in order to make and express their preferred choices.

Therefore, it is very important to look for nonverbal cues to express likes and dislikes. For instance, is the individual hesitant to initiate certain tasks? What do the person's facial expressions convey? Is the individual engaging in disruptive behaviors to express preferences? For individuals who have been employed previously, there is much to be learned from previous job separation. This includes future support needs and personal preferences. These experiences should be seen as opportunities for career development and growth.

CONCLUSION

The importance of using person-centered planning cannot be overemphasized or ignored. Getting to know the person and his or her preferences is a critical step toward positive inclusive employment outcomes. Specifically, negotiating jobs and customizing employment opportunities for individuals must be driven by the person's support needs and preferences. This can be accomplished by the types of person-centered planning activities described in this chapter. In addition, the profile information drawn from person-centered planning will be important during jobsite support because the individual's support needs are identified for developing and implementing effective support plans.

REFERENCES

Bolton, B.F. (2001). *Handbook of measurement and evaluation in rehabilitation* (3rd ed.). Gaithersburg, MD: Aspen Publishers.

Brooke, V., Inge, K.J., Armstrong, A., & Wehman, P. (1997). *Supported employment handbook: A customer-driven approach for persons with significant disabilities.* Richmond: Virginia Commonwealth University Rehabilitation Research and Training Center on Workplace Supports and Job Retention.

Butterworth, J., Hagner, D., Heikkinen, B., Faris, S., Demello, S., & McDonough, K. (1993). *Whole Life Planning: A guide for organizers and facilitators.* Boston: Institute for Community Inclusion.

Ducharme, G., Beeman, P., DeMarasse, R., & Ludlum, C. (1994). Building community one person at a time: One candle power. In V.J. Bradley, J.W. Ashbaugh, & B.C. Blaney (Eds.), *Creating individual supports for people with developmental disabilities: A mandate for change at many levels* (pp. 347–360). Baltimore: Paul H. Brookes Publishing Co.

Everson, J.M., & Reid, D.H. (1997). Using person-centered planning to determine employment preferences among people with the most severe developmental disabilities. *Journal of Vocational Rehabilitation, 9*(2), 99–108.

Falvey, M.A., Forest, M., Pearpoint, J., & Rosenberg, R.L. (1994). *All my life's a circle: Using the tools of circles, MAPS and PATH.* Toronto: Inclusion Press.

Inge, K.J., Strobel, W., Wehman, P., Todd, J., & Targett, P. (2000). Vocational outcomes for persons with severe physical disabilities: Design and implementation of assistive technology and workplace supports. *NeuroRehabilitation, 14*, 1–13.

Inge, K.J., & Targett, P. (2004). *Customized employment Q and A: Supporting community employment as an employment outcome.* Richmond: Virginia Commonwealth University, Training and Technical Assistance to Providers. Retrieved March 6, 2006, from http://www.t-tap.org/strategies/factsheet/supporting.html

Inge, K.J., Wehman, P., Kregel, J., & Targett, P.S. (1996). Vocational rehabilitation for persons with spinal cord injuries and other severe physical disabilities. *American Rehabilitation, 22*(4), 2–12.

Inge, K.J., Wehman, P., Strobel, W., Powell, D., & Todd, J. (1998). Supported employment and assistive technology for persons with spinal cord injury: Three illustrations of successful work supports. *Journal of Vocational Rehabilitation, 10*(2), 141–152.

Mount, B. (1991). *Dare to dream: An analysis of the conditions leading to personal change for people with disabilities.* Manchester, CT: Communitas.

Mount, B. (1994). Benefits and limitations of personal futures planning. In V.J. Bradley, J.W. Ashbaugh, & B.C. Blaney (Eds.), *Creating individual supports for people with developmental disabilities: A mandate for change at many levels* (pp. 97–108). Baltimore: Paul H. Brookes Publishing Co.

Mount, B., & Zwernik, K. (1988). *It's never too early. It's never too late: A booklet about personal futures planning.* St. Paul, MN: Governor's Planning Council on Developmental Disabilities.

O'Brien, J. (1987). A guide to lifestyle planning. In B. Wilcox & G.T. Bellamy (Eds.), *A comprehensive guide to the activities catalog: An alternative curriculum for youth and adults with severe disabilities* (pp. 175–189). Baltimore: Paul H. Brookes Publishing Co.

O'Brien, J., & O'Brien C.L. (Eds.). (1998). *A little book about person-centered planning.* Toronto: Inclusion Press.

Parent, W., Unger, D., & Inge, K.J. (1997). Customer profile. In V. Brooke, K.J. Inge, A. Armstrong, & P. Wehman (Eds.), *Supported employment handbook: A customer-driven approach for persons with significant disabilities* (pp. 46–97). Richmond: Virginia Commonwealth University Rehabilitation Research and Training Center on Workplace Supports and Job Retention.

Pearpoint, J., & Forest, M. (1994). *PATH training video* [Videotape]. Toronto: Inclusion Press.

Pearpoint, J., O'Brien, J., & Forest, M. (1993). *PATH: A workbook for planning positive possible futures: Planning alternative tomorrows with hope for schools, organizations, businesses, and families.* Toronto: Inclusion Press.

Smull, M. (1998). Revisiting choice. In J. O'Brien, & C.L. O'Brien (Eds.), *A little book about person-centered planning* (pp. 37–49). Toronto: Inclusion Press.

Targett, P. (2001). Situational assessment: Toward career planning. In P. Wehman (Ed.), *Supported employment in business: Expanding the capacity of workers with disabilities* (pp. 35–46). St. Augustine, FL: Training Resource Network.

U.S. Department of Labor. (2006). *Section 64c08: Students with disabilities and workers with disabilities who are enrolled in individual rehabilitation programs.* Retrieved March 31, 2006, from http://www.dol.gov/esa/whd/FOH/ch64/64c08.htm

Williams, R.K. (1991). Choices, communication, and control: A call for expanding them in the lives of people with severe disabilities. In L.H. Meyer, C.A. Peck, & L. Brown (Eds.), *Critical issues in the lives of people with severe disabilities* (pp. 543–544). Baltimore: Paul H. Brookes Publishing Co.

Chapter 5

Staff Selection, Training, and Development for Community Rehabilitation Programs

Pamela Sherron Targett

As work is done to increase the nation's resolve to promote employment for people with disabilities, one must look carefully at how supported employment and the personnel working in these programs might play a role. Wehman, Revell, and Kregel (1998) reported results of a 10-year effort to document growth and outcomes of supported employment by providing fiscal year (FY) 1995 data collected from state rehabilitation and other state-level agencies funding supported employment services across the United States. The study chronicled the successful impact of supported employment since the 1990s and revealed that, although too many people with significant disabilities are needlessly left out of this experience, tremendous progress has been made in a relatively short period of time. If one applies the annual 16% growth rate figure over 10 years, then more than 600,000 people with disabilities would be employed.

Their findings also reported that competitive employment is a positive and often therapeutic activity that directly influences self-esteem, personal value, and how people with significant disabilities see themselves. Going to a real job, getting paid, having co-workers, and getting into a normal daily work routine are critical aspects of life.

Finally, Wehman et al. (1998) found that supported employment is a program that works effectively when implemented by a committed organization with skilled staff. Employing quality personnel to help manage the employment process for people with the most severe disabilities is at the heart of program implementation. Therefore, staffing becomes one of the most important tasks facing managers of supported employment services (Grossi, Test, & Keul, 1991; Moore, Godbolt, Schwartz, Moriber, & Salzberg, 1991). This is true regardless of whether an organization is just starting a program, expanding services, or replacing personnel.

The first half of this chapter is reprinted by permission from Wehman, P., & Targett, P. (2002, December). Supported employment: The challenges of new staff recruitment, selection and retention. *Education and Training in Mental Retardation and Developmental Disabilities, 37*(4), 434–446. This article was made possible by Grant #H133B040011

Today, with more community-based organizations converting from segregated day programs to integrated competitive employment programs and an emphasis on improving services through the use of natural supports, expanding employer capacity, and self-instruction (Hagner, Fesko, Cadigan, Kiernan, & Butterworth, 1996; Parent, Cone, Turner, & Wehman, 1998), staffing becomes even more important. Effective staff will be a critical link to ensuring better outcomes for people with disabilities. Ineffective staff will result in poor employment outcomes for individuals with disabilities or, at best, a disproportionate investment of time, energy, and fiscal resources dedicated to training and monitoring those personnel (Pamenter, 1999; Shilling, 1998). Therefore, program managers are wise to invest the necessary time, energy, and resources into staff recruitment, training, and development.

The term *employment specialist* is used in this chapter to identify professionals who help identify, coordinate, and/or provide individualized employment and related services to people with significant disabilities. Using this approach, the employment specialist, sometimes referred to as a *job coach* or *employment consultant*, assists people with severe disabilities with gaining and maintaining work (Unger, Parent, Gibson, & Kane-Johnston, 1998). This usually includes assistance with locating job opportunities, on-the-job work supports (e.g., job and related skills training, accommodations), and ongoing follow-up services (Park, Shafer, & Drake, 1993; Wehman & Melia, 1985). The model does not require that the person with disabilities be "job ready" before going to work (Hanley-Maxwell, Bordieri, & Merz, 1999). Instead, the individual's existing preferences, talents, and abilities are identified and used to guide his or her job search (Wehman & Sherron-Targett, 1999). Once the individual is hired, the employment specialist arranges and/or provides supports either at or away from the workplace to enhance the new employee's performance and long-term job retention (Wehman, 1988).

Although the hiring of new staff presents an opportunity to enhance a supported employment program, it can also present a number of challenges (Powell et al., 1991). First, there has yet to be a consensus regarding the role of the employment specialist. The vocational rehabilitation (VR) field does not portray the role of employment specialist as a professional one. Instead, many consider employment specialists to be paraprofessionals. Second, salaries and benefits for employment specialists are often low when compared with others who perform similar duties (Everson, 1989). In addition to low annual salaries, staff may also face limited opportunities for career development (Park et al., 1993). Third, the work can be taxing as employment specialists are expected to function in a variety of roles (Brooke, Inge, Armstrong, & Wehman, 1997; LeRoy & Hartley-Malivuk, 1991) and work flexible schedules. If not properly managed, this can contribute to staff burnout and turnover (Gomez & Michaelis, 1995; Inge, Barcus, & Everson, 1988; Kregel & Sale, 1988). Because employment specialists play a central role in the employment process, turnover may result in a loss of rapport between the individual with disabilities and employer. In addition, key information related to retention may be lost (Moore et al., 1991).

INITIAL RECRUITING AND HIRING CONSIDERATIONS

Prior to recruiting personnel, it is wise for program managers to complete a thoughtful assessment of their organization (Larson & Hewitt, 2005; Pamenter, 1999). A close look at the organization's mission and values, an analysis of past staffing concerns, an examination of current personnel's strengths, and a review of staffing arrangements are recommended.

Mission/Values

An organization's mission statement should convey what the program intends to do or achieve and the values that underlie that purpose (Dileo & Langton, 1993; Powell et al., 1991). It should provide a strategic vision and direction for the organization. If a statement exists, then it should be reviewed and revised if needed. If one does not exist, then the organization should first determine its values, and then steps should be taken to formulate a mission statement. Some of the values related to best practices in supported employment are provided in Table 5.1. Generally, organizations providing supported employment services include these and other values embodied within their mission statement.

In addition to a formal statement, there are always informal missions that undergird every organization or unit. For example, organizations may choose to work only with individuals with certain types of disabilities, or an organization might choose to work with those individuals not served by others, regardless of disability labels. As another example, some organizations have extensive capital investments (e.g., large buildings, vans) and must generate money to continue these investments. These organizations may have different priorities than organizations with few capital investments.

Table 5.1.   Supported employment values

Values	Values clarification: A conviction that . . .
Presumption of employment	Everyone, regardless of his or her level or type of disability, has the capability and right to a job.
Competitive employment	Employment occurs within the local labor market in typical community businesses.
Control	When people with disabilities choose and regulate their own employment supports and services, career satisfaction will result.
Commensurate wages and benefits	People with disabilities should earn wages and benefits equal to that of co-workers performing the same or similar jobs.
Focus on capacity and capabilities	People with disabilities should be viewed in terms of their abilities, strengths, and interests rather than their disabilities.
Importance of relationships	Community relationships, both at and away from work, lead to mutual respect and acceptance.
Power of supports	People with disabilities need to determine their personal goals and receive assistance in assembling the supports necessary to achieve their ambitions.
Systems change	Traditional systems must be changed to ensure participant control, which is vital to the integrity of supported employment.
Importance of community	People need to be connected to the formal and informal networks of a community for acceptance, growth, and development.

From Brooke, V., Inge, K.J., Armstrong, A.J., & Wehman, P. (Eds.). (1997). *Supported employment handbook: A customer-driven approach for persons with significant disabilities* (p. 75). Richmond: Virginia Commonwealth University Rehabilitation Research and Training Center on Workplace Supports; reprinted by permission.

Whenever a vacancy is created, the manager should assess whether the program's mission is being met. If not, the manager should consider whether personnel decisions could enhance the organization's ability to achieve its goals. For example, if the manager determines that the program is not adequately meeting its mission of serving individuals with severe disabilities, then it is possible that hiring someone who is experienced in this area would increase the program's capacity to accomplish this goal.

Analysis of Past Staffing Concerns

Analysis of the data obtained from exit interviews should be considered by operational programs prior to recruitment. An exit interview is a discussion between the individual who is terminating his or her employment with the organization and the program manager or other representative. Outsourcing this task or using written questionnaires may encourage exiting employees to speak more freely and result in more valid results. The exiting employee may be asked questions that relate to the actual work involved in carrying out the job duties, obstacles that impeded effective performances, overall job satisfaction, and suggestions for improving services. Some sample questions are listed in Table 5.2. This type of feedback may offer insight into future staffing needs, characteristics of successful staff, and/or ways to meet the mission and improve program outcomes.

Examination of Current Personnel's Strengths

An analysis of the strengths and weaknesses of current staff should also be undertaken prior to recruitment. Positive vocational outcomes for people with disabilities are the result of teamwork. It becomes important, then, to look at the aggregate strengths and weaknesses of a staff and identify absent characteristics, which, if present, may help in

Table 5.2.   Sample exit interview questions

Please describe your day-to-day activities.

What did you like the most about the job?

What did you like the least about the job?

How can we improve our services?

Please rate the following statements using a scale of 1–5, with
1 meaning "do not agree" and 5 meaning "totally agree."

• My co-workers were supportive and team players.

• Management listened to my concerns.

• Management treated staff fairly and with respect.

• My customers appreciated the services I provided.

• Staff morale was high in my division.

Why did you decide to leave?

What could we do to make you withdraw your resignation?

From Wehman, P., and Targett, P. (2002, December). Supported employment: The challenges of new staff recruitment, selection and retention. *Education and Training in Mental Retardation and Developmental Disabilities, 37*(4), 437; reprinted by permission.

meeting the organization's mission. For example, it may be that existing staff members are quite knowledgeable about job development techniques yet know little about systematic instruction and other training techniques. It would then behoove the manager to emphasize instructional knowledge in the job description and advertisement for the vacant position. Alternatively, the program manager may decide a change in the staffing configuration would more effectively utilize personnel strengths.

Review of Staffing Arrangements

It is impossible to identify a finite set of staffing arrangements for supported employment programs. Program size, number of supported employment approaches offered by a program, and qualifications and experience of staff are a few of the factors contributing to staffing arrangement decisions. Optimal staffing arrangements are those that satisfy and lead to the best outcomes for the program's customers.

For example, consider the following arrangement. The employment specialist performs all direct-service duties, including assessing the strengths and desires of individuals with disabilities, supporting job development strategies, providing on-the-job supports, and ensuring follow-along for each person on his or her caseload. In this situation, there is a clear continuity of services provided, yet the employment specialist is significantly structured across all areas. A second arrangement might involve personnel specializing in selected duties. For example, each employment specialist performs job development and on-the-job support activities but does not provide follow-along services for his or her customers. To date, there is no empirical evidence that demonstrates one type of arrangement is better than another.

Nevertheless, this is a staffing management challenge. There are certainly pros and cons to both arrangements (Wehman & Sherron, 1993). For example, in some organizations there are different pay scales for job developers, jobsite trainers, and follow-along personnel. Although this may have economic merit, the notion that one component requires more skills and is more valued than another is antithetical to the supported employment concept. Indeed, some programs use the follow-along position as an entry-level position; however, this often requires the most sociable and savvy of staff members who can quickly assess problems and resolve them.

RECRUITMENT PROCESS

After this organizational assessment, recruitment can begin. This process usually involves a number of steps. It begins with determining a need for a position and a job analysis. Then, a job description is prepared using the job analysis. Next, selection criteria are determined. After that, an advertisement is written, and finally, a variety of recruitment sources are used to obtain a pool of qualified applicants.

Job Analysis

Job analysis examines the nature of a position and the workplace environment. It may include details such as what an employee does, why he or she performs certain tasks, how he or she does the job, the conditions under which work is performed, the relationship the job has to other jobs, competencies necessary to complete the work, and physical and mental requirements (Rebore, 1998). This information is used to develop

Table 5.3.   Job analysis techniques

Type	Description
Observation	The employee is observed performing his or her job duties.
Interview	In-depth individual or group interviews are conducted with select employees, and the results are included in the job analysis.
Diary	Employees maintain a written report to summarize daily activities for a specific period of time.
Questionnaire	Employees rate a set of predetermined tasks to indicate if the said duty is performed and add missing data.

From Wehman, P., and Targett, P. (2002, December). Supported employment: The challenges of new staff recruitment, selection and retention. *Education and Training in Mental Retardation and Developmental Disabilities, 37*(4), 438; reprinted by permission.

a job description. It may also be used to design tools for evaluating employee performance. A number of recognized techniques can be used in job analysis (Caruth, Noe, & Mondy, 1988; Shilling, 1998; Webb & Norton, 1999; see Table 5.3). These techniques are generally not used in isolation but instead should be used to complement one another. Use of multiple methods should lead to a superior job analysis. This then serves as a basis for the next step in the recruitment process, the preparation of the job description.

Job Description

Most job descriptions include the organization's objective, the purpose of the position, a specific listing of core duties and responsibilities, qualifications (e.g., physical and cognitive requirements; knowledge, skills, and abilities or competencies required; education, experience, or certification required), and salary and benefits (Webb & Norton, 1999).

Organization's Objective

The organization's objective is a statement that reflects what the organization plans to achieve. In many instances, it will be the formal mission statement or an abbreviated version of it.

Purpose of Position

The section describing the purpose of the position should convey the nature of the job and the overall parameters of the duties. In this general description, the affiliation of the position is often stated along with the major duties. Variations within the general description will be based primarily on the staffing configuration of the program (i.e., one employment specialist providing all services or separating job tasks) and possibly the types of disabilities that customers typically have.

Specific Duties/Responsibilities

This duties and responsibilities section should be specific, and each major duty should be depicted in enough detail to provide a clear understanding of expectations. Very often, supported employment duties are listed in the order in which a placement is secured and maintained. An alternative that is especially useful in organizations with employment specialists who perform a limited number of job functions is listing job duties in the order of the percentage of time that an employee performs those duties. For example, if a program uses a staffing configuration that has employment specialists separated by job function and wants to hire an individual to solely serve as a job developer, then the description should start with those duties specifically related to locating or creating job opportunities because this is what the employee does the majority of the time.

Although the general supported employment service-delivery approach is generic across disability categories, the specific duties associated with various customers may vary, and, if so, this variance should be conveyed in the job description. For example, if the position is for an employment specialist who works only with individuals who have traumatic brain injuries, then the customer assessment section might include information related to understanding neuropsychological test results; roles of other professionals, such as physicians; inpatient rehabilitation units; counseling and psychological services; and the signs and symptoms of substance abuse.

Likewise, the jobsite training section of the job description may emphasize a variety of instructional strategies, such as behavioral rehearsal, vocational counseling, and the development of compensatory strategies. In short, the specific job duty listing must be tailored to the supported employment program.

This part of the job description is often used as a foundation for an employee's performance plan and evaluation. For this reason, it is important to be as specific and as comprehensive as possible. As mentioned earlier, when a company is hiring, duties are often realigned to refine the position with respect to changing organizational needs and meeting the company's mission. This is the section that will most frequently reflect those needs.

Qualifications

The qualifications section of the job description delineates education, experience, and other attributes that the organization either requires or prefers as prerequisites to employment. This will serve as a sieve by allowing only applicants with certain qualifications to be considered for interviews.

Although there continues to be debate over the educational level needed by employment specialists, a desired educational level of employment specialists should be, at minimum, completion of a 2-year associate's degree in a related field and probably should require a bachelor's degree (Grossi et al., 1991). There are many examples, however, of competent employment specialists who do not have a degree, and currently no empirical data exists that education levels directly relate to better outcomes (Everson, 1991). Given the fact that educational and rehabilitation practices dictate these minimum levels of education for other professionals, such as special education teachers, rehabilitation counselors, and vocational evaluation specialists, employment specialists should probably hold the same.

The required or preferred type of experience also varies depending on the values of the organization. For example, some organizations prefer employment specialists with extensive business-related work histories as opposed to rehabilitation service-delivery experience. Among other reasons, it is believed that business experience can lead to more effective marketing and relations with community employers. Although the new employee training will be more extensive, molding staff to do things your way without having to change previously learned skills can offer many benefits.

Salary and Benefits

Salary level and benefit packages have been linked to the high turnover rate of professionals who perform direct-service duties similar to those of an employment specialist (Braddock & Mitchell, 1992; Larson, Hewitt, & Lakin, 2004; Larson & Larkin, 1999). Salary and benefits are a critical factor in attracting good personnel who will remain with an organization. Sometimes the organization will have classification schema that will make salary setting a relatively rigid process. In other instances, the organization can set the salary each time a position is filled. In either case, salaries should be determined based on an equitable salary system that is competitive with other programs.

Salary surveys by telephone or letter along with any published data can be used to gather information about salary programs. Research has revealed that money is an important motivator, no matter what the position or current pay status (Rebore, 1998). This highlights the need for a good starting salary as well as performance incentives such as the ability to earn more and assume greater responsibility.

The organization should also ensure parity among workers who have similar duties within an organization. It should be pointed out at this juncture that the duties and demands associated with supported employment vary drastically from those duties and demands of traditional rehabilitation direct-service staff, who provide training and other rehabilitation within workshops and other non–community-based settings. Employment specialists most often operate much more independently and within much more diverse environments than workshop personnel (Moore et al., 1991). Therefore, salaries should not be based on those paid to workers in such settings.

Salary range ultimately set for a position results from a mixture of data, values, and availability of resources. Organizational value is also important. For example, lower salaries could be indicative of the devaluing of the service being provided and the employment specialist position.

Most often, benefits are standard within an organization and evolve organizationally rather than position by position. It is important to remember that sometimes benefits can offset lower salary, depending on the applicant's situation. For example, single people may be most interested in education reimbursement, whereas older adults want to know about retirement benefits. Common benefits include sick and vacation leave, health plans, and accrual of compensatory time.

Several general points about job descriptions should be noted. First, the job description sections previously stated are typical but may vary among organizations. Second, job descriptions must be individually tailored to the organizational needs at a given point in time. Therefore, there is no one standardized description. Instead, general guidelines and prototypes are given to provide a foundation on which to build. It is imperative that program managers be intimately familiar with their own personnel policies prior to initiating the development of job descriptions, vacancy announcements, and hiring procedures. Third, even when a description exists, it should be reviewed to ensure that it is still accurate because working conditions and organizational needs change.

Selection Criteria

With an accurate job description in hand, the criteria against which candidates will be evaluated should be determined (Rebore, 1998). This is simply a listing of specific characteristics that, if present, would allow the candidate to successfully perform the job. It is particularly useful when more than one person is involved in the interview process. The criteria allow interviewers to quantify their opinions and provide documentation related to the final selection. For example, the selection criteria based on the job description in the previous section may include 1) personal characteristics and qualifications, 2) professional characteristics and qualifications, and 3) experience and training. Table 5.4 provides examples of selection criteria in these areas.

Job Advertisement

After the position description is updated or created and the selection criteria are chosen, the next step is to write an advertisement to let people know there is a vacancy within the organization. Then, the selection process can begin.

An effective job advertisement is crucial for recruiting quality staff. The content of the advertisement is determined by the job description and the criteria that will be used to select the most qualified candidate for the position. Effective advertisements reflect the major responsibilities of the position, the minimum qualifications, and instructions for submitting an application. This is no easy task because the advertisement must be brief enough to appear in a variety of recruitment sources. A sample

Table 5.4.   Selection criteria

Professional characteristics and qualifications

Bachelor's degree

Knowledge of supported employment

Knowledge of disability issues

Knowledge of employment practices

Knowledge of sales and marketing approaches

Knowledge of individualized instructional methods

Philosophy compatible with organization

Verbal communication skills

Written communication skills

Ability to plan, organize, and carry out activities

Ability to creatively problem-solve

Experience and training

Relevance of experience with people with disabilities

Relevance of past work experience

Relevance of life and nonprofessional experience

Personal characteristics and qualifications

Appearance

Personality

Enthusiasm

Flexibility

Willingness to learn and improve self

From Wehman, P., and Targett, P. (2002, December). Supported employment: The challenges of new staff recruitment, selection and retention. *Education and Training in Mental Retardation and Developmental Disabilities, 37*(4), 441; reprinted by permission.

Table 5.5.   Sample job advertisement

An established company is seeking an employment specialist. This individual will have the responsibility of assisting people with disabilities with gaining and maintaining employment, involving such activities as assessing vocational strengths and support needs, locating work opportunities, and arranging or providing on-the-job supports. We are seeking candidates with a college degree in education, business, psychology or a related field; experience; the ability to problem solve; and excellent communication skills. Excellent compensation and benefits package in addition to professional growth opportunities. Apply in confidence. Send résumé and salary requirements to Supported Employment, Anywhere, USA. We are an equal opportunity and affirmative action employer.

From Wehman, P., and Targett, P. (2002, December). Supported employment: The challenges of new staff recruitment, selection and retention. *Education and Training in Mental Retardation and Developmental Disabilities, 37*(4), 441; reprinted by permission.

advertisement is shown in Table 5.5. The advertisement should provide enough information for the prospective candidate to make a decision about applying, as well as give the program manager adequate criteria to narrow down the applicant pool. Existing advertisements should not be reused without thoughtful consideration.

Recruitment Sources

There are many ways to announce a position vacancy and recruit newcomers. Two strategies include networking and written advertisements posted in published resources or on carefully selected Internet sites (Webb & Norton, 1999).

Networking

Word of mouth is an excellent way to obtain applicants. The program manager should call colleagues who may know of individuals desired for the position that are not actively seeking new employment. Likewise, organizations that are frequented by potential applicants should also be sent a position description and application instructions. Sources may include organizations in the community that work with people who have disabilities, professional organizations, universities, or other educational settings that provide training. Present employees are also an important recruiting resource. Research indicates that employee referrals can be a highly effective recruitment source (Webb & Norton, 1999).

Written Advertisements

One of the most popular strategies is to post written advertisements, which may be listed in the local newspaper, industry trade journals, newsletters, or on the Internet. The Internet is becoming more popular and hosts a great number of sites that allow both job postings and résumés for review:

- America's Job Bank at http://www.ajb.dni.us—This web site is the result of a partnership between the U.S. Department of Labor and the state-operated Public

Employment Service. It provides a labor exchange service through a network of more than 1,800 offices throughout the United States. There is no cost to post a job or résumé.

- Hot Jobs at http://www.hotjobs.com—This web site allows job seekers to browse by location, job type, and company. There is no cost to search the site or to post a résumé .

- Virginia Commonwealth University Rehabilitation Research and Training Center on Workplace Supports and Job Retention at http://www.worksupport.com— This web site offers a wealth of information on employment and disability issues. Job advertisements can be posted free of charge.

On-line recruiting is transforming the recruitment process and will likely continue to gain acceptance (Rebore, 1998). A larger list of possible on-line recruitment resources is presented in Table 5.6.

Content of written advertisements and the frequency with which they appear in the newspaper or on the Internet will be dictated by the money budgeted within an organization for recruitment activities. Sometimes, posting an advertisement one time will not be enough; thus, it should appear until an adequate pool of candidates is obtained. However, caution should be used because repeated advertisements or postings in multiple sources can result in an inordinate number of *unqualified* applicants. Screening a large number of applications can be quite time consuming. Creating an accurate advertisement and using select strategies to announce the opening will help ensure a good balance.

Recruitment of Minorities

Programs should also take steps to enhance the success of their minority recruitment programs. First, administrative human resource policies that reflect a commitment to diversity should be adopted. Second, those involved in recruitment should be trained on the policy procedures to enhance minority recruitment efforts (Herman, 1994; Webb & Norton, 1999). Finally, recruitment practices should be reviewed to be sure they are not discriminatory and support the organization's commitment to diversity in the workplace. Placing advertisements in publications with a high minority readership and in minority-related publications—a statement that encourages minorities to apply—may help with recruitment.

SELECTION PROCESS

The result of effective advertising should be a broad pool of applicants who meet the minimum qualifications of the position. Usually, the desired breadth of the pool will vary, depending on the community size, demographics, and economic conditions. After the advertisement has been removed, the program manager should review the applicant pool to determine who to interview and to begin the selection process.

Applicant Screening

The initial screening step is to eliminate all applicants who do not meet the minimum qualifications as listed in the advertisement (e.g., education, experience). The second

Table 5.6.   Sample on-line recruiting web sites

Name of web site	Link	Description
Americas JobBank	http://www.ajb.dni.us/	Thousands of new jobs are posted daily by employers.
Bilingual Jobs	http://www.bilingual-jobs.com/ default_new.htm	This site is a job destination for bilingual career professionals.
CareerBuilder	http://www.careerbuilder.com	Visitors can search nationally for jobs, post résumés, and set up job alerts.
Career Magazine	http://www.careermag.com	This site provides industry-specific career channels with a wealth of information tailored to specific career goals.
Dice	http://www.dice.com/	This site was rated the number one technology job board to search for a permanent or contract position by key word, job title, skills, city, state, or area code.
East Coast Jobs	http://www.eastcoastjob.com/	This site sifts through the Internet to find the best resources and links and offers comprehensive indexes.
Euro Jobs	http://www.eurojobs.com/	This site provides global resourcing information.
Federal Jobs Central	http://www.fedjobs.com/	This database has 16,799 jobs, with new jobs being added weekly.
Fed World Jobs	http://www.fedworld.gov/	This site searches for federal government jobs and has a series of search tools, including by series, by grade, by state, and for-merit promotion jobs.
Global Careers	http://www.globalcareers.com	Global Careers is an established recruiting firm dedicated to providing quality recruitment and other cost-effective placement services to companies of all sizes with current job listings and an on-line job board.
Hot Jobs	http://hotjobs.yahoo.com/	Visitors can browse by industry and state.
Job Circle	http://www.jobcircle.com/	Job Circle provides regional employment opportunities, résumé submission, career development, monthly columns, discussion databases, news, and regional events.
JobOptions	http://www.jobweb.com/	JobOptions, a web site of career development and job search information for college students and new college graduates, is owned and sponsored by the National Association of Colleges and Employers.
Monster TRAK	http://www.monstertrak. monster.com/	Monster TRAK is a web site for students and alumni looking for full-time and part-time positions, internships, and on-campus employment.
Overseas Jobs	http://www.overseasjobs.com/	Overseas Jobs features international job opportunities for professionals, expatriates, and adventure seekers.
Saludos	http://www.saludos.com/	Saludos specializes in joining the Hispanic bilingual professional with companies looking for diversity in the workplace.
USA Jobs	http://www.usajobs.opm.gov/	This site is the federal government's one-stop source for federal jobs and employment information.
Vault	http://www.vault.com/	Vault provides general and targeted job boards for top opportunities, with career guides available for purchase.

step is to create a pool of "most viable" applicants by separating out applicants who appear to exceed the minimum qualifications by meeting one or more of the preferred qualifications. It is not uncommon for one or more seemingly minimally qualified applicants to be moved into the group of most viable candidates. Therefore, the manager should examine both the minimally qualified and the more-than-minimally-qualified pools of applicants at this time to ensure that the qualification criteria used results in applicants with the most desired qualities falling into the smaller of the two groups. This is a check to make sure that what was conveyed within the advertisement and/or position description matches the manager's perception of a "good" candidate. Candidates who may be desirable but who did not make the second application-screening cut should be moved into the pool of "viable" candidates. The final step in the screening process is to rank applicants based on the written documentation that has been obtained. During this step, the manager will identify which group of applicants to interview first.

Interviewing

Conducting effective interviews is crucial to the selection process. An interview is a structured conversation between an employer and job seeker that allows the employer to gather facts from the job seeker and to learn about experience, beliefs, and opinions relative to predetermined selection criteria (Webb & Norton, 1999). It provides an opportunity for the manager to determine if the candidate is qualified for the job and a good match for the organization. Essentially, the manager is trying to predict successful future performance. At the same time, the job seeker is also gathering information about the company and the corporate culture.

As an interviewer, the program manager has several important responsibilities. First, he or she must design the process, which includes determining the approach (i.e., individual or group interviews) and creating questions and/or other means for evaluating candidates. The interviewer must also facilitate the process, which involves creating a positive environment and conducting the interviews. Finally, the interviewer must decide whom to choose for the job.

Designing the Process

The manager should have a list of interview questions prepared in advance. One way to derive a list of interview questions is to start by reviewing the job description and selection criteria. Afterward, insightful questions can be created (see Table 5.7). Managers should also present situations that have been encountered by employment specialists within their program and ask candidates what they would have done in a similar situation (Grossi et al., 1991). Responses to these behavior-based questions can provide invaluable insight to a candidate's knowledge and problem-solving abilities.

Facilitating the Process

A pleasant environment and warm interview style will help put candidates at ease and facilitate effective communication. This can be achieved by moving away from being behind a desk and reducing any potential interruptions by turning off the telephone and letting other staff know that interviews are taking place. The program manager

Table 5.7. Sample interview questions

Knowledge of assessment techniques, workplace supports, instructional strategies, and relationships with people with disabilities

1. What type of experience do you have with individuals with disabilities?
2. What ideas do you have for exploring the job seeker's strengths and support needs?
3. What if the person is nonverbal?
4. JoAnn is a 40-year-old woman who has never worked. Her vocational strengths are as follows: She is highly motivated to work, she can read letters and numbers, she uses her left foot to operate her wheelchair for mobility, she has the ability to use her left hand, she can see and hear, her speech is usually understood by those who know her best, and she has a warm personality. What ideas do you have for job opportunities for JoAnn?
5. Our primary customers are people with disabilities. What ideas do you have to promote JoAnn's involvement in her job search?
6. What roles do parents or significant others play in the employment process?
7. What procedures would you use to evaluate the person's progress in 1) the job search process and 2) work performance? Should the person be involved in evaluating your performance?
8. Tell me about a time that you provided instruction to someone else. What made this a successful learning experience? What four words would a learner use to describe your teaching strategies?
9. How would you promote integration of the new worker within the employment setting?
10. You are providing on-the-job skills training and the new employee is stocking items on a shelf but not following the correct steps to complete the task correctly. You provide a verbal prompt, and the employee states, "You are not my supervisor. Stop telling me what to do. I know what I am doing, and this is right!" How would you respond?
11. An individual with disabilities who lives in an institutional setting tells you that she has requested to be bathed nightly but has been told that this is not possible. What steps would you follow?
12. How involved should the person with disabilities be in his or her job search and the selection of instructional strategies? How would you promote participation and choice?

Knowledge of sales and marketing techniques and relationships with business

1. Many Americans with disabilities are unemployed. What do you feel are the major barriers to their employment, and how would you promote the employment of people with disabilities in our community?
2. Why should businesses hire people with disabilities?
3. What techniques would you use to learn about local employment opportunities?
4. What would you say during the employer meeting?
5. What questions do you think employers might have, and how would you respond?
6. The job involves meeting with potential employers to identify work opportunities. Imagine you are meeting with an employer who states, "We cannot hire a person with disabilities. All of our employees must be physically fit and fast thinkers. We also require everyone to be cross-trained." How would you respond?
7. Not all employers are open to learning about our services and hiring people with disabilities. Tell me about the most irritating customer/person you have had to deal with, and how did you respond?
8. What ideas do you have for developing long-term relations with area businesses?
9. Should business be involved in evaluating your performance? Why?

Relationships with colleagues

1. What qualities do you have that would enhance our team?
2. What characteristics do you find desirable/undesirable in people?
3. Tell me about the busiest time you had on your last job.
4. Tell me about a time when you helped a co-worker with learning a task/solving a problem.
5. Why will our organization be better for having hired you?
6. What are your expectations of management?

General topics and background information

1. Why do you feel that you are qualified for this position?
2. What is your philosophy as it relates to the employment of people with disabilities?
3. Tell me about your duties and responsibilities at your most recent job that are related to the position.
4. Why do you want to work here and in this position?

From Wehman, P., and Targett, P. (2002, December). Supported employment: The challenges of new staff recruitment, selection and retention. *Education and Training in Mental Retardation and Developmental Disabilities, 37*(4), 444; reprinted by permission.

should also give the person a warm welcome and inquire about the person's travel to the office. Next, the process should be described. During the interview, the manager should make eye contact without staring, speak in a normal tone of voice, and use frequent body language to promote broader responses (i.e., nodding, smiling, brief acknowledgments of hearing what was said).

The interview is also a time for candidates to ask questions about the organization and the position. Thus, the manager should mention perks and have adequate information to answer questions. Options such as flex time and telecommuting can be attractive to some workers. Any benefits and programs that help employees' lives run smoothly should be emphasized (i.e., reimbursement for education, child care assistance). Ample time should also be allocated to respond to the applicant's questions. The types of questions and the manner in which they are asked will often provide the manager with additional information about the candidate's ability and desire to do the job.

Although often criticized for consuming significant time and resources, reference and background checks are another important step in the hiring process (Smith & Knab, 1996; Webb & Norton, 1999). This involves examining the person's character by questioning past employers about the candidate (Shilling, 1998). A great deal may be learned by talking to others who know the applicant well. Checking references may identify individuals who misrepresented their background or qualifications. A negative reference could disqualify a poor candidate and save the organization time and money. Due to a fear of being sued for defamation of character, it can sometimes be difficult to get more than dates of hire and a basic job description from previous employers. Background checks take an even closer look into a prospective employee's past. This may include verifying information related to the job requirements such as employment history, criminal background, and driver's record. This activity should be handled by the hiring manager (Pamenter, 1999) or outsourced. Ideally, checks are performed prior to making a job offer. Under either circumstance, information obtained must be kept strictly confidential.

Making a Choice

Once the interviews are completed, the manager should organize all relevant data and then carefully consider the choices. The data should include a rank ordering of scores against the selection criteria, verified credentials, applications, and any other relevant data. The program manager should review this material and then select the candidate who appears to be the most qualified. Once a decision is made (and approved if necessary), the program manager offers the job to the selected candidate and negotiates the necessary details. The manager should be prepared to handle the start date, salary negotiations (even if the money is not available), and other special considerations.

Accepting employment within a new organization can be a major decision. Therefore, the manager should be prepared to wait a few days for a final decision from the candidate. A set time limit for a response should be mutually agreed on, with an understanding that the offer will be withdrawn after the agreed-on date. If the candidate accepts the position, then it is imperative that the terms of the employment be documented in some type of employment agreement.

The final step of the hiring process is to establish a start date for the new hire and notify the unsuccessful applicants that the position has been filled. Obviously, because the top candidate may decline the job offer, notification should not occur until the employment agreement is confirmed and the start date has been established.

PREPARING STAFF TO PROVIDE QUALITY SERVICES

Once hired, new staff must be trained. Although the most significant factor influencing the quality of supported employment services is staff expertise (Rogan & Held, 1999), most staff members enter the field with limited education and little or no formal training or experience in supported employment. Agosta, Brown, and Melda (1993) found that 37% of employment specialists had only a high school education and that 51% had received no more than 8 hours of training prior to starting work. As a result, many supported employment programs have come to rely on staff members who are not professionally trained to provide services. This pathway into the field brings with it great learning opportunities as well as challenges.

The remainder of this chapter takes a closer look at these and other issues related to the training and development of supported employment staff. We begin by revisiting the critical role that the employment specialist plays in the implementation of supported employment. Next, a review of the literature on training needs is provided, followed by a brief look at programmatic barriers to staff development. The chapter will conclude with a discussion of a competency-based training approach for supported employment.

Role of the Employment Specialist

If supported employment providers are to develop and retain quality staff, then the rewards and demands inherent in the position must be recognized. To more fully appreciate this fact, it is necessary to revisit the role of the employment specialist. Working in the field of supported employment is highly demanding. In this position, employment specialists have the responsibility for facilitating and/or providing a wide range of services to ensure that individuals with disabilities become successfully employed in their communities. This requires the employment specialist to take on many roles and perform a multitude of job functions that are linked to the major service components of supported employment (i.e., career planning, job search, on-the-job support, extended/job retention services). Within each component, the specific activities performed must be individualized and specifically tailored to meet the needs and capitalize on the abilities of each person being served. At one time, this service option was primarily used to serve individuals with intellectual disabilities. Today's programs may serve people with other severe development disabilities, traumatic injuries (e.g., traumatic brain injury, spinal cord injury), mental illness, or multiple disabilities. Thus, in addition to knowledge in core areas, employment specialists often need some disability-specific training.

To further complicate matters, the employment specialist must also be business minded. For example, he or she must become skilled at marketing services and the job seekers' talents to potential employers, as well as savvy at negotiating viable work opportunities and facilitating or providing workplace supports. It will be critical for the employment specialist to understand and respond to the unique needs of both the job seeker with disabilities as well as the employer looking for job candidates. If this is not done correctly, then the effectiveness of service delivery will be compromised.

To successfully perform this vast array of functions, employment specialists must be skilled and comfortably move in and out of a number of roles. For example, they must focus on both planning and coordination of resources and on direct instruction and facilitation of workplace supports. They must also be able to interact effectively with people on many different levels, from corporate chief executive officers or small business owners to family members or individuals with disabilities who do not use verbal communication. Communications are often required with other professionals, too, such as VR counselors, physicians, and/or service coordinators.

Often times, there are ongoing organizational pressures present in the employment specialists' workplace. For instance, policies and procedures related to communication and documentation must be followed, and expectations related to the number of hours committed to service delivery must be met. Keeping customers satisfied can also become quite challenging when an employment specialist is working for a number of people, who are involved in various phases of the employment process. If one customer suddenly becomes employed, other customers may be on hold unless another staff member can take over job development.

Staff must also keep a flexible schedule and be prepared to work as needed. This may mean working outside of bankers' hours (9 A.M. to 5 P.M.) with little or no notice. Furthermore, because services are provided within the community, employment specialists may be isolated from immediate role models and support networks. Oftentimes, they must act independently, "think on their feet," and problem-solve without immediate in-house supervision or support.

These and other factors combined place great pressure on employment specialists, both personally and professionally, which can lead to problems with staff motivation and retention due to "burn out." In turn, high turnover rates create service gaps for both employers and individuals with disabilities. A study by Morehouse and Albright (1991) revealed that job coaches leave their positions primarily due to personal circumstances, lack of training, and inability to provide adequate support to individuals with disabilities. This finding further highlights the importance of providing staff with initial and ongoing training and development.

Review of the Literature

A review of the literature offers additional insight into supported employment staff training and development needs. Everson (1991) and Morgan, Ames, Loosli, Feng, and Taylor (1995) surveyed employment specialists to determine their self-reported training needs. Based on surveys from 519 direct-service personnel, Everson found that the skills ranked highest in terms of training needs included Social Security and medical coverage, behavior management techniques, job modifications technology, reinforcement techniques, integration strategies, parent/family advocacy techniques, and instructional training methods. Morgan et al. surveyed 131 personnel involved in providing on-the-job training and found a need for training in the areas of matching a job to an applicant, developing a job for an applicant, encouraging family and parent support, marketing the applicant, strengthening social behavior, encouraging employer/supervisor support, and strengthening job skills.

Sale (1990) wrote that supported employment curricula should include foundation, core, and disability specialty areas. He suggested that the foundation courses include content related to competencies in philosophical, historical, ethical, and legal issues associated with people who have disabilities. The core area should include information about implementation of the supported employment model and may include strategies for marketing, consumer assessment techniques, job placement activities, jobsite training, and follow-along interventions. Specific emphasis on the application of systematic instruction, behavioral analysis, and behavioral change strategies should be provided. Service coordination and advocacy should also be included in the core curriculum. Supported employment personnel should become familiar with ways to gain access to and coordinate community resources. Advocacy should also be explored, and content should emphasize techniques to facilitate decision making and involvement in the process. After receiving training in the foundation, core curriculum staff should receive specialty training to develop skills related to a specific disability and advanced implementation skills in supported employment that hit on any related nuances.

Test and Wood (1995) reviewed the skills and competencies direct-service staff need to train an individual with severe disabilities in an integrated employment setting. They indicated that, in order to provide quality job training, an employment specialist must have mastered systematic instruction skills and consultation skills. They noted that if staff members are not competent in systematic instruction and applied behavior analysis, then they will not be able to meet the needs of individuals with the most severe intellectual and behavioral disabilities, and job training will be prolonged due to an inability to fade from the jobsite.

As the field of supported employment has evolved, so have the roles and training needs of direct-service personnel. For example, traditional direct-service roles have adapted to the provision of customer-driven approaches and facilitating natural and other workplace supports. One study catalogued the kinds of service-delivery activities employment specialists actually engaged in when working in a community employment program that emphasized the use of community and workplace supports (Unger et al., 1998). Data indicated that employment specialists engage in a variety of activities. In addition, it suggested that the role of the employment specialist had evolved from that of the primary provider of services to a facilitator of services. Unger et al. indicated that if staff members are not competent in facilitating the natural involvement of co-workers and supervisors and maximizing the use of workplace supports, then the optimal integration of employees with disabilities would not be realized.

A national survey of training and information needs of organizations and professionals involved with VR service provision was conducted by Wehman, Barcus, and Wilson (2002). Thirty-five percent of those surveyed were supported employment direct-service providers. The overwhelming trend in this study was that rehabilitation providers are seeking information on working closely with businesses on the employment of people with disabilities. Similar to other studies (Griffin, 1997; Region IV Community Rehabilitation Provider Survey, 1996; Region X Training Needs Survey, 1998), Wehman et al. found that respondents indicated a high need for knowledge of employer/business cultures, marketing and job development methods, effective strategies for educating employers, strategies for building employer networks, and utilization of assistive technology in the workplace (i.e., working with employers, involving customers, environmental modifications). A second trend of the survey was the need for developing techniques that help empower individuals with disabilities such as person-centered planning, career planning, and facilitating self-determination. Employment specialists indicated that they need assistance with jobsite support interventions and creating good career options for people with the most severe disabilities.

Some researchers complain that too often staff development programs have been derived from reviews of literature, surveys of experts, or a combination of the two. Rothwell and Kazanas (1994) have argued that although the literature review and survey approach provides some useful information, this approach may not contain the degree of detail or direct applicability to practice needed to develop effective training.

Instead, they recommended analyzing worker functions during on-the-job tasks to develop the curriculum. One such method is the *critical incident technique*, in which experienced workers are asked to describe situations or incidents that are specifically indicative of or critical to effective job performance. This method has been widely used to identify work performance factors (Neale, Dunlap, Isenhour, & Carroll, 2000) and to develop critical thinking and problem-solving skills among paraprofessionals (Burgum & Bridge, 1997).

Hagner, Noll, and Donovan (2002) used this technique to identify competencies required to prepare employees for job development and employment specialist roles. In this pilot study, critical incidents from community employment personnel were used to generate a list of staff competencies for job development and job support. The authors reported that competencies recommended were surprisingly wide ranging and complex, including possessing a broad knowledge of disability-specific legislation and policies, assisting employers to develop job accommodations, and helping individuals with disabilities to identify and work toward jobs that match their vocational interests as well as their strengths and desires.

The scope and depth of the competencies identified underscores the fact that work competency is best viewed as a complex interaction of skills and knowledge in which identification of contextual factors is critical (Sandberg, 2000). Because these competencies are directly linked to real-life occurrences, the authors indicated that competencies developed through the critical incident method can be assumed to have a high degree of applicability to the practice of community rehabilitation. These competencies could be used to serve as training module topics or the basis to survey a more discreet subset of training needs. It was also recommended that an exploration of the critical incidents in a staff member's own practice with a supervisor or mentor is an effective on-the-job training technique that complements and enriches other training. The authors concluded that despite such study limitations to include intersubjectivity of raters, the critical incident method appears to be a promising approach to the development of effective training curriculum for staff.

Basic Training Concepts

Staff development initiatives generally focus on three interrelated areas of job performance: 1) attitudes, 2) knowledge, and 3) skills. Adult learners should develop an attitude of acceptance and respect toward others and ultimately learn to distinguish between people and ideas and to challenge ideas without threatening people (Smith, 2002). The *attitudes* held by supported employment staff will influence their desire and motivation to perform at work. Basic attitudes held by staff regarding the ability of people with disabilities to work and their right to make choices and take risks are examples of attitudinal issues that affect staff performance. Staff who do not believe in the abilities of people with disabilities will find it difficult to accept the core principles associated with the best practices in the field. For example, a staff person may know how to locate work opportunities; however, if that person does not believe that an individual with severe disabilities will be productive, then he or she is not likely to put forward the effort needed to achieve a positive result (i.e., a job offer). Staff must also understand, support, and value the organization's mission. Simply setting standards and performance expectations is not enough. Employment specialists who do not understand values or embrace the goals of supported employment are less likely to be committed to its success.

Knowledge refers to staff learning basic facts, terms, elements, or the conceptual classifications of categories, principles, theories, and/or models. Within a supported employment program, staff training programs that are designed to acquire knowledge will focus on such content areas as the history of supported employment, the components of a supported employment service, and disability classifications. The assumption is that, given proper input, support, and resources, staff will build a basic set of knowledge and, on request, will be able to convey information about supported employment in the course of their job.

Skills refers to a learner's procedural capability with techniques, criteria for procedures, and strategic ability. For example, an employment specialist may possess general knowledge about systematic instruction to assist an individual with significant disabilities but may not be skilled in using this procedure. Therefore, the employment specialist has gained knowledge of a procedure but has not advanced to an applied level of learning, actually possessing the skill to deliver service. When designing training programs, it is critical to consider the attitudes, knowledge, and skills necessary to allow staff to successfully perform their jobs.

As mentioned previously, historically, training programs have focused on increasing staff knowledge through lectures and discussions; however, today's high-quality training initiatives understand the importance of also providing direct training in the environment where performance based skills can be taught and evaluated.

Barriers to Staff Training and Development

The occupation of an employment specialist is truly a demanding and professional position, and there undoubtedly remains a shortage of skilled staff. Yet, most service providers have an unimpressive record of preparing and supporting their staff for what lies ahead, and few formal training programs exist. There are a number of barriers that prevent the establishment and maintenance of effective staff development programs. For example, problems associated with a lack of administrative support can hinder development, and these are often the first to be cut or eliminated when financial pressures increase.

Beyond administrative support, a lack of time, resources, or expertise to develop and evaluate training are common barriers. Then, there are logistics. Many programs count on staff to begin providing direct billable services as soon as possible. Thus, a new hire may be expected to enter the field quickly (i.e., hit the ground running) with little or limited training or ongoing field supervision. Although the program's intentions may be good, new support staff soon "sink" or "swim" without adequate training.

Without adequate training and development, employment specialists will not be able to adequately meet the needs of those individuals with the most severe disabilities; they will continue to remain underserved. In addition, ill-equipped staff will likely be less effective and efficient, affecting both the quality of service delivered and costs. The bottom line is staff must receive the skills training necessary to provide high-quality and effective supported employment services.

Staff Skills Training Opportunities

There has been a continuing national discussion through the Association of Persons in Supported Employment about the need to professionalize the job of an employment specialist by setting standards for credentialing and basic competency require-ments. To date, however, this organization has not set a national standard. By far, the majority of employment specialists do not have college degrees. As a result of the di-verse backgrounds of incumbent personnel, nondegree programs such as workshops, institutes, and national conferences have been commonly relied on for training.

These more traditional approaches to training have inherent logistical and fiscal problems associated with them. Participants must leave their home communities and workplaces, incur travel and per diem expenses, and lose the benefit of learning with their local peers. Today, live video teleconferencing, live web casts, and interactive on-line courses provide an alternative to traditional training.

Live teleconferencing and web casts can be interactive if designed appropriately. For example, participants can view a live presentation and then ask questions and present their views on the current subject matter. Afterward, the presentations can be stored and reviewed at a later date to supplement staff development training and re-inforce principles learned. More recently, on-line courses have been established that allow new and established personnel to study the "nuts and bolts" of supported em-ployment without the cost and burden of travel.

One such course is offered by Virginia Commonwealth University Rehabilitation Research and Training Center on Workplace Supports and Job Retention. This sup-ported employment web-based certificate series offers an extensive overview of sup-ported employment in six lessons over a 12-week period. Employment strategies that are covered include

- Assistive technology evaluation and application

- Developing business partnerships

- Career development

- Compensatory strategies

- Customer choice

- Instruction in the workplace

- Marketing and job development

- Job restructuring

- Person-centered planning

- Positive behavior supports

- Self-employment

- Social Security work incentives

- Workplace/co-worker supports

In addition to listening to on-line presentations, participants attend group discus-sions on related topics, link to valuable resources, and complete other activities to sup-plement their learning experience. Participants who successfully complete the course are given a certificate of completion, and continuing educational units are also avail-able. Because more and more on-line courses are cropping up, buyers should beware and take care to select a course that is offered by a reputable organization.

Although all of these training approaches can be useful in developing the employment specialist's general knowledge base, it is imperative that didactic information and simulations be supported with hands-on experience. For example, learners should be paired with other experienced staff so that their knowledge can be developed into practical skills.

Practical Training Model

The future of supported employment requires service providers to become more committed to training and ongoing staff development so that their employees can perform their job to the best of their abilities. Such training should offer structure and support to ensure that staff members gain the knowledge and develop the skills necessary to be effective and efficient in their roles. Today's more progressive programs have abandoned a "hire and hope" or "sink or swim" approach and are providing direct skills training in the natural work environment where performance-based skills can be taught and evaluated.

Although traditional methods of training may be used to improve knowledge and allow simulated skills practice in a formal setting, the implementation of these newly acquired skills often does not occur once staff members are back in the field. Thus, programs must recognize the need to balance traditional training approaches with a sound dose of practical field-based skills training.

CURRICULUM DESIGN

A performance-based training model used at one program is outlined next. It is anticipated that this conceptual information will assist those involved in developing their own staff development programs. Although general training in supported employment, such as that provided by an on-line course, is an effective way to build on or refine one's knowledge base, initiatives must also be designed within the context of each program's philosophy and program procedures.

Orientation

The orientation process is essentially a preservice educational program that sets the foundation for working in the field of supported employment. The emphasis is on helping the new staff member become more familiar with his or her role and how his or her role fits into the organization, policies and procedures, the supported employment process, orienting to the physical environment, staff, customers, and program philosophy. Table 5.8 provides an example of a 5-day orientation schedule. The content could be modified according to the strengths and weaknesses of a new staff member. Suggested materials to facilitate learning include readings (i.e., supported employment handbook, current research, and case studies), videotapes, organizational flow charts, policy and procedure manuals, sample reports, documentation forms, and easy-to-follow handouts.

The 5-day orientation is followed by additional readings, discussions, field observations, collaboration with senior staff, and hands-on experience. New staff gradually take on more responsibility during the workday and learn how to apply information presented during orientation to their direct work experience.

Table 5.8.   Sample content for a 5-day orientation

Day 1

Welcome and overview of training
Overview of organization and division
- Purpose and mission
- History
- Structure, function, and interfacing of various divisions
- Tour of worksite and introductions to others

Overview of supported employment
- Historical overview (normalization, integration, and key legislation)
- Definitions and key terminology
- Values and beliefs
- Best practices and quality indicators (commitment to excellence)
- Benefits
- Roles and responsibilities

Exploration of relationship building
- Customer service philosophy
- Privacy and confidentiality
- Assessing satisfaction
- Handling concerns and complaints
- Professional conduct

Debriefing from observation of employment specialist performing follow-along activities
Introduction to medical and psychosocial aspects of disability
- Program structure and outcome data
- Functional aspects and implications of various disabilities
- Person-centered services

Examination of program policies and other administrative issues

Day 2

Review of previous day's activities/questions and answers
Introduction to creative problem solving
Overview of business and employment practices
- Research related to employer disability hiring practices and attitudes
- State of local labor market
- Professional conduct and program image
- Features that benefit employers

Discussion on removing barriers to employment
- Negative attitudes (person-first language, media, in-house tools, modeling)
- Creative work designs
- Workplace supports
- Natural supports
- Transportation
- Social Security work incentives
- Disability legislation and regulations

Introduction to identifying strengths, abilities, supports, and career planning
- Purpose and outcomes of person-centered career planning
- Referral process
- Career exploration
- Functional assessment
- Customer profile
- Strategies for representing individual job seekers

(continued)

Table 5.8.   *(continued)*

- Creative work structures
- Individual marketing tools

Debriefing from observation of employment specialist performing or simulation of functional assessment activities and profile development

Discussion of strategies for customer involvement

Examination of documentation and communication for customer assessment activities

- Procedures
- Time management
- Team building

Day 3

Review of previous day's activities/questions and answers

Introduction to building relations and making connections with businesses

- Professional conduct and program image
- Service features as employer benefits
- Business needs
- Hidden job opportunities
- Employer concerns
- Positive closings
- Local labor market analysis
- Prospect list and job search plan
- "Warm Calls"
- Letters of introduction
- Telephone techniques
- Networks
- Tools and other resources

Debriefing from observation of employment specialists making employer contacts by telephone

Explanation of workplace and job analysis

- Techniques
- Deal breakers
- Review of job opportunity with job seeker
- Employer follow-up and future contact

Briefing on creative work structures

- Strategies
- Employer presentation
- Negotiation techniques

Debriefing from observation of employment specialist meeting with employer and workplace job analysis

Discussion of strategies for customer involvement

Examination of documentation and communication for job development activities

- Procedures
- Time management
- Team building

Day 4

Review of previous day's activities/questions and answers

Explanation of pre-employment supports

- Application process
- Interviewing
- Employment offer

Briefing on new employee supports

- Transportation training

- Off-site supports
- New employee orientation
- New employee skills training
- Learning styles
- Facilitation of workplace support
- Skill acquisition training (instructional strategies, data collection, analysis, and modifications)
- Production training (techniques, data collection, analysis, and modifications)
- Assistive technology
- Generalization and fading instructional support

Overview of natural supports
- Types
- Strategies for facilitating

Dialogue on prevention of and solutions to workplace problems
- Administrative
- Employer initiated
- Co-worker initiated
- Worker initiated

Debriefing from simulation of on-the-job skills training activity
Discussion of strategies for customer involvement
Examination of documentation and communication for on/off job support
- Procedures
- Time management
- Team building

Day 5
Review of previous day's activities/questions and answers
Exploration of long-term follow-up and job retention strategies
- Definition
- Funding sources
- Methods

Dialogue on preventing and solving workplace problems
- Administrative
- Employer initiated
- Co-worker initiated
- Work initiated

Overview of work termination and career advancement
- Support
- Next steps

Explanation of off-site support
- Role of employment specialist
- Community resources

Discussion of strategies for customer involvement
Examination of documentation and communication for job retention
- Procedures
- Time management
- Team building

Introduction to other topics in supported employment
- Strategies for return to pre-injury employment
- Positive behavior supports

Overview of on-the-job training curriculum
- Structural characteristics and content overview
- Training procedures and measurements

Structural Characteristics and Content Overview

The structure of the curriculum is performance based. This approach offers clarity in role expectations and provides a performance evaluation system to monitor both learning and ongoing performance. The primary focus of the curriculum content is to enhance the employment specialists' knowledge and skills while developing a healthy professional attitude.

There are a number of benefits to using this approach to ongoing skills training and development. First, the training, although structured, is also flexible. A new hire learns and is eventually evaluated as real-work activities occur. In addition, the training content can be modified or expanded to meet the needs of individual staff members. Second, the curriculum design is behaviorally specific and relevant. Performance ratings are based on observable skills and verbal knowledge, and the training occurs during actual work activities. Next, this approach facilitates self-directed learning and ensures ongoing feedback to management so that program design can respond to ongoing needs. Finally, and perhaps most important, new staff can immediately participate in developing the skills needed to become successful on the job. Table 5.8 provides an overview of the on-the-job training curriculum, and the employment specialist training forms in the appendix at the end of this chapter illustrate the tool used to measure performance and facilitate the learning process.

Training Procedures and Measurements

Training objectives cannot be addressed efficiently if the curriculum is difficult to understand and implement. To be effective, training initiatives need to be well conceived and strategically designed as well as practical and easy for staff to follow.

Training is provided to the new staff by experienced staff who have demonstrated the skills and knowledge necessary to competently perform the job. The skills and knowledge needed are taught using a variety of methods, such as verbal explanation, modeling, and on-the-job skills training or job coaching. The teaching methods are flexible and adjusted to meet the trainee's learning style. Eventually, after some field-based skills training, a trainee is observed and evaluated on the job. Most observations are made in the field; however, this may not always be feasible. Thus, verbal explanations or simulation may need to be used. Comments and additional goals are added to address ongoing staff development needs.

The curriculum provides the opportunity for new staff to receive positive feedback on the strengths and skills that they have acquired. It also offers them feedback on areas in need of improvement. Thus, additional instruction can be arranged to ensure skill acquisition and successful job performance. The training content is modified based on staff feedback and as changes occur. Obviously, other programs interested in utilizing such an approach would need to design materials that are in alignment with their particular program's philosophy, policies, practices, and procedures.

CONCLUSION

Test and Wood (1995) stated that the best way to invest in the future of supported employment is to ensure employment specialists are well trained and competent at performing their jobs; however, many questions remain about helping staff acquire, generalize, and maintain their skills. With advances in technology, leaders in the field are now offering on-line instruction worldwide. This allows experts to reach a larger audience and certainly helps advance the field, but supported employment providers must also remember that there is no substitute for practical field-based training and should take the time to develop and implement an effective method for recruitment, as well as staff development and training programs.

REFERENCES

Agosta, J., Brown, L., & Melda, K. (1993). *Job coaching in supported employment: Present conditions and emerging directions. National survey results. Data summaries.* Salem, OR: Human Services Research Institute.

Braddock, D., & Mitchell, D. (1992). *Residential services and developmental disabilities in the United States: A national survey of staff compensation, turnover and related issues.* Washington, DC: American Association on Mental Retardation.

Brooke, V., Inge, K.J., Armstrong, A.J., & Wehman, P. (Eds.). (1997). *Supported employment handbook: A customer-driven approach for persons with significant disabilities.* Richmond: Virginia Commonwealth University Rehabilitation Research and Training Center on Workplace Supports and Job Retention.

Burgum, M., & Bridge, C. (1997). Using critical incidents in professional education to develop skills of reflection and critical thinking. In R. Pospisil & L. Wilcoxson (Eds.), *Learning through teaching* (pp. 58–61). Perth, WA: Murdoch University.

Caruth, D.L., Noe, R.M., & Mondy, R.W. (1988). *Staffing the contemporary organization.* Westport, CT: Greenwood Press.

Dileo, D., & Langton, D. (1993). *Get the marketing edge: A job developer's toolkit for people with disabilities.* St. Augustine, FL: Training Resource Network.

Everson, J.M. (1989). A survey of personnel in supported employment programs in Rehabilitation Services Administration (RSA) Region III: A description of training needs, educational backgrounds, and previous employment experiences. *Dissertation Abstracts International, 51*(1A), 135.

Everson, J.M. (1991). Supported employment personnel: An assessment of their self-reported training needs, educational backgrounds, and previous employment experiences. *Journal of The Association for Persons with Severe Handicaps, 16,* 140–145.

Gomez, J.S., & Michaelis, R.C. (1995). An assessment of burnout in human service providers. *Journal of Rehabilitation, 61*(1), 23–25.

Griffin, C.C. (1997). *National rural supported employment focus group.* Presentation at the conference of the Association for Persons in Supported Employment, Orlando, FL.

Grossi, T.A., Test, D.W., & Keul, P.K. (1991). Strategies for hiring, training and supervising job coaches. *Journal of Rehabilitation, 57*(3), 37–43.

Hagner, D., Fesko, S.L., Cadigan, M., Kiernan, W., & Butterworth, J. (1996). Securing employment: Job search and employer negotiation strategies in rehabilitation. In E.M. Szymanski & R.M. Parker (Eds.), *Work and disability: Issues and strategies in career development and job placement* (pp. 309–340). Austin, TX: PRO-ED.

Hagner, D., Noll, A., & Donovan, L.E. (2002). Identifying community employment program staff competencies: A critical incident approach. *Journal of Rehabilitation, 68*(1), 45–51.

Hanley-Maxwell, C., Bordieri, J., & Merz, M.A. (1999). Supporting placement. In E.M. Szymanski & R.M. Parker (Eds.), *Work and disability: Issues and strategies in career development and job placement* (pp. 341–364). Austin, TX: PRO-ED.

Herman, S.J. (1994). *Hiring right: A practical guide.* Thousand Oaks, CA: Sage Publications.

Inge, K.J., Barcus, J.M., & Everson, J.M. (1988). Developing in-service training programs for supported employment personnel. In P. Wehman & M. Moon (Eds.), *Vocational rehabilitation and supported employment* (pp. 145–162). Baltimore: Paul H. Brookes Publishing Co.

Kregel, J., & Sale, P. (1988). Preservice preparation of supported employment professionals. In P. Wehman & M.S. Moon (Eds.), *Vocational rehabilitation and supported employment* (pp. 129–144). Baltimore: Paul H. Brookes Publishing Co.

Larson, S.A., & Hewitt, A.S. (with invited contributors). (2005). *Staff recruitment, retention, and training strategies for community human services organizations.* Baltimore: Paul H. Brookes Publishing Co.

Larson, S.A., Hewitt, A.S., & Lakin, K.C. (2004). Multiperspective analysis of workforce challenges and their effects on consumer and family quality of life. *American Journal on Mental
Retardation, 109,* 481–500.

Larson, S.A., & Larkin, K.C. (1999). Longitudinal study of recruitment and retention in small
community homes supporting persons with developmental disabilities. *Mental Retardation,
37,* 267–280.

LeRoy, B.W., & Hartley-Malivuk, T. (1991). Supported employment staff training model. *Journal of Rehabilitation, 57*(2), 51–55.

Moore, S.C., Godbolt, F., Schwartz, M., Moriber, L., & Salzberg, C.L. (1991). Factors contributing to the attrition of supported employment job coaches. *Journal of Rehabilitation,
57*(2), 47–51.

Morehouse, J.A., & Albright, L. (1991). Training trends and needs of paraprofessionals in transition service delivery agencies. *Teacher Education and Special Education, 14*(4), 248–256.

Morgan, R.L., Ames, H.N., Loosli, T.S., Feng, J., & Taylor, M.J. (1995). Training of supported
employment specialists and their supervisors: Identifying important training topics. *Education
and Training in Mental Retardation and Developmental Disabilities, 30,* 299–307.

Neale, D., Dunlap, D., Isenhour, P., & Carroll, J. (2000). *Collaborative critical incident development.* Proceedings of the 40th annual meeting of the Human Factors and Ergonomics Society, Santa Monica, CA.

Pamenter, F. (1999). Recruitment management. *Ivey Business Journal, 14,* 61–66.

Parent, W.S., Cone, A.A., Turner, E., & Wehman, P. (1998). Supported employment: Consumers leading the way. In P. Wehman & J. Kregel (Eds.), *More than a job: Securing satisfying
careers for people with disabilities* (pp. 149–182). Baltimore: Paul H. Brookes Publishing Co.

Park, H., Shafer, M.S., & Drake, L. (1993). Factors related to the working environment of employment specialists. *Journal of Rehabilitation, 59*(4), 38–44.

Powell, T.H., Pancsofar, E.L., Steere, D.E., Butterworth, J., Itzkowitz, J.S., & Rainforth, B.
(1991). *Supported employment: Providing integrated employment opportunities for persons with disabilities.* White Plains, NY: Longman Publishing.

Rebore, R.W. (1998). *Personnel administration in education* (5th ed.). Boston: Allyn & Bacon.

Region IV Community Rehabilitation Provider Survey. (1996). *The services and learning needs of
community rehabilitation providers survey.* Atlanta: Georgia State University, Program for Rehabilitation Leadership, and University of Tennessee, Center on Disability and Employment.

Region X Training Needs Survey. (1998). *Community rehabilitation program (CRP) training needs
survey.* Mountlake Terrace: Western Washington University, Center for Continuing Education in Rehabilitation.

Rogan, P., & Held, M. (1999). Paraprofessionals in job coach roles. *Journal of The Association for
Persons with Severe Handicaps, 24,* 273–280.

Rothwell, W., & Kazanas, H. (1994). *Improving on-the-job training.* San Francisco: Jossey-Bass.

Sale, P. (1990). Preparation of supported employment personnel. In A.P. Kaiser & C.M.
McWhorter (Eds.), *Preparing personnel to work with persons with severe disabilities* (pp. 227–
240). Baltimore: Paul H. Brookes Publishing Co.

Sandberg, J. (2000). Understanding human competence at work: An interpretive approach.
Academy of Management Journal, 43(1), 9–25.

Shilling, D. (1998). *The complete guide to human resources and the law.* Paramus, NJ: Prentice Hall.

Smith, M.C., & Knab, K.M. (1996). Designing and implementing teacher selection systems.
NASSP Bulletin, 80, 101–106.

Smith, M.K. (2002). *Malcolm Knowles, informal adult education, self-direction and anadragogy: The
encyclopedia of informal education.* Retrieved January 30, 2005, from http://www.infed.org/
thinkers/et-knowl.htm

Test, D.W., & Wood, W.M. (1995). It almost does take a rocket scientist to be an employment
specialist. *Journal of Vocational Rehabilitation, 5,* 257–259.

Unger, D.D., Parent, W.S., Gibson, K.E., & Kane-Johnston, K. (1998). Maximizing community and workplace supports: Defining the role of the employment specialist. In P. Wehman
& J. Kregel (Eds.), *More than a job: Securing satisfying careers for people with disabilities* (pp. 183–
223). Baltimore: Paul H. Brookes Publishing Co.

Webb, L.D., & Norton, M.S. (1999). *Human resources administration: Personnel issues and needs
in education.* Upper Saddle River, NJ: Prentice Hall.

Wehman, P. (1988). Supported employment: Toward zero exclusion of persons with severe disabilities. In P. Wehman & M.S. Moon (Eds.), *Vocational rehabilitation and supported employment*
(pp. 3–16). Baltimore: Paul H. Brookes Publishing Co.

Wehman, P., Barcus, M., & Wilson, K. (2002). A survey of training and technical assistance needs
of community-based rehabilitation providers. *Journal of Vocational Rehabilitation, 17,* 39–46.

Wehman, P., & Melia, R. (1985). The job coach: Function in transition and supported employment. *American Rehabilitation, 11*(2), 4–7.

Wehman, P., Revell, G., & Kregel, J. (1998). Supported employment: A decade of rapid growth
and impact. *American Rehabilitation, 24*(1), 31–43.

Wehman, P., & Sherron, P. (1993). Preparing personnel for implementation of supported employment services. In C.J. Durgin, N.D. Schmidt, & L.J. Fryer (Eds.), *Staff development and clinical
intervention in brain injury rehabilitation* (pp. 129–156). Gaithersburg, MD: Aspen Publishers.

Wehman, P., & Sherron-Targett, P. (1999). *Vocational curriculum for individuals with special needs:
Transition from school to adulthood.* Austin, TX: PRO-ED.

Wehman, P., & Targett, P. (2002, December). Supported employment: The challenges of new
staff recruitment, selection and retention. *Education and Training in Mental Retardation and
Developmental Disabilities, 37*(4), 434–446

Appendix

Staff Assessment
and Training Evaluation

Training section: Identifying skills, abilities, and support needs for career planning

Skill area: Home visit

Purpose: To demonstrate the ability to establish rapport; identify vocational skills, abilities, and support needs; and establish a direction for job search and/or additional assessment activities with the job seeker

Method of evaluation: The employment specialist is observed during a home visit after he or she has observed a minimum of two home visits led by senior personnel and has taken the lead on one visit. Repeat observations as needed until the employment specialist demonstrates the knowledge and skills necessary to satisfactorily conduct a home visit.

Skills and knowledge:

☐ Reviews relevant functional information provided by the referral source prior to the visit

☐ Uses the customer profile as a guide; interviews the individual with disabilities and significant others (if needed/if permission is granted) in his or her home; and discusses abilities, work preferences, supports available, and support needs

☐ Observes the abilities of the person with disabilities and the support use in the home environment

☐ Discusses how the program is presented and how disclosure will be handled (from both programmatic and individual point of view) during employer meetings

☐ Discusses what makes a "good job" and what is not acceptable for the job seeker

☐ Discusses ideas for the initial direction of the job search and support needs

☐ Discusses the role of the employment specialist and assists the job seeker with determining his or her role in the job search

☐ Investigates if the job seeker has the necessary documents to begin work (e.g., photo identification) and, if not, explains what needs to be done

☐ Discusses the need for additional assessment with the job seeker

☐ Establishes guidelines for future communications (with whom, type, how often)

☐ Summarizes the meeting outcomes and the next steps

☐ Projects a pleasant, positive, and confident attitude

☐ Dresses appropriately for the home visit

Comments:

Trainer signature: _____ Date: _____

Trainee signature: _____ Date: _____

Training section: Identifying skills, abilities, and support needs for career planning

Skill area: Customer vocational profile

Purpose: To demonstrate the ability to analyze and synthesize information from a variety of sources and use it to guide the direction of the job search and employment selection activities

Method of evaluation: The employment specialist is observed creating a profile after he or she has reviewed and discussed a minimum of two profiles of individuals who are currently employed and has taken the lead on creating a profile under the guidance of senior staff. Repeat observations as needed until the employment specialist demonstrates knowledge and skills necessary to satisfactorily create a customer vocational profile.

Skills and knowledge:

☐ Analyzes information obtained during home visits and other functional assessment activities

☐ Synthesizes information to create a customer vocational profile and form an initial direction for search activities (e.g., area to survey, businesses to reach, specific positions to pursue)

☐ Forms an individualized job representation strategy (e.g., general development, job restructuring, use of marketing tools, role of employment specialist)

☐ Communicates the abilities and support needs of the individual with disabilities

☐ Justifies the direction of the job search and explains what meaningful employment looks like to the job seeker

☐ Recommends and arranges additional assessment activities if desired/warranted (e.g., vocationally oriented PATH, community assessment, situational assessment, business tours, informational interviewing, job shadowing)

Comments:

Trainer signature: _____ Date: _____

Trainee signature: _____ Date: _____

Training section: Building relations and making connections with business

Skill area: Employer presentation

Purpose: To demonstrate the ability to deliver messages that appeal to businesses, address concerns, and develop working relationships

Method of evaluation: The employment specialist is observed while meeting with a business representative after he or she has observed a minimum of one face-to-face encounter by senior personnel and has taken the lead on one face-to-face encounter. Repeat observations as needed until the employment specialist demonstrates knowledge and skills necessary to satisfactorily meet with a business representative.

Skills and knowledge:

☐ Uses effective techniques to establish a positive rapport with the employer

☐ Conducts informational interviews as a first step to identify business needs

☐ Asks questions and listens to gain a better understanding of the business needs

☐ Explains the features of supported employment in a way that appeals to and benefits employers (e.g., offers "other" services to employer)

☐ Gauges his or her personal presentation style to the employer's personality

☐ Uses business terminology and avoids using professional lingo

☐ Establishes credibility by using testimonials of other businesses and program outcome data

☐ Alleviates employer concerns or fears by addressing common ones upfront (e.g., Will this work? Will I lose or spend too much money? Will any harm be caused?)

☐ Reframes objections into a question

☐ Uses the three-step process to address concerns (identify concern heard, comment on it, validate its importance)

☐ Combats negative beliefs by providing educational materials

☐ Approaches the subject of hiring at the right time

☐ Projects a pleasant, positive, and confident attitude

☐ Dresses appropriately for the business contact

☐ Uses marketing tools

☐ Answers the employer's questions related to the law and incentives

☐ Closes with a commitment (meeting with hiring team, conducting informal interview with job seeker, touring the workplace, giving a referral to another business)

Comments:

Trainer signature: _____ Date: _____

Trainee signature: _____ Date: _____

Training section: Building relations and making connections with businesses

Skill area: Job seeker representations

Purpose: To demonstrate the ability to represent the individual in an honest and positive way to potential employers while maintaining the job seeker's confidentiality

Method of evaluation: The employment specialist is observed during a meeting with an employer who is looking to hire after he or she has discussed positive representation strategies, observed two face-to-face employer contacts, and has taken the lead on one. Repeat observations as needed until the employment specialist demonstrates the skills and knowledge necessary to satisfactorily represent the job seeker to an employer.

Skills and knowledge:

☐ Approaches the subject of hiring at the right time

☐ Uses adjectives to describe the job seeker's personality

☐ Reflects on the job seeker's experiences at work, at school, or in life

☐ States why a particular job would be a good fit for both parties

☐ Presents support needs in a positive light

☐ Asks questions to detect the employer's fears or concerns

☐ Addresses the employer's questions and concerns

☐ Uses personal networking tools to represent the job seeker

Comments:

Trainer signature: _____ Date: _____

Trainee signature: _____ Date: _____

Training section: Supporting the job seeker in pre-employment activities

Skill area: Job application process

Purpose: To demonstrate the ability to facilitate or provide support with completing the application process

Method of evaluation: After discussing support strategies used with current individuals with disabilities and common barriers in the job application process, debrief with the employment specialist until he or she expresses knowledge and/or performs skills to successfully conduct this activity.

Skills and knowledge:

☐ Makes recommendations on how to document reasons for previous work terminations

☐ Assists with securing names and details for appropriate references

☐ Facilitates or provides minimal support necessary to complete the application process

☐ Provides transportation to and from the business

☐ Ensures the arrangement of in-house completion of the application

Comments:

Trainer signature: _____ Date: _____

Trainee signature: _____ Date: _____

Training section: Supporting the job seeker in pre-employment activities

Skill area: Job interview

Purpose: To demonstrate the ability to provide flexible, individualized supports to assist the job seeker with the job interview process

Method of evaluation: After discussing possible support and needs of the current individual with disabilities, hold a minimum of two debriefings with the employment specialist until he or she expresses knowledge and/or performs skills to successfully conduct this activity.

Skills and knowledge:

☐ Discusses types of assistance or supports needed before interview process (e.g., appropriate clothing, specific appointment time, directions to site, accessibility of site, transportation to and from interview, practice interviewing)

☐ Facilitates or provides support prior to the interview process

☐ Discusses types of assistance or supports needed during the interview process (e.g., disclosing disability, discussing accommodation/workplace support needs, explaining ability to perform the job, finding out about site accessibility, discussing criminal background, responding to questions related to past job separations)

☐ Facilitates or provides support during the interview process

☐ Disarms the employer's fears that come up during the interview process (knows what the person can do well and what support may be needed, explains why the job is a good fit for both parties)

☐ Discusses types of assistance or supports needed after the interview process (e.g., thank-you letter, alternate testing procedure, follow-up with employer about next steps/offer)

☐ Facilitates or provides supports after the interview

Comments:

Trainer signature: _____ Date: _____

Trainee signature: _____ Date: _____

Training section: Supporting the employee at work

Skill area: New employee orientation

Purpose: To demonstrate the ability to facilitate or provide the support needed to ensure the new hire completes orientation

Method of evaluation: Debrief with the employment specialist a minimum of three times after orientation.

Skills and knowledge:

☐ Dresses appropriately for the workplace

☐ Attends the new employee orientation with the new hire unless directed not to attend

☐ Reviews the employee handbook (if provided) with the new hire away from the jobsite to check understanding of important information and to identify supports

☐ Ensures the new hire is introduced to other co-workers by workplace personnel

☐ Facilitates communication between the new hire and work personnel by providing the minimal amount of support needed to request information or answer questions, encouraging workplace personnel to address the employee, modeling effective ways to communicate with the person (if appropriate), and so forth

☐ Communicates relevant information to family members/caregivers as indicated (e.g., information on schedule, policies) to reinforce or provide support

Comments:

Trainer signature: _____ Date: _____

Trainee signature: _____ Date: _____

Training section: Supporting the employee at work

Skill area: Employee training

Purpose: To demonstrate the ability to provide different types of supports that enhance the employee's workplace integration and job performance

Method of evaluation: Debrief with the employment specialist throughout training. Discuss strategies to support the individual, review documentation data, and, if possible, make on-the-job observations to evaluate instruction. If this is not possible, then use in-house simulations.

Skills and knowledge:

☐ Arrives to work on time

☐ Dresses appropriately for the workplace

☐ Participates in and provides individualized supports or facilitates existing workplace supports as indicated during the employer's new employee training (e.g., notetaking, asking questions) to assist the new hire with completing this activity

☐ Designs a baseline data collection tool and collects and analyzes data to determine areas for instruction

☐ Provides or facilitates additional skills training to the new hire after the employer's in-house training is complete

☐ Develops and implements systematic instructional strategies, if appropriate

☐ Ensures task completion while providing on-the-job skills training to the new hire, if appropriate

☐ Designs a tool to document the new employee's performance of job functions

☐ Collects data to document the new employee's performance

☐ Analyzes data on performance to evaluate the effectiveness of instruction and identify areas in need of additional skills training

☐ Identifies the need for assistive technology to improve learning or prompt performance

☐ Ensures assistive technology is put into place (input from new hire, employer, and others as needed)

☐ Teaches the new hire to use assistive technology, if applicable

☐ Ensures that supervision and feedback come from appropriate jobsite personnel

☐ Encourages the new hire to say hello/good-bye to others

☐ Projects a pleasant, positive, and confident attitude

Comments:

Trainer signature: _____   Date: _____

Trainee signature: _____   Date: _____

Training section: Communication

Skill area: Communicating with individuals with disabilities

Purpose: To demonstrate effective communication skills with individuals with disabilities

Method of evaluation: Debrief with the employment specialist throughout training. Discuss strategies to communicate with individuals with disabilities and, if possible, make on-the-job observations. If this is not possible, then use in-house simulations.

Skills and knowledge:

☐ Uses a private setting to discuss confidential or personal issues

☐ Minimizes environmental distractions and interruptions

☐ Appears comfortable and at ease while communicating with the person

☐ Uses clear, concise, and meaningful language that is respectful of the person's age (e.g., avoids jargon, uses of person-first language, does not use condescending style [baby talk] or words [*sweetie-pie, honey*])

☐ Adjusts his or her communication style to ensure that the person understands (e.g., repeats information, shortens sentences)

☐ Uses active listening skills (e.g., paraphrasing, leaning forward, making eye contact)

☐ Uses alternate means to communicate with individuals who do not use words to communicate

☐ Regains the person's attention if needed by providing prompts (e.g., redirection, touching, using person's name)

☐ Pauses after questioning and gives the person time to respond (e.g., patient, does not interrupt)

☐ Seeks confirmation of the person's understanding

☐ Displays appropriate nonverbal language (e.g., eye contact, use of gestures)

☐ Directs questions to the individual being served rather than to others who may be present

Comments:

Trainer signature: _____ Date: _____

Trainee signature: _____ Date: _____

Section II

Tools for Change

Chapter 6

Supported Employment and Workplace Supports

Overview and Background

PAUL WEHMAN, KATHERINE J. INGE, W. GRANT REVELL, JR., AND VALERIE A. BROOKE

In the early 1980s, published reports began to appear on supported employment as a means to assist people with significant disabilities to become competitively employed. Since then, a great deal has been learned about what works in supported employment (Mank, Cioffi, & Yovanoff, 1999, 2000); however, many challenging implementation issues and persistent philosophical differences continue to exist among practitioners that create major barriers to full implementation of supported employment (Kregel, Wehman, Revell, Hill, & Cimera, 2000; Mank, 1994; Wehman, Revell, & Kregel, 1998). Still, there are clear indicators of the progress achieved in developing the supports used by many individuals with significant disabilities to live and work more fully integrated within their home communities. Deinstitutionalization has increased (Hayden & Albery, 1994), state institutions have closed (Stancliffe & Lakin, 1999), and some sheltered workshops have downsized or closed with an accompanying selective reallocation of funds targeted from segregated programs to integrated programs (Murphy, Rogan, Handley, Kincaid, & Royce-Davis, 2002). People with disabilities have acquired a more significant voice via legal status and the advocacy movement in influencing the policies and services that affect their lives (Wehmeyer & Lawrence, 1995).

The changes made by the American Association on Mental Retardation (AAMR) in the classification of individuals with mental retardation are an excellent example of the movement away from a focus on perceived levels of impairment and toward use of supports by individuals with disabilities. AAMR has shifted from intelligent quotient labels derived from tests to classification based on a description of the supports, in both level and intensity, that are required by people with intellectual disabilities (AAMR, 2002). In fact, the "hot term" for the 1980s was *supports*, and the current "hot term" is *self-determination*. The use of supported employment, supported education, and supported living, when intertwined with self-determination, effectively marries supports as a programmatic strategy with self-determination as a philosophical foundation.

SUPPORTED VERSUS SHELTERED EMPLOYMENT

The goal of supported employment programs is to assist people with the most significant disabilities to be successful in paid employment in the integrated work setting of their choice. Supported employment programs began as early as 1980 (Wehman, 1981) and were marked by a paradigm shift from providing services in centers to support services in business and industry settings. *The focus has been paid employment in integrated settings.* Current federal regulations, issued by the Rehabilitation Services Administration to govern the national Vocational Rehabilitation (VR) Program, define an *integrated setting* as a setting typically found in the community where individuals with disabilities interact with individuals without disabilities, other than individuals without disabilities who are providing services to them, to the same extent that individuals without disabilities in comparable positions interact with other people (State Vocational Rehabilitation, Jan. 21, 2001).

The revised regulations that eliminated extended employment in a nonintegrated setting overturned a decades-old policy that allowed VR agencies to consider placement in segregated employment settings such as sheltered workshops to be an appropriate employment outcome for individuals with disabilities. Under the amended regulations, an *employment outcome* is defined as full- or part-time employment in the integrated labor market (State Vocational Rehabilitation, Jan. 22, 2001). Appropriate employment outcomes include not only supported employment but also self-employment, telecommuting, or business ownership.

The amended regulations have been controversial. The U.S. Department of Education received more than 3,000 comments in response to the initial notice of proposed rulemaking in June 2000. Proponents of the amended regulations contended that the change would significantly increase access to integrated employment settings, eliminate barriers to competitive jobs for people with significant disabilities, and improve the overall accountability of the VR program. Critics expressed concern that restricting the definition of appropriate employment outcome exclusively to integrated employment settings would unnecessarily limit the choices of individuals with disabilities, reduce the number of employment options available to such individuals, limit access to the VR system for individuals with the most significant support needs, and lead to the elimination of sheltered workshops where individuals currently work.

Virtually all forms of sheltered employment can generally be classified into two types. *Transitional employment programs* are intended to provide training and experience to individuals in segregated settings so that they will be able to acquire the skills necessary to succeed in subsequent competitive employment. *Extended employment programs* are designed to be long-term or permanent placements for individuals that will allow them to use their existing abilities to earn wages in the segregated workshop setting.

Sheltered employment programs are designed to assist individuals who, for whatever reason, are viewed as not capable of working in a competitive employment setting in their local community. The term *sheltered employment* is often used to refer to a wide range of segregated vocational and nonvocational programs for individuals with disabilities, such as sheltered workshops, adult activity centers, work activity centers, and day treatment centers. These programs differ extensively in terms of their mission, services provided, and funding sources. Most sheltered employment services are operated through private, not-for-profit organizations that are funded through a variety of state and federal funding sources.

In amending the regulations regarding employment outcome, the U.S. Department of Education recognized the two different types of sheltered employment settings. "Extended employment (i.e., sheltered or nonintegrated employment) remains both an initial step toward achieving integrated employment under the vocational rehabilitation program and a long-term employment option through sources of support other than the vocational rehabilitation program" (State Vocational Rehabilitation, Jan. 22, 2001, p. 7,254). In other words, the revised regulations still recognize the transitional (training) function of sheltered workshops by allowing the use of VR funds to support an individual's placement in a sheltered workshop if the purpose of that placement is to prepare for work in an integrated employment setting. Furthermore, the regulations acknowledge that placement in sheltered employment may still remain a long-term outcome for individuals with disabilities. The regulations merely require that funds other than VR monies be used to support this segregated placement.

The move by the U.S. Department of Education to focus the use of VR funds on the achievement of integrated employment outcomes is the most recent episode in a long and contentious debate over the appropriateness of sheltered employment for people with intellectual disabilities (McLoughlin, Garner, & Callahan, 1987; Wehman, 2001). Sheltered workshops and other segregated employment settings formed the core of the nation's system of vocational training and employment supports for adults with significant intellectual disabilities throughout the 20th century. The majority of adults with intellectual disabilities still work in segregated, sheltered employment settings, as opposed to integrated settings in the competitive labor force (Braddock, Rizzolo, & Hemp, 2004).

In reaction to these criticisms, supported employment has emerged as an alternative to sheltered employment, particularly for individuals with intellectual disabilities. Supported employment, developed in the federal/state VR program in 1986, is viewed as competitive employment in an integrated work setting for individuals traditionally unable to obtain or maintain employment in the open labor market. As recently as 1986, only 300 programs across the country provided supported employment services. In 2005, more than 3,000 agencies provided supported employment to more than 250,000 individuals across the nation (Kregel & Wehman, 1997).

Despite its rapid emergence as the preferred employment alternative for individuals with significant intellectual disabilities, supported employment has been occasionally criticized (Kregel & Wehman, 1989; Wehman & Kregel, 1995). Concerns have been raised that individuals with intellectual disabilities are frequently unable to retain their jobs for extended periods of time after initial placement, individuals are often placed in low-paying jobs that do not allow them to achieve economic self-sufficiency, and the program fails to effectively meet the needs of individuals with the most significant and ongoing support needs.

The ability of both sheltered and supported employment to have a long-term impact on the earnings and economic self-sufficiency of individuals with cognitive disabilities directly relates to the U.S. Department of Education's decision to modify the definition of *employment outcome*. The revised regulations reject sheltered employment as a meaningful employment outcome for the VR program, yet retain sheltered employment as in "interim step in the rehabilitation process" (State Vocational Rehabilitation, Jan. 22, 2001, p. 7,255).

Research by Kregel and Dean (2002) has helped to validate these policy changes by the Social Security Administration (2004). The long-term earnings impact of sheltered and supported employment on 877 individuals with intellectual disabilities was investigated through the implementation of a comprehensive analytical framework for assessing employment outcomes for people with disabilities who have been served by a VR agency in a single state. Information on demographic characteristics, pre- and postprogram earnings, and local economic conditions were merged to allow a comprehensive examination of the earnings outcomes of individuals who receive alternative types of VR services. Results indicated that people served in sheltered and supported employment differ in many ways from other individuals with intellectual disabilities successfully served by the VR agency. Individuals in the supported employment group were more likely to have worked in competitive, integrated employment prior to program entry as compared with their sheltered employment counterparts. The sheltered and supported employment groups differed slightly in terms of demographic characteristics. *Earnings of the supported employment group were 250% greater than the sheltered employment cohort across a 7-year postprogram period.* Supported employment also had a statistically greater impact on the earnings of people with disabilities than participation in sheltered employment.

QUALITY INDICATORS OF SUPPORTED EMPLOYMENT

It is clear that specific indicators about what supported employment is and is not needed to be identified. Wehman, Revell, and Brooke (2003) identified 10 indicators that address the quality of a supported employment program from a variety of critical perspectives (see Table 6.1). We will not describe all of them here; however, "informed choice, control, and satisfaction" is viewed as a crucial first step. Hence, the first perspective is the point of view of individuals with disabilities who turn to a supported employment program for support in getting and retaining a job. Do individuals served by the supported employment program consistently achieve truly meaningful job outcomes? Who selects these jobs, and do these employment opportunities reflect informed customer choice and control?

The indicators must also reflect the perspective of employers. Are employers satisfied with the work produced by the individuals in supported employment and the quality of the ongoing support services received from the supported employment program? The indicators must be responsive to the agencies funding the supported employment program. Does the provider have a well-coordinated job retention support system in place, and does the program's management information system accurately track and monitor employment outcomes? Finally, the combined set of indicators must serve as a means for self-assessment by the supported employment program itself to help identify areas of strength that can be used in marketing and areas that need priority attention for improvement.

An individual in supported employment works in a competitive job in an integrated work setting. What, in fact, characterizes the true quality of competitive work in an integrated setting? The preamble to the 1997 VR regulatory announcement frames paid employment in integrated settings in the context of the *parity principle* by asking the question: Is the experience of the person with disabilities at parity with the experiences of the co-worker without disabilities (State Vocational Rehabilitation, 1997)? The importance of this parity principle is supported by the research by Mank and his associates (1999, 2000) on the positive relations of typical employment features and co-worker involvement with higher wage and integration outcomes for individuals in supported employment.

Table 6.1.   Quality indicators for a supported employment program

Quality indicator	Example of functional measures
Meaningful, competitive employment in integrated work settings	An employee with disabilities is hired, supervised, and paid directly by the business where the job setting is located and receives wages/benefits that are commensurate with co-workers without disabilities.
Informed choice, control, and satisfaction	An employee selects his or her own service provider and job coach, selects a job and work conditions, and is satisfied with the job and supports.
Level and nature of supports	The program is skilled in identifying workplace support options and developing workplace support options.
Employment of individuals with truly significant disabilities	The program serves individuals whose intermittent competitive work history, disability profile, functional capabilities, and other barriers to employment are truly reflective of people who need ongoing workplace supports to retain employment.
Amount of hours worked weekly	The program achieves employment outcomes at 30 or more hours per week consistently; individuals receiving support are satisfied with their hours of competitive employment.
Number of people from the program working regularly	The program currently has a majority of its participants working in competitive employment; individuals receiving support are satisfied with their program of services.
Well-coordinated job retention system	The program maintains regular contact with its employed customers to monitor job stability and can respond effectively to both planned and unplanned job retention support needs; the program replaces individuals who do not retain employment.
Employment outcome monitoring and tracking system	The program maintains an information system that provides information readily to its customers on employment status, longevity, wages, benefits, hours of employment, and jobs.
Maximizing integration and community participation	Employees with disabilities work in jobs in which the work environment facilitates physical and social interaction with co-workers; employees are satisfied with the quality of their work and community integration.
Employer satisfaction	The program is viewed as an employment service agency rather than a human service provider; employers are seen as a customer of the service, and the program designs policies and procedures that are responsive to the business community.

From "Competitive employment: Has it become 'first choice' yet?" by Paul Wehman, W.G. Revell, Jr., and V. Brooke, 2003, *Journal of Disability Policy Studies, 14*(3), p. 166. Copyright 2003 by PRO-ED, Inc. Adapted by permission.

The goal of supported employment has always been to identify meaningful employment outcomes for people with disabilities, many of whom have never worked before. A meaningful employment outcome is a job with career possibilities. A worker at a jobsite who is actually the employee of an outside service provider has limited career opportunities. Most people are not interested in dead-end positions. As with other members of the labor force, people with disabilities are interested in jobs where they can build their résumés and/or employment positions and potentially grow with a company. Meaningful employment outcomes for individuals in supported employment are jobs that have full parity with other jobs within the workplace in terms of how people are hired, supervised and compensated; the opportunities they have to interact with co-workers; and the access they have to job advancement and career opportunities.

The opportunity to make choices concerning employment, living arrangements, and recreation has been limited or nonexistent for many individuals with disabilities. It has become increasingly evident that the powerlessness and lack of direction frequently felt by people with disabilities are related to attitudes and practices of service providers, caregivers, funding agencies, and society in general, rather than to any true limitations as a result of the individuals' disabilities (Brooke, Wehman, Inge, & Parent, 1995; Browder, Wood, Test, Karvonen, & Algozzine, 2001; Wehman, 1981). High-quality supported employment programs avoid this trap by empowering their customers to make choices and to take control of their career paths. A critical factor in assessing the overall quality of a supported employment program is analyzing the data to determine if the customers of the service have choice over the process and are truly in control of their rehabilitation outcomes. Organizations that support choice and control shape their service-delivery practices by the wants and needs of their customers.

Individuals with disabilities who use supported employment must be in a position not only to choose their service provider and employment support personnel but also to have some measure of control over the services they seek. Individuals who utilize supported employment must be free to participate in supported employment services by choosing a service provider and employment specialist, by accepting or declining a specific job, or by electing to resign or continue employment with a particular company without fear of reprisal. Informed choice and control must be a key feature to any employment support service assisting people with significant disabilities in their search for employment.

ONGOING WORKPLACE SUPPORTS AND JOB RETENTION

A major defining aspect of all quality supported employment programs are the *supports* provided; without support, clients placed into work are at risk for losing employment. Without well-implemented supports, there is no quality supported employment. Different types of supports are required for different types of working situations and different types of disabilities. We cover many of these in the section that follows.

Ongoing supports focused on job retention are provided in a variety of ways. A job coach/employment specialist can provide supports directly to employees with disabilities, or the job coach can take a more indirect role that involves advocacy and facilitation of supports, including training of co-workers to be the primary source of the support (Mank et al., 1999, 2000; Parent, Unger, Gibson, & Clements, 1994). Unger, Parent, Gibson, Kane-Johnston, and Kregel (1998), in researching the role of the on-site employment specialist in the provision of ongoing supports, found that employment interventions are drawn from a variety of sources. Although the job coach is the most frequent source for identifying and arranging supports, the person with disabilities, family members, and others in the community can be very active in developing supports.

Co-workers and supervisors can be primary support providers at the workplace (West, Kregel, Hernandez, & Hock, 1997). Employment-related interventions address a variety of support needs in areas such as learning how to do the job, assistance with completing the job, addressing work-related and non–work-related issues, and arranging transportation to and from work. The job coach can have a primary role in both developing and providing employment interventions; however, it is also important that employers, co-workers, individuals in the community, and family members act as primary sources for employment-related ongoing supports for an individual with disabilities. There is variation across programs in the extent to which supports are directly provided by a job coach or by other sources.

Although the employment strategies emphasizing ongoing supports were developed initially for individuals with moderate to severe intellectual disabilities, they have been modified effectively for individuals with many other types of disabilities, including severe mental illness (Bond et al., 2001; Drake et al., 1999; Leff et al., 2005), severe traumatic brain injury (Wehman et al., 1993; Wehman, West, Kregel, Sherron, & Kreutzer, 1995), and severe physical disabilities (Inge, 2001; Inge, Strobel, Wehman, Todd, & Targett, 2000; Inge, Wehman, Strobel, Powell, & Todd, 1998; Mast & West, 2001).

A growing body of knowledge exists regarding the use of ongoing supports with specific populations of individuals with disabilities. For example, there are a variety of employment interventions that have documented effectiveness in assisting people with severe mental illness to achieve a successful employment outcome (Bond, 2004; Cook & Razzano, 2000; Drake et al., 1999; Ford, 1995; McHugo, Drake, & Becker, 1998; Musser et al., 2004; Salyers, Becker, Drake, Torrey, & Wyzik, 2004). Ridgway and Rapp (1998) provided a synthesis of research on effective employment interventions for individuals with severe mental illness. The employment interventions identified by Ridgway and Rapp emphasized commitment to competitive work, rapid movement to employment, individualized job exploration, and ongoing support. Key examples of ongoing, flexible, and individualized supports identified in this report include:

1. Workplace accommodations, job coaching, supportive counseling, off-site assistance, on-site assistance, support groups linked to other community supports such as medication monitoring, case management, and housing

2. Ongoing assessment of support needs conducted after securing a job

3. Ongoing assessment of the workplace environment and modification of the environment to improve person–environment fit

Replacement assistance is another key ongoing support for individuals with severe mental illness to enhance long-term job retention. Examples of this support include assisting the client to learn more about what he or she wants by working in real jobs; building toward a better match between the person's strengths and desires compared with the job characteristics; and assisting the person to plan a move to a better, more fulfilling job.

For individuals with intellectual disabilities, employment interventions frequently emphasize training with a special focus on speed and productivity. Interventions emphasizing job retention can be employment supports directly related to the individual's job. These supports might include training to enhance work speed and work quality, orientation and mobility at the jobsite, generalization across tasks (to facilitate cross-training), training for supervisors and co-workers, and retraining in instances in which there is a change in job assignment. Interventions can also be related to individual and community supports away from the jobsite. Off-site training support might involve assistance in managing housing and personal living situations, use of leisure time, personal finances, transportation, and personal relationships (Wehman, 2001).

In a recent study, employers identified a variety of ongoing supports and job accommodations found to be effective with employees with intellectual disabilities (Olson, Cioffi, Yovanoff, & Mank, 2001). These accommodations included providing extra attention to the employee; utilizing a job coach at the worksite; providing flexible hours of employment; addressing issues around the physical accessibility of the jobsite; restructuring job tasks; and providing longer periods of training. These accommodations were viewed to be of minimal cost to the employer, and the employers viewed employees with intellectual disabilities favorably.

People who experience physical disabilities such as cerebral palsy or spinal cord injury face a variety of different issues in retaining employment than people with intellectual or psychiatric disabilities. The physical ability to complete assigned work tasks and to be mobile around the worksite are two primary employment issues faced by this population (Dowler, Batiste, & Whitten, 1998). Also, employment service providers and employers have difficulty, at times, in determining how a person with limited physical abilities can perform the required job duties (Inge et al., 1998). Fortunately, a number of employment supports have demonstrated effectiveness in addressing the employment challenges faced by people with a primary significant physical disability. These workplace supports include compensatory strategies, personal assistance at the workplace, co-worker supports, assistive technology, and jobsite training (Inge, 2001).

Individuals who experience traumatic brain injury also face significant employment challenges. Traumatic brain injuries occur suddenly, leaving the injured person significantly changed immediately after the injury, often leaving substantial effects on learning, personality, and/or physical dexterity and mobility (Wehman et al., 1995). There are a variety of employment interventions that have demonstrated effectiveness in assisting people who have experienced a traumatic brain injury to successfully obtain and retain employment. These strategies include on-the-job skills training utilizing an employment specialist working closely with the employer to identify and develop workplace supports. Also, learning essential job skills can be promoted by restructuring the job environment and by using job adaptations and modifications (Wehman, Targett, & West, 2005).

Although there are substantial references in the literature to the provision of ongoing supports to enhance job retention, many of the studies are focused largely on the initial phase of employment over the first 3–6 months. There is a lack of longitudinal research studies on the impact of ongoing supports on job retention and career advancement over a period 12–24 months after job placement. The political landscape in which the provision of publicly funded ongoing supports operates is a primary contributor to limited longitudinal data on job retention.

Nationally, ongoing supports provided after the first 3–6 months of employment may be funded and administered through multiple state agencies, including mental health, mental retardation/developmental disability, Medicaid, health, labor, and VR (West, Johnson, Cone, Hernandez, & Revell, 1998). Data collection and reporting requirements and capabilities vary not only across states, but also across agencies within each state. Thus, it is much more difficult to determine, both across and within states, how ongoing supports operate and how successful they are in achieving desired customer outcomes such as earnings, fringe benefits, job retention, and career advancement. For a variety of reasons, consistent information is needed on what is happening to individual workers with disabilities after initial placement and support plans have been established. From the perspective of making effective decisions about funding, policy development, and program management, access to accurate information on service needs, use, and outcomes is critical.

Job terminations and changes are fairly common experiences for supported employment customers, particularly for individuals with intellectual disabilities (Moran, McDermott, & Butkus, 2002). Many individuals who are separated from their first supported employment positions remain out of the work force or return to segregated work settings (Murphy et al., 2002). Strategies for promoting long-term job maintenance and smooth job transitions are critical needs for provider agencies (Mank, Cioffi, & Yovanoff, 1998). Research on the relationship of ongoing supports to job retention is essential to improving service efficiency and quality and enhancing long-term customer employment outcomes, such as job retention and career advancement (Storey & Certo, 1996). Chapter 7 will present much more detailed information on how to design and develop natural supports and other tools for behavior change.

EVIDENCE-BASED EMPLOYMENT PRACTICES

The research literature on supported employment outcomes has been steadily growing since the early case studies published in the 1980s (e.g., Wehman, Hill, & Koehler, 1982). Gradually, the number of people studied increased; however, the most scientifically rigorous research comes from leading clinical research in the psychiatric disability field. There are six evidence-based principles for supported employment for people with severe mental illness that are predictive of better employment outcomes (Bond, 2004).

1. Eligibility is based on customer choice.

2. Supported employment is integrated with mental health treatment.

3. The goal is to focus services on competitive employment.

4. A rapid job search approach is used.

5. Job finding is individualized with attention to customer preferences.

6. Follow-along supports are continuous.

Programs that provide supported employment services consistent with these practices achieve better employment outcomes as compared with individuals with disabilities who do not participate in supported employment programs. Together, these principles serve as a foundation for evidence-based guidelines for providing effective supported employment services. As noted previously, these principles were derived from rigorous research performed with those with severe mental illness. Therefore, it is not possible to extrapolate these findings to those with other disabilities, despite the fact that many employment specialists in the field will probably affirm their validity. A brief summary of the six evidence-based principles follows.

The first principle is that eligibility is based on customer choice. Unlike many traditional vocational programs, an evidence-based supported employment program does not screen out individuals with disabilities who may not appear to be ideal candidates for employment because of their psychiatric, substance abuse, or work histories. Instead, supported employment operates on the principle of *zero exclusion*—anyone who expresses a desire to work and makes an informed choice to participate in a supported employment program is deemed eligible.

The evidence behind this principle is drawn from research suggesting that customer characteristics do not predict success in supported employment. Individuals with disabilities consistently have better competitive employment outcomes in supported employment than in alternative programs, regardless of their gender, ethnicity, diagnosis, hospitalization history, cognitive functioning, education, or substance use.

There are some compelling reasons not to assess individuals with disabilities for work readiness using conventional methods (e.g., standardized aptitude tests). First, these assessment methods screen out individuals with mental illnesses at a high rate, including many who could successfully work. Second, these assessment methods take resources away from services that could be better directed to helping people find jobs. Third, most standardized assessment approaches do not actually predict which individuals will work. And, finally, the assessments typically do not give information about what interventions to offer as a way to help individuals with disabilities become work ready.

The second principle is that supported employment should be integrated with the mental health treatment being received by each individual with disabilities. Among other things, this means that supported employment is unlikely to be effective if an individual is not concurrently receiving adequate clinical case management (i.e., good follow through between the case manager and client in helping to arrange services). In addition, this principle means that employment specialists are in frequent communication with mental health case managers and attend their team meetings. To accomplish this integration of employment and mental health services, it is best that the supported employment team and the mental health treatment team be part of the same agency (Bond et al., 2004).

The third evidence-based principle is that supported employment programs devote their resources and energy to assist individuals with disabilities in finding competitive jobs. This is in contrast to programs that seek to develop an array of rehabilitation activities, such as day treatment programs, or protected job options, such as sheltered workshops or agency-run businesses. The research is clear that these activities do not promote competitive employment. Individuals with disabilities may spend years in day treatment, including individuals who could work. When day treatment programs are closed down and converted to supported employment, individuals with disabilities who have been regular attendees of day treatment typically do well in competitive jobs (Bond et al., 2001).

The fourth evidence-based principle is that supported employment programs assist individuals with disabilities in looking for jobs soon after they enroll in the supported employment program. Contrary to conventional wisdom, there are no advantages to prevocational preparation, extended career counseling, or other work-readiness activities. Customer surveys have consistently indicated that most individuals with disabilities prefer to work toward community jobs instead of attending preparatory activities. Rapid job search means that employment specialists have an expectation that the job search typically will begin with a contact with an employer within the first month after an individual with disabilities enters the supported employment program; however, the job search process is individualized, which means that it will vary in strategy and timing.

The fifth principle is that job finding is a collaborative process between the individual with disabilities and the service provider (i.e., a partnership between employment specialist and job seeker). This collaborative process emphasizes use of a customer's preferences, strengths, and prior work experiences. Job selection takes into account job duties, location, hours of employment, work environment, and other factors related to satisfaction and success in working. Several studies have examined the role of occupational preferences. These studies have found that individuals with disabilities whose initial supported employment positions are consistent with their job preferences are much less likely to quit their jobs. Moreover, individuals with disabilities working in a field consistent with their preferences also have higher job satisfaction.

The sixth principle is that assistance from the supported employment program is not arbitrarily discontinued after a fixed period of time. In many states, funding for supported employment services is time limited, triggering rules about how long someone is eligible. Or, the funding may shift from one source (e.g., VR) to a second source (e.g., Medicaid) after a specific period of time that an individual with disabilities is employed. It is very apparent from clinical experience that arbitrary time limits can be detrimental to the design of a supported employment program. Therefore, programs that find ways to individualize the support for individuals with disabilities and to continue to stay in touch over the long term appear to be more effective than those that establish strict rules about time limits.

The six evidence-based principles have direct implications for employment service providers, agencies that purchase employment services, and customers of these services. For providers, the principles provide clear guidelines for program development. For funding agencies, the principles establish a basis for purchase of service guidelines and quality indicators. For service customers, the principles provide a measure for making informed choices about service providers and identifying which provider will be most effective in supporting the achievement of individualized employment goals. The data that have been presented provide strong evidence for the use of supported employment especially for those with severe mental illness.

CUSTOMIZED EMPLOYMENT

As supported employment has evolved and been utilized with different populations, new forms of workplace supports have been developed. In addition, there have been new or expanded approaches to supporting people with disabilities such as self-employment (see Chapter 12) or telework (see Chapter 13). Customized employment has also emerged as another form of supported employment that has received increasing attention.

The term *customized employment* was coined in 2001 when the Office of Disability Employment Policy (ODEP) was created within the U.S. Department of Labor (ODEP, 2004). Customized employment was conceived as a way for One Stop Career Centers to welcome and serve individuals with disabilities (Callahan, 2004c). It also was designed to apply to and benefit anyone who has unique circumstances that affect employment, including individuals who do not have disabilities (ODEP, 2005). In order to build the capacity of One Stop Career Centers to implement customized employment, ODEP has funded demonstration efforts with 20 projects currently operating throughout the country. The One Stop service-delivery system was established under the Workforce Investment Act (WIA) of 1998 (PL 105-220). One of the core principles of the WIA is to provide universal access to services by "giving all Americans [including those with disabilities] access to comprehensive services, information and resources that can help them in achieving their career goals" (Workforce Investment Act, 2004, p. 18,629). The intent is to provide access to a network of programs and services within a central location.

Definition

Customized employment has been defined as "the voluntary negotiation of a personalized employment relationship between a specific individual and an employer" (ODEP, 2005). The negotiation process is driven by the abilities and interests of each job seeker, resulting in job responsibilities that fit the needs of a specific individual while also meeting the employment needs of the business. The *Federal Register* (Agency Information Collection Activities, 2002) defined *customized employment* as the following:

> Customized employment means individualizing the employment relationship between employees and employers in ways that meet the needs of both. It is based on an individualized determination of the strengths, needs, and interests of the person with a disability, and is also designed to meet the specific needs of the employer.
>
> It may include employment developed through job carving, self-employment, or entrepreneurial initiatives, or other job development or restructuring strategies that result in job responsibilities being customized and individually negotiated to fit the needs of individuals with a disability. Customized employment assumes the provision of reasonable accommodations and supports necessary for the individual to perform the functions of a job that is individually negotiated and developed. (pp. 43,154–43,149)

ODEP (2005) has identified a set of principles that are fundamental to the implementation of customized employment (see Table 6.2). In addition, ODEP has described a set of indicators that must be present in order for the relationship between

Table 6.2.   Customized employment principles

The employer voluntarily negotiates specific job duties or employee expectations.

The negotiated employment relationship meets both the unique needs, strengths, and interests of the job seeker or employee and the discrete needs of the employer.

The job seeker is the primary source of information and decides the direction to explore the job market.

The job seeker controls the planning process that captures his or her preferences, interests, and connections in the community.

Even prior to planning, exploratory time is essential to uncover the job seeker's unique needs, abilities, and interests. More formal or traditional assessment may supplement this exploratory phase if necessary but should not be used as the primary source of information for planning.

Customized employment results in jobs that fit the individual and therefore have the potential for advancement for job seekers who have been chronically unemployed or underemployed.

Work occurs in an integrated, individualized work situation in the community or in a personal business alongside people who do not have disabilities.

Employment results in pay at the prevailing wage or "going rate."

Employment outcomes may include creating a job through self-employment.

The process is facilitated through a blend of supports and resources that include the work force system and other public private partners such as disability service providers. These resources are coordinated to meet the needs of the job seeker.

Source: ODEP (2005).

Table 6.3.   Customized employment indicators

The employee has a personalized job description and/or employer
   expectations that did not exist prior to the negotiation process.

The individual makes a tangible contribution to the employer's enterprise.

The individual is hired and paid directly by the employer.

Customized employment can be utilized either prior to or after employment
   as a strategy to modify job duties and/or other employer expectations for
   an individual who has complex needs.

Customized employment offers the opportunity for personal representation
   by a job developer, as appropriate, to assist the job seeker in negotiating
   with employers.

Customized employment is based on an array of strategies that allow for
   job duties to be tailored to satisfy both job seeker and employer needs.

Personal budgets, individual training accounts, and other forms of
   individualized funding that provide choice and control to the person and
   promote self-determination are used in customized employment.

The employer, the One Stop system, and/or funders of services should
   offer all accommodations and supports needed by the job seeker for
   success.

Source: ODEP (2005).

an individual with disabilities and an employer to be considered customized employment (see Table 6.3).

There has been some debate in the field regarding the definition of *customized employment* and its relationship to *supported employment* (Callahan & Rogan, 2004). Callahan (2004a) stated that customized employment is "much like supported employment in many ways" and is, in fact, the "progeny" of supported employment. In reality, the principles and indicators of customized employment are not new ideas but have developed since the 1980s with the inclusion of individuals with disabilities in their communities. Employment opportunities have expanded from segregated programs as the only work outcome to now include competitive employment with the development of supported employment, person-centered planning, self-determination, assistive technology, co-worker supports, instructional strategies, and other workplace accommodations and supports (Wehman, 2001). Professionals who worked during the 1980s and 1990s to expand the employment outcomes for this unemployed or underemployed group will recognize the principles and indicators of customized employment as best practices for facilitating inclusive employment. The following section will provide an overview of how these principles and indicators have evolved.

Foundations

Early supported employment efforts at placing individuals in paid community jobs focused on the labor market's available jobs and matching individuals from a pool of potential candidates to existing employment opportunities (Moon, Goodall, Barcus, & Brooke, 1985). Most of this initial focus was on how to contact employers, analyze the local labor market, and identify jobs that already existed in the business community;

however, supported employment professionals soon began to suggest that jobs be developed for a specific individual rather than for a group of potential job candidates (McLoughlin et al., 1987). McLoughlin and colleagues stated that individuals with more significant disabilities may require "individualized representation" rather than the use of a multiple applicant approach to representing individuals during job development activities. They went on to suggest negotiating with employers to create jobs that "jointly meet the needs of the employer and the prospective employee" (p. 90).

Moon, Inge, Wehman, Brooke, and Barcus (1990) recommended that the analysis of the local labor market be coordinated with community-based situational assessments to better match the job seeker's interests and strengths to potential jobs in the community. They wrote,

> Finding a job opening or assisting a company in creating a job that is well suited to both the individual strengths and desires of a person with [a disability] and to the particular needs and work demands of a company is finding an employment niche. (1990, p. 94)

Finding an employment or job niche was further described as working with a business to determine its specific needs that could result in the creation of a job that did not exist prior to the analysis of the company's labor needs. Other authors at this time, however, continued to discuss the multiple applicant approach to job development by matching existing jobs in the labor market to a pool of potential job applicants (Parent, Sherron, & Groah, 1992).

The terms *job carving* (Griffin, 1994; Nietupski, 1993a, 1993b) and *job restructuring* (Brooke, Inge, Armstrong, & Wehman, 1997) also have been used to refer to job creation. All of these sources essentially describe the identification of job duties that can be redistributed and tailored to the job seeker's unique skills and abilities. Once these job duties have been identified, the job developer or employment specialist negotiates with the employer to restructure or create a position. This may include the redistribution of job tasks from an existing position that cannot be performed by the job seeker to co-workers in exchange for job duties that the individual with disabilities can do or will learn on the job with the assistance of the employment specialist. Other authors have since recommended negotiating positions using employment proposals to meet the unique interests and abilities of job seekers (Inge, 2001; Inge et al., 2000; Luecking, Fabian, & Tilson, 2004; Nietupski & Hamre-Nietupski, 2001).

Bissonnette (1994) described the development of an *employment proposal* for job creation that is clearly a core aspect of customized employment yet is one of the more creative ways to solve challenges faced by job seekers unable to find employment. She used the term to refer to the process of matching the skills and abilities of individuals with disabilities with the needs of businesses. Bissonnette also suggested that job developers should not only determine what people can do, or their abilities, but also what they enjoy doing. After determining a person's interests and abilities, the job developer would identify businesses where the job seeker with disabilities could bring those skills and approach the employer with a written proposal. The proposal could be a letter, memo, or an outlined formal proposal to include the benefits to the employer, a summary of the service, a description of the employee, and the desired employment conditions. This employment proposal is an essential element in negotiating with employers for the purpose of job creation. Finally, Bissonnette stated that there are two types of job creation: applicant focused and employer focused. Indeed, the two are interdependent. Without a labor market need, jobs could not be created for individuals with disabilities who have skills and abilities to bring to the workplace.

Customer Choice and Self-Determination

The evolution of customer choice and self-determination is closely linked with negotiating jobs through an individualized approach. Prior to 1992, few programs provided choice to individuals with disabilities regarding how services were provided or what their employment outcomes should be (West & Parent, 1992). Changes in public policy at that time, such as the Rehabilitation Act Amendments of 1992 (PL 102-569), affected customer choice by requiring that individuals with disabilities participate and have a voice in the development of their rehabilitation programs.

Wehmeyer is one of the leaders in self-determination through his research beginning in the early 1990s. He defined *self-determination* as "acting as the primary causal agent in one's life and making choices and decisions regarding one's quality of life free from undue external influence or interference" (Wehmeyer, 2003). Recent research has demonstrated that individuals with disabilities are more likely to be successful in employment if they have self-determination skills.

Wehman stated,

> Supported employment was developed to give individuals with disabilities a choice in the labor force. This service model focuses on customer interest and provides an opportunity for individuals to identify a job, specify the working conditions, determine the wage level, select the job location, and decide the hours that they will work (1992, p. 1).

Kregel (1992) made a number of recommendations regarding the empowerment of individuals to guide their own careers. He suggested that federal, state, and local governments should experiment with different funding mechanisms and program regulations that place individuals with disabilities in control of purchasing or selecting their supported employment services. During this time period, Brooke and her colleagues began to write about a "customer-driven" approach to the selection and identification of a career path (Brooke et al., 1997; Brooke et al., 1995). They suggested that analyzing outcome data to determine if services are truly customer driven best identifies the overall quality of a supported employment program. Agencies that are customer driven shape their service-delivery practices by the wants and needs of individuals with disabilities, not on the existing services and supports that are available.

The ability of agencies to facilitate customer self-determination and choice has been influenced by the development of person-centered planning philosophies and approaches (Falvey, Forest, Pearpoint, & Rosenberg, 1993; Mount, 1994; Pearpoint, O'Brien, & Forest, 1993; Perske, 1989). The core values of person-centered planning are as follows.

1. Services are "driven" or directed by the individual with disabilities.

2. Focus is placed on the individual's abilities and dreams.

3. Community participation and membership is the goal.

4. Emphasis is placed on needed supports rather than the person's disabilities.

5. Planning needs to be individualized and not driven by the service system.

Callahan and Garner (1997) stressed that person-centered career planning should occur prior to job development to establish a picture of the ideal job for an individual with disabilities. Everson and Reid (1997) also discussed how to use person-centered planning to determine employment preferences among individuals with the most severe developmental disabilities, as did a number of authors during this time period (Brooke et al., 1997; Inge, Wehman, Kregel, & Targett, 1996; Inge et al., 1998).

The merger of person-centered planning strategies with customized employment methods has been a positive advancement for promoting inclusive employment outcomes. Another key piece of the process is focusing on identifying a person's abilities and strengths. McLoughlin and colleagues (1987) referred to this process as a *vocational profile*. Moon and colleagues (1985) used the term *consumer assessment*, whereas Brooke and her associates (1997) used the term *customer profile*.

As previously mentioned, Moon and colleagues (1990) presented a functional approach to identifying an individual's skills in the community by using *situational assessments* as a means to learn about the individual's skills and work preferences. Targett (2001) also discussed the use of situational assessments for the purpose of career planning and the identification of a person's skills and interests related to work. Callahan (2004b) used the term *discovery* to refer to this person-centered planning process. Although different terms have been used, all authors advocated for functional assessments and the identification of individual preferences rather than the use of standardized tests and vocational evaluations.

Comparison of Supported and Customized Employment

In reviewing the previous information, supported employment and customized employment have much in common and share the same philosophical foundation. Customized employment has embraced the principles and best practices that developed from supported employment implementation. Some of the critical components of both include 1) customer choice, 2) the belief that individuals should be viewed from an abilities versus disabilities perspective, 3) workplace integration, 4) jobs/careers of choice, 5) competitive/prevailing wages, and 6) customer-directed services with individualized workplace supports.

The fundamental differences between the two involve how supported employment has been implemented rather than how it was intended. There are still individuals earning less than minimum wage in enclave group settings that are maintained by community rehabilitation programs. Individuals with disabilities are still being placed in jobs that are driven by the local labor market rather than by the identification of nonstereotypical careers. Unfortunately, the opportunity to choose a job and to make decisions about the delivery of services may still be driven more by the person's perceived disabilities than through personal choice and abilities.

The inclusion of a more narrow interpretation of job negotiation in the current definition of customized employment is one potential difference between the conceptualization of customized and supported employment. Callahan (2004c) stated that customized employment is not driven by the local labor market but by the needs of the individual with disabilities. The outcome from the negotiation process with employers is that the employee has a personalized job description and/or employer expectations that did not exist prior to the negotiation process. Supported employment research has found that individuals with disabilities whose hiring practices and supports are more typical to current business practices have better employment outcomes (Mank et al., 2000). Research is needed to determine if all jobs for individuals with disabilities must be negotiated and a personalized job description created in order for a customized employment relationship to exist.

As previously mentioned, the term *customized employment* was created to bring the concept of providing services and supports to individuals with disabilities within the One Stop service-delivery system. The WIA created the One Stop service-delivery system and provides individuals with disabilities with the ability to gain access to an array of services and supports at One Stop Career Centers that are also potentially used by individuals without disabilities when seeking jobs. With the implementation of the WIA, the potential for customer choice, inclusion, and self-determination has become a possibility for many individuals with disabilities, who may no longer have to depend on a specialized service system to obtain employment (Bader, 2003). Therefore, the real promise of customized employment may lie in the blending of services, supports, and funding that exist for individuals with disabilities to achieve inclusive employment outcomes within the One Stop service-delivery system. A good example of this blended service approach to customized employment is the Tennessee Customized Employment Partnership (2004), a funded program under the ODEP initiatives. A posting found on its web site states, "Customized employment is not a single service, but a blend of services designed to increase employment options for individuals with significant disabilities."

The *Federal Register* (Office of Disability Employment Policy, 2002) also supports the idea of blending services and supports under the umbrella term of *customized employment*. The published definition of *customized employment* stated:

> It may include employment developed through job carving, self-employment, or entrepreneurial initiatives, or other job development or restructuring strategies that result in job responsibilities being customized and individually negotiated to fit the needs of individuals with a disability. Customized employment assumes the provision of reasonable accommodations and supports necessary for the individual to perform the functions of a job that is individually negotiated and developed. (p. 50698)

Customized employment as an approach to providing employment supports to individuals with disabilities is best viewed as an all-embracing "umbrella" term that includes supported employment, job negotiation, assistive technology, accommodations, resource ownership, microenterprises, self-employment, and person-centered planning. By picking from the menu of customized employment services and supports available in the One Stop service-delivery system, individuals are supported in identifying what services and supports are needed to achieve integrated competitive employment outcomes. It is important to note that the One Stop system is designed to include key partner agencies in the community providing funding, services, and resources supporting the employment of individuals with disabilities. Therefore, the service plan through the One Stop Career Center could include funding from VR blended with creative uses of the Individual Training Accounts to achieve inclusive employment outcomes (Butterworth, Ghiloni, Revell, & Brooks-Lane, 2004). Some individuals with the most significant disabilities may need the most intensive supports, including supported employment and a job coach. Others may only need minimal support that can be provided by the One Stop Career Center, such as assisting with career-path identification. All of these services would fall under the concept of providing customized supports to an individual to facilitate competitive outcomes.

CONCLUSION

Competitive employment remains an elusive goal for the vast majority of people with disabilities despite clear research-generated evidence that a variety of effective workplace and related supports exist that assist these individuals in increasing earnings and satisfaction from the work experience. The U.S. Department of Labor described the current employment challenges facing individuals with disabilities as follows:

> Negative stereotyping, unemployment, underemployment, and placement in segregated work and non-work settings are likely to continue until there are systemic changes undertaken. One such change is increasing provider capacity to provide individually determined, customized employment in non-stereotypic jobs for people with disabilities. (Grants to Cooperative Agreements, 2002, p. 50,697)

This statement was made within an announcement describing the planned creation of a national technical assistance and training effort designed to increase community-integrated employment outcomes achieved by people with disabilities through community rehabilitation programs and other community-based service providers that currently operate programs that result in segregated work outcomes and nonwork options. The U.S. Department of Labor's initiative is clear evidence that the critical value of supported employment and workplace supports is recognized as a means for programs working with people with disabilities in more center-based, segregated settings to move to providing integrated employment outcomes in nonstereotypical jobs based on customized employment strategies and individual choice.

This chapter has detailed the critical value of supported employment and workplace supports in achieving competitive employment outcomes by individuals with disabilities. These supports have proven effective across a full range of individuals with a variety of disabilities. It is critically important that these supports be provided with attention to quality and effectiveness. The quality indicators detailed in the chapter are clear measures for determining the extent to which the workplace supports provided truly reflect, for example, attention to customer choice in the support plan and job match, the availability of critically important ongoing supports, and the earnings and benefits achieved. Knowledge about workplace supports and employment outcomes is substantial and evolving continually. The ongoing challenge at the national, state, and community level is to assure that quality supports, customized as needed for each individual with disabilities, are readily and consistently available.

REFERENCES

American Association on Mental Retardation (AAMR). (2002). *Mental retardation: Definition, classification and systems of support.* Washington, DC: Author.

Bader, B.A. (2003). *Identification of best practices in One Stop Career Centers that facilitate use by people with disabilities seeking employment.* Unpublished doctoral dissertation, Virginia Commonwealth University.

Bissonnette, D. (1994). *Beyond traditional job development: The art of creating job opportunity.* Granada Hills, CA: Milt Wright & Associates.

Bond, G. (2004). Supported employment: Evidence for an evidence-based practice. *Psychiatric Rehabilitation Journal, 27*(4), 345–359.

Bond, G., Campbell, K., Gervey, R., Pascaris, A., Tice, S., & Revell, G. (2004). *Does type of provider organization affect fidelity to evidence-based supported employment?* Manuscript submitted for publication.

Bond, G.B., Becker, D.R., Drake, R.E., Rapp, C.A., Meisler, N., Lehman, A.F., et al. (2001). Implementing supported employment as an evidence-based practice. *Psychiatric Services, 52,* 313–322.

Braddock, D., Rizzolo, M., & Hemp, R. (2004). Most employment services growth in developmental disabilities during 1988–2002 was in segregated settings. *Mental Retardation, 42*(4), 317–320.

Brooke, V., Inge, K.J., Armstrong, A.J., & Wehman, P. (1997). *A customer-driven approach for persons with significant disabilities.* Richmond: Virginia Commonwealth University Rehabilitation Research and Training Center on Workplace Supports and Job Retention.

Brooke, V., Wehman, P., Inge, K., & Parent, W. (1995, December). Toward a customer-driven approach of supported employment. *Education and Training in Mental Retardation and Developmental Disabilities,* 308–320.

Browder, D., Wood, W., Test, D., Karvonen, M., & Algozzine, B. (2001). Reviewing resources on self-determination: A map for teachers. *Remedial and Special Education, 22*(4), 233–244.

Butterworth, J., Ghiloni, C., Revell, G., & Brooks-Lane, N. (2004). *Customized employment Q & A: Creating a diversified funding base* [On-line]. Richmond: Virginia Commonwealth University Rehabilitation Research and Training Center on Workplace Supports and Job Retention, Training and Technical Assistance to Programs (T-TAP). Retrieved February 7, 2006, from http://www.t-tap.org/strategies/factsheet/diversifiedfunding.html

Callahan, M. (2004a, July). *Customized and supported employment.* Paper presented at the 15th Annual Conference and Training Event for APSE: The Network on Employment, Indianapolis.

Callahan, M. (2004b). *Employment: From competitive to customized.* Gautier, MS: Employment for All.

Callahan, M. (2004c, June). What is customized employment? *The Advance, 15*(1), 2.

Callahan, M.J., & Garner, J.B. (1997). *Keys to the workplace: Skills and supports for people with disabilities.* Baltimore: Paul H. Brookes Publishing Co.

Callahan, M., & Rogan, P. (2004, June). Customized employment—a discussion: An interesting "model" or the next generation of supported employment. *The Advance, 15*(1), 2.

Cook, J., & Razzano, J. (2000). Vocational rehabilitation for persons with schizophrenia: Recent research and implications for practice. *Schizophrenic Bulletin 26*(1), 87–103.

Dowler, D., Batiste, L., & Whitten, E. (1998). Accommodating workers with spinal cord injury. *Journal of Vocational Rehabilitation, 10,* 115–122.

Drake, R.E., McHugo, G.J., Bebout, R.R., Becker, D.R., Harris, M., Bond, G.R., et al. (1999). A randomized clinical trial of supported employment for inner-city patients with severe mental retardation. *Archives of General Psychiatry, 56,* 627–633.

Everson, J.M., & Reid, D.H. (1997). Using person-centered planning concepts to determine employment preferences among people with the most severe developmental disabilities. *Journal of Vocational Rehabilitation, 9,* 99–108.

Falvey, M.A., Forest, M., Pearpoint, J., & Rosenberg, R.L. (1993). *All my life's a circle: Using the tools of circles, MAPS and PATH.* Toronto: Inclusion Press.

Ford, L.H. (1995). *Providing employment support for people with long-term mental illness: Choices, resources, and practical strategies.* Baltimore: Paul H. Brookes Publishing Co.

Grants to Cooperative Agreements: Customized Employment Program, 67(123) Fed. Reg. 43, 154–43,149 (June 26, 2002) (to be codified at 34 C.F.R. pt. 361).

Griffin, C. (1994). Job carving: A guide for job developers and employment specialists. In W.M. Wood, J.M. Everson, E. Panscofar, & P. Bourbeau (Eds.), *APSE papers* (Vol. 1, pp. 1–6). Richmond, VA: APSE.

Hayden, M.F., & Albery, B.H. (Eds.). (1994). *Challenges for a service system in transition: Ensuring quality community experiences for persons with developmental disabilities.* Baltimore: Paul H. Brookes Publishing Co.

Inge, K. (2001). Supported employment for individuals with physical disabilities. In P. Wehman (Ed.), *Supported employment in business: Expanding the capacity of workers with disabilities* (pp. 153–180). St. Augustine, FL: Training Resource Network.

Inge, K., Strobel, W., Wehman, P., Todd, J., & Targett, P. (2000). Vocational outcomes for persons with severe physical disabilities: Design and implementation of workplace supports. *NeuroRehabilitation, 15*(3), 175–188.

Inge, K., Wehman, P., Kregel, J., & Targett, P.S. (1996). Vocational rehabilitation for persons with spinal cord injuries and other severe physical disabilities. *American Rehabilitation, 22*(4), 2–12.

Inge, K.J., Wehman, P., Strobel, W., Powell, D., & Todd, J. (1998). Supported employment and assistive technology for persons with spinal cord injury: Three illustrations of successful work supports. *Journal of Vocational Rehabilitation, 10*(2), 141–152.

Kregel, J. (1992). A consumer empowerment approach to the design of service systems: Implications for supported employment. In V. Brooke, M. Barcus, & K.J. Inge (Eds.), *Consumer advocacy and supported employment: A vision for the future* (pp 33–48). Richmond: Virginia Commonwealth University Rehabilitation Research and Training Center on Workplace Supports and Job Retention.

Kregel, J., & Dean, D. (2002). Sheltered versus supported employment: A direct comparison of long-term earnings outcomes for individuals with cognitive disabilities. In J. Kregel, D. Dean, & P. Wehman (Eds.), *Achievements and challenges in employment services for people with disabilities: The longitudinal impact of workplace supports* (pp. 63–82). Richmond: Virginia Commonwealth University Rehabilitation Research and Training Center on Workplace Supports and Job Retention.

Kregel, J., & Wehman, P. (1989). An analysis of the employment outcomes of young adults with mental retardation. In P. Wehman & J. Kregel (Eds.), *Supported employment for persons with disabilities: Focus on excellence.* New York: Human Sciences Press.

Kregel, J., & Wehman, P. (1997). Supported employment: A decade of employment outcomes for individuals with significant disabilities. In W.E. Kiernan & R.L. Schalock (Eds.), *Integrated employment: Current status and future directions* (pp. 31–48). Washington, DC: American Association on Mental Retardation.

Kregel, J., Wehman, P., Revell, G., Hill, J., & Cimera, R. (2000). Supported employment benefit–cost analysis: Preliminary findings. *Journal of Vocational Rehabilitation, 14*(3), 153–161.

Leff, H.S., Cook, J.A., Gold, P.B., Toprac, M., Blyler, C., Goldberg, R.W., et al. (2005). Effects of job development and job support on competitive employment of persons with severe mental illness. *Psychiatric Services, 56*(10), 1237–1244.

Luecking, R.G., Fabian, E.S., & Tilson, G.P. (2004). *Working relationships: Creating career opportunities for job seekers with disabilities through employer partnerships.* Baltimore: Paul H. Brookes Publishing Co.

Mank, D. (1994). The underachievement of supported employment: A call for reinvestment. *Journal of Disability Policy Studies, 5*(2), 1–24.

Mank, D., Cioffi, A., & Yovanoff, P. (1998). Employment outcomes for people with severe disabilities: Opportunities for improvement. *Mental Retardation, 36*(3), 205–216.

Mank, D., Cioffi, A., & Yovanoff, P. (1999). Impact of coworker involvement with supported employees on wage and integration outcomes. *Mental Retardation, 37*(5), 383–394.

Mank, D., Cioffi, A., & Yovanoff, P. (2000). Direct support in supported employment and its relation to job typicalness, coworker involvement, and employment outcomes. *Mental Retardation, 38*(6), 506–516.

Mast, M., & West, M. (2001). Are individuals with severe physical impairments underserved in supported employment? *Journal of Vocational Rehabilitation, 16,* 3–7.

McHugo, G., Drake, R., & Becker, D. (1998). The durability of supported employment effects. *Psychiatric Rehabilitation Journal, 22*(1), 55–61.

McLoughlin, C.S., Garner, J.B., & Callahan, M. (1987). *Getting employed, staying employed: Job development and training for persons with severe handicaps.* Baltimore: Paul H. Brookes Publishing Co.

Moon, M.S., Goodall, P., Barcus, M., & Brooke, V. (1985). *The supported work model of competitive employment for citizens with severe handicaps: A guide for job trainers.* Richmond: Virginia Commonwealth University Rehabilitation Research and Training Center on Workplace Supports and Job Retention.

Moon, M.S., Inge, K.J., Wehman, P., Brooke, V., & Barcus, J.M. (1990). *Helping persons with severe mental retardation get and keep employment: Supported employment issues and strategies.* Baltimore: Paul H. Brookes Publishing Co.

Moran, R.R., McDermott, S., & Butkus, S. (2002). Getting a job, sustaining a job, and losing a job for individuals with mental retardation. *Journal of Vocational Rehabilitation, 16,* 237–244.

Mount, B. (1994). Benefits and limitations of personal futures planning. In V.J. Bradley, J.W. Ashbaugh, & B.C. Blaney (Eds.), *Creating individual supports for people with developmental disabilities: A mandate for change at many levels* (pp. 97–108). Baltimore: Paul H. Brookes Publishing Co.

Murphy, S.T., Rogan, P.M., Handley, M., Kincaid, C., & Royce-Davis, J. (2002). People's situations and perspectives eight years after workshop conversion. *Mental Retardation, 40,* 30–40.

Musser, K., Clark, R., Haines, M., Drake, R., McHugo, G., Bond, G., et al. (2004). The Hartford Study of supported employment for persons with severe mental illness. *Journal of Consulting and Clinical Psychology, 72,* 479–490.

Nietupski, J. (1993a). Tips for job carving: Part 1. *Job Training and Placement Report, 15*(12), 5.

Nietupski, J. (1993b). Tips for job carving: Part 2. *Job Training and Placement Report, 16*(1), 4.

Nietupski, J., & Hamre-Nietupski, S. (2001). A business approach to finding and restructuring supported employment opportunities. In P. Wehman (Ed.), *Supported employment in business: Expanding the capacity of workers with disabilities* (pp. 59–73). St. Augustine, FL: Training Resource Network.

Office of Disability Employment Policy: Disability Technical Assistance for Providers (TAP) Cooperative Agreement, 67(150) Fed. Reg. 50,697–50,710 (August 5, 2002).

Office of Disability Employment Policy (ODEP). (2004). *About the Office of Disability Employment Policy.* Retrieved February 7, 2006, from http://www.dol.gov/odep/about/about.htm

Office of Disability Employment Policy (ODEP). (2005, June). *Customized employment—Practical solutions for employment success.* Washington, DC: U.S. Department of Labor, ODEP and the National Center on Workforce and Disability/Adult. Retrieved March 30, 2006, from http://www.dol.gov/odep/pubs/custom/index.htm

Olson, D., Cioffi, A., Yovanoff, P., & Mank, D. (2001). Employer's perceptions of employees with mental retardation. *Journal of Vocational Rehabilitation, 1*(3), 30–44.

Parent, W.S., Sherron, P., & Groah, C. (1992). Consumer assessment, job development, and job placement. In P. Wehman, P. Sale, & W. Parent (Eds.), *Supported employment: Strategies for integration of workers with disabilities* (pp. 105–148). Stoneham, MA: Andover Medical Publishers.

Parent, W., Unger, D., Gibson, K., & Clements, C. (1994). The role of job coach: Orchestrating community and workplace supports. *American Rehabilitation, 20*(3), 2–11.

Pearpoint, J., O'Brien, J., & Forest, M. (1993). *PATH: A workbook for planning positive personal futures.* Toronto: Inclusion Press.

Perske, R. (1989). *Circle of friends: People with disabilities and their friends enrich the lives of others.* Nashville: Abington Press.

Rehabilitation Act Amendments of 1992, PL 102-569, 29 U.S.C. §§ 701 et seq.

Ridgway, P., & Rapp, C. (1998). *The active ingredients in achieving competitive employment for people with psychiatric disabilities: A research synthesis.* Lawrence: University of Kansas, School of Welfare.

Salyers, M., Becker, D., Drake, R., Torrey, W., & Wyzik, R. (2004). Ten-year follow-up of clients in a supported employment program. *Psychiatric Services, 55,* 302–308.

Social Security Administration (SSA). (2004). *Redbook.* Retrieved April 19, 2004, from http://www.socialsecurity.gov/work/ResourcesToolkit/redbook_page.html

Stancliffe, R.J., & Lakin, K.C. (1999). A longitudinal comparison of day program services and outcomes of people who left institutions and those who stayed. *Journal of The Association for Persons with Severe Handicaps, 24*(1), 44–57.

State Vocational Rehabilitation Program, 62(28) Fed. Reg. 6311 (Feb. 11, 1997) (to be codified at 34 C.F.R. pt. 361).

State Vocational Rehabilitation Services Program, 66(11) Fed. Reg. 4,382–4,389 (Jan. 21, 2001) (to be codified at 34 C.F.R. pt. 361).

State Vocational Rehabilitation Services Program, 66(14) Fed. Reg. 7,249–7,258 (Jan. 22, 2001) (to be codified at 34 C.F.R. pt. 361).

Storey, K., & Certo, N.J. (1996). Natural supports for increasing integration in the workplace for people with disabilities: A review of the literature and guidelines for implementation. *Rehabilitation Counseling Bulletin, 40,* 62–76.

Targett, P. (2001). Situational assessment: Toward career planning. In P. Wehman (Ed.), *Supported employment in business: Expanding the capacity of workers with disabilities* (pp. 35–46). St. Augustine, FL: Training Resource Network.

Tennessee Customized Employment Partnership. (2004). *Customized employment: Updating approaches to help people achieve jobs they want.* Retrieved February 7, 2006, from http://www.tcep online.org/topics/customized_employment.htm

Unger, D., Parent, W., Gibson, K., Kane-Johnston, K., & Kregel, J. (1998). An analysis of the activities of employment specialists in a natural support approach to supported employment. *Focus on Autism and Other Developmental Disabilities, 13*(1), 27–38.

Wehman, P. (1981). *Competitive employment: New horizons for severely disabled individuals.* Baltimore: Paul H. Brookes Publishing Co.

Wehman, P. (1992). Consumer advocacy and supported employment. In V. Brooke, M. Barcus, & K.J. Inge (Eds.), *Consumer advocacy and supported employment: A vision for the future* (pp. 2–12). Richmond: Virginia Commonwealth University Rehabilitation Research and Training Center on Workplace Supports and Job Retention.

Wehman, P. (2001). *Supported employment in business: Expanding the capacity of workers with disabilities*. St. Augustine, FL: Training Resource Network.

Wehman, P., Hill, M., & Koehler, F. (1982). Job placement and follow-up of moderately and severely handicapped individuals into competitive employment. *Journal of The Association for Severely Handicapped, 7*, 5–16.

Wehman, P., & Kregel, J. (1995). Supported employment: At the crossroads. *Journal of The Association for Persons with Severe Handicaps, 20*(4), 286–299.

Wehman, P., Revell, W.G., & Brooke, V. (2003). Competitive employment: Has it become the "first choice" yet? *Journal of Disability Policy Studies, 14*(3), 163–173.

Wehman, P., Revell, W.G., & Kregel, J. (1998). Supported employment: A decade of rapid growth and impact. *American Rehabilitation, 24*(1), 31–43.

Wehman, P., Sherron, P., Kregel, J., Kreutzer, J., Tran, S., & Cifu, D. (1993). Return to work for patients following severe traumatic brain injury: Supported employment outcomes after five years. *American Journal of Physical Medicine and Rehabilitation, 72*(6), 355–363.

Wehman, P., Targett, P., & West, M. (2005). Productive work and employment for persons with TBI: What have we learned after 20 years? *Journal of Head Trauma Rehabilitation 20*(2), 115–127.

Wehman, P., West, M.D., Kregel, J., Sherron, P., & Kreutzer, J.S. (1995). Return to work for persons with severe traumatic brain injury: A databased approach to program development. *Journal of Head Trauma Rehabilitation, 10*(1), 27–39.

Wehmeyer, M. (2003). Self-determination, vocational rehabilitation, and workplace supports. *Journal of Vocational Rehabilitation, 19*(2), 67–69.

Wehmeyer, M.L., & Lawrence, M. (1995). Whose future is it anyway? Promoting student involvement in transition planning. *Career Development for Exceptional Individuals, 18* (2), 68–84.

West, M., Kregel, J., Hernandez, A., & Hock, T. (1997). Everybody's doing it: A national study of the use of natural supports in supported employment. *Focus on Autism and Other Developmental Disabilities, 12*(3), 175–181, 192.

West, M., Johnson, A., Cone, A., Hernandez, A., & Revell, G. (1998). Extended employment support: Analysis of implementation and funding issues. *Education and Training in Mental Retardation and Developmental Disabilities, 33*, 357–366.

West, M., & Parent, W. (1992). Consumer choice and empowerment in supported employment. In P. Wehman, P. Sale, & W. Parent (Eds.), *Supported employment: Strategies for integration of workers with disabilities* (pp. 29–48). Boston: Andover Medical Publishers.

Workforce Investment Act (WIA) of 1998, PL 105-220, 29 U.S.C. §§ 2801 *et seq.*

Workforce Investment Act—Work Incentive Program, 69(68) Fed. Reg. 18629 (April 8, 2004).

Chapter 7

Supported Employment and Workplace Supports

Tools for Change

KATHERINE J. INGE, PAUL WEHMAN, W. GRANT REVELL, JR., AND VALERIE A. BROOKE

JAMES

James is a "soft line hanger" and an employee of a large department store, earning $7.00 per hour. His co-workers recently named him employee of the month. James is supported in his job by a company-built hanging apparatus, co-workers who aid him in walking throughout the store, and modifications to the process for preparing and distributing clothing.

CARLOS

Carlos works at a company that sells industrial equipment, compiling binders of marketing brochures for the sales staff. His job was customized for him by negotiating a duty that typically was performed by the office receptionist. The company was paying the receptionist overtime to complete the binders and was very receptive to paying Carlos $5.75 per hour and creating a position for him. He completes the job with the support of co-workers who set up his workstation, a specialized device made by a rehabilitation engineer for his power chair and desk, and initial training and ongoing supports from an employment specialist and co-workers.

MINGMEI

Mingmei works at a neighborhood store as a cashier and stock clerk, earns more than $5.50 per hour, and has opportunities for increased hours and career advancement. She received assistance from a retired co-worker who taught her how to do the job, instruction to learn how to stock despite an inability to read, and ongoing support from co-workers who provide prompts and assistance as needed.

What do these workers have in common? All are employed by community businesses in inclusive jobs making competitive wages. All work alongside their co-workers;

however, unlike their co-workers, James, Carlos, and Mingmei are individuals with significant disabilities. They are working successfully with the individualized support available through supported employment (Wehman, 2001; Wehman, Sale, & Parent, 1992).

In recent years, a strong shift has occurred toward designing services that emphasize the role of supports in enhancing the success of individuals with disabilities (Grossi, Banks, & Pinnyei, 2001; Unger, Parent, Gibson, Kane-Johnston, & Kregel, 1998; Wehman, 2001). Every individual, with or without disabilities, needs some level of assistance to succeed. There are some people with very significant disabilities, for example, who will need a greater level of support to succeed in school, work, home, and the community. As noted in the previous chapter, workplace supports are one way to help them become more independent and able to control the direction of their lives.

An individual with significant disabilities may have difficulty taking advantage of workplace support resources. He or she may be unaware of the potential supports that are available, how to choose among the alternatives, or how to go about gaining access to them. A critical factor toward achieving inclusive employment is the presence of a knowledgeable resource assistant or employment specialist who assists the individual in identifying, choosing, and gaining access to needed supports at the level of assistance preferred by the person with significant disabilities.

In addition, a commitment to ongoing supports is the unique feature of supported employment that makes it possible for people with significant disabilities to sustain employment over time. Supports that continue indefinitely are provided both at and away from the jobsite, an approach significantly different from services provided in day programs and other segregated models. For example, more traditional models move people through a continuum of job-readiness criteria before attempting to help them make the transition to competitive work. Unfortunately, people with significant disabilities, when served through this approach, rarely achieve actual successful movement to inclusive employment.

ROLE OF THE JOB COACH IN SUPPORTED EMPLOYMENT

The use of instructional strategies for training individuals on supported employment jobsites has been well documented (Brooke, Inge, Armstrong, & Wehman, 1997; Grossi, Regan, & Regan, 1998; Moon, Inge, Wehman, Brooke, & Barcus, 1990). Specific strategies have included the use of job duty and task analyses, natural supports, natural cues, compensatory strategies, prompting procedures, reinforcers, and self-management procedures (e.g., self-reinforcement, self-monitoring). Some critics of providing instruction at the jobsite have argued that training by an employment specialist draws attention to and isolates an individual from co-workers and supervisors; however, well-designed instructional programs that are "customer driven" will not segregate individuals with disabilities. Rather, poor practices isolate workers with disabilities from their co-workers.

Employment specialists must have knowledge of training strategies, the individual's support needs, the employer's support needs, and the demands of the workplace in order to select the least intrusive method for providing support (Inge & Tilson, 1997). Use of best-practice strategies can quickly facilitate independence from the job coach and transfer of support to the supervisor and co-workers of the company. This chapter discusses facilitating customer independence on the job by using a variety of workplace-support instructional strategies.

An analysis of the duties and daily routine associated with a job is the first step in determining what instruction is needed. This analysis includes identifying the areas in which various job tasks are performed, determining the essential and nonessential job functions, establishing a work routine, identifying natural supports and natural cues in the workplace, and designing appropriate training and support strategies. Usually, working one shift prior to introducing the individual with significant disabilities to the position is sufficient for completing these activities. Working the job gives the employment specialist the opportunity to note the major job duties and estimate the amount of time required for task completion. A Sequence of Job Duties Form (see Figure 7.1) can be used to record this information, including the movement required between workstations. If the sequence of job duties varies from day to day, then this also is noted on the form.

Once the sequence of major job duties has been determined, the next step is to analyze the skills required to perform each major duty. During this step, the employment specialist identifies and describes the skills, as well as the tools and equipment, that are

Position _____

Jobsite _____

☐ Job duties remain the same   ☐ Job duties vary from day to day (If checked, complete a separate form for each different sequence; circle day for which this form is completed.)

Mon. Tues. Wed. Thus. Fri. Sat. Sun.

Approximate times	Job duty

Comments:

Signature:

Figure 7.1.   Sequence of Job Duties Form. (From Moon, M.S., Inge, K.J., Wehman, P., Brooke, V., & Barcus, J.M. [1990]. *Helping persons with mental retardation get and keep employment: Supported employment issues and strategies* [p. 104]. Baltimore: Paul H. Brookes Publishing Co., adapted by permission.)

needed. Information may be obtained by interviewing the employer, co-workers, and supervisors; observing co-workers perform the skills; and by personally completing the job duties. Typically, each duty will have several associated skills. As an example, a worker is responsible for pricing merchandise at a department store. When he arrives in the morning, the first task in his sequence of job duties is setting up the workstation. The skills associated with this include:

- Locating stock for pricing

- Opening and emptying boxes

- Obtaining inventory sheets and the day's price tickets from his supervisor

- Locating and collecting equipment, including the price gun, pencil, and inventory stamp

During this stage of analysis, the employment specialist should concentrate on how the job duty is performed by the co-worker(s). Once this has been established, the employment specialist considers how the task can be organized or modified specific to the worker who will master it. Suggestions for completing a job duty analysis can be found in Table 7.1.

Determining the most efficient procedure to complete each skill as well as analyzing how to eliminate or reduce unnecessary movement will be important when assisting workers with significant disabilities. Using the example of setting up a workstation, the individual with significant disabilities may not realize that gathering all supplies and making one trip is more efficient than carrying one item at a time. An employment specialist may be tempted to let an individual work using unnecessary movements because he or she is doing the task without prompting; however, using unnecessary movements can increase task completion time, result in the person not being on schedule, and affect the individual's ability to perform to the company's production standards. Establishing and following a sequence of job duties from the first day of employment can quickly minimize the need for an employment specialist's

Table 7.1.   Guidelines for a job duty analysis

1.   Interview the employer/supervisor for his or her input.

2.   Observe a co-worker completing the job duty.

3.   Identify the skills that must be completed successfully to perform the job duty.

4.   Identify all tools and machinery that are required. Consider any modifications or accommodations that may be needed to this equipment.

5.   Determine the most efficient procedure to complete each skill.

6.   Try to eliminate or reduce unnecessary movement when completing the job duty analysis.

7.   If changes are made in the "usual way of doing business," be sure to clear the modifications with the employer and/or supervisor.

From Brooke, V., Inge, K.J., Armstrong, A., and Wehman, P. (1997). *Supported employment handbook: A customer-driven approach for persons with significant disabilities.* Richmond: Virginia Commonwealth University Rehabilitation Research and Training Center on Workplace Supports and Job Retention; adapted by permission.

Table 7.2.   Guidelines for writing a task analysis

1.   State the steps in terms of observable behaviors.

2.   Write the steps in adequate detail, with only one behavior per step.

3.   Test the task analysis to ensure that each step results in a visible change in the task or process.

4.   Order the steps from first to last.

5.   Word the steps as verbal cues.

6.   Build natural cues and compensatory strategies into the task analysis.

7.   Consider efficiency; use both hands with the least amount of movement.

8.   Eliminate discrimination by building judgment into the task.

From Brooke, V., Inge, K.J., Armstrong, A., and Wehman, P. (1997). *Supported employment handbook: A customer-driven approach for persons with significant disabilities.* Richmond: Virginia Commonwealth University Rehabilitation Research and Training Center on Workplace Supports and Job Retention; adapted by permission.

presence and eliminate the need to correct any error patterns that the person develops during the initial on-site support phase.

Once the major job duties, specific skills, schedule for completion, and any needed supplies and tools have been identified, the employment specialist must develop a written task analysis for each skill to be performed. Steps in a task analysis should be stated in terms of observable behaviors with each step representing one distinct movement. Once the step is complete, a visible change in the task or process has occurred. Wording steps in the form of a verbal cue (e.g., Push the "off" button) allows the employment specialist to use the steps of the task analysis as verbal prompts of instruction if required. Table 7.2 presents a list of suggestions for writing a task analysis (Inge, 1997).

INSTRUCTIONAL STRATEGIES

Once the job duties are identified and a task analysis is developed, the employment specialist must design instructional programs for each job duty or other related skills to be taught. The design should include input from the individual with disabilities, the supervisor, and co-workers. Each program includes 1) natural supports, 2) natural cues, 3) training objectives, 4) data collection guidelines, 5) prompting procedures, and 6) compensatory strategies.

Natural Supports

Employment success for an individual with significant disabilities may be determined by the natural supports provided by co-workers as well as by training on the actual work tasks. Once a job duty analysis and task analysis have been developed, the next step is to identify the supports that are naturally available in the workplace. The purpose is to determine what supports can be obtained that will minimize the need for the employment specialist's intervention. If a worker with disabilities is perceived as reliable, cooperative, and competent by co-workers from the first day of employment, then the chances for long-term job retention are increased.

The use of natural supports implies that the supports are ones that are typically available to all workers and not artificially created by the employment specialist. Orientation training, company videotapes, co-worker mentors, performance incentives, staff development, checklists, car pooling, flexible scheduling, and employee assistance programs are but a few of the many strategies used by employers to develop skills, encourage motivation, and promote retention of employees. Utilizing the support typically offered by a company provides workers with disabilities the advantages of greater opportunities for assistance, enhanced integration, increased socialization, and more resources from which to choose the type and amount of support that they would like (Storey & Certo, 1996; Storey & Garff, 1997). In addition, natural supports have been found to enhance supported employment outcomes in terms of cost-effectiveness, quality service-delivery practices, and customer satisfaction (Zivolich, Shueman, & Weiner, 1997).

Natural supports can provide the assistance that a worker with disabilities needs to get through a typical day, and they can be a source of interaction that an individual looks forward to as part of the daily routine. This may include a ride to work from a neighbor, a greeting and reminder to go to lunch by a co-worker, or a word of praise and quality-control check by a supervisor. It is not unusual for co-workers to help each other with a complicated task, for an employer to offer an alternative work schedule, or for a family member to share home responsibilities. Individuals with disabilities also need similar kinds of help for many of the same things. The main difference may be the intensity of the support, the number of supports needed, the length of time during which support is required, or how the person gains access to using the support. Many individuals with disabilities may not have the skills to ask for assistance, others may not be able to identify the best way assistance should be provided, and still others may be faced with people who want to help but don't know how.

The role of the employment specialist is to assist the individual in identifying and reviewing the variety of supports available and in selecting the ones that meet the needs of the worker with disabilities. For instance, one company may have a classroom orientation and training program, whereas another company may have a co-worker mentor program. In addition, the support must be analyzed to determine if it meets the needs of the individual. A one time, 2-hour classroom lecture on company policies may be of little benefit to the individual with disabilities, whereas a co-worker who explains the "unwritten rules" of the workplace to all new employees may be an extremely valuable resource.

Some co-workers may initially not feel comfortable providing instruction and supervision to an individual with disabilities. The employment specialist can model interactions and training strategies that will allow co-workers and supervisors to become proficient in assisting the worker. This can be as subtle as encouraging a co-worker to direct questions and conversation to the individual rather than to the employment specialist. Another example is instructing the worker with disabilities to interact with and ask questions of the other company employees. For instance, instead of the employment specialist asking about where the work supplies are kept, the individual with disabilities is encouraged to interact with the supervisor from the first day of employment.

In general, the employment specialist wants to foster inclusion in the workplace rather than dependence on the job coach. Too often, the assumption is made that co-workers would not want to or be capable of providing the assistance that an employment specialist may be required to do. Quite to the contrary, an abundance of supports are in existence, and individuals with disabilities can use them very effectively to be able to complete their jobs with reduced support from a paid provider. The key is to think creatively, keep an open mind, believe in the notion that supports exist, and not be surprised at anything.

Natural Cues

A *natural cue* represents some feature of the work environment, job tasks, or activities that signals what to do next. It is typically something that a worker can see, hear, touch/feel, or smell. Examples include an on/off indicator light, a service-door buzzer, the ringing of a telephone or fax machine, an announcement over the loud speaker, the smell of cookies ready to be removed from the oven, and the placement or location of work materials such as paper in an in-box. Obviously, if a worker with disabilities responds to a natural cue, instruction is not required. Some individuals, however, may need to learn to recognize and attend to the cues in the workplace. The employment specialist should collaborate with co-workers and supervisors to identify the natural cues that can assist the individual in completing his or her job duties successfully.

Some individuals may fail to respond to or recognize a cue even after it is pointed out to them. One way to call attention to a cue may be to initially add an extra cue to the natural one. This extra cue can enhance the relevant features of the naturally occurring one. For example, taping a red arrow pointing to the "start" button on the copy machine. Whenever cues are added, the employment specialist should discuss them with the employer and obtain permission. Discussions with the employer and co-workers also may ensure ownership of the strategy by all individuals involved as well as guarantee that changes are not made that the supervisor would not approve.

In addition, the co-workers and supervisor should be approached about assisting the individual with added cues. Shifting responsibility from the employment specialist to co-workers and the supervisor must occur in order for a relationship to develop between the individual with disabilities and his or her co-workers. This would include checking that cues are not removed by other employees who are unfamiliar with the individual's training program. When assisting the worker with disabilities, co-workers may find that cues added for the person with disabilities are beneficial to them as well.

Training Objectives

Training objectives are written to include observable skills, the conditions under which they occur, and the criteria that will be used to evaluate performance. Each skill to be trained has a corresponding training objective. The following is an example for entering data into a company's mailing list.

Conditions under which work performance will occur:

- Give a list of addresses and cue, "Add the names to the mailing list."

Observable work skills:

- Ramona will enter the names and addresses.

Criteria for evaluation of worker performance:

- Performance with 100% accuracy according to the steps in the task analysis for three consecutive probe trials

Data Collection Guidelines

Recording and graphing data is critical to the success of jobsite training and knowing when the worker with disabilities is independent of the employment specialist's assistance. Measurement procedures are a vital component because they allow the employment specialist to monitor the employee's progress. They will show whether a particular training strategy is effective or needs modification (e.g., changing strategies, adding external cues, modifying tasks). Data collection also can provide documentation for the individual's continued funding. Measurement procedures continue throughout initial jobsite training when the employment specialist is on site into long-term supports when the employment specialist is only making follow-along visits. This will assist the employment specialist in identifying additional training or retraining needs for the individual with disabilities. It is important to remember that data collection should never be an intrusive or obvious process.

Baseline, probe, and prompt data are based on the task analysis of each major job duty and indicate whether the individual is working independently. The initial data collection before instruction begins is referred to as *baseline* and should be conducted at least once prior to the initiation of a skill acquisition program. Data that is collected after training begins is referred to as *probe data*. The procedures for baseline and probe data are essentially the same and provide information on how well the individual performs a job duty without prompting or feedback from the employment specialist, supervisor, or co-workers. Probe data should be collected at least once each week. Typically, a job task is considered learned when the employee independently and correctly performs every step for a minimum of three consecutive probe trials.

There are two different strategies that an employment specialist can use to collect data on a jobsite to include a single- or multiple-opportunity probe. Regardless of which procedure is used, the employment specialist shows the individual how to perform the specific job duty prior to conducting baseline assessment. After training begins, the worker with disabilities is asked to perform the job duty without any prompting or demonstrations. Steps for using a single-opportunity probe are listed in Table 7.3.

There is one major benefit to using a single-opportunity probe for data collection. Specifically, assessment should not be time consuming or interrupt the natural flow of the workplace. Discontinuing the probe as soon as the individual makes an error allows for instruction to begin immediately on that specific step of the task analysis. In contrast, use of a multiple-opportunity probe shows which steps of the task the individual is having difficulty performing without assistance, prompting, or feedback. Table 7.4 outlines the steps for a multiple-opportunity probe procedure. The employment specialist must assess the work environment and length of task to determine the most appropriate strategy for data collection.

Prompting Procedures

The majority of the literature on teaching vocational tasks to individuals with significant disabilities focuses on the use of least prompts as the teaching strategy of choice (Brooke et al., 1997; Cuvo, Leaf, & Borakove, 1978; Test, Grossi, & Keul, 1988). This strategy is also referred to as a *response prompt hierarchy* because the employment specialist or trainer progresses from the least amount of assistance (usually a verbal prompt) to the most intrusive (usually a physical prompt) until one prompt results in

Table 7.3.   Guidelines for using a single-opportunity probe

1. Have the individual move to the appropriate work area unless movement is part of the task analysis.

2. Stand beside or behind the individual so that data collection does not interrupt the work flow.

3. Tell the individual that he or she is going to work without assistance to see what he or she can do independently.

4. Provide the work cue (e.g., "Enter the names into the mailing list.")

5. Do not provide prompts or reinforcement.

6. Wait 3–5 seconds for the individual to make a response.

7. If he or she does not begin to work or makes an error, then discontinue the probe, and score a – for all steps in the task analysis.

8. If he or she begins work, then continue as long as correct responses are made, scoring a + for correct performance.

9. As soon as an error occurs, discontinue the probe, and score a – for all remaining steps in the task analysis.

From Moon, M.S., Inge, K.J., Wehman, P., Brooke, V., and Barcus, J.M. (1990). *Helping persons with mental retardation get and keep employment: Supported employment issues and strategies* (p. 131). Baltimore: Paul H. Brookes Publishing Co.; adapted by permission.

Table 7.4.   Guidelines for using a multiple-opportunity probe

1. Have the individual move to the appropriate work area unless movement is the first step in the task analysis.

2. Stand beside or behind the individual so that data collection does not interrupt the work flow.

3. Provide the work cue (e.g., "Enter the names into the mailing list.")

4. Do not provide verbal instruction, prompts, or reinforcement during the data collection.

5. Wait a specified time (e.g., 3–5 seconds) for the individual to initiate a response.

6. Record a + if the individual completes the step correctly.

7. If there is no response or the individual is incorrect, then position him or her to perform the next step in the task analysis or complete the step yourself (if necessary).

8. Repeat items 5, 6, and 7 as needed in order to test all steps in the task analysis from first to last.

From Moon, M.S., Inge, K.J., Wehman, P., Brooke, V., and Barcus, J.M. (1990). *Helping persons with mental retardation get and keep employment: Supported employment issues and strategies* (p. 131). Baltimore: Paul H. Brookes Publishing Co.; adapted by permission.

the individual correctly completing the step in the task. Employment specialists are encouraged to consider various types of prompts to use in addition to the traditional verbal, model, physical sequence. For instance, as an individual becomes more proficient performing his or her job duties, the employment specialist can try using an indirect verbal prompt in the sequence before using the verbal prompt specific to the step in the task analysis, such as, "What do you do next?" This may be effective also for training individuals who have been dependent on agency staff or human service providers for verbal instruction. In addition, gestures can be used instead of a model prompt. Or, a partial physical prompt (e.g., touching the individual's arm) can be used instead of total physical assistance. Table 7.5 lists prompts that can be used to assist a person in learning his or her job tasks.

Regardless of the types of prompts selected, the employment specialist must establish the length of time that he or she will wait for the individual to respond before providing the next level of assistance. Usually, a worker with disabilities should be given approximately 3 or 5 seconds to respond independently. Individuals with physical disabilities, however, may require longer response times based on their movement limitations, and this should be determined on an individual basis (Inge, 2001; Sowers & Powers, 1991). Finally, the employment specialist is cautioned to deliver each prompt only once before moving to the next, more intrusive level of assistance that results in a step of the task being completed correctly. Table 7.6 provides step-by-step guidelines on how to implement this prompting strategy.

Teaching the individual to complete a job duty should occur at the same pace or production standard that co-workers perform in the workplace. If the employment specialist provides instruction that exceeds the normal time to complete a task, then the worker with disabilities may learn to perform at standards less than those required by the jobsite. If this occurs, then the employment specialist needs to consider the types of prompts that are used in the least-to-most prompting procedure as well as potentially modify the amount of time between prompts. Successful use of this strategy should be seen quickly in the form of the individual requiring lesser amounts of assistance. Careful monitoring of the data can help the employment specialist identify problem steps in the task analysis that may require additional cues, co-worker feedback, or adding other compensatory strategies that will be discussed later in this chapter.

Least Intrusive Prompt System

The same task analysis used for probe data collection is used for recording prompt data. In the case of least prompts, the employment specialist records a symbol representing either independent performance of a step (+) or use of a specific prompt. For instance, a verbal prompt can be scored by a v, a model prompt by an m, a gestural prompt by a g, or a physical prompt by a p. By keeping track of the number and types of prompts that the worker requires over time, the employment specialist will be able to determine when it is possible to start gradually moving away from the individual during training. How often prompt data is collected depends on each worker and the amount of training required for him or her to learn the job duty. Individuals with more significant disabilities may require prompting over the course of several weeks to independence, whereas others may learn particular tasks very quickly. Each employment specialist will have to make judgments about how to best monitor the worker's performance.

Initially, the employment specialist may be located beside or behind the individual in a position to provide direct instruction. When the worker is independently per-

Table 7.5.   Prompt examples

Indirect verbal instructions:

In response to a natural cue such as a light blinking on the copy machine, the employment specialist might say:

- "What do you do now?"
- "What do you do next?"
- "What happens now?"

Direct verbal instructions:

The employment specialist might say:

- "Get your time card."
- "Stock the cart."
- "Open the filing cabinet drawer."

Gestures:

The employment specialist points to the time clock (to prompt the individual to punch in/out).

The employment specialist taps a wristwatch (to prompt the individual to take a lunch break).

The employment specialist touches the in-box with files (to prompt the individual to begin copying files).

Model prompts:

A co-worker shows the individual how to go to the employee break room.

The supervisor demonstrates how to use the time clock to punch in/out.

Partial physical assistance:

The employment specialist taps the individual on the elbow to prompt him or her to reach for the time card.

The employment specialist guides the individual's elbow to prompt him or her to pick up a file folder.

Full physical assistance:

The employment specialist, with his or her hand over the individual's hand, selects the time card from the rack.

The employment specialist, with his or her hand on the individual's hand, guides the individual in placing a security sticker on a blouse.

---

forming approximately 70%–80% of the steps in the task analysis for the job duty and performs the remaining steps with a verbal prompt, the employment specialist can move 3'–6' away from the individual. If a prompt is needed at this point in training, then the employment specialist can move toward the worker. Once a correct response is initiated, the trainer should move back to the designated distance.

Table 7.6.   Guidelines for using a least prompt hierarchy

1. Have the worker with disabilities move to the appropriate work area unless movement is part of the task analysis.

2. Stand behind or beside the individual so that you can quickly provide prompts if necessary.

3. Provide the cue to begin the task (e.g., "Clock in." "Enter the addresses into the mailing list.").

4. Wait 3 seconds for self-initiation of Step 1 of the task analysis.

5. If the individual completes the step independently, then provide feedback on the correct response and proceed to Step 2 of the task analysis.

6. If the individual is incorrect or does not respond within 3 seconds, then provide a verbal prompt specific to Step 1 of the task analysis (e.g., "Find your time card.").

7. If the individual completes the step with a verbal prompt, then provide feedback and move to Step 2.

8. If the individual is incorrect or does not respond within 3 seconds, then use a gesture or model the response (e.g., point to the time card).

9. If the individual completes the step with a model prompt, then provide feedback and move to Step 2.

10. If the individual is incorrect or does not respond within 3 seconds, then physically guide him or her through the response (e.g., guide the individual's hand to pick up the time card.).

11. Begin instruction on Step 2 of the task analysis.

12. Repeat this procedure for each step in the task analysis until the task is completed.

13. Always interrupt an error with the next prompt in the least prompt system.

Sources: Barcus, Brooke, Inge, Moon, and Goodall (1987); Brooke, Inge, Armstrong, and Wehman (1997); Moon, Inge, Wehman, Brooke, and Barcus (1990).

In this manner, the employment specialist can fade his or her physical proximity to the person as he or she begins to independently perform the steps of the task analysis with fewer prompts. Ultimately, the employment specialist must remove his or her presence from the immediate work area in which the job duty is performed and eventually from the jobsite altogether. Removal of the trainer's presence from the immediate work area must be systematically planned and based on the performance of the individual.

Graphing Data

Improvement in a person's ability to perform job duties independently is easier to analyze if the data are displayed graphically. Tracking the percentage of steps the individual performs without prompts and feedback allows the employment specialist to determine the rate at which the worker is acquiring the job skills. When plotting data on a graph, information such as frequency, percent, number of steps, and other finite data are placed on the vertical axis. Number of sessions, weeks, days, and other infinite numbers go along the horizontal axis. Data analysis can indicate whether a change or modification is needed to the training program. For instance, if the individual gradually shows an increase in performing steps independently, then the employment specialist would continue the instructional program. If there is no change in either prompt or probe data within several days, the employment specialist must reevaluate the instructional plan and change components of the program.

Prompting Strategies

Time delay is another way to systematically fade instructional prompts (Inge, Moon, & Parent, 1993; Moon et al., 1990). There are several critical components to a time-delay procedure (Gast, Ault, Wolery, Doyle, & Belanger, 1988; Snell & Gast, 1981). First, the employment specialist must select a single prompt that consistently assists the individual in performing the job duty correctly. Initially, the prompt is given simultaneously with the request to perform the job duty. Gradually, increasing amounts of time (usually seconds) are waited between giving the request to perform the task and providing the prompt to complete the skill correctly. The number of trials at each delay level and length of the delay should be determined prior to initiation of training.

By pairing the prompt with the request to perform a work task, the individual is not allowed to make errors initially. The delay procedure allows the employment specialist to gradually fade assistance until the individual performs without prompting. For example, a set number of trials are determined for a 0-second delay, the next set at a 2-second delay, the next at a 4-second delay, and so forth until the individual performs without assistance. Unlike the system of least prompts, time delay requires that the employment specialist select one prompt for use during training. Therefore, the procedure is particularly useful if an individual consistently demonstrates a preference for one type of prompt. For example, if a worker with disabilities has shown that he or she always responds to a model prompt without making errors, then the employment specialist can select it to place on delay.

Monitoring the training data is essential to ensure that the worker with disabilities is not constantly making errors during the procedure. If an error occurs during training, then the employment specialist should implement an error-correction procedure. Typically, an error may occur once increasing amounts of time are waited before the prompt is provided. Usually, error correction consists of immediately interrupting the individual's mistake and providing the prompt. If the individual makes three or more errors in a row, then the trainer may consider reverting to a number of trials at 0 seconds before again delaying the prompt.

Constant time delay is a variation on the previous strategy. Training also begins with a predetermined number of trials at a 0-second delay; however, after the initial trials are conducted, a constant interval (e.g., 5 seconds) is selected for all remaining trials. Guidelines for training using a time-delay strategy can be found in Table 7.7.

MONICA

Monica is a young woman with cerebral palsy who is responsible for maintaining her company's mailing list. Initially, she could type using a head pointer, but she did not know how to use the company's software program to enter names and addresses into the mailing list format. She learned this job duty with the assistance of an employment specialist and a time-delay program.

First, the employment specialist loaded a software program called Sticky Keys onto Monica's computer to eliminate Monica's having to press two keys si-

Table 7.7.   Guidelines for time delay

1.   Specify the number of training trials to be conducted at 0-second delay (e.g., all trials on the first day of work will be at 0-second delay).

2.   Specify the time-delay intervals (e.g., 2, 4, 6 or 1, 2, 3, 4 seconds).

3.   Determine the number of training trials to be conducted at each interval (e.g., all trials on the second day of work will be at a 2-second delay; all trials on the third day of work will be at a 4-second delay).

4.   Select one prompt for training that the individual consistently responds to correctly.

5.   Design an error-correction procedure (e.g., all errors will be interrupted immediately). If three errors occur consecutively, then return to a predetermined number of trials at 0-second delay. When these trials are completed, return to the previous delay level.

6.   Implement the following procedure:

   •   Have the worker move to the work area unless movement is part of the task analysis.

   •   Provide the overall cue to begin work.

   •   Wait the specified delay level.

   •   If the worker performs independently, then provide reinforcement and move to the next step of the task analysis.

   •   If no response occurs within the specified time, then provide the prompt and reinforce the worker for step completion. Move to the next step of the task.

   •   Interrupt all errors immediately, regardless of the time-delay level, and provide the selected prompt.

   •   Implement the error-correction procedure if the worker makes three errors in a row on the same step of the task analysis.

Source: Inge (1997).

Note: The guidelines for a constant time-delay procedure follow the same steps outlined above with one exception. After the initial trials at 0 seconds are completed, training during all other trials is done at the selected constant delay (e.g., 3 seconds) until the worker meets skill acquisition.

multaneously (e.g., holding down the SHIFT key while typing the first letter of a name). Second, she developed a task analysis type for data entry. Third, the employment specialist selected a verbal prompt of choice because Monica always followed verbal instructions successfully. The task analysis for entering one name and the corresponding address can be found in Table 7.8.

Monica's time-delay program consisted of 1 day of work with a 0-second time delay. For instance, as soon as the instructional cue "enter a name and address" was given, the employment specialist gave the first verbal cue, "press the up arrow key." As soon as Monica pressed the up arrow key, the next verbal prompt was given, "press the SHIFT key," and so forth. In this manner, the employment specialist verbally walked Monica successfully through the first day of data entry.

On the next day of instruction, the employment specialist used a 2-second delay procedure. This meant that she paused for 2 seconds between prompts. The employment specialist gave the instructional cue to begin work. She waited 2 seconds for Monica to perform independently. If Monica began without a specific verbal prompt, then she was told that she had correctly initiated the first step in the task. If there was no response, then Monica was provided with a verbal cue specific to the first step in the task analysis. If Monica began to make a mistake while the employment specialist was waiting between steps, then she was interrupted immediately with the next verbal prompt. The delay level between steps was gradually increased each day until Monica was working independently.

Table 7.8.   Task analysis for entering names into the mailing list

Instructional cue to begin work: "Enter a name and address"

1.   Press the up arrow key.

2.   Press CONTROL key.

3.   Type *F*.

4.   Press the SHIFT key.

5.   Type the first name.

6.   Press the ENTER key.

7.   Press the SHIFT key.

8.   Type the last name.

9.   Press the ENTER key.

10.   Type the company name.

11.   Press the ENTER key 2 times.

12.   Type the street name.

13.   Press the ENTER key 2 times.

14.   Type the zip code.

15.   Press the ENTER key 2 times.

16.   Type today's date.

17.   Press the ENTER key 3 times.

18.   Type 1.

19.   Press the ENTER key 3 times.

20.   Begin the next entry.

Compensatory Strategies

Adding compensatory strategies to jobsite training can enhance a worker's ability to learn and perform independently. In some instances, using a compensatory strategy can eliminate instruction by the employment specialist and allow the individual to participate in activities that he or she otherwise would not be able to enjoy. For instance, a person may use a money card to purchase a soda from the break room vending machine. The money card eliminates the need for the individual to learn the difference between coins or the actual amount that is required to gain access to the machine; however, the steps in using a compensatory strategy may require instruction and should be included within any task analyses that are developed.

If compensatory strategies are targeted, then they must be designed with input from the individual, employer, and co-workers. In addition, care should be given to the design and construction of materials to ensure that they do not stigmatize the individual. Materials should be age appropriate, accessible by an adult within a work environment, and accepted by the work culture in which they are used. For instance, if a picture book is selected to assist a person in remembering his or her work schedule, then the employment specialist and person should work together in the design of the booklet. Some of the things they may want to consider include:

- Pictures should be concise and eliminate unnecessary information.

- The number of pictures in the booklet should be evaluated. Too many may distract or confuse the individual rather than assist in task completion.

- The size of the booklet must be evaluated. Does it draw attention to the individual? Could it be made small enough to fit in a pocket?

- The materials must be those that any adult would use.

- The booklet should be durable. How often will it need to be replaced? Who will be assisting the individual after the employment specialist has faded from the workplace?

- The materials should be simple to use. Is there a less complicated strategy that is just as effective? For instance, could the individual learn to use a written list of job tasks rather than a bulky picture book?

The same concepts or ideas could be applied to almost any compensatory strategy used on a jobsite. The strategy should be simple to use, concise, and the least intrusive to assist the individual in performing his or her job duties.

RANDY

Randy learned to perform his job duty of vacuuming the second floor of a local department store; however, he had difficulty moving from one department to another. For instance, one day he would remember to vacuum women's shoes, whereas on another day, he would skip it entirely. On yet another day, he would remember to vacuum women's shoes but forget to vacuum women's coats. The employment specialist discussed this with Randy and his employer, and they came up with the following solution.

There were five areas Randy needed to vacuum in a day: women's coats, women's shoes, women's dresses, women's accessories, and cosmetics. The employment specialist copied pictures that represented each area of the second floor. The pictures were approximately 3" × 3". Booklets were developed by stapling five pictures together in a packet. Randy's supervisor agreed to make sure that there were booklets always available in Randy's locker.

At the beginning of a workday, Randy took out one booklet from his locker. He proceeded to the area of the store to be vacuumed as represented by the first picture in the packet. After he completed vacuuming the section, Randy tore the top picture from the booklet and threw it in the trash. He then moved to the next area. In this manner, Randy was able to sequence the sections of the store for vacuuming. Throwing away a picture after the work was completed seemed to be very reinforcing and helped Randy move through his workday.

Employment specialists are encouraged to design other compensatory strategies specific to individuals whom they are intended to benefit. Many types of added cues and prompts can be used. Table 7.9 provides some additional suggestions.

Some individuals with brain injury will have specific memory difficulties related to their disability (Keyser-Marcus et al., 2002; Kreutzer & Wehman, 1990; Penn & Cleary, 1988), including problems with auditory and visual memory and learning, as well as short- and long-term memory. Compensatory strategies, such as use of imagery, number chunking, memory notebooks, verbal labeling, and verbal rehearsal, are ways to deal with these issues (see Table 7.10).

Table 7.9.   Compensatory strategy ideas

Challenge: The individual can't remember his or her sequence of job duties.

Strategies: Written list, audiocassette, picture book, assignment board, flow chart

Challenge: The individual has difficulty reading copy requests to determine work assignments.

Strategies: In/out boxes for each co-worker requesting work with name or picture of co-worker on box, special form highlighting relevant features of the task such as thick outlined box where number of copies is located, audiocassette requests for copy work

Challenge: The individual cannot count using one-to-one correspondence in order to package work materials.

Strategies: Strips of tape on table that correspond to number of items in package, picture of number of items in the package, box with number of dividers that correspond to number of items in package, sample of package for matching work

From Inge, K.J., and Tilson, G. (1997). Ensuring support systems that work: Getting beyond the natural supports vs. job coach controversy. *Journal of Vocational Rehabilitation, 9*(2), 133–142; adapted by permission.

Table 7.10.   Compensatory memory strategies

Assignment board—presenting a list of task assignments as a graphic (e.g., a worker lists her job duties with specific times for completion on a bulletin board on the door of her locker to refer to throughout the day).

Imagery—using mental pictures/images of information to be recalled (e.g., an individual visualizes him- or herself walking a specific route to assist in remembering how to find his or her jobsite).

Location and place markers—placing a visual cue at some point in a task sequence to indicate where the task is to be resumed (e.g., a warehouse worker who straightens shelf inventory ties a bandana on the shelf to cue himself for coming back to where he left off).

Memory notebook—maintaining written cues systematically in a log to keep up with things that have been done or need to be accomplished (e.g., a date or daytime organizer book is used by employees to remember appointments).

Mnemonic—imposing an organizational structure on verbal information to cue recall of several elements (e.g., a clerical assistant recalls her sequence of job duties by remembering the word *code*: *C,* clock in; *O,* open mail; *D,* deliver mail; *E,* enter data)

Numbering grouping—recalling numbers by perceptually reorganizing them into fewer elements (e.g., a worker remembers a 4-digit code by looking at a computer printout of the four numbers 1,7,2, and 5 and recalling the information as the date 1725).

Verbal rehearsal—repeating key information to facilitate memory recall (e.g., an inventory control specialist sets up her workstation by stating the following aloud: 1) turn on monitor, 2) turn on computer, 3) enter my password, 4) hit ENTER; she eventually learns to internalize this process by repeating the instruction quietly until she no longer needs to verbalize the information).

SELF-MANAGEMENT

Self-management has been referred to as *self-monitoring, self-observation, self-evaluation, self-reinforcement, self-instruction,* and *self-assessment* (Browder & Shapiro, 1985; Karoly, 1977; Kazdin, 1984; Shapiro, 1981). Self-management strategies may be applied either before or after the targeted job duty or skill to assist the worker in performing a task successfully. For instance, the worker may use a preset alarm on a watch to determine when it is time to take a break. Another example may be a worker who uses a compensatory strategy such as a picture book of tasks that need to be completed during the day.

The effectiveness of self-management procedures has been documented by Shafer and Brooke (1985). They used a self-recording strategy to increase the punctuality of a young woman in her job. The individual recorded her checkout time on a piece of paper that was printed with a calendar grid. She was responsible for recording the time that her supervisor told her to leave the jobsite on this card, as well as using the time clock to punch out. The employment specialist compared her self-recording card with the actual punch-out time every 3 or 4 days. This self-monitoring strategy was successful in decreasing the number of days that the worker left the job-site prior to schedule without daily supervision from the employment specialist.

Self-management usually entails instructing the worker with disabilities to independently self-monitor by using such things as natural cues, external cues and prompts, compensatory strategies, assistive technology devices, and so forth. This instruction can be provided by the employment specialist, friends, family members, co-workers, and/or the supervisor depending on the person's support needs. For instance, a family member may assist the person in learning to check off days on a calendar to determine when he or she goes to work. A co-worker may instruct the same individual in using a timer to monitor production, whereas the employment specialist may assist the individual in developing a self-reinforcement strategy to use on the job when he or she meets the production standard. Regardless of who provides the person instruction and support, the guidelines outlined in Table 7.11 should be considered.

JESSICA

Jessica works part time at a restaurant from 9:00 A.M. to noon, Tuesday, Thursday, and Saturday and 9:00 A.M. to 3:00 P.M. on Friday. From the first day of work, Jessica has earned $5.25 per hour for a total of 15 hours per week. During the times of the week that Jessica does not work, she attends her regular school program. Her primary job duty is to roll silverware and distribute it to the bus stations. She also occasionally greets customers as they enter the restaurant. Her position was identified based on her preference to work at a restaurant in a position where she could also greet and meet people. This job was customized for Jessica by the restaurant manager and her employment specialist. It was determined during the

Table 7.11.   Considerations for self-management programs

1. Review training data. If the employee is having specific difficulties in sequencing, discriminating, or meeting production, then consider using self-management procedures.

2. Consider the learning style of the person. Does he or she respond best to visual, auditory, or tactile information, or is a combination of these needed?

3. Determine if the self-management strategies are stigmatizing. For instance, self-instruction may not be appropriate for a person who is in frequent contact with co-workers and the public.

4. Always have the person assist in the design and selection of self-management strategies.

5. Include the supervisor and/or co-workers in the process. Do not implement a strategy without approval.

6. Decide who will be responsible for supporting the person in learning how to self-monitor.

7. Evaluate the procedure, and modify if necessary.

8. Fade the self-management procedure if necessary.

Source: Inge (1997).

initial interview that the waitresses had difficulty keeping an adequate supply of silverware during the workday. As such, the manager was very receptive to creating a position for Jessica that freed up the waitresses from this part of their job responsibility.

Initial jobsite training took place throughout the restaurant; however, the majority of the instruction occurred at a small workstation located between two dining rooms. Waitresses and other employees constantly move in and out of this area because it houses supplies for setting the tables, as well as serving nonalcoholic beverages. Initially, Jessica was trained by her employment specialist to roll silverware using a least prompt strategy. She successfully learned the task and could perform it without prompting; however, an analysis of her program data indicated that Jessica did not meet the production standards for rolling silverware. Jessica, her employment specialist, and her supervisor decided that she should try using a self-management procedure.

MEASUREMENT AND RECORDING PROCEDURES

The first step in assisting Jessica in meeting production was to set and verify a company standard for rolling silverware. The manager wanted this task completed at a steady, constant work pace, but he did not have a specific predetermined standard for Jessica to follow. Therefore, the employment specialist observed co-workers, observed Jessica's production without reinforcement or prompting, and completed the task himself to determine a reasonable rate of performance. A production standard of 10 pieces of silverware in 8 minutes was set, and the manager and co-workers agreed that the rate would be satisfactory. Prior to implementing the program design, the employment specialist took a baseline of Jessica's performance. When measured unobtrusively, she completed one piece of silverware an average of every 90 seconds (10 pieces of silverware in 15 minutes.)

PROGRAM DESIGN

Self-Monitoring

Two cues were selected based on Jessica's learning style to assist her in self-monitoring production. First, an auditory cue (i.e., digital kitchen timer) was purchased by the employment specialist, and 8 minutes was placed in its stored memory. Next, a visual cue (i.e., 10 strips of colored tape) were placed on the table to the right side of Jessica's workstation. Each piece of tape corresponded to one piece of rolled silverware. Jessica was trained to punch the "start/stop" button on the timer as the first step in beginning her silverware task. After rolling one piece of silverware, she placed the completed work on a strip of tape. Essentially, Jessica was instructed to fill the "cue area" with silverware prior to the alarm sounding on the timer.

Self-Reinforcement

The second component of the program was the design of a reinforcement booklet. A line drawing of four pieces of silverware positioned on a napkin was created by the employment specialist. He then divided one page of standard white bond paper into five sections approximately 8" by 2½". Within these five sections, 10 line drawings were positioned. Next, the employment specialist used the copy machine to produce multiple pages of the reinforcer. After producing the pages, he cut them into strips and stapled five reinforcer sheets together to make a booklet.

Self-reinforcement occurred after Jessica picked up the 10 rolls of silverware from the "tape grid" and placed them in a silverware bin. If the timer had not rung, then she pushed the "start/stop" button, picked up the "reinforcer booklet", tore off a sheet, and placed it on the table beside her work. At the end of the day, Jessica could take these "earned" pages to show at school and at home. If the timer rang prior to completion of 10 pieces of silverware, then Jessica was to tear off a reinforcer sheet and throw it in the trashcan. She then finished the remainder of the 10, put the silverware in the finished silverware bin, and started on the next set of 10 by setting the timer.

Five sections of 10 were selected for each reinforcer sheet because this corresponded to the number of napkins in a pack, as well as approximately 1 hour of work. It was felt that this could further assist Jessica in self-monitoring her production/ speed. In other words, at the end of 1 hour of work, Jessica should have an empty pack of napkins, a full bin of rolled silverware, and a reinforcer sheet that she could take to school or home at the end of the day. The extra time was allowed for getting new supplies and distributing the silverware to the waitress stations. In addition, Jessica's co-workers assisted her by agreeing to check on her at the end of each hour. If Jessica had completed the task, then she was able to assist her co-worker as a door greeter until the beginning of the next hour of work.

The employment specialist took the responsibility of assisting Jessica in learning how to use the self-monitoring program. Once she learned the task, her production standard was maintained with the support of her co-workers. Initially, Jessica did not fully understand the concept of working at a constant speed. The use of the self-management procedures assisted her in meeting production without constant interference from the employment specialist until she began to do so independently. In addition, it is suggested that the natural consequences of working at an acceptable speed (e.g., positive interactions from her supervisor and co-workers) began to influence Jessica's work performance. The self-management procedures quickly lead to the transfer of control from artificial prompts and reinforcers to the naturally occurring supports on the jobsite. By using a self-management procedure, Jessica is in control of her training and presents a competent image to her co-workers.

FADING FROM THE JOBSITE

Once the worker with disabilities has learned to perform all of the job duties correctly and independently, the employment specialist must ensure that the performance of these duties is maintained to company standards under the naturally occurring supervision. The focus of training at this point is to increase the worker's independence while fading the employment specialist's presence from the jobsite. Much of this will occur naturally if the employment specialist has paid attention to including the supervisor and co-workers in the program design from the first day of employment.

For instance, as the individual with disabilities begins performing steps in the task analysis independently, the employment specialist fades his or her presence from the immediate work area (e.g., is 3' away, then 5'). If planning has been done correctly, the employment specialist is ready to develop a fading schedule for leaving the jobsite. The individual's first time alone for part of the day will be a major step for the individual. The employment specialist should explain to the individual, the employer, and the co-workers that he or she can be contacted and will return if needed. As the individual with disabilities continues to do well based on supervisor and co-worker comments, the employment specialist gradually fades his or her presence until the worker is alone the entire workday. Initially, the employment specialist should stop by the jobsite at the end of the day to ensure that the individual is comfortable with the fading schedule. The guidelines in Table 7.12 may be useful when fading from the jobsite.

Table 7.12.   Guidelines for fading from the jobsite

1. Discuss the fading schedule with the worker with disabilities and the supervisor.

2. Agree on a day to begin fading your presence.

3. Inform the individual and co-workers (if appropriate) that you are leaving and for how long.

4. Give the worker and the supervisor a telephone number where you can be reached.

5. Leave for 1–2 hours for the first fading session.

6. Continue to collect probe and production data on the job duties.

7. Gradually increase the time off the site as the individual continues to be independent until he or she is working for the entire day with the naturally occurring support of the workplace.

From Brooke, V., Inge, K.J., Armstrong, A., and Wehman, P. (1997). *Supported employment handbook: A customer-driven approach for persons with significant disabilities.* Richmond: Virginia Commonwealth University Rehabilitation Research and Training Center on Workplace Supports and Job Retention; adapted by permission.

CONCLUSION

The most effective workplace support and training is the one that results in the worker being independent on the job. For every support and training need that is identified, there will be a variety of support resources available. All of the generated ideas should be discussed with the individual, the employer, and co-workers, including an explanation of what using the specific strategy will entail. The availability of the support option, the pros and cons of each, and the level of interest expressed by the individual can be explored at the same time.

In general, strategies should blend into the workplace and not make the worker with disabilities stand out. Effective supports are designed with the input of the employee with disabilities as well as the employer. A variety of factors need to be considered in order to determine if a support is effective. Is the individual with disabilities satisfied with the training procedures and supports? Be aware that an individual who is not using a workplace strategy or support may actually be thinking any of the following: "I feel uncomfortable using this strategy." "I do not need training." "I do not know how to use the support."

Always include the person with disabilities when providing skills training. Make sure that the person is learning to be independent on the job without the support of an employment specialist. Is integration and inclusion being enhanced? It is important to remember that a workplace support is only as good as the outcomes that are achieved. How is the support affecting employment, such as wages, hours, quality, and production of the employee? Is the employee with disabilities satisfied with his or her job? Flexibility, creativity, and resourcefulness are essential elements contributing to a combination of workplace supports that will meet the individual's needs and result in a job of choice in a community business.

REFERENCES

Barcus, M., Brooke, V., Inge, K., Moon, S., & Goodall, P. (1987). *An instructional guide for training on a job site: A supported employment resource.* Richmond: Virginia Commonwealth University Rehabilitation Research and Training Center on Workplace Supports and Job Retention.

Brooke, V., Inge, K.J., Armstrong, A., & Wehman, P. (1997). *Supported employment handbook: A customer-driven approach for persons with significant disabilities.* Richmond: Virginia Commonwealth University Rehabilitation Research and Training Center on Workplace Supports and Job Retention.

Browder, D.M., & Shapiro, E.S. (1985). Applications of self-management to individuals with severe handicaps: A review. *Journal of The Association for Persons with Severe Handicaps, 10*(4), 200–208.

Cuvo, A.J., Leaf, R.B., & Borakove, L.S. (1978). Teaching janitorial skills to the mentally retarded: Acquisition, generalization, and maintenance. *Journal of Applied Behavior Analysis, 11,* 345–355.

Gast, D.L., Ault, M.F., Wolery, M., Doyle, P.M., & Belanger, J. (1988). Comparison of constant time delay and the system of least prompts in teaching sight word reading to students with moderate retardation. *Education and Training in Mental Retardation, 23,* 117–128.

Grossi, T., Banks, B., & Pinnyei, D. (2001). Facilitating job site training and supports: The evolving role of the job coach. In P. Wehman (Ed.), *Supported employment in business: Expanding the capacity of workers with disabilities* (pp. 75–92). St. Augustine, FL: Training Resource Network.

Grossi, T.A., Regan, J., & Regan, B. (1998). Consumer-driven training techniques. In P. Wehman & J. Kregel, (Eds.), *More than a job: Securing satisfying careers for people with disabilities* (pp. 119–148). Baltimore: Paul H. Brookes Publishing Co.

Inge, K. (1997). Job site training. In V. Brooke, K.J. Inge, A. Armstrong, & P. Wehman (Eds.), *Supported employment handbook: A customer-driven approach for persons with significant disabilities* (pp. 159–200). Richmond: Virginia Commonwealth University Rehabilitation Research and Training Center on Workplace Supports and Job Retention.

Inge, K. (2001). Supported employment for individuals with physical disabilities. In P. Wehman (Ed.), *Supported employment in business: Expanding the capacity of workers with disabilities* (pp. 153–180). St. Augustine, FL: Training Resource Network.

Inge, K.J., Moon, M.S., & Parent, W. (1993). Applied behavior analysis in supported employment settings. *Journal of Vocational Rehabilitation, 3*(3), 53–60.

Inge, K.J., & Tilson, G. (1997). Ensuring support systems that work: Getting beyond the natural supports versus. job coach controversy. *Journal of Vocational Rehabilitation, 9*(2), 133–142.

Karoly, P. (1977). Behavioral self-management in children: Concepts, methods, issues, and directions. In M. Hersen, R.M. Eisler, & P.M. Miller (Eds.), *Progress in behavior modification* (Vol. 5, pp. 197–262). San Diego: Academic Press.

Kazdin, A.E. (1984). *Behavior modification in applied settings* (3rd ed.). Hometown, IL: Dorsey Press.

Keyser-Marcus, L., Briel, L., Sherron-Targett, P., Yasuda, S., Johnson, S., & Wehman, P. (2002). Enhancing the schooling of students with traumatic brain injury. *Teaching Exceptional Children, 34*(4), 62–67.

Kreutzer, J.S., & Wehman, P. (Eds.). (1990). *Community integration following traumatic brain injury.* Baltimore: Paul H. Brookes Publishing Co.

Moon, M.S., Inge K.J., Wehman, P., Brooke, V., & Barcus, J.M. (1990). *Helping persons with severe mental retardation get and keep employment: Supported employment issues and strategies.* Baltimore: Paul H. Brookes Publishing Co.

Penn, C., & Cleary, J. (1988). Compensatory strategies in the language of closed head-injured patients. *Brain Injury, 2*(1), 3–17.

Shafer, M.S., & Brooke, V. (1985). The development of punctuality in a mentally retarded worker through self-recording. In P. Wehman & J. Hill (Eds.), *Competitive employment for persons with mental retardation: From research to practice* (Vol. 1, pp. 416–428). Richmond: Virginia Commonwealth University Rehabilitation Research and Training Center on Workplace Supports and Job Retention.

Shapiro, E.S. (1981). Self-control procedures with the mentally retarded. In M. Hersen, R.M. Eisler, & P.M. Miller (Eds.), *Progress in behavior modification* (Vol. 12, pp. 265–297). San Diego: Academic Press.

Snell, M., & Gast, D.L. (1981). Applying delay procedures to the instruction of the severely handicapped. *Journal of The Association of the Severely Handicapped, 5*(4), 3–14.

Sowers, J.-A., & Powers, L. (1991). *Vocational preparation and employment of students with physical and multiple disabilities.* Baltimore: Paul H. Brookes Publishing Co.

Storey, K., & Certo, N.J. (1996). Natural supports for increasing integration in the workplace for people with disabilities: A review of the literature and guidelines for implementation. *Rehabilitation Counseling Bulletin, 40,* 62–76.

Storey, K., & Garff, J. (1997). The cumulative effect of natural support strategies and social skills instruction on the integration of a worker in supported employment. *Journal of Vocational Rehabilitation, 9*(2), 143–152.

Test, D.W., Grossi, T., & Keul, P. (1988). A functional analysis of the acquisition and maintenance of janitorial skills in competitive work setting. *Journal of The Association for Persons with Severe Handicaps, 13,* 1–7.

Unger, D., Parent, W., Gibson, K., Kane-Johnston, K., & Kregel, J. (1998). An analysis of the activities of employment specialists in a natural support approach to supported employment. *Focus on Autism and Other Developmental Disabilities, 13*(1), 27–38.

Wehman, P. (Ed.). (2001). *Supported employment in business: Expanding the capacity of workers with disabilities.* St. Augustine, FL: Training Resource Network.

Wehman, P., Sale, P., & Parent, W. (1992). *Supported employment: Strategies for integration of workers with disabilities.* Boston: Andover Medical Publishers.

Zivolich, S., Shueman, S., & Weiner, J. (1997). An exploratory cost–benefit analysis of natural support strategies in the employment of people with severe disabilities. *Journal of Vocational Rehabilitation, 8*(3), 211–221.

Chapter 8

Systematic Instruction
for Applied Behavior Analysis

Supporting People with
Significant Disabilities in Community Jobs

Dennis H. Reid and Carolyn W. Green

The benefits of community-based employment for people with developmental disabilities have become readily apparent. Increased income, enhanced social integration and acceptance, and improved job satisfaction are all common outcomes of community-based employment (Wehman & Kregel, 1995). In short, working in real jobs in typical communities is now a well-recognized component of a desirable quality of life for people with developmental disabilities.

Although the advantages of community-based employment have become well established, the benefits of working in community jobs have not been experienced proportionally across the population of people with developmental disabilities. In particular, individuals who have highly significant disabilities have experienced far fewer opportunities to work in community jobs than people with less serious disabilities. People with severe or profound intellectual disabilities, for example, generally represent less than 10% of individuals in supported employment (Mank, Cioffi, & Yovanoff, 1998). An even smaller number of people who have severe multiple disabilities (e.g., severe intellectual and physical disabilities) work in community jobs (Kregel, 1995). Most people with the latter types of disabilities work in segregated settings of a congregate nature or do not work at all (Reid, Parsons, & Green, 2001).

The relative lack of participation of people with highly significant disabilities in community-based employment is due to a number of reasons, including untrained staff, attitudes of businesses and the community, Social Security disincentives, fear of loss of health care, and transportation issues. Nonetheless, there is now convincing evidence that, with proper support, people who have among the most severe disabilities can successfully work in community jobs to varying degrees (e.g., Mautz, Storey, & Certo, 2001). There is also evidence that when people with highly significant disabilities obtain community-based employment, they experience beneficial outcomes similar to people with less serious disabilities, especially relative to spending their weekdays in segregated day treatment settings of a congregate nature (Reid, Green, & Parsons, 1998).

Proclaiming that people who have among the most severe disabilities can work in community jobs if provided appropriate support often evokes controversy among practitioners and service providers. Essentially, stating that successful work experience is a function of adequate support provision represents an assertion that cannot be proven false. If community work is unsuccessful for an individual, then it can simply be claimed that the lack of success was due to inadequate support. The reasoning continues that if appropriate support had been provided, then the work experience would have been more likely to succeed. This type of circular reasoning has left many practitioners who work with people with highly significant disabilities frustrated and skeptical about involving this population in community jobs.

If more people with highly significant disabilities are to obtain and maintain community employment, then additional information will be needed for practitioners beyond the general assertion that success in community work is a function of appropriate support; precisely what is meant by *appropriate support* must be specified. Human services and related personnel attempting to involve individuals with highly significant disabilities in community jobs must be given specific tools that translate into effective support. Information is needed regarding specifically what should be done to assist an individual with highly significant disabilities to function successfully in a community job.

In addition to translating "support" into specific actions, practitioners and their customers will benefit most if those actions are *evidence based*, which means that actions to enhance work involvement are based on research that demonstrates the effectiveness of the actions (e.g., McDonnell & O'Neill, 2003). Procedures that have an evidence base to support their effectiveness increase the likelihood that the procedures will prove successful when applied by practitioners relative to procedures for which there is no supporting evidence.

One means of providing support for people with severe disabilities that consists of specific procedures and an underlying evidence base is the application of behavior analysis (Becker-Cottrill, McFarland, & Anderson, 2003; Bird & Luiselli, 2000; Gardner, Bird, Maguire, Carreiro, & Abenaim, 2003). Applied behavior analysis (ABA) is a research-based discipline that focuses on understanding and improving human behavior (Cooper, Heron, & Heward, 1987). Relying on principles of learning and behavior change established through systematic research, ABA focuses on applying those learning and behavior change principles to improve behavior in socially relevant contexts. The purpose of this chapter is to describe how ABA can enhance community-based employment among people who have highly significant disabilities.

ETHEL

Ethel is an older adult with many challenges. She has severe intellectual disabilities, does not speak, has partial use of her hands, and uses an electric wheelchair for mobility. Ethel is also very opinionated, expressing her likes and dislikes through distinct facial gestures, loud utterances, laughter, and physical refusal to participate in certain activities. By asking Ethel a series of yes/no questions, it became clear to people who knew her well that she desired to work in a real job outside of her residence. A part-time job performing clerical duties was obtained in a small publishing company.

On-the-job behavioral teaching sessions were provided to teach Ethel relevant job skills, supplemented with brief but intensive teaching sessions on how to perform specific work tasks that were conducted at times when Ethel was not at work. While on the job, Ethel performed some duties readily, whereas with other job duties she required considerable job coach assistance and periodically refused to complete her assigned tasks. Following a series of behavioral preference assessments on the job, several distinct work-related preferences were identified. Her job routine was then altered to allow her to work in a preferred location at the job (an office separate from other supported workers with disabilities) with a preferred job coach. Following the work alterations, Ethel worked with minimal assistance, rarely refused to complete tasks, and often laughed and indicated enjoyment with her work and interactions. On her seventy-third birthday, Ethel celebrated 7 continuous years of part-time employment at the publishing company.

Initial applications of behavior analysis to the work performance of individuals with developmental disabilities occurred in sheltered work situations in the 1960s and 1970s (see Whitman, Scibak, & Reid, 1983). As increased national attention was directed to supporting people with disabilities in community jobs, behavior analysis applications were then extended to community work situations (Luecking, Fabian, & Tilson, 2004; Rusch & Hughes, 1989; Wehman, 2001). For the most part, the latter extensions involved workers with mild or moderate disabilities (Mautz et al., 2001). More recently, applications of behavior analysis have begun to address means of supporting people with more significant disabilities in community-based jobs. The latter applications of behavior analysis represent the focus of this chapter.

Before discussing how principles and procedures of ABA can be used to support people with highly significant disabilities in community-based employment, clarification is warranted regarding what is meant by people who have highly significant disabilities. For purposes here, *highly significant disabilities* refer to severe and profound intellectual disabilities. In addition, the term refers to individuals who have challenges beyond intellectual disabilities, including severe autism, sensory and/or physical disabilities, and challenging or problem behavior (e.g., aggression, self-injury, property destruction). People with these types of disabilities arguably require the most support, and the most specialized support, to successfully participate in community-based employment. These are also individuals for whom behavior analysis applications are usually most needed in the workplace if the individuals are to succeed in community-based employment.

It is far beyond the scope of this chapter to provide an in-depth discussion of the entire range of principles and practices of ABA as they relate to supporting people with developmental disabilities in work situations. As just indicated, behavioral procedures have been used in vocational contexts with people with disabilities for many years. Hence, the focus here is on several recent advances in ABA that are particularly relevant in regard to community-based employment for people with highly significant disabilities. Three areas of relevance will be addressed: 1) matching job tasks to individual preferences, 2) increasing independent performance on the job, and 3) overcoming challenging behavior.

MATCHING JOB TASKS TO INDIVIDUAL PREFERENCES

A central premise of supported employment has always been that attention should be directed to the work-related preferences of individuals with disabilities when identifying potential jobs (Luecking et al., 2004; Wehman, Revell, & Brooke, 2003; West &

Parent, 1992). Matching jobs to the work-related preferences of supported workers is also a component of supported employment legislation (West, 1995). Helping workers with disabilities obtain jobs they prefer relative to jobs they do not prefer has strong logical appeal—most workers, regardless of whether they have disabilities, would rather spend their work time engaging in work duties that they like relative to duties that they do not like (Wehmeyer & Gragoudas, 2004).

In addition to the logical appeal of matching jobs to individual worker preferences, applied behavior analytic research has demonstrated several more specific benefits of determining supported worker job assignments based on identified work preferences. Initially, research with people with severe disabilities in sheltered work situations demonstrated that workers tend to spend more time engaging in desired work behavior when given opportunities to work on preferred work tasks relative to working on nonpreferred work tasks (Bambara, Ager, & Koger, 1994; Parsons, Reid, Reynolds, & Bumgarner, 1990). Similar effects were subsequently demonstrated in community-based, supported work situations (Parsons, Reid, & Green, 2001). As will be discussed later, matching work duties to work preferences is also a primary component of a behavior analytic approach for preventing and reducing challenging behavior that occurs among some workers with highly significant disabilities.

In light of the benefits of working on preferred versus nonpreferred jobs, it is highly recommended that efforts be made to identify work-related preferences before determining job placements; however, special consideration is warranted regarding how to identify preferences for people who have highly significant disabilities. Traditional methods for assessing work preferences used with supported workers who have less serious disabilities often are not suitable for people with highly significant disabilities (Parsons, Reid, & Green, 1998). The latter individuals often lack the necessary communication skills to express preferences in a manner required by traditional assessment procedures (Wehman, 2001).

Although research to date has not demonstrated means of accurately identifying preferences among people with highly significant disabilities across entire jobs, research has validated means of identifying preferences for specific work tasks that comprise important parts of jobs (Parsons et al., 1998). Because the specific tasks that a worker is expected to perform as part of a job represent a significant part of the overall job, it can be quite valuable to determine what tasks a worker prefers when attempting to find a suitable job placement.

The most common means of identifying work-task preferences among people with highly significant disabilities involves a systematic item/activity choice-sampling process. A potential worker is provided repeated opportunities to choose from two or more work materials that are necessary to complete respective job tasks and then provided instructional assistance to work with the materials to perform the chosen task for a few minutes. This process is then repeated until all relevant items/activities have been offered for choice with all other items/activities on at least three occasions. Subsequently, the items/activities chosen most often by the worker across all choice opportunities represent the most preferred work tasks. Generally, those items/activities that are chosen on 70% or more of the opportunities represent most preferred work tasks, and those chosen less than 50% of opportunities represent least preferred work tasks (Lattimore, Parsons, & Reid, 2003). Descriptions for how to conduct these types of systematic preference assessments for people with highly significant disabilities are provided elsewhere (e.g., Lohrmann-O'Rourke, Browder, & Brown, 2000).

The item/activity choice-sampling process has proven accurate in predicting work tasks that workers with a variety of severe disabilities prefer to work on as part of their daily job routine. The process has predicted work-task preferences among people with severe and profound intellectual and physical disabilities (Reid, Parsons, & Green, 1998), as well as severe autism (Lattimore, Parsons, & Reid, 2002). The process has also been used successfully with a supported worker with severe multiple disabilities including deafblindness (Parsons et al., 1998).

When conducting systematic preference assessments to determine the types of work tasks that people with highly significant disabilities prefer, several concerns warrant attention. A primary concern is to make sure that preferences identified in pre-work assessments accurately reflect subsequent on-the-job preferences of individual workers.

Concern over the degree to which preferences identified prior to beginning a job accurately match preferences during the regular job routine exists because of difficulty individuals with highly significant disabilities have in generalizing from one situation to another. Typically, the greater the difference between the prework assessment situation and the actual job situation, the more likely it is that preferences identified in the former situation will not be the same as preferences displayed in the latter. Hence, it is critical that prework preference assessments be conducted in a manner that is as similar to a given worker's subsequent job situation as possible. Key components of conducting prework preference assessments that make it likely that preferences identified in the assessment will subsequently represent preferences while on the job include

- Use of the same work materials during the prework assessment that will be used on the job

- Having the regular job coach conduct the prework assessment

- Ensuring that the worker practices using the materials for a few minutes during the assessment in the same way that the materials will be used on the job to perform assigned work tasks

Another concern is that some jobs do not lend themselves to this type of prework assessment. The task sampling process involves presenting potential supported workers with repeated choices of work tasks that constitute a given job. Some jobs involve a large number of different tasks to perform such that it would not be feasible to repeatedly present pairs or groups of all tasks for choice comparisons. In addition, some jobs involve tasks that are difficult to present in a meaningful choice situation because of the abstract nature of the choices presented (see Hanley, Iwata, & Lindberg, 1999). Some tasks are heavily activity oriented and involve different materials and locations (e.g., yard maintenance work). Providing choices for these types of jobs with the choice-sampling format may lack validity in that potential workers with highly significant disabilities can experience difficulties in associating the choices with the actual tasks and locations (Parsons, Reid, & Green, 2001).

With the types of jobs just noted, an alternative means of identifying work-task preferences is through a situational preference assessment that has been used with workers with milder disabilities. In a situational assessment, a worker is given opportunities to work on various job tasks and then the worker is questioned as to which tasks are preferred. Although questioning workers with highly significant disabilities about work preferences can be problematic because of their intellectual and communication challenges, initial research has suggested that situational assessments can be modified for application with these workers (Parsons, Reid, & Green, 2001).

In contrast to asking workers about their task preferences, situational preference assessments can be modified for workers with highly significant disabilities by allowing workers opportunities to work briefly on different tasks and observing their reactions. Such reactions may be the frequency of indices of happiness or enjoyment versus indices of unhappiness (Green & Reid, 1996; Ivancic, Barrett, Simonow, & Kimberly, 1997). Working on tasks that are accompanied by more indices of happiness and/or less indices of unhappiness tend to reflect the tasks that are more preferred (Parsons et al., 2001). In addition, worker performance on different tasks can be systematically observed in that workers tend to work more on preferred tasks than less-preferred tasks, as indicated previously. The occurrence of resistive behavior (i.e., tending to refuse to work) and other types of challenging behavior can also be systematically observed. Generally, individuals show less problem behavior when they are enjoying what they are doing (Reid & Parsons, 2001).

INCREASING INDEPENDENT PERFORMANCE ON THE JOB

Due to the severity and multiplicity of their various challenges, most supported workers with highly significant disabilities require continued support after obtaining a community job in order to perform the job successfully. Often, that support is in the form of assistance in performing tasks by job coaches or other employment specialists. In practice, a frequent problem that arises is that the job coaches perform work tasks for the supported workers. Observations have indicated, for example, that in some work settings involving workers with severe multiple disabilities, support personnel actually perform most of the job tasks that the supported workers are expected to complete (Parsons, Reid, Green, & Browning, 1999).

A seemingly logical solution to this issue is to ensure that staff teach the workers how to perform their work more independently while on the job. In this regard, arguably the most important contribution of ABA in the vocational area is the development of means of teaching people with very severe disabilities how to perform job tasks independently or with minimal assistance. In current practice though, on-the-job teaching of work skills with this population of supported workers has been problematic.

There are a number of reasons why support personnel perform job tasks for workers with highly significant disabilities in contrast to teaching the workers how to perform the tasks themselves. One reason is that many personnel who function as job coaches or in similar roles have not been adequately trained in how to teach people with highly significant or multiple disabilities while on the job. Another reason is that the staff are justifiably concerned that work will not be completed and work placements may be jeopardized if they do not perform work tasks for the supported workers (Wehman et al., 2003).

Behavior analysis research has investigated means of increasing supported worker independence in completing community job tasks by reducing the amount of assistance provided by support staff. One approach involves an alternative application of a common behavioral procedure used in work situations—task analysis (Wehman, 2001; Wehman & Parent, 1996). In contrast to the usual approach of task analyzing a work skill into a series of discrete behaviors to be taught to a potential worker with disabilities as part of a job preparation process, a task analysis is conducted of both the job coach's behavior and the supported worker's behavior involved in completing respective duties (Parsons et al., 1999). An ongoing work situation is observed, and each step necessary to complete a given task is noted. Next, how each step in the task is completed is specified in terms of whether the supported worker completes the step independently, the worker completes the step with assistance from the job coach, or the step is completed entirely by the job coach.

Once the analysis of ongoing worker and job coach support is conducted, then the job coach is assisted in reviewing each step in the work task that is not completed independently by the worker. A decision is then made based on the coach's familiarity with the worker regarding: 1) the likelihood of teaching the worker to perform the step with brief but intensive teaching trials and 2) the likelihood of not being able to quickly teach the skills necessary to perform the step but making the step easier to perform through a physical adaptation of the step or use of an adaptive device or work jig.

Following the task analysis and decision-making process, the work task is altered where possible through physical adaptations, and intensive teaching sessions are conducted for each step that the worker could learn to perform. The teaching is considered intensive because repeated instructional trials are conducted with the one step of concern until the step is mastered by the worker (i.e., in contrast to teaching the entire range of steps that comprise the whole job task). Sometimes the intensive teaching trials are conducted while the supported worker is at the jobsite (Parsons et al., 1999). It is not always possible to provide the intensive teaching while on the job because conducting repeated instructional trials with selected steps of a job task can interfere with the actual job being completed.

Another approach to reducing job coach assistance by providing intensive teaching on specific steps of a job task involves providing the instructional trials when the worker is not at the jobsite. In this alternative off-site/on-site model (Parsons, Reid, Green, & Browning, 2001), the main focus while on the job is completing the necessary work, and some teaching is conducted on the job where possible; however, most teaching is conducted away from the job such that the repeated instructional trials on selected task steps do not interfere with completing the necessary work.

The off-site/on-site model has been demonstrated as a relatively efficient means of reducing job coach assistance when a worker with highly significant disabilities obtains a community job. In one sense though, this approach can be subject to criticism in that it may be viewed as a return to the more traditional "train-and-place" (Langford & Lawson, 1994) approach to vocational services for people with disabilities. In the typical train-and-place approach, the intent was to train work skills to people with disabilities in segregated, nonwork settings and place them in real jobs once they obtained relevant work skills. The problem with the train-and-place approach was that it rarely resulted in individuals with severe disabilities obtaining community jobs (Kemp & Carr, 1995); the individuals usually remained in the nonwork settings indefinitely. The skills taught in the nonwork situation frequently had little to do with what the individuals needed to learn to succeed in a real job.

On closer examination, the off-site/on-site model avoids the problems with the traditional train-and-place model. Most important, off-site training on selected task steps of a job does not begin until the worker is in a community-based job. Hence, job obtainment is not delayed or withheld while teaching is occurring. The off-site training represents a supplement to on-the-job training, not a prerequisite to obtaining a community job. In addition, the off-site/on-site model seems advantageous for people with highly significant disabilities when considering that when these individuals do obtain community-based jobs, it is almost always on a part-time basis (Kregel, Wehman, & Banks, 1989). Instead of spending the nonwork time in traditional day treatment activities that often are of questionable value (Kregel, 1991; Reid et al., 2001), free time can focus on actively assisting the individuals in becoming more independent with their real work duties.

When considering the off-site/on-site model for reducing job coach assistance, special attention is warranted to the degree to which the job skills taught away from the worksite carry over or generalize to the work setting. Problems that people with highly significant disabilities experience in generalizing skills from one setting to another were noted previously; however, if the suggestions for enhancing generalization described with the prework preference assessment are adhered to when conducting off-site training of job skills, then the problems with generalization can be overcome relatively easily.

Another approach to reducing job coach assistance involves a shared-work (Hood, Test, Spooner, & Steele, 1996) or job-carving model (Griffin & Targett, 2001). In the shared-work model, several workers work in a given job, and the duties comprising the job are shared or distributed among various workers. Although much of the focus with this approach has centered on workers with mild disabilities sharing a job with workers who do not have disabilities (Mank, Cioffi, & Yovanoff, 1999), the approach has also proven helpful with workers with highly significant disabilities (Parsons, Reid, Green, Browning, & Hensley, 2002).

Applying the shared-work approach to workers with highly significant disabilities involves a task-analysis approach in order to assess how a respective job is being completed in the same manner as described previously (i.e., determining parts of a job that supported workers are performing independently or with job coach assistance versus which parts are being completed by the coaches). Following the analysis, different parts of the job are reassigned across several supported workers in a work crew or enclave such that workers are expected to perform only those task steps for which they are already independent. The intent is to combine independently completed steps across workers such that when taken as a whole, the steps function to complete the entire job. In cases in which every step cannot be reassigned such that all steps will be completed independently across workers because some steps cannot be completed by any worker, the shared-work model can be supplemented by the procedures described previously involving either on- or off-site intensive teaching of specific task steps with one or more workers.

OVERCOMING CHALLENGING BEHAVIOR

Similar to applications of ABA to teach work-related skills to people with developmental disabilities, behavioral procedures for overcoming challenging behavior have existed for years; however, how behavioral principles have been applied and the range of behavior change procedures available for preventing and reducing challenging behavior have broadened significantly. Beginning in the 1980s, a major development occurred within ABA that has significant implications for overcoming challenging behavior among people with highly significant disabilities in community jobs. Essentially, behavioral research and application began to refocus on understanding the motivation for an individual's display of problem behavior and designing treatment plans relevant to the motivating factors for the behavior. Although behavior analysis from its inception concentrated on the variables that tended to motivate an individual's behavior, in routine practice that attention often became a secondary concern. When an individual displayed challenging behavior of a serious nature, such as aggression or self-injury, the primary focus among behavioral practitioners was on changing or stopping the behavior. As long as the problem behavior was substantially reduced, relatively little attention was directed to the individual's motivation, or reason, for engaging in the behavior.

Currently, recommended practice in ABA requires careful attention to the variables that occasion the problem behavior of concern. Recommended practice calls for the design of interventions that relate to the individual's motivation for the behavior. There is a growing evidence base as well as professional consensus that interventions for reducing challenging behavior are more likely to be effective if the behavior change procedures take into account an individual's motivation for the behavior (Scotti & Kennedy, 2000). In essence, the intent is to empirically determine the reason for the problem behavior and then design intervention programs such that the individual no longer has a reason to engage in the problematic behavior.

Before summarizing advances in developing treatment plans for challenging behavior based on an individual's motivation for the behavior, two related developments that are also relevant to community employment for people with highly significant disabilities warrant mention. The first development is the growing field of positive behavior support. *Positive behavior support* is defined by the application of positive behavioral interventions and systems to achieve socially significant behavior change among people with developmental disabilities and challenging behavior (Sugai et al., 2000). A key component of positive behavior support is ABA, which in large part represents the science on which positive behavior support is based. ABA also forms the basis for many of the procedural applications of a positive behavior support approach. Positive behavior support, however, is broader than ABA. This approach to overcoming challenging behavior among people with disabilities openly espouses certain values that are closely aligned with the underlying values of supported employment.

Positive behavior support focuses on assisting people with disabilities in functioning in typical societal settings with people who do not have disabilities (Hieneman & Dunlap, 2000), just as supported employment focuses on workers with disabilities working alongside workers without disabilities in real jobs. Positive behavior support is also grounded in a person-centered philosophy (Wehman, Everson, & Reid, 2001) that attempts to give an individual with disabilities as much control and choice as possible over his or her life, including the selection of type and place of employment.

It is becoming increasingly apparent that applications of behavior analysis for overcoming challenging behavior in the workplace are likely to be better accepted among practitioners, individuals with disabilities, and society at large if they are practiced within a positive behavior support paradigm. Behavior analysis applications are arguably also likely to be more effective if used within the context of positive behavior support. A number of sources are now available that describe use of behavior analytic procedures in accordance with the values and practices of positive behavior support (Becker-Cottrill et al., 2003; Bird & Luiselli, 2000; Carr et al., 2002; Gardner et al., 2003). Curricula are likewise becoming available for training service providers and direct-support staff in positive behavior support (Reid, Parsons, Rotholz, Braswell, & Morris, 2004). This chapter's discussion on using ABA to overcome challenging behavior among people with highly significant disabilities in community jobs is presented within a positive behavior support framework.

A second development related to advances in ABA pertains to the *prevention* of challenging behavior in the workplace. Although much more behavioral research has addressed treating challenging behavior once it occurs than preventing its occurrence, understanding ways to prevent such behavior from occurring has also improved. In particular, it is becoming more recognized that if people with disabilities are working on jobs that they prefer relative to jobs obtained without regard to individual worker preferences, challenging behavior is less likely to be a concern. This is one reason that an emphasis should be placed on prework assessment of worker preferences prior to finalizing job placements, as discussed previously.

There are several general approaches to assessing the motivational variables for challenging behavior and designing relevant treatment approaches. Probably the most widely used approach, and one that is readily applicable in work settings, is the antecedent-behavior-consequence (ABC) model (Iwata, Kahng, Wallace, & Lindberg, 2000). The ABC model has long been used within behavior analysis for understanding the variables accounting for a behavior's occurrence and for promoting desired behavior change in applied settings. This approach begins with carefully identifying the behavior of concern and then identifying antecedents and consequences that coincide with the behavior's occurrence. The antecedents refer to environmental events that tend to occur just before the behavior and are considered to occasion the behavior. The consequences refer to what happens right after or as a result of the behavior and are likely to maintain the behavior's occurrence.

There are two general applications of the ABC model within job situations. The first is to apply the model to promote desirable work-related behavior, including working productively on a job task and acting in accordance with social norms and workplace expectations. The ABC model is an underlying conceptual basis for developing the types of procedures discussed in preceding chapter sections for increasing worker independence.

The second application of the ABC model pertains to reducing challenging behavior that may occur in the workplace. When a worker engages in challenging behavior on the job that can interfere with successful work performance, applications of the ABC model typically begin with attempts to identify antecedents to the problem behavior. Any number of events can occasion challenging behavior on the job including, for example, the manner in which task instructions are provided, the behavior of co-workers, changes in the usual job routine, and presentations of nonpreferred work tasks.

Once likely antecedents to the problem behavior of concern are identified, the intent is to either alter the antecedents such that they no longer occasion the problem behavior or remove the antecedents altogether. Antecedents may be altered in a variety of ways, including changing the way instructions are provided such as by slowing the pace of instructions, changing certain behavior of co-workers, providing cues as to pending changes in the work routine, and altering a job task to make it more preferred. Allowing a worker to work in a location separate from a co-worker whose behavior serves as an antecedent for the worker's problem behavior is a common example of removing an antecedent to a problem behavior.

JEFF

Jeff worked in a consulting firm on a part-time basis performing clerical duties. Jeff had profound intellectual disabilities, walked for only short distances without assistance, and did not speak. Although Jeff was proficient in performing his assigned duties with relatively minimal assistance from a job coach, he often refused to complete certain tasks and repeatedly stomped his foot and slammed the table with his fist. Observations indicated his work refusal and problem behavior usually followed instructions to perform work at a table in the center of a workroom.

Following reports from some of Jeff's friends that he enjoyed looking at cars and trucks, a preference assessment was conducted on the job that involved comparing preferences for performing his work in different locations at the firm's offices. The preference assessment indicated that Jeff preferred completing tasks at a workstand next to a window (which allowed him opportunities to watch vehicles on a road that was visible from the window). Jeff's work area was then moved beside the window. Subsequently, Jeff rarely refused to complete his assignments and stopped stomping his foot and pounding the table.

Changing or removing antecedent events can be an effective means of overcoming challenging behavior and is an important focus of positive behavior support applications; however, often a more powerful means of reducing or eliminating challenging behavior is by changing the consequences to the behavior. The first step in overcoming problem behavior from a consequence perspective is to determine what consequence typically results from the behavior of concern. Systematic observations using the ABC model represent one approach to identifying existing consequences for problem behavior. There are also several other *functional assessment* instruments (Targett & Armstrong, 2002) and procedures that have been developed for determining the naturally occurring consequences of problem behavior (see Iwata et al., 2000, for a summary).

Functional assessments are used to identify consequences for challenging behavior in order to determine what function the behavior serves for an individual. In work situations, challenging behavior typically serves one of two functions: 1) the behavior functions to get something the worker wants, or 2) the behavior functions to allow the worker to get out of something that is unwanted. These two functions relate to two basic principles of human behavior that are central to ABA. The first principle is positive reinforcement, in which a behavior's occurrence increases as a result of the behavior obtaining something for the worker. A common example is a worker acting inappropriately in order to obtain social attention from a co-worker or job coach. The second principle is negative reinforcement, in which a behavior's occurrence increases as a result of the behavior discontinuing something undesired by the worker. A typical example is a worker who destroys work materials in order to avoid, or escape from, having to perform a particular job task.

Once a functional assessment provides information regarding the likely function of a problem behavior in the workplace, then a treatment plan can be devised to help overcome the behavior. The plan should be based on the identified function whenever possible. For example, if the function of the behavior appears to be to obtain social attention, then the plan might call for increased attention from the job coach or co-workers when the worker is appropriately performing work (e.g., praising work performance) or at other times such as during work breaks. In this manner, the supported worker can receive desired attention without resorting to inappropriate work behavior. Alternatively, if the problem behavior serves to allow the worker to avoid having to work on a task, then the plan may involve making the task more desirable for the worker or, if possible, changing the assigned work task altogether.

Procedures for reducing challenging behavior maintained by positive and negative reinforcement have proliferated in recent years. The procedures are far too numerous to sufficiently describe here, and the interested reader is referred to existing summaries (e.g., Becker-Cottrill et al., 2003; Carr et al., 2002; Carr, Coriaty, & Dozier, 2000). It may be helpful, though, to note a general guideline for designing plans to overcome challenging behavior based on the function that the behavior serves for an individual worker. The guideline has two components. First, when a worker begins to display problem behavior in the workplace, attempts should be made to answer the question of what the behavior seems to be achieving for the worker. Second, attempts should be made to find a way for the worker to achieve the outcome identified by answering the first question without resorting to problem behavior. Persistence in adhering to this guideline often can have a major effect on helping a worker overcome problem behavior.

CONCLUSION

ABA represents one of many types of support often needed for individuals with highly significant disabilities to succeed in community-based employment. Due in large part to the specificity of its procedures and the underlying evidence base of the procedures, this approach to workplace support is often both practical and effective. To date, behavior analytic approaches have made important advances in matching supported workers who have highly significant disabilities with job duties that they prefer, reducing the amount of job coach assistance typically provided for these workers to successfully complete their work duties, and overcoming challenging behavior that occurs among some workers with highly significant disabilities. Continued research and application with behavior analysis may help many more workers with highly significant disabilities experience the desirable outcomes associated with obtaining and maintaining a community job.

REFERENCES

Bambara, L.M., Ager, C., & Koger, F. (1994). The effects of choice and task preference on the work performance of adults with severe disabilities. *Journal of Applied Behavior Analysis, 27,* 555–556.

Becker-Cottrill, B., McFarland, J., & Anderson, V. (2003). A model of positive behavioral support for individuals with autism and their families. *Focus on Autism and Other Developmental Disabilities, 18*(2), 113–123.

Bird, F.L., & Luiselli, J.K. (2000). Positive behavioral support of adults with developmental disabilities: Assessment of long-term adjustment and habilitation following restrictive treatment histories. *Journal of Behavior Therapy and Experimental Psychiatry, 31*(1), 5–20.

Carr, E.G., Dunlap, G., Horner, R.H., Hoegel, R.L., Turnbull, A.P., Sailor, W., et al. (2002). Positive behavior support: Evolution of an applied science. *Journal of Positive Behavior Interventions, 4*(1), 4–17.

Carr, J.E., Coriaty, S., & Dozier, C.L. (2000). Current issues in the function-based treatment of aberrant behavior in individuals with developmental disabilities. In J. Austin & J.E. Carr (Eds.), *Handbook of applied behavior analysis* (pp. 113–135). Reno, NV: Context Press.

Cooper, J.O., Heron, T.E., & Heward, W.L. (1987). *Applied behavior analysis.* Columbus, OH: Charles E. Merrill Publishing.

Gardner, R.M., Bird, F.L., Maguire, H., Carreiro, R., & Abenaim, N. (2003). Intensive positive behavior supports for adolescents with acquired brain injury: Long-term outcomes in community settings. *Journal of Head Trauma Rehabilitation, 18*(1), 52–74.

Green, C.W., & Reid, D.H. (1996). Defining, validating, and increasing indices of happiness among people with profound multiple disabilities. *Journal of Applied Behavior Analysis, 29,* 67–78.

Griffin, C., & Targett, P.S. (2001). Finding jobs for young people with disabilities. In P. Wehman (Ed.), *Life beyond the classroom: Transition strategies for young people with disabilities* (3rd ed., pp. 171–198). Baltimore: Paul H. Brookes Publishing Co.

Hanley, G.P., Iwata, B.A., & Lindberg, J.S. (1999). Analysis of activity preferences as a function of differential consequences. *Journal of Applied Behavior Analysis, 32,* 419–435.

Hieneman, M., & Dunlap, G. (2000). Factors affecting the outcomes of community-based behavioral support: I. Identification and description of factor categories. *Journal of Positive Behavior Interventions, 2,* 161–169.

Hood, E.L., Test, D.W., Spooner, F., & Steele, R. (1996). Paid coworker support for individuals with severe and multiple disabilities. *Education and Training in Mental Retardation and Developmental Disabilities, 31,* 251–265.

Ivancic, M.T., Barrett, G.T., Simonow, A., & Kimberly, A. (1997). A replication to increase happiness indices among some people with profound multiple disabilities. *Research in Developmental Disabilities, 18,* 79–89.

Iwata, B.A., Kahng, S.W., Wallace, M.D., & Lindberg, J.S. (2000). The functional analysis model of behavioral assessment. In J. Austin & J.E. Carr (Eds.), *Handbook of applied behavior analysis* (pp. 61–89). Reno, NV: Context Press.

Kemp, D.C., & Carr, E.G. (1995). Reduction of severe problem behavior in community employment using a hypothesis-driven multicomponent intervention approach. *Journal of The Association for Persons with Severe Handicaps, 20,* 229–247.

Kregel, J. (1991). Introduction to the issue. *Journal of Vocational Rehabilitation, 1,* 6–7.

Kregel, J. (1995). Personal and functional characteristics of supported employment participants with severe mental retardation. *Journal of Vocational Rehabilitation, 5,* 221–231.

Kregel, J., Wehman, P., & Banks, P.D. (1989). The effects of consumer characteristics and type of employment model on individual outcomes in supported employment. *Journal of Applied Behavior Analysis, 22,* 407–415.

Langford, C.A., & Lawson, S. (1994). Changes in assessment procedures for supported employment. *Assessment in Rehabilitation and Exceptionality, 1,* 307–322.

Lattimore, L.P., Parsons, M.B., & Reid, D.H. (2002). A prework assessment of task preferences among adults with autism beginning a supported job. *Journal of Applied Behavior Analysis, 35,* 85–88.

Lattimore, L.P., Parsons, M.B., & Reid, D.H. (2003). Assessing preferred work among adults with autism beginning supported jobs: Identification of constant and alternating task preferences. *Behavioral Interventions, 18,* 161–177.

Lohrmann-O'Rourke, S., Browder, D.M., & Brown, F. (2000). Guidelines for conducting socially valid systematic preference assessments. *Journal of The Association for Persons with Severe Handicaps, 25,* 42–53.

Luecking, R.G., Fabian, E.S., & Tilson, G.P. (2004). *Working relationships: Creating career opportunities for job seekers with disabilities through employer partnerships.* Baltimore: Paul H. Brookes Publishing Co.

Mank, D., Cioffi, A., & Yovanoff, P. (1998). Employment outcomes for people with severe disabilities: Opportunities for improvement. *Mental Retardation, 36,* 205–216.

Mank, D., Cioffi, A., & Yovanoff, P. (1999). Impact of coworker involvement with supported employees on wage and integration outcomes. *Mental Retardation, 37,* 383–394.

Mautz, D., Storey, K., & Certo, N. (2001). Increasing integrated workplace social interactions: The effects of job modification, natural supports, adaptive communication instruction, and job coach training. *Journal of The Association for Persons with Severe Handicaps, 26,* 257–269.

McDonnell, J., & O'Neill, R. (2003). A perspective on single/within subject research methods and "scientifically based research." *Research and Practice for Persons with Severe Disabilities, 28,* 138–142.

Parsons, M.B., Reid, D.H., & Green, C.W. (1998). Identifying work preferences prior to supported work for an individual with multiple severe disabilities including deaf-blindness. *Journal of The Association for Persons with Severe Handicaps, 23,* 329–333.

Parsons, M.B., Reid, D.H., & Green, C.W. (2001). Situational assessment of task preferences among adults with multiple severe disabilities in supported work. *Journal of The Association for Persons with Severe Handicaps, 26,* 50–55.

Parsons, M.B., Reid, D.H., Green, C.W., & Browning, L.B. (1999). Reducing job coach assistance provided to supported workers with severe multiple disabilities. *Journal of The Association for Persons with Severe Handicaps, 24,* 292–297.

Parsons, M.B., Reid, D.H., Green, C.W., & Browning, L.B. (2001). Reducing job coach assistance for supported workers with severe multiple disabilities: An alternative off-site/on-site model. *Research in Developmental Disabilities, 21,* 151–164.

Parsons, M.B., Reid, D.H., Green, C.W., Browning, L.B., & Hensley, M.B. (2002). Evaluation of a shared-work program for reducing assistance provided to supported workers with severe multiple disabilities. *Research in Developmental Disabilities, 23,* 1–16.

Parsons, M.B., Reid, D.H., Reynolds, J., & Bumgarner, M. (1990). Effects of chosen versus assigned jobs on the work performance of persons with severe handicaps. *Journal of Applied Behavior Analysis, 23,* 253–258.

Reid, D.H., Green, C.W., & Parsons, M.B. (1998). A comparison of supported work versus center-based program services on selected outcomes for individuals with multiple severe disabilities. *Journal of The Association for Persons with Severe Handicaps, 23,* 69–76.

Reid, D.H., & Parsons, M.B. (2001). *Working with staff to overcome challenging behavior among people who have severe disabilities: A guide for getting support plans carried out.* Morganton, NC: Habilitative Management Consultants.

Reid, D.H., Parsons, M.B., & Green, C.W. (1998). Identifying work preferences among individuals with severe multiple disabilities prior to beginning supported work. *Journal of Applied Behavior Analysis, 31,* 281–285.

Reid, D.H., Parsons, M.B., & Green, C.W. (2001). Evaluating the functional utility of congregate day treatment activities for adults with severe disabilities. *American Journal on Mental Retardation, 106,* 460–469.

Reid, D.H., Parsons, M.B., Rotholz, D.A., Braswell, B.A., & Morris, L. (2004). *Positive behavior support training curriculum: Direct support edition.* Washington, DC: American Association on Mental Retardation.

Rusch, F.R., & Hughes, C. (1989). Overview of supported employment. *Journal of Applied Behavior Analysis, 22,* 351–363.

Scotti, J.R., & Kennedy, C.H. (2000). Introduction to issues in the application of functional assessment. *Journal of The Association for Persons with Severe Handicaps, 25,* 195–196.

Sugai, G., Horner, R.H., Dunlap, G., Hieneman, M., Lewis, T.J., Nelson, C.M., et al. (2000). Applying positive behavior support and functional behavioral assessment in schools. *Journal of Positive Behavior Interventions, 2,* 131–143.

Targett, P., & Armstrong, A. (2002). Assessment for transition. In P. Wehman (Ed.), *Individual transition plans: The teacher's guide for helping youth with special needs* (2nd ed., pp. 37–56). Austin, TX: PRO-ED.

Wehman, P. (2001). *Supported employment in business: Expanding the capacity of workers with disabilities.* St. Augustine, FL: TRIN Publishing.

Wehman, P., Everson, J.M., & Reid, D.H. (2001). Beyond programs and placements: Using person-centered practices to individualize the transition process and outcomes. In P. Wehman (Ed.), *Life beyond the classroom: Transition strategies for young people with disabilities* (3rd ed., pp. 91–124). Baltimore: Paul H. Brookes Publishing Co.

Wehman, P., & Kregel, J. (1995). At the crossroads: Supported employment a decade later. *Journal of The Association for Persons with Severe Handicaps, 20,* 286–299.

Wehman, P., & Parent, W. (1996). Supported employment. In P.J. McLaughlin & P. Wehman (Eds.), *Mental retardation and developmental disabilities* (2nd ed., pp. 317–338). Austin, TX: PRO-ED.

Wehman, P., Revell, W.G., & Brooke, V. (2003). Competitive employment: Has it become the "first choice" yet? *Journal of Disability Policy Studies, 14*(3), 163–173.

Wehmeyer, M.L., & Gragoudas, S. (2004). Centers for independent living and transition-age youth: Empowerment and self-determination. *Journal of Vocational Rehabilitation, 20*(1), 53–58.

West, M.D. (1995). Choice, self-determination and VR services: Systemic barriers for consumers with severe disabilities. *Journal of Vocational Rehabilitation, 5,* 281–290.

West, M.D., & Parent, W.S. (1992). Consumer choice and empowerment in supported employment services: Issues and strategies. *Journal of The Association for Persons with Severe Handicaps, 17,* 47–52.

Whitman, T.L., Scibak, J.W., & Reid, D.H. (1983). *Behavior modification with the severely and profoundly retarded: Research and application.* San Diego: Academic Press.

Chapter 9

Assistive Technology as a Workplace Support

KATHERINE J. INGE AND PAMELA SHERRON TARGETT

According to the 2004 National Organization on Disability's Harris Survey of Americans with Disabilities, there are 54 million Americans with disabilities, more than half of whom are of working age (18–64). As of October 2004, individuals with disabilities have an employment rate of 35%, compared with 78% for those without disabilities (Bureau of Labor Statistics, 2004). They are three times more likely to live in poverty with annual household incomes below $15,000 (National Organization on Disability, 2004).

People who experience significant physical disabilities usually are challenged by work entry or reentry. Kaye, Kang, and LaPlante (2001) reported that fewer than one fifth of individuals who use wheelchairs or walkers and are of working age are employed. Health issues, transportation, health care costs and other funding disincentives, and personal care needs have been documented as barriers to employment for this group of underemployed or unemployed individuals (Croser, 1999; Wehman et al., 1999).

Reasons for physical disabilities vary and may relate to complications before, during, or soon after birth (e.g., cerebral palsy) or may be caused by a traumatic injury (e.g., spinal cord injury), progressive disease (e.g., multiple sclerosis), or illness (e.g., polio). Often, multiple impairments will coexist. For example, a young man in an automobile accident who sustained a spinal cord injury may also have other disabilities such as a traumatic brain injury. Although the focus of assisting individuals should not be on "fixing" their disabilities, there is a wide range of supports, including assistive technology, that can make life easier and facilitate community inclusion.

Assistive technology can play a major role in bridging the accessibility gap by enhancing a person's abilities in all of life's daily activities to increase independence at home, at work, and in the community. Many workplace challenges can be overcome or at least ameliorated by using assistive technology in combination with other types of workplace supports (Inge, 2001; Inge, Strobel, Wehman, Todd, & Targett, 2000; Inge, Wehman, Kregel, & Sherron-Targett, 1996; Inge, Wehman, Strobel, Powell, & Todd, 1998; Sowers, 1995). This chapter focuses on assistive technology in the workplace and how it can be used to promote the employment of individuals with physical disabilities. The chapter begins with the definition of *assistive technology* and an overview of the most recent legislation, including funding options. Next, a description is provided of how assistive technology can be combined with other workplace supports such as supported employment. Then, case study examples are presented that illustrate how individuals with the most significant physical disabilities have become productive members of their local communities' work force.

ASSISTIVE TECHNOLOGY DEFINED

The most frequently quoted definition of *assistive technology* comes from the Technology-Related Assistance for Individuals with Disabilities Act of 1988 (PL 100-407), which was reauthorized in 1993, 1998, and most recently in 2004. In 1998, the act was renamed the Assistive Technology Act (PL 105-394). This law defines *assistive technology* as any item, piece of equipment, or product system, whether acquired commercially or off the shelf, modified or customized, that increases, maintains or improves functional capabilities of individuals with disabilities. The act also defines *assistive technology services* to mean any services that directly assist an individual with disabilities in the selection, acquisition, or use of an assistive technology device.

The Technology-Related Assistance for Individuals with Disabilities Act allowed states to establish systems to help individuals with disabilities gain access to assistive technology (United Cerebral Palsy, 2004). The Assistive Technology Act of 2004 (PL 108-364) changed this focus to direct aid to individuals (Boehner, 2004). Under the new act, states will be able to apply for grants, and the majority of the funds are to be spent on direct services for individuals with disabilities. States will have the option of using 60% of the state grants to fund assistive technology reutilization programs, assistive technology demonstration programs, alternative financing programs, and device loan programs. Or, states may choose to use 70% of the grants having full discretion on how to allocate the money for at least two, and up to four, of the programs listed previously.

For this chapter, *assistive technology* will be defined as any new, modified, or fabricated device, material, or equipment that increases a person's ability to function and become independent at work. Although the primary focus of the chapter will be on assistive technology, successful employment typically occurs using a mix and interplay of different types of workplace supports and services. This key point will become apparent in the case studies as each exemplifies the versatility and application of assistive technology in combination with other supports.

Assistive technology may be classified as either low or high technology based on a continuum of complexity related to the devices as well as the materials used to produce them. Low-technology devices usually are inexpensive and easy to purchase or fabricate. Materials to make low-technology devices can be found at many generic merchandise stores (e.g., hardware, home improvement, computer stores) or ordered from catalogues. Consider the following low-technology examples:

- A person with unsteady hand movements uses a nonskid mat to stabilize work materials.

- An individual with limited coordination uses a keyguard over a computer keyboard to enable him or her to strike the correct key.

- A person who uses a wheelchair has a reaching device to retrieve items that have fallen to the floor.

Modified items or purchased materials can also produce low-technology solutions. These solutions do not necessarily require specialized training to identify or make and are relatively easy to implement for individuals with disabilities. For example, a stapler could be mounted on a base with a paper guide so that an individual who uses only one hand can staple papers.

High-technology devices are characterized by the use of electronics, special manufacturing techniques, and unique materials. Usually, high-technology devices are obtained through specialized vendors and require an assistive technology service provider such as a rehabilitation engineer; a rehabilitation counselor; or an occupational, physical, or speech-language therapist to acquire and install the accommodation. Acquisition of devices and services is discussed later in the chapter.

Today, there are many new and emerging high technologies. For example, individuals who cannot speak can use augmentative communication devices with synthesized speech. A person with limited vision may "read" by using a computer software program that converts typed words or text into an electronic voice. Or, a person with limited mobility might use any number of high-technology options such as voice-activated software, various input devices, and modified keyboards to enter information into a computer without using a standard keyboard. For instance, a person could gain access to a software program that creates an on-screen keyboard in combination with an alternative input device to "type." These kinds of programs, although once novel, are now becoming available in the mainstream, and individuals without disabilities are taking advantage of technologies such as voice-activated software and computer trackballs.

FUNDING ASSISTIVE TECHNOLOGY

There are a number of public and private options for funding assistive technology services and devices. These potential resources include state grants, as funded through the Assistive Technology Act of 2004; vocational rehabilitation (VR); employers, as mandated under the Americans with Disabilities Act (ADA) of 1990 (PL 101-336); Social Security Work Incentives; Medicaid; private insurance; and other charitable sources such as foundations. Each of these options has specific requirements and guidelines that must be followed in order to gain access to funds for the purchase of assistive technology services and devices.

Assistive Technology Act of 2004

As previously mentioned, the Assistive Technology Act of 1998 has been amended to allow states to apply for grants that will fund direct services for individuals with disabilities. The amended act creates greater accountability for the states on how they use these grants. Each state will be required to submit an application that details the planned activities as well as measurable goals related to education, employment, telecommunication or information technology, and community living. In addition, the programs must be evaluated on an ongoing basis regarding their effectiveness (Boehner, 2004). The potential for alternative financing programs and device loan programs directly to individuals with disabilities has great potential for facilitating community inclusion and employment. Individuals with disabilities should contact their state's assistive technology office or program to determine what supports are available that can assist them in obtaining assistive technology services and devices for employment.

Rehabilitation Act Amendments

Although some individuals with physical disabilities are able to independently conduct a successful job search and advocate for accommodations in the workplace, others cannot. In order for these individuals to join the nation's work force, assistive technology and other workplace supports such as supported employment will be needed (Inge, 2001; Inge et al., 2000). Eligible individuals with disabilities can gain access to these services through their state's VR program funded by the Rehabilitation Act Amendments. The Rehabilitation Act of 1973 (PL 93-112) was the first federal statute to prohibit discrimination in employment against people with disabilities (West, 1991). Reauthorization of the act in 1986 (PL 99-506) included supported employment as a VR strategy (Brooke, Inge, Armstrong, & Wehman, 1997). The act was subsequently amended in 1992 (PL 102-569) and then reauthorized as part of the Workforce Investment Act (WIA) in 1998 (PL 105-220).

The Rehabilitation Act Amendments as part of WIA require each state plan to contain

> [A] description of the methods to be used to expand and improve services to individuals with disabilities, including how a broad range of *assistive technology services and assistive technology devices* will be provided to such individuals at each stage of the rehabilitation process and how such services and devices will be provided to such individuals on a statewide basis. (PL 105-220, Title I, Part A, Sec. 101 [15] [D] [i])

In addition, each individual's individualized plan for employment (IPE) must include a description of the specific services that are to be provided to achieve an employment outcome "including, as appropriate, the provision of *assistive technology devices and assistive technology services,* and personal assistance services, including training in the management of such services" (PL 105-220, Title I, Part A, Sec. 102 [3] [B] [i] [I]).

Individuals with physical disabilities who need vocational supports (i.e., assistive technology, supported employment) must apply and have their cases open to receive these services. When seeking funding from VR for assistive technology, an individual must provide information as to how the technology will be used to achieve an employment outcome. Assistive technology that is needed for independent living also potentially can be paid for under the Independent Living provision of the Rehabilitation Act Amendments.

Under the Rehabilitation Act Amendments of 1992 (PL 102-569), counselors were mandated to provide rehabilitation technology to an individual if it was needed to achieve a person's rehabilitation goals. Technology was exempt from the comparable services and benefits requirement that applied to all other services under the act. The 1998 amendments modified this provision, and comparable sources funding must be sought before VR will purchase assistive technology devices and services. Comparable funding sources could include the individual's private health insurance, Medicaid, the employer as mandated by ADA, and other sources; however, if the search for comparable sources of funding would delay or interrupt the progress of achieving the employment outcome identified in the IPE, then the counselor immediately can provide the service or device (U.S. Department of Education, 1998).

If needed technology is denied or there are delays in its acquisition, then an individual with disabilities does have options. The first is to ask for a meeting with the VR counselor and/or his or her supervisor to determine if a solution can be found. The second is to seek assistance from the Client Assistance Program (CAP). CAP can provide assistance and advocacy for obtaining needed services. All states are mandated to have such programs, and they can provide assistance and advocacy in receiving services that are directly related to the individual's employment.

Americans with Disabilities Act

The provision of assistive technology also may be the responsibility of the business as a reasonable accommodation under the ADA. The law provides equal opportunity for individuals with disabilities in employment, public accommodations, transportation, state and local government services, and telecommunications. The implementation of the ADA can be seen in a number of architectural and equipment modifications such as sidewalk curb cuts to the street, ramps leading into buildings, Braille instructions on ATM machines, picture menus at restaurants, or televisions equipped with closed-captioning decoders.

Title I of the ADA sets requirements and gives guidance to employers to ensure that people with disabilities do not incur discrimination in any aspect of the employment process or work environment (Sec. 102 [A]). Many of the provisions are based on Section 504 of the Rehabilitation Act and its regulations; however, the Rehabilitation Act applies only to entities that receive funding from the federal government. The ADA extends these requirements to most of the private sector and state and local government agencies and programs that they sponsor. Although the primary focus in this chapter is Title I employment provisions, the reader should note that this legislation does not supplant the requirements under any other federal or state laws that prohibit discrimination against individuals with disabilities. Because laws vary widely from state to state, the reader needs to become familiar with those that apply in his or her location.

An employer may be required to provide and pay for a reasonable accommodation to a qualified applicant or worker with disabilities unless undue hardship would result. The ADA defines *reasonable accommodation* as efforts that may include, among other adjustments, making the workplace accessible, restructuring a job to best use a person's skills, modifying work schedules, modifying equipment, adjusting training materials or policies, and providing qualified readers or interpreters (ADA, Sec. 101 [9] [A, B]; Equal Employment Opportunity Commission [EEOC], 1992). The type of accommodation provided is also determined on a case-by-case basis and depends on the person's needs and the possible solutions; however, at no time is the employer required to reduce the productivity expectations.

The applicant/person with disabilities must be able to satisfy the job-related requirements of the position such as educational requirements, training, skills, and experience. He or she also must be able to perform the essential job functions with or without reasonable accommodation. Requiring a person to perform essential functions assures that an individual with disabilities will not be disqualified due to an inability to perform some marginal or incidental job function. In essence, a reasonable accommodation is a change in the way things are typically done that allows the person with disabilities to participate in all aspects of the employment process. This can include the application of assistive technology devices and services. An individual who can perform the essential functions with an accommodation is considered a qualified applicant and cannot be screened out because the individual needs accommodation.

Although the possibilities of accommodations in the workplace can be limitless, the following points should be noted. First, employers are only required to make reasonable job-related accommodations. They are not obligated to provide employees with personal devices and services such as hearing aids, wheelchairs, or augmentative communication devices. A reasonable accommodation, however, may include permitting an individual with disabilities to provide and use equipment, aids, or services that an employer is not required to supply. For example, a person may purchase and use a scooter to travel around the worksite, or a personal assistant hired by the person may provide assistance with eating lunch and taking a restroom break on the jobsite (see Chapter 11).

Second, an employer is obligated to discuss reasonable accommodations with an applicant or employee with disabilities after receiving notification that one may be needed, unless providing the accommodation would impose undue hardship on the employer (ADA, Sec. 101 [10] [A]). Although an employer is required to consider an employee's recommendations for accommodation, any accommodation may be chosen as long as it allows the employee to perform the essential job functions. When choosing between two or more effective accommodations, the employer has the final say and may select the one that is less expensive or less disruptive. Federal regulations suggest that an employer should initiate an "informal, interactive process" with the employee when trying to determine possible accommodations.

If an employer purchases assistive technology as a reasonable accommodation, then the assistive technology belongs to the business. When the employee leaves, the assistive technology ordinarily remains with the owner or company. As previously mentioned, a state's VR agency can also fund assistive technology. Employees with disabilities who have separated from their jobs may request that the state VR department purchase the technology from a former employer or talk with the new employer about purchasing the technology. This would allow the individual to take the technology to the new place of employment. If an employer obtains financial assistance for the purchase of devices or cost shares with VR, then the assistive technology usually belongs to the user.

Resolving Accommodation Issues

Counselors, employment specialists, and other advocates working with individuals with disabilities to obtain employment should take a proactive stance on the issue of undue hardship. Taking a positive, rather than an aggressive, approach to ADA compliance with employers can set the foundation for supporting individuals with disabilities in the workplace. For instance, the individual and his or her advocate should provide information demonstrating how accommodations do not have to be costly. Inge and her colleagues (2000) found that the average cost of an accommodation in their program for individuals with significant physical disabilities was $112.35 per accommodation. This data supports the Job Accommodation Network's (JAN) information, which indicates that most accommodations cost less than $500 each. JAN is a free consulting service designed to increase the employability of people with disabilities by 1) providing individualized worksite accommodations solutions, 2) providing technical assistance regarding the ADA and other disability-related legislation, and 3) educating callers about self-employment options. Additional information on the ADA and accommodations can be obtained from JAN by visiting http://www.jan.wvu.edu/ or calling 800-526-7234.

Most employers will work collaboratively with people with disabilities to resolve accommodation issues; however, if an employer is not meeting his or her duty of reasonable accommodation, there are several places to go for assistance. More information on the ADA can be obtained through the U.S. Department of Justice and the EEOC. The Department of Justice is the primary enforcing entity for civil rights discrimination under the ADA and enforces the ADA's requirements in three areas:

1. Title I: Employment practices by units of state and local government

2. Title II: Programs, services, and activities of state and local government

3. Title III: Public accommodations and commercial facilities (private sector)

The Department of Justice publishes quarterly reports of its enforcement activities that include ADA litigation, formal settlement agreements, other settlements, and mediation. Publications are available at http://www.usdoj.gov/crt/ada/adahom1.htm.

The EEOC enforces Title I provisions prohibiting discrimination in employment against qualified individuals with disabilities. It investigates complaints filed by job applicants or employees who believe that they have been discriminated against under the ADA. The EEOC web site (http://www.eeoc.gov/) has a section on enforcement activities, guidance, and policies.

Tax Incentives for Improving Accessibility

There are two tax incentives for employers to make accommodations (Internal Revenue Service [IRS], 2003). If a business makes access improvements for ADA compliance, then it can use these tax incentives to reduce its federal taxes in the year that the expenses were incurred. One incentive is a tax credit that is subtracted from the business's tax liability after taxes are calculated. The other is a tax deduction that is subtracted as part of determining the business's tax liability (Adaptive Environments Center, 1998).

The tax credit is for small businesses that have revenues of $1 million or less or 30 or fewer full-time employees and can be used for architectural adaptations, equipment acquisitions, and services such as sign language interpreters. The tax deduction can be used for architectural or transportation adaptations by a business of any size. A small business can use the tax credit and the tax deduction together if the expenses qualify.

There are maximum allowed expenses per year for both the tax credit and the tax deduction. Either can be used annually, but expenses may not be carried over from one year to the next. In other words, a business may not claim a credit or deduction for a previous year's expense. Only the costs associated with adaptations or renovations to existing facilities for ADA compliance are allowed under both the tax credit and tax deduction. For more information, request IRS Publication 334, *Tax Guide for Small Business*, and Form 8826, Disabled Access Credit, or gain access to these publications on the IRS web site (http://www.irs.gov). Businesses should be encouraged to consult their accountants or a representative of an IRS office to ensure that all requirements are being met and that the correct tax form is submitted.

State Educational System

Under the Individuals with Disabilities Education Act (IDEA) Amendments of 1991 (PL 102-119), schools have a responsibility to provide assistive technology services and devices to eligible students with disabilities. Individuals with disabilities who need assistive technology devices to facilitate employment outcomes may be eligible to receive funding for assistive technology if specified as part of the student's individualized education program (IEP). Devices and equipment that are purchased by the school system, however, remain the property of the district (Inge & Shepherd, 1995). A student with disabilities who is working or participating in community-based vocational training as part of his or her IEP goals and using equipment purchased by the school system will need to have other long-term funding options explored.

For instance, VR may purchase assistive technology for students who are still in special education and who have been identified as needing VR services for the transition from school to work. IDEA regulations envision other agencies providing services to students in transition, including VR agencies (34 C.F.R. § 300.348). VR regulations require that the state VR plan specify the financial responsibility of the various state agencies serving students with disabilities (§ 361.22[a] [2] [v]).

More specifically, beginning when the student is age 16 (or younger, if appropriate), the IEP must include the transition services that are needed to help him or her prepare for exiting the school program. These transition services can include assistive technology devices and services as specified in the student's IEP. Whenever there is a meeting to consider needed transition services, the school must invite a representative of any other agency that is likely to be responsible for providing or paying for transition services, such as a VR counselor, when a goal is to make the transition from school to work. This individual can help the team plan any transition services that the student needs. He or she can also commit the resources of the agency to pay for or provide needed transition services (U.S. Department of Education, 2005).

For instance, if a graduating student will need assistive technology services and/or devices to obtain and maintain employment, then the VR counselor should be invited to attend meetings to discuss and plan for providing the needed transition services. Depending on the interagency agreements between the school system and the VR agency, a reasonable request may be for VR to pay for the needed assistive technology service or purchase the device. In some states, VR has paid for services that occur during the last 6 months of the student's educational program. Or, the VR agency may be able to purchase a device from the school district when the student graduates. The need for a device must be reflected in the IEP, with reference to the VR agency as payer (or purchaser) of the existing device after the student's graduation. The assistive technology device would also appear in the IPE, which must be developed by the VR agency before the individual finishes school. This type of funding arrangement should be worked out on an individual basis during transition planning.

As an example, a young woman with a grade three traumatic brain injury as a result of a car accident was in her last year of high school. The brain injury resulted in right-side hemiplegia, severe ataxia in her hands, an unsteady gait, severe short-term memory impairment, and a slow speech pattern. One of her IEP transition goals was to be employed upon graduation and included community-based work experiences that reflected her personal interests and skills. During these community experiences, the need for assistive technology to facilitate independence from school personnel became apparent. The school purchased and provided the modifications that were needed during these community-based work experiences.

In the last 6 months of high school, a part-time job was identified at the student's local gym. Work tasks included scanning patrons' membership cards, passing out keys to the lockers, and handing out towels at the front desk. Several modifications needed to be fabricated in order for the student to be independent, including a device to hold the scanner and a Plexiglas container at the front desk to hold keys within her reach. A meeting was held with school representatives, the young woman, her parents, and a representative from the VR agency. The VR agency agreed to pay for the services of a rehabilitation engineer to modify the student's work environment while she was in the last months of her school program. The collaboration between the school system and the VR agency resulted in a part-time paid position during the last year of her school experience.

ASSISTIVE TECHNOLOGY ASSESSMENT

Supported employment services for individuals with physical disabilities should not differ significantly from services and strategies traditionally used by supported employment programs (Inge, 2001). The only difference would be the inclusion of assistive technology services and devices as part of the supports provided for this group of individuals. It is critical to determine what a person wants to do for employment prior to the identification, purchase, or application of technology. The individual should not be evaluated for technology needs prior to determining his or her abilities, interests, and preferences for employment as an employment specialist would learn about any job seeker.

No one individual or professional discipline will possess all of the information available on assistive technology, including software, hardware, and the most recent technology devices available (Inge & Shepherd, 1995). In addition, no one individual will have all of the expertise needed to design, fabricate, or modify existing devices that are needed by an individual for work. Typically, a team approach is needed for assessment purposes, beginning with a group of individuals who know the person well, such as family members, and who will be able to provide information on devices and services already used by the individual. Professionals and other individuals who may have input into the person's technology needs can include rehabilitation professionals (e.g., rehabilitation counselors, rehabilitation engineers), therapists (e.g., speech-language, occupational, and physical therapists), social workers, and teachers, as well as individuals who are carpenters or construction workers.

Employment specialists also can learn to identify, purchase, or fabricate simple workplace accommodations for individuals with disabilities. Caution needs to be taken when purchasing assistive technology for the workplace from catalogues, office supply stores, or other sources. A common temptation may be to "shop" assistive technology catalogues, which can lead to the acquisition of technology that does not match the person's physical needs if the purchaser does not understand the customer's physical capacity.

For instance, there are a wide variety of input devices that can be used for data entry. There are *head pointers* that have the pointer extending from the forehead and others that extend from the chin. Use of these two types of head pointers requires different motor control. There are also high-technology devices that use switch controls and computer software for data entry. These devices require varying levels of motor ability to operate. For example, one high-technology device uses a small dot on the person's forehead with associated computer software and hardware. The individual inputs information by aiming the dot at the computer hardware, which in turn activates the software. An individual who is unable to hold his or her head steady for any length of time may not be very successful with this option.

Therefore, supported employment programs need to establish relationships with the professionals and individuals in the community who provide assistive technology services and devices. The professional who evaluates the person's assistive technology needs is usually linked closely to how the recommended devices will be funded. For instance, a physician must write a prescription for assistive technology services for Medicaid to fund the technology as durable medical equipment. If a device is to be paid for by VR, then a rehabilitation counselor must approve the individual's referral for assistive technology services. For instance, the VR counselor can fund the services of a rehabilitation engineer when a device needs fabricating to meet work goals.

Physical, occupational, and speech-language therapists can provide valuable assistive technology services. Referrals for these services may come from the physician or the rehabilitation counselor. Again, the referral source should correspond to the requirements of the funding agency. The employment specialist may be the individual who recognizes the need for the specific services within the workplace and then assists the individual in obtaining a referral from the appropriate professional.

Remember, whenever possible, evaluations for assistive technology should occur within the workplace to ensure the usefulness of the device. In addition, being able to test out or try a device in the workplace for a brief period of time before purchase can be an invaluable experience. One approach is to establish relationships with various assistive technology vendors in the community. Sometimes devices can be rented, if not borrowed. Also, there may be a lending library for assistive technology associated with a local Center for Independent Living or the state's Assistive Technology Project. In addition, an individual with disabilities may know someone else who also uses the device, or an assistive technology vendor may be able to refer the individual to another user of the same technology. This assistive technology user may be able to share firsthand experiences and give advice on purchase and upkeep.

Purchasing technology without knowing the person's preferences, understanding his or her physical capacity, or seeking the assistance of someone who understands the match between the person and the assistive technology device can result in the acquisition of equipment that is never used. This is not to imply that a person with physical disabilities cannot learn to use various devices. It does emphasize, however, that there needs to be a "best fit" between an individual's physical capacity and a device.

Assessing Functional Capacity

An employment specialist can gain a wealth of information by interviewing and observing a job seeker in the community. Interviews should take place in a setting selected by the job seeker (e.g., the person's home, the local One Stop Career Center, a local restaurant, mall, other community setting). During the initial interview, the employment specialist and job seeker privately meet to discuss work preferences, personal interests, vocational strengths, and support needs (both on and off the job). Although significant others may want to help and should be involved, they should give their input at a later time. Afterward, time is spent together in community settings.

During a visit at the job seeker's home, the employment specialist may get a firsthand view of how the individual uses technology (Inge et al., 2000). This can provide some additional insight into what assistive technology may be helpful in the workplace. For example, a person might answer the telephone and gain access to a computer using a mouth stick. Thus, work opportunities that use this skill may be pursued (e.g., positions as a receptionist or customer-service representative).

Accompanying a job seeker on a community outing, such as meeting at the library to research businesses over the Internet, going to a mall to explore retail jobs, or attending a community event to network with potential employers, provides important information for both parties (Inge et al., 2000). For example, when setting up the appointment to meet, the specialist could learn if the person makes his or her own transportation arrangements. If not, then the job seeker could learn about possible transportation support services. Upon arriving at the desired destination, such as a local shopping mall, the specialist could observe the person while engaged in a number of practical activities such as making purchases, reading letters and numbers, attending to personal care needs outside the home, following directions, orienting to large and small areas, and using his or her hands. Positive feedback from the specialist on abilities may give the job seeker additional insight into his or her vocational strengths and may boost his or her self-esteem.

An informal exploration of various occupations and job tasks in the retail industry could also take place. Consider how much a job seeker could learn while chatting with a worker who is performing the job. For example, the job seeker may learn about the task involved, pace of work, or whether the employee likes working there. More information about possible workplace assistive technology could also be gained. This type of practical assessment of assistive technology needs—one that occurs within the context of "real life" rather than a clinical setting—can help ensure the "usefulness" of the technology and decrease the likelihood of abandonment. In addition, this helps ensure that the job seeker, not the assistive technology, drives the direction of the job search.

It is important to note that not having immediate or specific ideas about assistive technology should not delay the job search. Later on, when a viable job lead is found, assistive technology solutions and other types of workplace supports can be identified (Inge et al. 2000; Inge et al., 1996; Inge et al., 1998; Parent, Unger, & Inge, 1997; Sowers, 1995). This information can then be presented to the employer, either verbally or in writing, using an employment proposal that documents what assistive technology may be needed to get the job done. Also, while waiting to get the assistive technology in place, whether it is being fabricated or purchased, the vocational specialist can provide the necessary assistance to make sure the work is done. For example, a person who was hired as a customer-service representative needed a modified keyboard, track mouse, and automatic page-turner to perform the job independently. While waiting for the technology to be put in place, the specialist turned the pages for the worker and helped maintain production standards by typing in customer contact information while the employee took calls.

ON-THE-JOB SUPPORTS AND ASSISTIVE TECHNOLOGY

Once a job seeker is hired, a variety of different types of workplace supports are either provided for the employee or facilitated by the employment specialist. There are many well-documented strategies for assisting an individual with disabilities to learn new job duties, including the use of natural cues, compensatory strategies, self-management procedures, task analysis, and prompting procedures (Inge, 1997). These strategies, however, are not discussed because the focus of this chapter is on using assistive technology in the workplace. As mentioned previously, assistive technology is only one type of workplace support, and it is the unique mix of workplace supports and strategies that culminates in the "right package of supports," which in turn leads to success at work (Inge, 2001).

Employment Specialist Support

An employment specialist accompanies a new employee to work in order to provide or facilitate whatever supports are needed to help the person succeed. The employment specialist should be thinking about what assistive technology is needed to help the new employee get the job done. Sometimes the effectiveness for the assistive technology suggested in the employment proposal may be confirmed; at other times, new ideas may emerge. Either way, the employment specialist must take the necessary steps to ensure that the new employee is involved in selecting his or her technology. Also, whenever a new idea emerges, employer permission may also need to be obtained, depending on the situation. When the employer's new employee training stops, the employment specialist steps in and provides additional skills training or other services such as selecting assistive technology to aid the worker in learning or performing the job. Once the assistive technology needs are assessed and intervention is designed, the employment specialist helps the business and worker implement accordingly.

Long-Term Follow-Up and Job-Retention Services

Supported employment offers ongoing support to promote success at work. The support required varies from person to person and changes over time. Although some supports may be required on the job, such as those described in the previous section, others will be work related. Over time, the employment specialist's intensive on-the-job assistance is gradually removed as the employee begins to perform the job to meet the employer's standards. For example, after the employee gets the needed assistive technology in place and learns to use it, the employment specialist begins to fade his or her presence from the jobsite until he or she is no longer there on a continual basis. At this stage, the specialist moves into an ongoing advocacy role and periodically checks in with the employee and/or employer to evaluate how things are going and to inquire about the need for any additional services.

For example, an employee may receive another job duty and need new assistive technology to get the job done, or current assistive technology may become ineffective and need to be replaced. Or, new management may join the work force, and the employee may need some advice or direct advocacy services to help build rapport and address questions related to certain accommodations (e.g., on-the-job personal assistance service, scheduling adjustments, job coaching). The specialist keeps a pulse on how things are going from both the employee's and employer's perspectives in order to be proactive in reducing threats to job retention.

JOBSITE TRAINING AND SUPPORT NEEDS

There are many well-documented strategies for assisting an individual with disabilities to learn the job duties associated with his or her position, including using natural cues, natural supports, compensatory strategies, self-management procedures, task analysis, and prompting procedures (Inge, 1997; Inge & Tilson, 1997). The intent of this section is not to define these practices; instead, the section provides information related to the more unique needs of individuals with significant physical disabilities. These best practice strategies should be used in combination with those discussed here when assisting individuals with disabilities in becoming independent in the workplace.

The development of a task analysis for an individual's job duties is a best practice for any supported employment placement. For an individual with physical disabilities, this is true when determining the most efficient way to complete a task. By determining the most effective way to physically complete a job duty given the person's motor abilities, production issues or other problems can be addressed before they become barriers to success.

When developing any intervention strategy for the workplace, the goal is always to fade the employment specialist's assistance and presence as quickly as possible. There may be a natural tendency to physically provide assistance to someone who has limited motor skills; however, this will not benefit the person or promote his or her independence on the jobsite. The employment specialist must determine as quickly as possible how the individual will learn to use accommodations and other supports to complete all the requirements of the job, including the physical demands. Considering this issue when developing a task analysis is one strategy for ensuring that the employment specialist is not assisting the individual with disabilities any longer than is necessary.

When writing a task analysis, the employment specialist should critically analyze the individual's motor abilities and how they can be maximized. Assistance with this can be obtained from a physical or occupational therapist if needed; however, the employment specialist also can complete the task simulating the physical abilities of the individual with disabilities. Although role playing will not completely correspond to the person's skills, it should provide insight regarding the difficulty that the person will have when completing a specific job task. For instance, if the individual has the use of only one hand, then the employment specialist can physically try doing the task with one hand. In addition, seeking another co-worker's opinion may be helpful because this will provide a different viewpoint. The first two case studies are offered as examples of how developing a task analysis with the individual's physical capacity in mind would have prevented the subsequent problems on these jobsites. The third case study provides information on how an individual with significant physical disabilities can be assisted using supported employment to obtain and maintain a competitive job.

PATTY

An employment specialist developed a task analysis for Patty, whose job was attaching coupons to pizza boxes at a delivery- and pick-up–only pizzeria. Patty was unable to use her left hand, and a rehabilitation engineer fabricated a device to assist her in managing the coupon stickers.

Patty used a wheelchair for mobility, and her workstation was small. Essentially, there was enough room for her to drive into the area but not enough to turn around once she got there. Driving into the workstation meant that the stacked boxes were on her left side, which was the hand that she did not use. Immediately to her right was the order counter. Patty could not reach across her body to put a box on the stack once she had attached the coupon. Nor was there enough room on her right side to allow for the boxes to be stacked there. When it came time to put the completed box on the stack, she handed the box to her employment specialist who then completed that step of the task analysis. Even though this occurred during initial instruction while the focus was on learning to use the technology, the employment specialist still was fostering dependence.

When developing the task analysis, the employment specialist had not thought about the ramifications of driving into versus backing into the work area.

She had inserted her physical assistance as part of the task analysis in her haste to teach the use of the technology. The problem was solved by teaching Patty to back into her work area as the first steps of the task analysis for attaching coupons to the boxes. This adjustment quickly eliminated the need for the physical assistance that would have prolonged the employment specialist's presence on the jobsite.

MARGARET

Margaret, who has some difficulty with grasping small objects and papers, was matched to a job at a bank. Her primary responsibility was to open mail and sort it into letters that included checks for data entry and those that did not. A low-technology device fabricated by a rehabilitation engineer assisted Margaret in opening the envelopes.

Margaret did not require any instruction on using the device; therefore, the employment specialist did not develop a task analysis for the job duty. Within a few weeks of employment, however, the supervisor reported to the supported employment agency that Margaret was not meeting the production standard of the job. Margaret was in jeopardy of losing her position.

An analysis of the way Margaret performed the task revealed that she was not completing it as efficiently as possible. There were many unnecessary movements that took extra seconds not needed by her co-workers without disabilities. Specifically, observation showed that she was picking up and putting down the envelope more times than were necessary. Because Margaret had difficulty opening and closing her hand, this increased the amount of time that it took her to sort the mail. The task was analyzed, and a new task analysis developed. In the new task analysis, Margaret was asked to pick up the envelope and do as much of the job duty as possible. By reducing the number of times that she had to open and close her hand, Margaret was able to increase her production. A comparison of the two task analyses can be found in Table 9.1.

Unfortunately, the employer still was not satisfied with Margaret's production. The intervention was "too little, too late," and Margaret was terminated from the position. The critical lesson learned from this example is to be proactive. Know the production requirements from the first day of employment. Do not assume that an employer will accept less than the company standard for someone with physical disabilities. Renegotiate the production standard as part of the job restructuring process. Or, make sure that the task analysis and other workplace accommodations are quickly implemented in order for the person to meet the agreed-on requirements of the job. If this had occurred from the first day, then job separation may have been prevented.

AMAR

Four years ago, Amar decided to use supported employment services to assist him with employment. At age 36, Amar remained very eager to work. Over the years, he had volunteered on occasion but had never been able to find a "real" job. Amar invited his employment specialist, Willis, to meet him in his home to determine a career direction.

During the home visit, Willis asked Amar to describe a typical day. Amar said that he had two personal assistants. One aide arrived at his home around 9 A.M.

Table 9.1.   Task analysis for opening envelopes

First task analysis	Revised task analysis
1. Pick up an envelope, and slide it on the jig.	1. Pick up the envelope, and slide it on jig.
2. Pop open the envelope.	2. Pop open the envelope.
3. Pick up the envelope.	3. Pick up the envelope.
4. Lay the envelope on the table.	4. Shake out the contents onto the table.
5. Close the jig.	5. Throw the envelope away.
6. Pick up the envelope.	6. Pick up the checks and insert them into the bill statement.
7. Open the envelope.	7. Stack the bill statement on the pile of statements.
8. Take out the checks and bill statement.	8. Close the jig.
9. Put the checks and bill statement on table.	
10. Put the envelope on the table.	
11. Pick up the checks and insert them into the bill statement.	
12. Stack the bill statement on the pile of statements.	
13. Pick up the envelope.	
14. Throw the envelope away.	

and stayed a couple of hours to assist him with getting dressed, preparing and eating breakfast, and some light housekeeping. After the morning aide left, Amar said he spent most of his days, except for Fridays when he went shopping and Sundays when he attended church, watching television, typing letters to friends, and surfing the Internet. The other aide arrived around 6 P.M. and assisted Amar with preparing a simple meal, eating, and preparing for and getting into the bed.

Next, Willis asked Amar to show him how he typed letters. He observed that Amar was slow but methodical. He also noted that Amar did not use any assistive technology. Then, Willis asked Amar some questions about what he expected from work. During the interview, Amar described some of his life experiences and identified work preferences. He also decided that he would assist with his job search by networking with members of his church and family, as well as surfing the Internet to identify businesses where he might like to work. This information would be forwarded to Willis. In addition, they agreed that they would communicate with each other by e-mail at least one time per week.

Prior to leaving, Willis and Amar decided to meet at the local mall the following week to have coffee and take a look at different types of jobs that might require the use of a computer. During this outing, Willis was able to learn more about Amar's abilities. For example, he learned that Amar could make his own transportation arrangements, locate the main mall entrance, order coffee, know if he received the right change back, ask for assistance, and use a map to find a store. Amar saw that there were a lot of different types of jobs that required the use of a keyboard and monitor. He also learned about how a job could possibly be restructured or created to capitalize on his unique abilities. Based on the information gained during the home visit and the community outing, Willis began to form a vocational profile that outlined a direction for Amar's job search (see Table 9.2).

The following day, Amar's job search went in to full swing. Willis knew that the best way to locate a job lead was to diversify his approach and tap into the

Table 9.2.   Information included on Amar's vocational profile

Topic	Amar's remarks and Willis's observations
Supports needed to complete the employment application and screening process	Amar prefers that the job coach assist him with completing an application at a business. He will need advance notice to arrange a specialized transportation provider, and the job site must be wheelchair accessible.
Assistance needed before, during, and after the job interview process	Amar requests assistance with reviewing a job description disclosing his disability, and identifying and selecting accommodations and workplace supports. If required, assistance will be needed for identifying alternate modes for applicant testing and presenting accommodation/ support needs and qualifications to a potential employer.
Work preferences	Amar's work preferences include: having a part-time day structured work schedule, earning more than minimum wage, wearing business-like attire to work, having a 15-minute commute from home, working with a computer (but not data processing), being in a professional atmosphere in a temperature-controlled environment, experiencing daily changes in assignments, working alongside co-workers, having occasional public contact, and having a moderate level of supervision.
Good worker traits	Amar is a hard worker, conscientious, cooperative, dependable, and a team player. He has a positive outlook.
Current abilities	Amar learns new information without too much difficulty. He has good eyesight and hearing. Amar is most alert before 5 P.M. and can work 3–4 hours without a break. He reads, uses his computer to e-mail or type letters to friends, and surfs the Internet.
Potential vocational support needs	Willis will locate work opportunities (see previous on pre-employment assistance), assist with identifying and selecting assistive technology, and provide on-the-job skills training (prefers verbal explanation and modeling if needed) to ensure that quality (error correction) and production standards are met.

hidden job market, so he immediately began making contact with employers he had met in the past, sending out letters to new prospects, and cold-calling smaller businesses. He also knew that it was highly likely that a job would need to be carved or created for Amar.

One day, after an informational interview with a large firm, Willis noted a number of smaller businesses across the street. He grabbed a piece of scrap paper out of his jacket pocket and jotted down the names of 10 businesses. Back in the office, Willis pulled out the telephone book, got their telephone numbers, and started making telephone calls. He was able to get through to one employer/ owner, Mr. Kovack at Sound Works, a local music company, who somewhat reluctantly agreed to meet with him the following week.

The meeting went very well. During their talks, Mr. Kovack showed Willis around as he explained the operation. While touring, Willis noted a room filled with various samples of floor tiles and product information sheets. He inquired about what they did in there and discovered that it was the mailroom. He also learned that no one person was responsible for the job, and it was completed by whoever had the time, oftentimes by the owner and his wife on weeknights and weekends.

Hearing opportunity knock, Willis asked if Mr. Kovack might consider hiring a part-time worker to send out product information. He explained that if he could come in for a couple of hours the next day to learn more about the job tasks, he may be able to recommend someone. Mr. Kovack agreed that Willis could come back the following morning and "shadow" his wife as she sent out promotional materials.

The workplace and job analysis provided a lot of information and gave Willis the insight he needed to recommend Amar for an interview. For example, he was able to look at accessibility in the work and work-related areas (e.g., entrance, bathroom, breakroom) and begin to think about possible assistive technology and other supports that would help Amar complete the job. He also began to get a sense for the workplace culture. Everyone seemed friendly and genuinely happy with his or her jobs. Meals were often taken on the premises, and everyone seemed to enjoy joking around and chatting about current events. He also noted that although everyone was very busy, they were also team oriented.

Severe physical disabilities sometimes create apprehension and concern for some employers. Simply said, some people fail to recognize how a person can get the job done. Amar and Willis had discussed this reality in advance, and it was agreed that, if needed, Amar's disability could be revealed to an interested employer prior to the interview to help avoid the "shock effect."

Willis told Mr. Kovack that he felt like he knew a perfect candidate for the job. He went on to describe some of Amar's positive traits and attributes. He also explained that although Amar had a physical disability, he would be able to get the job done with the right supports. Mr. Kovack asked about the type of disability. Willis said Amar has cerebral palsy, which makes his speech and some of his movements slow. He then went back to describing Amar's vocational strengths, emphasizing the facts that he lived close by, had volunteered for the Sunny Side Memorial Fund, and was very motivated to work.

Mr. Kovack said that he was not really sure that someone with that type of disability could do the job. Willis reiterated that he offered a service that allowed him to accompany the new employee to work. He indicated that he would help ensure that the new employee could perform the job to meet his standards. After a few moments, Mr. Kovack agreed to meet Amar or someone else if Amar was not interested in the job.

Willis went straight to Amar's house to tell him about the job. Information from the workplace and job analysis was compared with Amar's vocational profile. This led to discussions on how this opportunity did and did not meet his preferences. In addition, it shed light on how the task capitalized on Amar's vocational strengths and what supports might be needed.

Amar was interested, and an interview was set up a few days later. In the meantime, Willis and Amar wrote an employment proposal describing how Amar would be able to get the job done. Amar interviewed with both Mr. and Mrs. Kovack. During the interview, Willis helped interpret Amar's responses whenever the Kovacks seemed confused, and Amar handed the employment proposal to them for review. After the interview, Amar was given a tour of the workplace. He left with a promise from the Kovacks that they needed to think this through and would make a decision in a few days. Willis and Amar followed up with thank-you letters that reiterated how the work would get done. A few days passed without any contact, so Willis and Amar decided to call Mr. Kovack. He said he and his wife had given it a lot of thought and decided to give Amar "a try."

Amar was hired to do promotional mailings, which involved preparing and sending promotional packets to customers and keeping the database up to date. Willis accompanied Amar to work from day one and facilitated or provided a number of

Table 9.3.   Examples of Amar's workplace supports

Challenge	Solution
The front entrance to the office was not accessible. There are two steps leading up to the office door, and there is a loading dock in the back of the building. Amar uses a wheelchair for mobility and could not gain access to the workplace.	Willis rented a portable ramp for the interview. Once Amar was hired, the employer and the state vocational rehabilitation (VR) agency shared the cost to purchase a portable ramp. A co-worker sets out and brings in the ramp as needed.
Amar had to learn to prioritize his work each day.	Willis and Amar worked with the employer to develop a flow chart of "recommended daily work flow" and a decision-making tree that could be referred to when questioning daily priorities.
Amar had to learn to differentiate between which requests to fill and which ones to leave for someone else to complete.	Initially, the manager separated the requests for Amar. Willis provided instruction, and Amar learned to identify more complex requests that someone else should complete.
A copier and printer were located on a table. Amar could not get close enough to use the equipment.	The copier and printer were moved to a wheelchair-accessible table that allowed Amar to reach them.
Amar had to match the correct literature with the corresponding sample to send out to prospective customers.	The literature and samples were reorganized and stored alongside one another.
Amar had to package the materials to send out. He had a difficult time gaining access to the materials.	Materials were stored on lower shelves, and dividers were used to ease access.
Amar experienced difficulty with placing labels on envelopes.	A rehabilitation engineer was called in to discuss possible solutions. The engineer created a simple device that assisted Amar with peeling the labels. Amar learned how to use the device so that the labels would not wrinkle. Willis assisted Amar with developing techniques for placing labels on the envelopes.
Amar could type but needed to increase his speed and accuracy.	A keyguard was placed directly over the keys of the computer keyboard so that Amar only hit the intended key. The computer's accessibility features were turned on.
Amar could not reach the button to operate the mail postage machine.	The machine was moved to a lower level so that Amar could have access to it.

workplace supports, as well as assisted with identifying and implementing assistive technology. Table 9.3 highlights some of the major challenges Amar faced at work and the workplace supports used to address these challenges.

Amar has been employed for more than 5 years. Today, Willis continues to check in with Amar and the Kovacks a couple of times per month to ensure all is well. Over the years, Willis has provided additional support as needed. When the company moved to a new building, Willis provided assistance to Amar and the employer by identifying ways to make the new site more accessible. For example, Willis recommended tile flooring, a new desk for Amar, and built-in accessible shelving. Fortunately, the employer made sure his new business location had an accessible entrance, so the portable ramp was no longer necessary.

A recent performance evaluation stated, "Amar fits in real well with our company. He is an asset for us and a pleasure to work with." When asked to give other people with disabilities advice on employment, Amar said, "Never assume that an employer is not interested."

CONCLUSION

Clearly, the need for a skilled labor pool is great in today's economy. The job market is booming with jobs that do not require physical competence. There is a need to develop strategies that can effectively empower individuals with significant physical disabilities to become part of the nation's labor force. The general public, business personnel, people with disabilities, and VR professionals need to embrace a stronger and more powerful conviction that every person has the right to work when given the proper workplace supports. Individuals with significant physical disabilities can make a meaningful contribution to a business and society when their abilities are matched to a customized job and they are provided with assistive technology devices and services. As more people with significant disabilities go to work, positive changes should occur in the attitudes of others related to the abilities of people with significant disabilities. A more aggressive national media campaign is needed that highlights the idea that "disability does not mean inability." Such a campaign could promote the value that people with disabilities should work while combating existing stereotypes and myths.

REFERENCES

Adaptive Environments Center. (1998). *Tax incentives for improving accessibility: The Americans with disabilities fact sheet series.* Retrieved February 9, 2006, from http://www.usdoj.gov/crt/ada/taxpack.htm#anchor297649

Americans with Disabilities Act (ADA) of 1990, PL 101-336, 42 U.S.C. §§ 12101 *et seq.*

Assistive Technology Act of 1998, PL 105-394, 29 U.S.C. §§ 3001 *et seq.*

Assistive Technology Act of 2004, PL 108-364, 118 Stat. 1707.

Boehner, J. (2004). *Assistive Technology Act of 2004: Putting technology into the hands of individuals with disabilities.* Retrieved November 3, 2004, from http://edworkforce.house.gov/issues/108th/education/at/billsummary.htm

Brooke, V., Inge, K.J., Armstrong, A.J., & Wehman, P. (1997). *Supported employment handbook: A customer-driven approach for persons with significant disabilities* (Monograph). Richmond: Virginia Commonwealth University Rehabilitation Research and Training Center on Workplace Supports and Job Retention.

Bureau of Labor Statistics. (2004). *Current population survey.* Retrieved November 5, 2004, from http://www.bls.gov/cps/home.htm

Croser, M.D. (1999, March/April). Every little bit helps. *AAMR News & Notes, 2.*

Equal Employment Opportunity Commission. (1992). *A technical assistance manual on the employment provisions of (Title 1) of the Americans with Disabilities Act.* Washington, DC: Author.

Individuals with Disabilities Education Act (IDEA) Amendments of 1991, PL 102-119, 20 U.S.C. §§ 1400 *et seq.*

Inge, K.J. (1997). Job site training. In V. Brooke, K.J. Inge, A. Armstrong, & P. Wehman (Eds.), *Supported employment handbook: A customer-driven approach for persons with significant disabilities* (pp. 159–200). Richmond: Virginia Commonwealth University Rehabilitation Research and Training Center on Workplace Supports and Job Retention.

Inge, K.J. (2001). Supported employment for individuals with physical disabilities. In P. Wehman (Ed.), *Supported employment in business: Expanding the capacity of workers with disabilities* (pp. 153–180). St Augustine, FL: Training Resource Network.

Inge, K.J., & Shepherd, J. (1995). Assistive technology applications and strategies for school system personnel. In K.F. Flippo, K.J. Inge, & J.M. Barcus (Eds.), *Assistive technology: A resource for school, work, and community* (pp. 106–132). Baltimore: Paul H. Brookes Publishing Co.

Inge, K.J., Strobel, W., Wehman, P., Todd, J., & Targett, P. (2000). Vocational outcomes for persons with severe physical disabilities: Design and implementation of workplace supports. *NeuroRehabilitation, 15*(3), 175–188.

Inge, K.J., & Tilson, G. (1997). Ensuring support systems that work: Getting beyond the natural supports versus job coach controversy. *Journal of Vocational Rehabilitation, 9*(2), 133–142.

Inge, K.J., Wehman, P., Kregel, J., & Sherron-Targett, P. (1996). Vocational rehabilitation for persons with spinal cord injuries and other severe physical disabilities. *American Rehabilitation, 2*(2), 2–12.

Inge, K.J., Wehman, P., Strobel, W., Powell, D., & Todd, J. (1998). Supported employment and assistive technology for persons with spinal cord injury: Three illustrations of successful work supports. *Journal of Vocational Rehabilitation, 10*(2), 141–152.

Internal Revenue Service. (2003). *Know the rules and regulations for improving accessibility for the disabled.* Retrieved February 9, 2006, from http://www.irs.gov/businesses/small/article/0,,id=113382,00.html

Kaye, H.S., Kang, T., & LaPlante, M.P. (2001). *Mobility device use in the United States.* San Francisco: University of California, Disability Statistics Center Institute for Health and Aging.

National Organization on Disability. (2004). *Harris survey of Americans with disabilities.* Retrieved October 27, 2004, from http://www.nod.org/content.cfm?id=1537

Parent, W., Unger, D., & Inge, K.J. (1997). Customer profile. In V. Brooke, K.J. Inge, A.J. Armstrong, & P. Wehman (Eds.), *Supported employment handbook: A customer-driven approach for persons with significant disabilities* (pp. 46–97). Richmond: Virginia Commonwealth University Rehabilitation Research and Training Center on Workplace Supports and Job Retention.

Rehabilitation Act Amendments of 1986, PL 99-506, 29 U.S.C. §§ 701 *et seq.*

Rehabilitation Act Amendments of 1992, PL 102-569, 29 U.S.C. §§ 701 *et seq.*

Rehabilitation Act of 1973, PL 93-112, 29 U.S.C. §§ 701 *et seq.*

Sowers, J.A. (1995). Adaptive environments in the workplace. In K.F. Flippo, K.J. Inge, & J.M. Barcus (Eds.), *Assistive technology: A resource for school, work, and community* (pp. 167–186). Baltimore: Paul H. Brookes Publishing Co.

Technology-Related Assistance for Individuals with Disabilities Act of 1988, PL 100-407, 29 U.S.C. §§ 2201 *et seq.*

United Cerebral Palsy. (2004, January 12). *Assistive Technology Act still awaiting reauthorization.* Retrieved November 8, 2004, from http://www.ucp.org/ucp_generaldoc.cfm/1/8/33/33-12110/5270

U.S. Department of Education. (2005). *My child's special needs: A guide to the individualized education program.* Retrieved February 17, 2005, from http://www.ed.gov/parents/needs/speced/iepguide/index.html

U.S. Department of Education, Office of Special Education and Rehabilitation Services Administration. (1998). *The Rehabilitation Act Amendments of 1998* (Information Memorandum RSA-IM-98-20). Washington, DC: Author.

Wehman, P., Wilson, K., Targett, P., West, M., Bricout, J., & McKinley, W. (1999). Removing transportation barriers for persons with spinal cord injuries: An ongoing challenge to community reintegration. *Journal of Vocational Rehabilitation, 13,* 21–30.

West, J. (1991). *The Americans with Disabilities Act: From policy to practice.* New York: Milbank Memorial Fund.

Workforce Investment Act (WIA) of 1998, PL 105-220, 29 U.S.C. §§ 2801 *et seq.*

Chapter 10

Personal Assistants
in the Workplace

EDMOND TURNER, PAUL WEHMAN, W. GRANT REVELL, JR., AND VALERIE A. BROOKE

Historically, personal assistance services have been viewed as an essential way of supporting individuals with physical disabilities in their independent living. The use of personal assistance services has been an important extension of empowering individuals with disabilities to live at home and to move about the community with a greater degree of independence. Without personal assistance services, thousands of people with physical and other significant disabilities would be confined to institutionalized nursing home environments or other segregated living situations that were predicated on the need for group care. Fortunately, since the mid-1980s, there has been both a philosophical and programmatic move away from institutional living arrangements accompanied by an understanding that a personal assistant can play a critically vital role in allowing for improved quality of community living for many people with significant disabilities.

Unfortunately, myriad problems hold back the expansion of personal assistance services. First, there is a scarcity of personnel who are willing and able to fulfill this role (Hinton, 2003). Personal assistants have responsibilities for the lives in their hands, and if they are indifferent or not trained properly in how to perform their duties, particularly in a crisis situation, it can be the difference between life and death. This can deter a number of potential personal assistants from entering this career. The second problem is that there are very few well-developed training programs for guiding people who wish to become competent personal assistants. The third, and perhaps the most significant, obstacle is the lack of a clear stream of funding from the state and federal governments in helping to underwrite the costs of personal-care services as a genuine long-term support priority (Silverstein, 2003).

It is reasonable to argue that if the federal government is going to pay for wheelchairs, respirators, cochlear implants, job coaches, and other types of long-term support services and devices, then public funding for the use of personal assistants to help people enjoy a better quality of life and reduce institutionalization would also be a good investment. To date, this critical shortage of skilled personal care attendants, the lack of quality training resources, and the limited funding are primary obstacles that have made independent living more difficult for people with significant disabilities. Effective implementation by states of the Medicaid Buy-In provision of the Ticket to

Work and Work Incentives Improvement Act of 1999 (PL 106-170) would help to reduce these obstacles.

This chapter addresses the role of a personal assistant in the workplace. Although modern medicine and contemporary rehabilitation, as well as families and friends, have helped individuals with disabilities become individually empowered at home, employment must not be left out. In fact, one could very reasonably argue that returning to a previous job, entering new employment, starting a business, or telecommuting are all important elements of closing the rehabilitation loop for people who have suffered serious injuries or experienced significant and/or life-changing disabilities. Living with independence at home is vital. Moving about the community is essential, but productive work provides that final stage of fulfillment and meaningfulness that home living by itself cannot provide. The importance of employment is especially true for younger Americans with disabilities, who are full of energy and excitement and looking forward to making an impact on the world.

This chapter focuses on the premise that personal assistants are crucial in the workplace. Employers have learned to accept employment specialists and job coaches for short-term periods, and they will also accept competent and well-trained personal assistants who can help individuals with disabilities with critical functions that are necessary in their work performance. For example, in the Virginia Commonwealth University Rehabilitation Research and Training Center (VCU-RRTC) on Workplace Supports and Job Retention, which is comprised predominantly of people without disabilities, some employees have very significant disabilities, such as cerebral palsy. These individuals are highly intelligent and motivated but in some cases are unable to handle utensils. Therefore, for these individuals, the services of a personal assistant are used to enhance their ability to get their job done with a maximum of productivity and efficiency. In another case, a personal assistant helps an extremely intelligent and highly motivated individual to complete work tasks by operating equipment that the employee with disabilities is physically unable to operate. In short, personal assistants in the workplace, as well as in a home environment, should be seen as what they are—*an important extension or support* that enables a person with disabilities to be all that he or she can be.

Virtually all people at some point in their work tenure need help or support. It may be a special type of chair, a different type of schedule, or help within the Employee Assistance Program. There really is no end to the different types of assistance that good employers will make available for employees who have shown themselves to be good workers. Yes, the concept of a personal assistant is different, but when you get past the issue of funding, does it really matter? If the employee being supported by a personal assistant effectively and efficiently delivers products or services valuable to the employer, then why not utilize this personal support mechanism?

Finally, this chapter presents strategies for making an extension of the personal assistant into the workplace a reality. These strategies emphasize the primary role and responsibility of the person who utilizes these services to hire, train, guide, and supervise the personal assistant. They also involve accurate assessments of the need for personal assistance services at the workplace, careful consideration of the employer's critical involvement in planning for these services, access to needed funding, and consideration of resources such as assistive technology to help with needed workplace supports.

Personal assistants have proven themselves to be viable, reasonable accommodations (Hinton, 2003); failure to use this resource when appropriate to the functions of the job constitutes discrimination against potential employees who have disabilities. It is accepted that a personal assistant can help an individual live with independence at home and move with freedom about the community. Why, then, should there be any doubt that a personal assistant can help that same person with significant disabilities earn a living wage and be more productive in the workplace? The answer to this question is simple: Personal assistants can function just as effectively in the workplace as they do in other situations in the community.

DESCRIPTION OF WORKPLACE PERSONAL ASSISTANCE SERVICES

For many people with significant disabilities, the use of personal assistance services as a workplace support is as essential to successful employment as these services are for successful community living. During the 1980s, great disability rights leaders and self-advocates such as Ed Roberts and Judy Heumann proved the value and cost-effectiveness of customer-directed personal assistance services through their work in the independent living movement and at the World Institute on Disability. These two pioneers demonstrated that customer-directed personal assistance services could enable people with significant disabilities to live and actively participate in their communities. This historic work was documented in the research monograph *Attending to America* (Litvak, Zukas, & Heumann, 1987).

Many people with disabilities who have managed personal assistants in their home environments realize similar supports are needed on the job. Knowing how to manage a personal assistant at work could mean the difference between maintaining or losing a job. Even with the vast array of assistive technology now available, some tasks require the intellectual skills and abilities of another human being. To be successful in a career, the employee with significant disabilities must balance the right assistive technology with the appropriate level of support from a workplace personal assistant. Effectively managing a personal assistant involves having the skills needed to direct a support person to do those tasks that would be physically impossible or extremely time consuming for the employee with disabilities to do without assistance.

Unlike home- and community-based personal assistance services, when personal assistance services are used as a workplace support, they are not based on medical need because having a work support to accomplish job tasks is not medically necessary. As a result, employees with disabilities have great difficulty using traditional resources to find qualified workplace personal assistants. This difficulty is especially true of home health care agencies that only recruit personal assistants to do personal care and some minor medical services; these individuals would possibly have limited understanding of how to support an individual on the job. Even individuals with disabilities who have experience recruiting, hiring, and managing a personal assistant for home-based duties have to learn new skills in order to find competent support in the workplace.

Before an employee can successfully use personal assistance services in the workplace, he or she must understand that from a legal and regulatory standpoint, personal assistance services as a job accommodation are not necessarily services of a personal nature. Instead, personal assistance services in the workplace involve services that the employee needs to complete essential job functions in a timely manner. Title I of the Americans with Disabilities Act (ADA) of 1990 (PL 101-336) stated that services of a personal nature are not the responsibility of the employer. Therefore, personal assistance services in the workplace would not typically include tasks such as feeding, grooming, or toileting. Rather, personal assistance services would involve job-related functions that assist in the completion of essential job functions in a timely manner (Silverstein, 2003).

Grooming might be a possible exception to personal assistance services as a workplace job accommodation. Certainly in business, academic, and other professional settings, it is essential that the employee be well groomed; however, in most other cases, it is the responsibility of the employee with disabilities, not the employer, to find someone to perform services that are deemed personal. To avoid possible undue hardships for employers, writers of Title I of the ADA were very specific in how workplace personal assistance services are defined as a reasonable accommodation. Although the business community may consider the ADA definition a fair concession, it presents many challenges to employees with more significant disabilities.

The Job Accommodation Network and the President's Committee on Employment of People with Disabilities (PCEPD) developed the following definition of personal assistance services in the workplace shortly after the passage of the ADA. The PCEPD has become the Office of Disability Employment Policy (ODEP) in the U.S. Department of Labor, and the Job Accommodation Network is now affiliated with ODEP. This definition of personal assistance services in the workplace includes examples of tasks that can be performed by personal assistants for employees with different disabilities.

> In the workplace, PAS [personal assistance services] is provided as a reasonable accommodation to enable an employee to perform the functions of a job. The employer's responsibility for providing reasonable accommodations begins when the employee reaches the job site and concludes when the workday ends. PAS in the workplace does not include skilled medical care. Work-related PAS might include filing, retrieving work materials that are out of reach, or providing travel assistance for an employee with a mobility impairment; helping an employee with a cognitive disability with planning or decision making; reading handwritten mail to an employee with a visual impairment; or ensuring that a sign language interpreter is present during staff meetings to accommodate an employee with a hearing impairment. Each person with a disability has different needs and may require a unique combination of PAS. (ODEP, 2006, p. 1)

Another definition of personal assistance services as a workplace support was developed by the VCU-RRTC on Workplace Supports and Job Retention in 1998. The purpose of this definition is to assist employees with disabilities, workplace personal assistants, and employers (including human resource managers) to better understand personal assistance services as a workplace support. It was generated after conducting two focus group sessions: one group contained experienced users of workplace personal assistance services; the other group had mostly very inexperienced users of personal assistance services.

The first session was held during the 1998 National Council of Independent Living Conference in Washington, D.C. This group included experienced users of personal assistance services in the workplace. The second session was held as an activity in a demonstration supported-employment project involving individuals with very significant disabilities. Many of the people in this group lived in a residential care facility with very little or no control over how their care was provided. The definition developed by these two groups is as follows:

> Personal assistance services in the workplace are services provided to an employee with a disability by a personal assistant to enable the employee to perform the essential duties of a job more efficiently. (Turner, 2000, p. 4)

It is important that personal assistance services that support needs related to personal care be differentiated from those involving the performance of essential duties of the job. The following are examples of personal assistance services at the workplace that respond to personal needs:

- Assist with grooming tasks
- Assist with getting beverages
- Assist with getting and eating food
- Assist with toileting (if necessary)
- Assist with transportation
- Assist with dressing and grooming tasks on business trips

The following are examples of personal assistance services at the workplace that respond directly to efficiently performing essential job duties:

- Assist with making telephone calls
- Assist with filing
- Assist with taking dictation
- Assist with voice interpretation
- Assist with making copies
- Assist with data entry
- Assist with taking notes in meetings
- Assist with reading documents
- Assist with getting and opening mail
- Assist with keeping work space organized
- Assist with traveling on business trips

As noted, the definition of personal assistance services at the workplace developed from the ADA clearly differentiates personal assistance services responding to personal needs from those necessary to perform essential job functions. Negotiating clear differentiations between these two types of workplace personal assistance service needs can be a challenge for a job seeker with disabilities and a potential employer. The self-assessment example contained in Table 10.1 shows how a checklist can help clearly identify workplace personal assistance service needs.

Even though personal assistance services such as grooming, assistance with restroom needs, and eating are not normally services that are paid for by employers, they can be essential for many employees with significant disabilities. In many employment settings, particularly more professional settings, it is critically important for the employee's appearance to reflect a positive image for the business represented. For example, the employee may represent his or her business in arenas such as banking, in which a professional appearance is viewed as essential to effective job performance. Also, the employee must be able to take care of personal needs in a timely manner. Having a personal assistant to help with personal needs will frequently make the

Table 10.1.   Self-assessment checklist for a training associate

Essential function	How function will be accomplished	Assistive devices used	Tasks needing personal assistance	Estimated time personal assistance service needed
Develop training materials, reports, and related correspondence	Assistance from a workplace personal assistant	Appropriate computer software	Word processing skills in a timely manner	12 hours per week
Acquire speakers and coordinate trainings	Assistance from a workplace personal assistant	Telephone with speaker device	Assistance with dialing elephone, recording dates, and maintaining telephone data base	5 hours per week
Track training outcomes	Assistance from a workplace personal assistant	Appropriate computer software and telephone with speaker device	Assistance with dialing telephone numbers	2 hours per week
Prepare and participate in presentations	Assistance from a workplace personal assistant	Appropriate computer software	Word processing and using PowerPoint in a timely manner	3 hours per week
Represent company at national meetings	Assistance from a workplace personal assistant	Appropriate computer software	Word processing, personal grooming, and travel assistance	As needed
Coordinate activities across various projects	Assistance from a workplace personal assistant	Appropriate computer software and telephone with speaker device	Word processing, personal grooming, and travel assistance	5 hours per week
Necessary systems advocacy	Assistance from a workplace personal assistant	Appropriate computer software and telephone with speaker device	Word processing and using PowerPoint in a timely manner	As needed

employee more efficient. In some cases, the professional employee with disabilities can successfully make this case to the employer and gain personal services as part of their workplace personal assistance services package.

Accurately describing the specific duties that will be required of the personal assistant in the workplace is vital. In one case in which a large national bank agreed to provide personal services as part of workplace personal assistance services because grooming requirements were an important part of the work culture, neither the employee nor the employer thought to describe the specific work tasks of the workplace personal assistance services. As a result, the employer got very angry when the professional employee asked his workplace personal assistant to pick up his dry cleaning before returning from lunch. It was extremely natural for the employee to make this request of the personal assistant that assists him at home; however, the supervisor did not see this as part of the duties of a workplace personal assistant and began to view the employee in a negative light. This situation could have been avoided if the new employee and the employer had specifically described the duties of the workplace personal assistant. In cases where the employee is paying for his or her own personal assistant, it is still a good idea to compose a list of job duties that will be expected of the personal assistant.

REASONS FOR WORKPLACE PERSONAL ASSISTANCE SERVICES

Like all employees, workers with disabilities have very different and unique needs. Therefore, what is successful for one employee might not work for another employee who has the same type of disability. Some individuals can use assistive technology or simply have their workstation modified to do their job efficiently without the support of a personal assistant, whereas others may need a personal assistant in combination with some type of assistive technology.

The type of support used will depend on the person's level of need. Assistive technology can help in some cases, but there are many job-related tasks that may need the support of a personal assistant to be accomplished. Thus, it is important that employers/human resource managers not judge an employee's request for personal assistance services as a reasonable accommodation solely by disability types. Employers/human resource managers should get to know the individual to better understand what their employee's needs are and how to accommodate those needs. If necessary, the employer should consult with a rehabilitation professional before making a decision about granting personal assistance services as a reasonable accommodation. There are many reasons that may not be obvious to the employer why the employee might require the services of a personal assistant to be efficient. Both the employee and employer should have all the necessary information before determining the role of the personal assistant.

Maintaining physical stamina on the job is a big issue for many people who have disabilities. If a person spends a lot of time doing labor-intensive tasks that are not deemed as essential functions of the job, then he or she will not be physically or mentally able to do the essential functions of that job. An employee with disabilities expending large amounts of energy doing tasks that could more easily be done by a workplace personal assistant is simply not cost-effective for the employer. For example, a person who has poor hand coordination might spend several hours keying in information on a word processor and could become too physically exhausted to think properly about what needs to be written. Voice-activated computer software programs can alleviate the data-entry problem, but these programs have not proved effective for people with speech impairments. In this case, it would be more cost-effective to have a qualified workplace personal assistant take dictation from the employee with disabilities. It would also increase the employee's efficiency and productivity on the job by allowing him or her to focus on developing the material.

Another example might be an employee with visual impairments utilizing a reader instead of a reading machine (e.g., a Kurswald Reader) that could possibly break down and leave the person unable to read (hear) critical documents. Also, a machine requires the person to place documents in precisely the right position to be read properly. With a personal assistant, the task could be done more efficiently, giving the employee time to respond to the reading matter. These are two examples in which the use of a personal assistant makes the employee with disabilities more effective and, therefore, reduces the cost of wasted time for the employer. The decision to utilize personal assistance services as a reasonable job accommodation should be made through a joint agreement between the employer and employee. Additional examples matched to specific disability areas are provided from the Job Accommodation Network (2004) and are helpful when exploring possibilities.

BARRIERS TO ADEQUATE
WORKPLACE PERSONAL ASSISTANCE SERVICES

Employees with disabilities who utilize personal assistance services in the workplace face many potential challenges. There is the challenge of recruiting a qualified, reliable, and punctual personal assistant. In addition, the personal assistant must have the skills and personality needed to provide support effectively within a work environment. Next, the employee must be able to effectively explain the need for personal assistance services to the employer/supervisor and establish an agreement on how the personal assistant will function. To meet these challenges, the employee with disabilities must be knowledgeable about his or her personal assistance services support needs and self-confident in explaining these needs to both potential personal assistants and to employers.

Some employers still do not understand their responsibility to provide personal assistance services as a reasonable accommodation. They still may perceive it as two people doing the same job. Here, the employee must be very patient in making the case for personal assistance services to be provided as a reasonable accommodation. If the employer recommends some assistive technology that might address the employee's needs, then the suggestion should be considered courteously. If personal assistance services would be a better accommodation, however, then the employee should remain firm in explaining how the personal assistant will help in getting the job done more efficiently. Employees with disabilities should understand that it is the employer's decision to approve and agree to pay for personal assistance services as a reasonable accommodation. When such a request is denied, the employee has to decide whether to accept a lesser accommodation or turn down the job and seek other employment that will provide more adequate accommodations.

Even after the employer has agreed to pay for the employee to have a personal assistant as a reasonable accommodation on the job, the employee may have many barriers to overcome before the support is in place. The employee may still have to come up with funding to cover such tasks as feeding and assistance in the restroom. The employee's salary might be too low to offset that expense. There are ways to overcome this expense by using Social Security Work Incentives. The cost of the personal assistance services can either be claimed as an Impairment-Related Work Expense (IRWE) or can be covered under a Plan for Achieving Self-Support (PASS). By utilizing either of these Social Security Administration work incentives, the employee could keep some level of Social Security benefits to pay for that assistance. Chapter 17 provides a detailed description of use of Social Security Work Incentives such as PASS and IRWE.

When the employee is able to pay for personal assistance services of a more personal nature, he or she still must find a person who is willing to come to the job for a limited number of hours. Driving for one half hour to one hour just to work a limited number of hours is not very cost-effective for the personal assistant. Therefore, the employee must try to come up with creative ways of finding this type of support. One of the best ways to solve the problem of getting someone to assist with lunch and restroom needs is to convince the person who is assisting with work-related personal as-sistance services to also assist with personal needs. Also, some employees have used other co-workers who may need extra cash to perform these intimate services. This approach may work if the employee is frank and honest about the level of support needed and if it is agreeable to the other co-worker.

One tip the employee might want to consider is asking a co-worker who is not directly connected to his or her department for assistance, thus avoiding the possible embarrassment some people feel in asking more immediate co-workers for assistance with personal needs. Again, the essential point is to be frank and honest. Also, the use of casual conversation and humor can increase the comfort level of the co-worker who has agreed to assist. These relationships take time to develop and will either work or not work depending on the personalities and attitudes of the parties involved.

Because personal assistance services as a workplace support is relatively new, some employees lack the skills to train and manage personal assistants for workplace duties. In these cases, the employee with disabilities should enroll in a training program known as Personal Assistant Management Training Program that is usually provided by a local Center for Independent Living (CIL). A CIL is a nonresidential place of ac-tion and coalition where people with disabilities learn empowerment and develop the skills necessary to make lifestyle choices. These centers are funded by state, federal, local, and private dollars. Part C of Title VII of the Workforce Investment Act of 1998 (PL 105-220) provides general operations money for CILs across the country. Even though the dynamics may be a little different for managing personal assistants in the workplace compared with the home, many of the same management techniques can be utilized when training personal assistants for workplace and home-based duties. The basic rule for managing personal assistants in any environment is clearly articulating the support needed and specifying how those needs can best be met.

Personal assistance services as a workplace support will potentially unlock the door to employment for thousands of people with significant disabilities. It can have the same impact for people with severe physical disabilities as supported employment has had for more than 200,000 individuals with all types of disabilities (Braddock et al., 2004). To achieve this level of impact, however, personal assistance services as a workplace support must be fully understood by employees with significant disabilities, potential workplace personal assistants, and employers.

WORKPLACE PERSONAL ASSISTANCE SERVICES AS A REASONABLE ACCOMMODATION

The same economic forces that are driving the financial markets are also creating one of the greatest challenges faced by today's employers: low unemployment. Thus, many employers are turning to the large and untapped labor pool of employees with disabili-ties. The use of personal assistance services as a reasonable accommodation is new to many businesses. In the workplace, personal assistance services are considered a reason-able accommodation to enable an employee to perform the essential functions of the job. According to Section 1630.9 of the ADA Handbook (EEOC, 1992b), the em-ployer's obligation to make a reasonable accommodation is a form of nondiscrimination.

Section 1630.9: Not Making Reasonable Accommodation
  (a) It is unlawful for a covered entity not to make reasonable accommodations to the known physical or mental limitations of an otherwise qualified applicant or employee

with a disability, unless such covered entity can demonstrate that the accommodation would impose an undue hardship on the operation of its business.

(b) It is unlawful for a covered entity to deny employment opportunities to an otherwise qualified job applicant or employee with a disability based on the need of such covered entity to make reasonable accommodation to such individuals' physical or mental impairments.

A covered entity shall not be excused from the requirements of this part because of any failure to receive technical assistance authorized by Section 506 of the ADA, including any failure in the development or dissemination of any technical assistance manual authorized by that Act.

A qualified individual with a disability is not required to accept an accommodation, aid, service, opportunity or benefit that such qualified individual chooses to accept. However, if such individual rejects a reasonable accommodation, aid, service, opportunity or benefit that is necessary to enable the individual to perform the essential functions of the position held or desired, and cannot, as a result of that rejection, perform the essential functions of the position, the individual will not be considered a qualified individual with a disability. (Equal Employment Opportunity Commission [EEOC], 1992b, p. A-33)

If an adjustment or modification specifically assists the individual in performing the duties of a particular job, then it may be considered a type of reasonable accommodation (EEOC, 1992b). For instance, an employer may provide an individual who is blind with a workplace personal assistant to act as a sighted guide on business trips; however, if a modification assists the individual throughout his or her daily activities, on or off the job, then it is considered a "personal" item that the employer is not required to provide. An employer does not have to provide an employee with a workplace personal assistant for personal needs such as grooming, eating, or personal hygiene unless such non–job-related supports are provided to employees without disabilities (EEOC, 1992a). Daily-living activities on or off the job are not the responsibility of the employer.

Table 10.2 provides sample personal assistant job functions for readers, interpreters/ transliterators, and personal attendants. Table 10.3 shows examples of personal assistance services that employers have provided for their employees with disabilities. It is important to note that professionals who provide reader and interpreter/transliterator services usually do not refer to themselves as personal assistants or workplace personal assistants.

The classification of readers and interpreters/transliterators as a personal assistance service is a business perspective driven by the EEOC's interpretation of the ADA. For example, when asked what personal assistance services are provided to employees with disabilities, representatives from IBM, UnumProvident, and SunTrust Bank indicated they routinely provide personal assistants such as readers and interpreters (Jon Ehret, personal communication, March 17, 2000; Susan Olson, personal communication, April 17, 2000; and Meg O'Connell, personal communication, April 11, 2000); however, with the exception of UnumProvident, it was indicated that these businesses had no experience in providing personal assistants in the workplace for their employees.

In the business community, the current view is that a personal assistant is to be provided as a reasonable accommodation for job-related functions only. In the disability field, a personal assistant is viewed as a person who assists people who have activities of daily living or instrumental activities of daily living deficiencies with their personal care or other daily activities (Dautel & Frieden, 1999). Activities of daily living are considered basic self-care functions such as bathing, dressing, and using the toilet. Instrumental activities of daily living refer to tasks that require physical dexterity,

Table 10.2.   Sample job functions for workplace personal assistants

Reader	Assist an employee with disabilities with reading:
	• Resource and reference materials
	• Technical materials in specialized areas
	• Field reports, surveys, and other documents
	• Legislation
	• Regulations
	• Policies
	• Incoming correspondence
	Identify significant information and/or issues in incoming correspondence as per directions from the employee with disabilities.
	Highlight and condense pertinent information as per directions from the employee with disabilities.
Interpreter/ transliterator	Interpret spoken words using the communication mode of the individual who is deaf or who has a hearing impairment (manual code for English or American Sign Language) to facilitate communication between employees who are hearing and employees with hearing impairments.
	Interpret manual code for English or American Sign Language to spoken words for hearing individuals to facilitate communication between hearing employees and employees with hearing impairments.
	Transliterate spoken words to manual coded English/pidgin signed English to facilitate communication between hearing employees and employees with hearing impairments.
	Transliterate manual coded English/pidgin signed English to spoken words to facilitate communication between hearing employees and employees with hearing impairments.

strength, speech, hearing, vision, memory, and cognitive reasoning (e.g., cooking, cleaning, shopping, doing laundry, using a telephone, paying bills).

The disability rights movement has pushed for the utilization of personal assistants who provide assistance with activities of daily living and instrumental activities of daily living to people with disabilities throughout the community, including the workplace. It is important to note that there is nothing in the law that prohibits an employer from paying for personal assistance services if the employer chooses to do so. For example, UnumProvident has an attendance service policy that subsidizes the cost of personal attendance services to employees who need these services in order to work (Susan Olson, personal communication, April 17, 2000). The UnumProvident attendance service policy includes eating, toileting, hygiene, and job-specific assistance.

When applying for a job, an applicant with significant disabilities may need assistance to complete an application or a pre-employment test. For example, an employer may provide a reader to assist someone with a visual impairment with completing a job application or a pre-employment test. A workplace personal assistant may also be needed to assist an employee with performing certain job functions. In this case, the workplace personal assistant assists with, but does not perform, essential job functions. For example, a reader may be needed on a daily basis to help a customer service representative who has a visual impairment and limited use of his or her hands to perform the essential job function of responding *to written correspondence*. This might include performing a job-related function such as *reading written letters aloud* to the employee and/or *typing a response* dictated by the employee. Workplace personal assistants may also be needed to allow an employee to participate in or enjoy equal benefits and privileges of the job. For example, a driver may be hired from time to time to transport an employee to the annual company picnic or holiday celebration.

Table 10.3.   Examples of the use of workplace personal assistants

A state agency maintenance mechanic had difficulties climbing stairs and carrying materials. The job was restructured so that this individual always worked in a team with another mechanic. The co-worker was easily able to carry the equipment and do the required lifting on the job while this worker performed other necessary tasks. Because the facility had no elevator, the worker was assigned only to jobs on the first floor.

A college professor with physical limitations resulting from a stroke was assigned a student worker to assist with transport of materials to and from classes. The cost was minimal as the worker was already assigned to the department and performed other duties.

An engineer who uses a wheelchair worked in a manufacturing company that required employees to move around the facility inspecting buildings by climbing and crawling into small spaces. They worked in teams. A member of the team videotaped the areas that this worker could not enter. The engineer used the videotape to gather pertinent information.

A proofreader in a publishing company who uses a wheelchair was not able to transport materials from an inaccessible location to her workstation. She was provided a low file cabinet and drawer unit to help her gain access to the necessary materials placed within her reach. Co-workers periodically stocked this area for her. Materials that were housed elsewhere were brought to her on a daily basis by co-workers who were also obtaining or returning their own materials.

A federal agency employed two full-time sign language interpreters to accommodate communication needs of numerous employees who were deaf. Having interpreters on staff eliminated the need to contract out for this service. This eliminated the need to schedule interpreters in advance, allowing for impromptu meetings. In addition, these interpreters were familiar with the agency's vocabulary, protocols, and individuals, therefore enabling them to perform their duties better.

An insurance company program analyst who is deaf had to communicate frequently with others. The person worked with a team, but team members rotated throughout various projects. An interpreter was hired to facilitate communication between this worker and other team members.

A private school employed a counselor who is blind. Accommodations included providing a screen reader and voice synthesizer for computer activities. A part-time support service assistant was hired to complete handwritten paperwork and read print materials.

A health care service coordinator who is blind was provided a driver to assist him in making home visits. The same driver also was used for other driving needs of the health care facility. As often as possible, trips were scheduled so that the driver was transporting this individual and meeting other needs at the same time.

Adapted from Office of Disability Employment Policy, U.S. Department of Labor. (n.d.). *Personal assistance service in the workplace.* Washington, DC: Author.

Sometimes a person outside of the company is hired to provide assistance, whereas at other times a co-worker may provide the assistance needed. For example, a major manufacturing corporation in Richmond, Virginia, temporarily employed three sign language interpreters through the Virginia Department for the Deaf and Hard of Hearing (VDDHH) to accommodate the communication needs of employees who are deaf during the company's annual shareholders meeting. In another situation, which illustrates the use of existing workplace supports, a human resource assistant with a bank assisted an applicant (who could not write) with completing a job application.

EMPLOYER CONCERNS ABOUT WORKPLACE PERSONAL ASSISTANCE SERVICES

In general, it is the employer's responsibility to provide a workplace personal assistant for job-related functions and the employee's responsibility to provide a personal assistant for personal needs. Employers often have no previous experience with providing a workplace personal assistant and may not realize that providing a workplace personal assistant can be easy to implement and inexpensive. Some common employer questions are addressed next.

"I Am Concerned About the Cost of Providing a Workplace Personal Assistant."

Oftentimes, cost is minimal; however, if the cost of the service is expensive, then employers should inquire about financial assistance available to either pay or help pay for the service. This might include assistance from state and local vocational rehabilitation (VR) agencies or tax incentives from the Internal Revenue Service, such as the tax credit to small businesses who provide job accommodations (see Chapter 9). Also, employers must give the applicant/employee the opportunity to pay a portion of an accommodation that proves undue hardship for the business. In some cases, the applicant/employee may be able to write off the cost for the service by using a Social Security Work Incentive (see Chapter 17). Also, in some states such as West Virginia, Medicaid state plans have been amended to allow provision of personal assistance services at the workplace to individuals with disabilities who are employed (Hinton, 2003).

"I Believe This Would Be Disruptive to My Place of Business."

Keep in mind that in some instances, the provision of workplace personal assistants may not require another employee to be hired. In many cases, a co-worker can quickly and effectively assist the employee with whatever is needed. If indeed a workplace personal assistant would be needed on a consistent basis, then the employer needs to keep in mind that the workplace personal assistant would be an employee and, therefore, is required to follow workplace policies like any other employee.

"Employees Should Take Care of Their Own Personal Care Needs."

Employers are not required to pay services not related to enabling the person to complete essential job functions. Workplace personal assistants are not paid to take care of an employee's personal needs while at work. If an individual needs assistance eating or going to the restroom while at work, then it is up to him or her to make necessary arrangements and get his or her employer's permission to allow the personal assistant on the premises.

WHAT SHOULD AN EMPLOYER DO FOLLOWING A REQUEST?

A job applicant or an employee with disabilities may request a workplace accommodation at any time during employment. There are several considerations when determining reasonable accommodation requests, including the demands of the job, the employee's skills and functional limitations, available technology, and cost. After the employer and employee agree that a workplace accommodation is needed, they should determine an appropriate accommodation. The following process may be helpful when determining the use of a workplace personal assistant as a reasonable accommodation.

- Identify the employee's personal assistance service needs.

- Use job descriptions and job analyses to identify the essential functions of the job.

- Consult with the employee and identify his or her functional limitations and potential accommodations.

- Consult with rehabilitation professionals, if needed.

- Select and provide the personal assistance services that are most appropriate.

- Select the personal assistant together with the employee.

- If equipment is used, the employee should try the product or piece of equipment prior to purchase (it is best, if possible, to try the product, modification, or equipment on the job).

- If a person is used, the employee should direct the selection of the personal assistant.

- Examine the personal assistance services utilized to see if they enable the employee to complete the necessary work tasks.

- Evaluate regularly the personal assistance services to ensure effectiveness.

- Provide regular follow-up. If needed, modify the personal assistance services plan as necessary.

When a request is made for a workplace personal assistant or other personal assistance services, employers should test the "reasonableness" of the accommodation. First, the employer and the employee need to identify the job functions that require personal assistance services. Next, a variety of personal assistance services should be identified that may reduce or remove the barrier and increase productivity. Finally, in partnership with the employee, the employer should implement the most appropriate accommodation with the least economic impact.

An employer is only required to offer an effective accommodation; it may not be the "best" accommodation in the eyes of the applicant or employee. For example, a customer service representative may want a personal attendant to come in daily to help respond to written correspondence, but the employer may either decide that having the workplace personal assistant there once a week is enough to get the job done or may ask another worker to assist the person on a scheduled basis. If the employer decides that the workplace personal assistant request as an accommodation presents undue hardship, then another alternative accommodation should be considered. Undue hardship is determined on an individual basis using the following criteria: the cost, overall financial resources of the business, and the type of operation of the employer. If the alternatives are deemed "unreasonable," then the individual who made the request must be given a chance to pay for a portion of the service.

CONCLUSION

People with disabilities remain a largely untapped labor source. If greater numbers of people with disabilities are going to gain access to employment, then increased understanding and use of personal assistance services is needed. When personal assistance services are more widely used in the workplace, they can help reduce the 70% unemployment rate among people with significant disabilities. Before large numbers of employees can begin gaining access to this support, though, additional regulatory clarification must be given to define the supports considered to be personal in nature and potentially funded by Medicare or other funding sources.

To address the need for personal assistance services, the disability rights movement has pushed for a fundamental change in federal and state long-term care policies (Dautel & Frieden, 1999). Current efforts are focused on legislation to establish a national program of community-based attendance services and supports for people with disabilities, regardless of age or disability. Although these important issues are being addressed, it is vital that health and human services agencies, CILs, or personnel instructors begin to develop personal assistance services training curricula and packages to recruit, train, and maintain personal assistants and other nonmedical home caregivers. It will be important that these packages present a candid and balanced overview of the services to be rendered and include the perspectives of people with disabilities, caregivers, and agency managers.

The national trend for people with disabilities is a move away from institutional life and toward options for living in the community, participating in the nation's labor force, and owning their own homes. The result is an increasing demand for trained personal assistants; yet, there is no registry for such training. Furthermore, there is a large and growing need for personal assistants who understand customer-directed care. Agencies who train and place personal assistants need to be prepared with updated training resources. When it becomes the norm to utilize personal assistance services as a career support, all Americans with and without disabilities will be in a win-win situation.

REFERENCES

Americans with Disabilities Act (ADA) of 1990, PL 101-336, 42 U.S.C. §§ 12101 *et seq.*

Braddock, D., Rizzolo, M., & Hemp, R. (2004). Most employment services growth in developmental disabilities during 1998–2002 was in segregated settings. *Mental Retardation, 42*(4), 317–320.

Dautel, P., & Frieden, L. (1999). *Consumer choice and control: Personal assistant services and supports in America.* Houston, TX: Independent Living Research Utilization.

Equal Employment Opportunity Commission, U.S. Justice Department. (1992a). *A technical assistance manual of the provisions of Title 1 of the ADA.* Washington, DC: Author.

Equal Employment Opportunity Commission, U.S. Justice Department. (1992b). *Americans with Disabilities Act handbook: Appendix*. Washington, DC: Author. Retrieved March 9, 2006, from http://www.jan.wvu.edu/links/ADAtam1app.html

Hinton, D. (2003). *Personal assistance services on the job*. Retrieved March 9, 2006, from http://www.ncwd-youth.info/assets/info_briefs/infobrief_issue6.pdf

Job Accommodation Network. (2004). *Personal assistance services (PAS) in the workplace*. Morgantown: West Virginia University.

Litvak, S., Zukas, H., & Heumann, J.E. (1987). *Attending to America: Personal assistance for independent living. A survey of attendant service programs in the United States for people of all ages with disabilities*. Berkeley, CA: World Institute of Disability.

Office of Disability Employment Policy, U.S. Department of Labor. (n.d.). *Personal assistance services in the workplace*. Washington, DC: Author. Retrieved March 9, 2006, from http://www.dol.gov/odep/pubs/ek97/personal.htm

Silverstein, R. (2003). *The applicability of the ADA to personal assistance services in the workplace*. Boston: University of Massachusetts.

Ticket to Work and Work Incentives Improvement Act of 1999, PL 106-170, 42 U.S.C. §§ 1305 *et seq.*

Turner, E. (2000). Role of a personal assistant in the workplace. In V. Brooke, G. Revell, & P. Wehman (Eds.), *The customer is right: A newsletter for customers from the Rehabilitation Research and Training Center on Workplace Supports* (pp. 4). Richmond: Virginia Commonwealth University Rehabilitation Research and Training Center on Workplace Supports and Job Retention.

Workforce Investment Act of 1998, PL 105-220, 112 Stat. 936.

Chapter 11

Self-Employment

Owning the American Dream

CARY GRIFFIN, NANCY BROOKS-LANE, DAVID G. HAMMIS, AND DOUG CRANDELL

JIM

Jim has known for quite some time that his dream job would be in construction. He wanted, in his words, a manly job using equipment and helping to build things. He graduated with a special education diploma. His employment history includes working in a grocery store, a bowling alley, a food service job, and a hotel. He also attended a segregated day program between jobs.

Jim's day program began an aggressive systems-change effort involving downsizing, moving out of a warehouse to a professional office park, and creating an organizational philosophy focused on employment and community-based supports. Knowing of Jim's interest in a construction job, staff contacted the builder of the new offices to determine if there might be a place for Jim in his company. A job was carved out after a period of negotiating, and Jim began employment within the month. He was quickly accepted as part of the work crew. The power of natural supports was evident when co-workers invited Jim to go with them on a short working trip out of state.

During follow-up person-centered planning meetings, a concern was addressed regarding the seasonal nature of construction work and how this could affect Jim's financial well-being. There was no immediate answer to this concern, but ongoing creative planning resulted in the idea that Jim might be interested in owning a piece of equipment that he could rent out. Jim was particularly interested in nail guns and some of the heavy equipment he was becoming familiar with at his worksites.

Market analysis revealed that small front-end loaders were in high demand. If Jim was able to purchase a loader, then he could couple his wage employment from the construction job with the income he would earn renting out the equipment. The connections he had made through his construction job could serve as a network that could help him market his rental business.

The construction company Jim works for rents loaders often. But, like many small businesses, they are undercapitalized and cannot justify purchasing expensive equipment that sits idle several days per week. Jim's ability to buy a used loader posed a unique opportunity for collaboration and mutual gain. After negotiations, Jim agreed to rent the loader to the construction company at a slightly reduced cost. In return, on the days that it does not need the loader, the company acts as Jim's agent, renting the loader out to other nearby construction companies. Jim's activity in this area is privately run through his newly established rental company. He supplements his wage job with a small business on the side, the way many Americans do.

The construction company is also providing natural supports in terms of teaching Jim how to drive the loader and perform some of the routine maintenance. Without Jim's active involvement in his equipment rental business, the Social Security Administration (SSA) would consider his earnings as passive income that counts dollar for dollar against his Medicaid and Supplemental Security Income (SSI) benefit (Hammis & Griffin, 2002).

Because Jim's business was supported with cash from a Customized Employment Project through the U.S Department of Labor, this unique business trial was possible without a full-blown business plan. Instead, the idea was tested in real time, and now the plan is being written to strengthen the concept, to anticipate income impacts on benefits, to create a business bank account that circumvents the $2,000 resource limit imposed on SSI recipients, and to consider reinvestment of profits into more construction rental equipment. At some point, Jim may decide to work in his small business full time, but for now, the mix of wage employment and business ownership represents a creative person-centered approach to customized employment, career development, and self-determination. The steps involved to establish Jim's employment are shown in Table 11.1.

RATIONALE FOR SELF-EMPLOYMENT

In 1776, Scottish political economist Adam Smith published *The Wealth of Nations*. Smith's Labor Theory of Value, although a direct assault on the often violent acquisition of physical property by the landed gentry, also revolutionized thinking about opportunity. Smith reasoned that anyone capable of producing goods or services, whether they owned land, could trade that physical effort for money (Smith, 2003). Certainly laborers and farmers alike had existed in Europe for many years, but the theme of amassing wealth; selling in a free market; and moving well beyond the traditions of feudal farming, strictly regulated craft guilds, and indentures signaled the rise of economic democracy.

In the United States, the theme of community melded with the cult of the individual. Tocqueville (2001) noted in *Democracy in America* that both farmers and townspeople on the cusp of the Industrial Revolution exuded a hopefulness about the future not yet widely apparent in western Europe. The country was already imbued with fresh individualism and frontier capitalism where personal effort mattered more than family lineage and where anyone (except most women and people of color) could strike out on their own; support their family; and continue the spread of independence, hope, and financial freedom. Jefferson's (2001) romanticized version of the yeoman farmer; Thoreau's (1902) rugged, but free-thinking, individualist; Jackson's roughneck frontiersmen (Schlesinger, 1945); and even Twain's (1996) Nevada gold miners all had one thing in common—they were all pursuing the founders' democratic principle of happiness through individual effort, mixed with the civilizing communal and commercial contributions of growing settlements. Herein grow the roots of self-determination.

Of course, Western capitalism, fueled by the underpinnings of manifest destiny, was consistently brutal, too (Merk, 1995). The savagery of slavery (Fogel & Enger-

Table 11.1. Summary of critical resources for Jim

Employment component	Source/description	Cost
Person-centered planning	Jim, significant people in Jim's life, community services board (CSB)	Day support/supported employment Medicaid waiver funding: $10,000
Vocational profile, community-based assessment	Jim, CSB	Included in waiver supports
Customized employment–wage job	Jim, CSB	Included in waiver supports (Vocational rehabilitation funds were expended during previous employment; successful closure status)
Job coaching	CSB	Included in waiver supports
Person-centered planning, follow-up/consultation	Jim, significant people in Jim's life, CSB, consulting company	Included in waiver supports, consulting agreement
Marketing research	Jim, CSB	Included in waiver supports
Business plan development	Jim, CSB, consulting company	Included in waiver supports, consulting agreement
Purchase of loader	Jim, CSB	U.S. Department of Labor/Office of Disability Employment Policy Customized Employment Grant: $10,000

man, 1994), the greed of America's industrialists (Norris, 1994; Twain, 2001), and the plight of the working poor are well documented (Riis, 1985; Sinclair, 2003). American economic history cannot be accurately recounted without revealing the obvious exclusion and struggles of many devalued classes and races. Certainly, people with disabilities share little mention in this history due to high mortality rates and the rise of institutional care (Shapiro, 1993; Trent, 1995).

Still, the hopefulness that fueled the democracy grew, even as the west was settled and populated, as the gold played out, and as the dustbowl drought ravaged the plains (Steinbeck, 1992; Turner, 1985). Through the Emancipation Proclamation, *Brown v. Board of Education* (1954), the Civil Rights Act of 1964 (PL 88-352), and the Americans with Disabilities Act (ADA) of 1990 (PL 101-336), the history of the United States, although littered with inequity and contradiction, is still one of optimism, growth, community, and opportunity (Couto, 1999; Lewis, 1990; Putnam, 2000).

That spirit of individual enterprise, coupled with the soothing balm of community and the historic promise of equality, is the starting point for discussing *customized employment* and small-business ownership by individuals with disabilities. For the general population, small-business ownership represents the largest market segment of new and expanding employment options in the United States. The self-employment rate is growing at more than 20% annually, and microenterprises (companies comprising 1–5 workers) generated more than 40% of all new jobs since the mid-1990s. Currently, small businesses in this country create more jobs than the Fortune 500 companies (Access to Credit, 1998; Brodsky, 2002; Friedman, 1996; Sirolli, 1999; U.S. Census Bureau, 2001).

Self-employment for individuals with disabilities represents another customized employment option and has its roots in the supported-employment processes of matching a person's dreams and talents to economic activity, earning wages commensurate with others, and designing support strategies that promote a successful tenure (Wehman & Kregel, 1998). Self-employment is also a rehabilitative option under the Rehabilitation Act of 1973 (PL 93-112) and its amendments and the Workforce Investment Act (WIA) of 1998 (PL 105-220). Both systems can help a person with disabilities purchase business equipment and/or assistive technology, training, and the supports necessary to run his or her business (e.g., legal, marketing, accounting). The SSA is also actively promoting the use of business ownership to stimulate employment of individuals with disabilities through the Plan for Achieving Self-Support (PASS). A PASS is one of the few financial options providing actual operating cash to businesses and is a critical complement to vocational rehabilitation (VR) and/or WIA resources (Griffin & Hammis, 2003).

SELF-EMPLOYMENT PROCESS

BOB

Initially, Bob's support team thought he was unmotivated or unable to focus as a result of his disabilities. This job, his first since graduating from high school, required him to stock and clean shelves in a department store. Bob was feeling increasing pressure and disappointment in himself for not doing a good enough job.

Bob was unfocused and unmotivated because of a bad job match. The support team rallied around Bob and planned for his ideal job, which would involve dogs because of his passion for animals. An analysis of potential employment opportunities within his neighborhood included pet stores, veterinarians, groomers, and dog walkers. Bob was presented with the option of owning his own business, a plan that his family also liked and wished to help start. Bob made it clear that a dog walking business interested him, so he and his employment consultant began the development process by exploring the option of creating an apprenticeship with a kennel. Together, they located a kennel four blocks from his home and met with the owner to propose wage employment with "resource ownership."

In this particular case, Bob purchased a treadmill on which to exercise pets in bad weather and to provide extra exercise for energetic dogs. The resource allowed Bob to create a position within an existing business. Bob is an apprentice, and owning his own equipment allows the employer to satisfy more customers and create more profit, much the same way hiring someone with a veterinary degree would allow a pet groomer to increase profits through a value-added medical service. The treadmill remains in Bob's ownership. Once he has learned the business through his apprenticeship, Bob will open his own business. Table 11.2 illustrates this process.

It is important to note that Bob is not "getting ready" to own a small business. He is ready now, but the opportunity for the apprenticeship cuts down on the need for intensive and expensive supports that would be necessary at this point. Instead, the apprenticeship represents an opportunity for the kennel host business to benefit from Bob's labor and his new equipment, and Bob learns about customer service and dog care. There is no prerequisite for owning a business, but, for some people, learning the trade first is a beneficial approach to launching their own profitable enterprise and avoiding common start-up mistakes made by those who have little experience in running an enterprise.

Table 11.2. Summary of critical resources for Bob

Employment component	Source/description	Cost
Person-centered planning	Bob, significant people in Bob's life, community services board (CSB)	Supported employment/state grant in aid (GIA) funding: $6,000
Vocational profile, community-based assessment	Bob, CSB	Included in GIA funding
Marketing research	Bob, CSB	Included in GIA funding
Customized employment–wage job	Bob, CSB	Included in GIA funding
Consultation	Bob, Bob's father, CSB, consulting company	Consulting agreement
Job coaching	CSB	Included in GIA funding
Purchase of treadmill	Bob, CSB	U.S. Department of Labor/Office of Disability Employment Policy Customized Employment Grant: $4,600
Natural supports	Bob's co-workers	No cost

Bob currently has the support of his employment specialist (being paid for through the local VR office), the natural support of the business owner and staff, and the support and love of his family. What became immediately obvious was that Bob, now in a position that meets his career dreams, has a very strong work ethic, is highly motivated, and is driven by his passion for animals. What was at first assumed to be lack of focus and lack of motivation in a traditional experience was an erroneous view of Bob that could have resulted in a life of chronic under-employment or unemployment.

Resource ownership is acquiring materials, equipment, or skills that an employer uses to make a profit. For instance, many people spend $50,000 or more on a college degree, and that degree is a symbol of exploitable resources. Employers reason that they can profit from a graduate's intellect, so people with degrees get hired. In essence, the graduate gives the employer that degree in trade for wages. The same occurs when a truck driver who owns a tractor-trailer applies for a hauling job. Without the trucking equipment, the trucker is possibly forced to face unemployment or a less satisfactory, lower paying trucking job. The point is that people need exploitable resources to get a good job, and by putting the means of production in the hands of people with disabilities, it makes them more employable (Griffin & Hammis, 2003).

Self-employment is not for everyone, but it is a reasonable option for consideration. All careers involve personal choice that should be balanced by a variety of life circumstances, including financial circumstance and funding, availability and quality of business and personal supports, and the quality of the business idea. As in supported employment, the dominant principle remains that everyone is ready to work, and it is the responsibility of special education and rehabilitation professionals to provide or facilitate the supports that make success possible. In some cases, allowing the person to experiment with different career options is the greatest support available.

The reason some small businesses are successful and others are not has a tremendous amount to do with the processes used to establish an enterprise. In supported

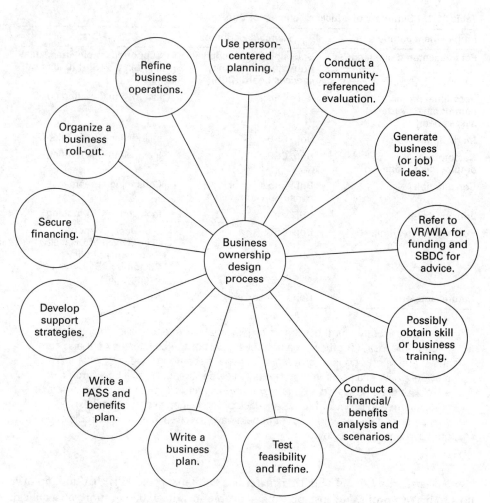

Figure 11.1.   The business ownership design process. (*Key:* SBDC, Small Business Development Center; VR, Vocational Rehabilitation; WIA, Workforce Investment Act of 1998 [PL 105-220].)

employment, for instance, the quality of the job match has long been known to make or break job retention and satisfaction (Callahan & Garner, 1997; Griffin & Hammis, 1996; Wehman, 2000). Using solid approaches coupled with inventive problem solving is a must in any career design and is especially critical when applied to people with significant support needs. Figure 11.1 shows the various components of the self-employment process. The approach is not always linear, with one step naturally following another, but instead it is one of deviations and adjustments based on the individual involved, the funding and financing climate, the potential for supports, and the market conditions. Still, the components of self-employment remain typical for almost any start-up business.

ROLE OF PERSON-CENTERED PLANNING

Person-centered planning is crucial to business development regardless of the approach utilized. The work of Beth Mount, Marsha Forest, and John and Connie O'Brien provided adequate tools for planning (Forest & Pearpoint, 1992; Mount, 1987; O'Brien & Mount, 1991). Basically, person-centered planning entails collecting functional information about the prospective business owner's life, dreams, talents, supports, and relationships. From here, a picture, both literally and figuratively, can be drawn of the best possible future. The support team concentrates on achieving the best of all possible futures, recognizing that along the way, new experiences will likely cause the prospective business owner to alter course as he or she discovers new likes and dislikes.

Community-referenced evaluation, the next component to discovering a person's possible future through real-life exposure and experience, stands in contradiction to formal testing and vocational evaluation. This self-determination process relies on ecological and not predictive validity. In other words, the team should be interested in discovering where the person feels best, performs best, and learns best. This is accomplished by focusing on the person's interests, as the team did in Bob's example, and creating opportunities to experience job tasks and environments in several community settings. Paid work experiences, informational interviews with business owners in related fields, apprenticeships, and sometimes classes all go into developing a formal, written vocational profile that further highlights the individual's career aspirations and best possible work environments (Callahan & Nisbet, 1997; Condon, Moses, Brown, & Jurica, 2003).

Oftentimes, it is mentioned that both transition-age students and adults served in the rehabilitation system have low motivation to work. Using a community-based exploration of interests and talents is a good method of finding the right fit. Many people with disabilities have not been exposed to the myriad of job choices that exist in the world, or they have been subjected to entry-level employment that failed to match their interests or engage their passions. Still others were placed in unpaid work experiences that reinforced work more as punishment than as reward.

Community-referenced evaluation is a legitimate function of habilitative services for those receiving school transition services, can be funded by adult developmental disability and mental health agencies, is an allowable cost under Medicaid, and can be supported as on-the-job training or assessment services by both VR and the WIA programs. Once a few short work experiences are completed, in keeping with job choices outlined in the person-centered plan, a job development plan or a business idea takes shape. The key is remembering that good employment practice is focused on assistance, not assessment (Griffin & Hammis, 2002).

Generating Business Ideas

Generating business ideas is the job of the individual and the team. Often, families are the best source of information, business support, and ideas in this part of the process. Many family members are already self-employed or have extensive experience in business and are invaluable in designing the approach. For example, Maryland's Project Income, funded through the state's Developmental Disabilities Council and operated by the Howard County and the Anne Arundel County Arcs, supported a young woman interested in food vending. Her father, also a food vendor and an accountant, wrote her business plan, assisted with a PASS, and helped negotiate with VR. The result was a custom-made mobile hotdog stand, a series of vending sites at local sports fields, and a stable and growing income for someone who had previously been marginally employed in wage jobs. The idea for the hotdog stand came from reviewing the young lady's interests, her unique family supports, and the availability of a market for her goods.

The process is often the same for others. In North Carolina, a young man with autism showed an interest in gardens and tractors. He started a greenhouse operation located on a farm with a produce stand. Natural supports came from the farmers who instructed him in planting seedlings, cultivating, and watering. Business supports came from the Arc of Stanly County with the understanding that, when affordable, the man would purchase bookkeeping services from a local accountant (Griffin & Hammis, 2003).

Idea generation is a process involving common sense, brainstorming, and mining of the data derived from community work experiences. Typically, it is best to throw out the first idea because it is too basic, too obvious, and too unimaginative. Instead of creating another paper shredding business, for instance, look to the motivations behind a person's interest in shredding. Perhaps it is the only job task the individual has been exposed to, the money was good enough that interest was sustained for a while longer than with other workers in the same job, or perhaps the person simply likes the co-workers and tolerates the repetitive tasks. And, of course, there are people who really do enjoy paper shredding, and thus the job is a perfect fit for them.

Thoroughly examine business ideas that are based on hobbies. Many people do not wish their hobby to be converted into a money-making opportunity, although many people certainly do evolve from hobbyists to business owners. Avoid arts and crafts hobbies that may stereotype people with significant disabilities as incapable of greater contribution. For instance, in one community, a young man makes patriotic costume jewelry. He makes only one item in his group home at night because he is bored. He derives great joy from the products, but other than selling a few at church and in the sheltered workshop, he is a far cry from running a profitable business. His team is looking beneath his love of beadwork and patriotism to see if there is a company that has a job that matches his profile or if there is a market for an expanded line of patriotic beaded jewelry.

Vocational Rehabilitation and Workforce Investment Act

Referral to VR and WIA is one of the steps along the way to self-employment and can happen at the beginning of the career exploration process or later as development occurs. It is recommended that both VR counselors and work-force center staff have a meaningful role in the development and generation of business ideas because they are experts in understanding the local market and the support strategies people often need.

VR policies on self-employment vary from state to state, but the Rehabilitation Act does indeed consider business ownership a reasonable outcome of services, and, in fact, VR nationally succeeds in assisting more than 5,000 people annually with their self-employment goals (Arnold, 1998). Counselors can use their general case services funding and their supported employment allocation for self-employment. VR can pay for such things as business classes, business plan development, marketing services, business/job coaching, work experience, vehicle repairs, capital equipment, tools, and other necessities of a small business. WIA programs, such as One Stop Career Centers, have less experience with both disability and self-employment, but the U.S. Department of Labor, their funder and administrative unit in the government, is clear that business ownership is a reasonable outcome of services (Callahan, 2003; Griffin & Hammis, 2004b). WIA programs can fund the same list of services as the rehabilitation system using the intensive training or individual training account options of their program, and numerous special projects exist across the country funded with WIA dollars to test self-employment and other customized approaches.

Skill training and business training are also available through the VR and the WIA systems, as well as through many Small Business Administration (SBA) programs. The list is long, but the SBA funds or supports in part such programs as the Small Business Development Centers (SBDC); Women's Entrepreneurship programs; the Tribal Business Information Centers (TBIC); the Senior Corps of Retired Executives (SCORE); community kitchens where space to produce food products is available at low cost; and business incubators that provide mentoring, production space, and office equipment to start-up enterprises at low cost, and numerous special projects (Griffin-Hammis, 2003; see also the SBA web site at http://www.sba.gov).

Business Training

Business training involves a multiweek commitment by those who are interested in starting an enterprise or expanding an existing one. This inclusive setting can lead to profitable business relationships; however, it appears that these classes are used to screen people out if they cannot grasp the academics involved. Of course, this is discriminatory against people with significant disabilities. The issue in self-employment is support, so if someone cannot read or write and produce a business plan, but he or she has someone else working with him or her who can perform these tasks, then funding should continue based on the business idea, not on the person's perceived limitations.

Small business ownership for individuals with significant disabilities is based on the principle of partial participation (Brown et al., 1987). Simply stated, a person who performs part of a task still has value and can contribute in a work setting. This concept is the foundation of outsourcing in business in which tasks are carved out for other subcontractors to perform and of the rehabilitation concept of job carving in which emphasis is focused on the contribution of the individual in a worksite and not on the tasks he or she cannot perform or does not enjoy (Griffin & Targett, 2000).

The classes are quite relevant to many people and introduce the topics of business planning; marketing and sales; financial management; cash-flow analysis; financing options; production and supplier refinement; hiring and management; and so forth. In some instances, it will make more sense for the support staff and/or family members to complete the coursework and use their knowledge to support the individual with disabilities. Regardless of how it is approached, learning more about the formal operations of a business is a valuable consideration, but again, not a prerequisite to owning a business. As mentioned previously, most small businesses in the United States do not have business plans, yet 80% of them succeed and achieve a tenure of 8 years on average (U.S. Department of Commerce, 2000).

As mentioned, both VR and WIA programs, as well as various Community Rehabilitation Programs, can also fund vocational training necessary to perform the vital tasks of a trade. Both VR and WIA have funded degree and certificate programs, as well as short courses so that people can become truck drivers, welders, carpenters, musical instrument renovators, accountants and bookkeepers, meteorologists, car painters, mechanics, farmers, artists, and so forth. This skill training is often an important element in determining a person's interests (i.e., through the community-based evaluation), testing one's commitment to a business idea, or expanding an existing business by learning about new or better (more profitable) techniques and equipment. Again, depending on the person's situation, a team member may need to take the classes alongside the business owner and then support the individual in applying the new information in his or her business.

Financial and Benefits Planning

Financial and benefits analysis is another key aspect in any vocational planning but can be especially critical when starting a business due to the impact of earnings on benefits and the advantages that self-employment can have over wage employment. During person-centered planning, it is critical to add a financial map to the process (Griffin & Hammis, 2003).

When developing a business or working with an ongoing small business, there are a series of critical factors that need to be accounted for by small business owners with disabilities who receive SSI and/or Social Security Disability Insurance (SSDI) benefits. SSI and SSDI have different policies and laws regarding self-employment than are used for wage employment. Medicaid, Medicare, Section 8 Housing, food stamps, and other support programs are generally affected by self-employment income as well. In some cases, significant monetary gains occur as a result of small business earnings and resource exclusions. In other cases, substantial losses occur if not planned for. Preparing a small-business benefits analysis or examining how a small business will affect the business owner's benefits is a very important initial step in the process of developing an enterprise and identifying ongoing supports needed for long-term business success.

Cash-Flow Analysis

Cash-flow analysis for the business needs to take Social Security benefits into consideration. Often, general practice small-business advisors, such as those at the SBDC, do not know how or why such income is affected and, therefore, do not include benefits information when developing cash-flow projections. SSDI, for example, is an "all or nothing" check each month. If someone receiving a $900 SSDI check loses that check unexpectedly due to poor planning, it could be difficult to recover from a sudden loss of $900 per month and still develop a small business. Some people receive both SSI and SSDI checks, thus doubling the complications. The good news is that these issues are relatively easy to anticipate through a benefits analysis.

SSI and SSDI hold potential for additional business start-up funding through a work incentive from the SSA called a PASS. PASS does not work for every small business, but it can provide substantial start-up funds for a business over an 18-month or longer period.

Both Medicare and Medicaid present opportunities for small business owners in health care coverage and long-term living supports or can have a critical impact if SSI and/or SSDI are lost due to poor benefits planning. Self-employment allows for wealth accumulation in the SSI and Medicaid systems through a work incentive called Property Essential to Self-Support (PESS). This policy allows a small business owner with SSI and/or Medicaid to have unlimited cash funds in a business account and unlimited business resources and property. Such opportunities do not exist in regular wage employment. A single person receiving SSI is required to have less than $2,000 in cash resources if employed in a wage job. PESS neutralizes that resource limit and allows the individual to accumulate wealth in the business account that can be harvested later for personal and business purchases.

Small-business owners with disabilities are often involved in a wide array of support programs beyond SSI, SSDI, Medicare, and Medicaid, including programs such as Section 8 housing, Home and Community-Based Medicaid Waiver funding, food stamps, Supported Living funding, other programs unique to veterans or children of veterans with disabilities, annuities from insurance accident funds, and possibly some welfare assistance. Each program views self-employment roughly the same as Social Security and Medicaid but varies from state to state. For instance, food-stamp programs in some states insist on monthly accounting of gross business sales and net earnings from self-employment (NESE), with each month's NESE fluctuations reported, whereas SSI divides yearly NESE by 12, resulting in NESE applied to SSI's check reduction formulas that occur evenly each month. It is important to stress again that an individual with disabilities can experience tremendous financial difficulties by not planning and considering the impact that self-employment income can have on other support programs.

For years, Section 8 housing programs did not allow a small business to be operated out of a residence. There are currently some exceptions in Section 8 small-business policies that allow parent(s) on welfare to operate child care businesses in some situations. Also, Section 8 rental policies now allow small-business activities to be operated out of tenant-based apartments if the primary use of the apartment is for housing and the incidental use is for legal profit-making activities. Knowing how SSA benefits, Section 8, Medicaid and Medicare, and other benefits programs interact is crucial in small-business planning (Hammis & Griffin, 2002).

EVAN

The "system" had not done a good job of helping Evan know what being employed meant. After high school, he entered a segregated day program. When asked about jobs he might be interested in applying for, Evan often responded with the classic "fireman" or "policeman" because he had never had the opportunity to work or understand the array of choices available.

During his person-centered planning, support staff commented on how Evan dresses in the latest hip hop styles and that cool hats, clothes, sunglasses, and shoes are of interest to him. Evan liked the idea of having a business-within-a-business selling urban wear. Through a business coalition, staff knew whom to contact to discuss such a plan. One of the members of the coalition was in contact with a woman who owned a dress shop who might be interested. Evan and his employment consultant went to the shop to negotiate a business-within-a-business in which Evan could sell urban wear.

The meeting was a disaster. The owner had very specific ideas about the environment of her business. There could be no playing of loud rap music, no magazines that conflicted with her strong religious beliefs, and, because her clientele were mainly older professionals, the attire sold would need to conform to this customer profile. Obviously, this was not a good match for Evan.

Continued planning resulted in an idea that Evan is currently testing out. It was important to him to be able to have hip hop and rap music playing in the space where his wares are sold. He also wants to focus on clothing for younger men. In addition, because Evan sometimes curses, the culture of the workplace needs to accommodate this. Evan's support staff was aware of a flea market in town where those conditions existed. Evan could rent a booth for a couple of months, and he and the staff could evaluate the viability of this self-employment option. Thus, Evan's Hip Hop Shop was born.

Initially, a Customized Employment Grant funded by the U.S. Department of Labor supported the business start-up. If successful, Evan and his employment consultant will present Evan's business plan to VR requesting funding to grow the business. The start-up cash expended for this 2-month trial totaled $3,380. Renting a booth for 2 months cost $500, and Evan, with the assistance from staff and his mother, selected $2,880 in clothing and accessories inventory to begin operations.

Resources in addition to the start-up costs included job coaching, which was funded through VR. His booth is open Fridays from noon to 8:00 P.M., Saturdays from 11 A.M. until 8:00 P.M., and Sundays from noon to 6:00 P.M. A schedule was developed with staff, Evan, and his mother detailing the sharing of on-site support. Preliminary financial analysis at midpoint in the testing of this idea shows a profit of $1,000 after only a month. Table 11.3 outlines the steps involved in establishing Evan's Hip Hop Shop.

Table 11.3.   Summary of critical resources for Evan

Employment component	Source/description	Cost
Person-centered planning	Evan, significant people in Evan's life, community services board (CSB)	Day support/supported employment Medicaid waiver funding: $10,000
Vocational profile, community-based assessment	Evan, CSB	Included in waiver supports
Interview at potential business	Evan, CSB, business owner	Included in waiver supports
Community research for alternative business location	Evan, CSB	Included in waiver supports
Consultation	Evan, Evan's mother, CSB, consulting company	Consulting agreement
Two-month demonstration self-employment business plan	Evan, Evan's mother, CSB	Included in waiver funding
Purchase of clothing and accessories, booth rental fee	Evan, CSB	U.S. Department of Labor/Office of Disability Employment Policy Customized Employment Grant: $3380
Financial analysis of demonstration business outcomes	Evan, Evan's mother, CSB, consulting company	Consulting agreement
Business plan development	Evan, CSB, consulting company	Consulting agreement
Presentation of business plan and demonstration business outcomes to vocational rehabilitation (VR) for job coach funding	Evan, CSB	VR funding for job coaching: $2,000
Ongoing business analysis to assess self-employment plans	Evan, CSB, consulting company	Consulting agreement

Evan's example illustrates that a little investment of time and money can have impressive results. The alternative was that Evan stay in entry-level jobs or day programs, neither of which satisfies the intent of rehabilitation or honors the trust that Evan places in the system charged with helping him attain a better life. Of course, not all business ideas are as easy to test, especially those that require a large investment in machinery, vehicles, training, or facilities. Still, there are some options for testing almost any idea (Griffin & Hammis, 2003).

One of the simplest methods of testing ideas is to draw up a brief survey and ask people at the local mall, on the street, or via telephone a few short questions about the idea. Evan, for instance, might have gone to the flea market and, with the permission of the owners, asked shoppers:

- Are you interested in purchasing the latest in urban wear?

- Would you shop here for those items if such a booth existed?

- What items would you be most interested in?

Because the shoppers are at a flea market, it might be assumed they are looking for low- or moderate-cost items and that they want a booth layout and environment that allows them to look through the goods at their own pace. Of course, every question and answer presents the opportunity for a follow-up question to glean more information about customer preferences.

Another option for testing the idea is to do a competitive analysis. That is, survey the community or conduct an Internet search for similar businesses to identify other possible competitors, visit some of the businesses, and discern their unique market niche. Planning a similar business involves differentiating the enterprise from the others. For instance, there are thousands of jewelry makers, but their designs differ and appeal to various customers. Some sell high-cost items, whereas others sell lower-cost goods for the budget conscious. Some use precious stones, whereas others employ precious metals. Some rely on classic styles, whereas others produce modern designs. The role of testing is to meld the owner's interests with those of the marketplace to find a match. Then, marketing and sales approaches are refined to attract customers and motivate them to buy.

Feasibility testing centers on making certain that the individual truly wants to operate the business and then addresses these basic questions:

- I know this is my customer base because . . .

- My business will provide the following services/products . . .

- This business is unique and different from the competition because . . .

- Customers will buy my product/service because . . .

- I know who my customers are because they purchased the following from me . . .

- I think I know who my customers are because they will purchase the following from me . . .

- I believe the best avenues for reaching my customers is through these channels (e.g., web site, retail sales, direct mail and catalogs, door-to-door sales, Yellow Pages advertising) . . .

Writing a Business Plan

Writing a business plan derives from all of the previous steps and puts the information in a logical sequence. The plan is essential in acquiring funding through most systems, and banks or loan funds will certainly require a comprehensive plan as well. The flow chart in Figure 11.2 represents a step-by-step approach to gathering and detailing information for the plan. Business plan templates are available from numerous sources including the local VR office, the SBA web site, and the local SBDC. Before writing the plan, check with the funder to ask which format the funder prefers or requires.

Product/Service

A precise statement describing the product or service is written, followed by an examination of the market environment and location. This statement includes information regarding the market and reasons why the business will succeed and a short assessment of the person's situation and support strategies, his or her talents, the availability of SSA work incentives, his or her love for making the product or delivering the service, and a discussion of why this business makes sense for him or her. The feasibility examination draws on the market data collected and a clarification of which tasks the owner will undertake and how he or she sees the business growing.

Three C's

The 3 C's critical to a business plan are *customer, competitors,* and *capabilities.* First, the business's potential customers are examined.

- Who are they?
- Where do they live?
- Why would they buy this product/service?
- Are they one-time buyers or will they want/need more?

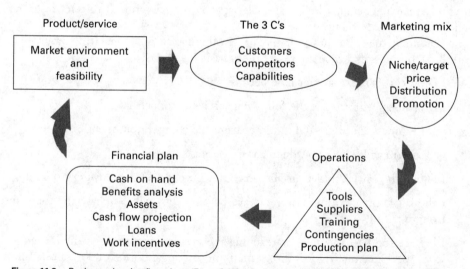

Figure 11.2. Business planning flow chart. (From Griffin, C., & Hammis, D. [2003]. *Making self-employment work for people with disabilities* [p. 47]. Baltimore: Paul H. Brookes Publishing Co. Adapted from Griffin, C., & Hamis, D. [2002]. Jimbo's Jumbos: A primer on small business planning. *Journal of Vocational Rehabilitation, 17*[2], p. 92.)

- Is price a consideration for them?

- What quality of product/service do they expect?

- What level of customer service will they require?

The evaluation of competitors is similar.

- Who are competitors?

- Will it be easy for another competitor to enter the market with a similar idea?

- Will the business compete on price, quality, or both?

- Is there a plan to turn competitors into partners or suppliers of needed parts/ services?

- What makes this product/service better or different from the competitors'?

Posing a series of questions emanating from the customer/competitor analysis sums up the capabilities of the business.

- How many customers can we potentially reach?

- How many repeat customers will we have?

- Will our competitors supply us with raw materials or component parts? Can we supply them with finished items or subassembly work?

- How will we grow into other markets such as opening other retail outlets, securing contracts from wholesale buyers, or creating an Internet presence?

The questions are endless with one prompting yet another. They are used to explore the myriad opportunities and challenges facing the business. This questioning also points out potential problems or weaknesses in the initial business design, illustrates positive market trends, and reveals capacity needs (e.g., retail sales require the business to invest in display cabinets, credit card capacity, shipping, and inventory space). A good part of this information is collected during the feasibility study.

Marketing Mix

This portion of the business plan expands on the information collected about customers, competitors, and capabilities. Based on this information, the target market is clarified. If, for instance, the research reveals that hip hop clothing buyers are young with expendable incomes, then the distribution and promotion of these products should focus on places frequented by these customers.

Pricing is determined not simply by the labor and materials used in producing the product. The price also includes burden costs such as salary and benefits, rent, legal fees, business licensing, insurance, shipping and handling, tooling and equipment, communications, advertising, depreciation, and other fixed and variable costs. There is also a psychological aspect to pricing. Some customers seek bargains, and at other times they insist on high-priced name brands. Knowing the market helps determine the price. Some manufacturers offer the same product at various levels of quality. This is why companies make several models of washing machines and why furniture comes with different wear guarantees.

Distribution and promotion refers to where and how customers get the product and the methods used to attract customers (e.g., networking, advertising, sales, marketing). Distribution planning includes determining the boundaries of the sales territory, if any; reserving shelf space; the form of delivery; and the planned approach for reaching the customer. Promotion refers to the method used to advertise and market the business and its goods or services. Most small enterprises use word-of-mouth (networking) to advertise and supplement that activity with web sites, guest appearances on local radio shows, press releases to the business editor of the local newspaper, phonebook listings, and the occasional radio or print advertisement.

Operations

The operations category concerns production of the product or service and using appropriate processes and support strategies. Listing the tools and equipment necessary for production is an essential component here, and if high-technology equipment is available, then its purchase must be planned for and amortized profitably. Suppliers must be secured and training for the business owner and employees arranged.

Contingency plans are also necessary in the operations section. If a supplier is unable to deliver, then alternative suppliers should be known, and, if the business is seasonal (e.g., tourist-related service), a plan for bad weather should be outlined so that the business does not falter. There should also be a discussion of equipment repair plans. The contingencies do not have to take into account anything that could go wrong, but some thought must go into reasonable expected interruptions in business.

Financial Plan

The financial plan is perhaps the most critically developed and managed portion of the business plan. Here, the benefits analysis is merged with available funding and the long-term (2–5 years generally) estimation of income and expenses. Typically, the business develops an operating budget, a cash-flow projection, a break-even analysis that illustrates when sales income exceeds expenses, and a PASS if applicable. All of these forms are available through the local VR office, the SBA web site, and the local SBDC. Funders want to see that the company will be profitable in a reasonable amount of time and that the operator is making money. The scope of this chapter does not allow space to cover financials, but many resources exist locally for assistance and training (Griffin & Hammis, 2004a).

Writing the PASS plan occurs at this point, or sooner if the business idea is solid and the benefits analysis indicates the opportunity. The PASS provides cash to a business owner, something no other system can provide, and requires at least an 18-month business plan projection before approval. PASS can buy such items as starting inventory, vehicles, equipment or assistive devices, marketing and sales assistance, classes or training, and a host of business essentials. The PASS forms and regulations are available at http://www.ssa.gov, and sample PASS plans can be viewed at the Rural Institute, University of Montana, web site at http://www.passplan.org. A thorough discussion of PASS and self-employment is also available in *Making Self Employment Work for People with Disabilities* (Griffin & Hammis, 2003) and at http://www.griffinhammis.com

Developing support strategies is the result of good person-centered planning and should be detailed in both the business plan operations section and in the PASS.

Family support is a typical approach in most American businesses (Doyel, 2000), and rehabilitative supports through an employment specialist or job coach are often available long term. Still, the desire for emancipation from the system should be a driving consideration while using various funding sources to maximize benefits before cutting free.

One of the most natural means of attaining support in a small business is to make certain that the cost of identified supports is built into the pricing structure and that these costs can be covered once disability system financial support is diminished. In many typical small businesses, the owner does not perform the accounting functions because most business owners are more interested and skilled in producing their particular product or service. Therefore, the accounting functions are outsourced to a local accountant, and the cost for those services becomes a consideration in the pricing of the products sold.

Another method of designing supports mentioned throughout this chapter is the business within a business. This arrangement makes sense when a complimentary service or product is brought inside an existing enterprise. Hence, a person interested in weaving custom sweaters sets up shop inside a woolens retailer, an espresso maker collocates inside a pastry shop, or a manicurist adds a chair in the local beauty parlor. The host business attracts customers, and the existing staff can naturally assist the new enterprise by teaching the tricks of the trade. The host business also benefits from having a value-added service in-house and from the rent generally paid by the new occupant. In these cases, support and assistance have taken the form of joint advertising; assistance with customer and production scheduling; training in the use of tools and equipment; help with pricing and bookkeeping; and assistance with inventory, supply ordering, transportation, and delivery.

In some cases, the business-within-a-business strategy can be used to create opportunities that are not obvious.

TRICIA

Tricia, a woman with significant disabilities, wished to work in a child care center. She also enjoyed working with computers, but her lack of reading and writing skills severely limited her job choices. Job development failed to find a child care job but did identify an employer interested in Tricia. As with many small businesses, the child care center in question did not have ready cash to risk nor any positions open. A proposal for Tricia to manage a computer tutoring service was developed, which blended her interest in children and computers. The employer was still reluctant of the risk, so a further refinement involved Tricia purchasing the equipment and operating her own computer lab inside the child care facility. The child care center would then be satisfying a known customer need and would increase revenues from Tricia's payments for rent.

The owner hesitated until a feasibility survey to the parents indicated a strong desire for computer tutoring using the latest interactive and intuitive software. In fact, approximately 20 families signed their children up for the classes. Within a few months of operating, the employer saw the value of the service and offered Tricia a position on staff. Although this meant that Tricia closed her sole proprietorship, it also meant she no longer had to manage the business, which actually came as a relief to her. Table 11.4 summarizes the process utilized for supporting Tricia and her employment dream.

Table 11.4.   Summary of critical resources

Employment component	Source/description	Cost
Person-centered planning	Tricia, significant people in Tricia's life, community services board (CSB)	Day support Medicaid waiver: $10,000
Vocational profile, community-based assessment	Tricia, CSB	Included in waiver support
Meeting with vocational rehabilitation (VR)	Tricia, CSB	Included in waiver support
Interview at potential child care businesses	Tricia, CSB, business owners	VR supported employment funding: $3,500
Consultation	Tricia, CSB, consulting company	Consulting agreement
Customized employment wage job with resource ownership negotiated	Tricia, CSB, business owner	Included in VR funding
Purchase of printer, computer, learning stations, software	Tricia, CSB	U.S. Department of Labor/Office of Disability Employment Policy Customized Employment Grant: $4,000
Training in use of resources	Tricia, CSB	Included in VR funding
Job coaching	CSB	Included in VR funding
Ongoing financial and benefits analysis	Tricia, CSB, consulting company	Consulting agreement
Natural supports	Co-workers	No cost

In Tricia's case, a business-within-a-business approach reduced an employer's risk and stress at creating a position, utilized natural supports in a worksite, and proved previous vocational assessments wrong. Traditional vocational evaluations had indicated that Tricia could not succeed in her dream job, but the small business coupled with the resource-ownership technique served as a transitional approach to securing a desirable wage position.

Securing financing is a consideration from the start of the business planning process. But, now that the plan is basically complete, solid commitments can be added to the plan through the negotiation process with VR, WIA, or the CRP providing supports. Once the sources of income and amounts are known, the financial projections can be updated. An important technical aspect to consider is the depreciation schedule for capital equipment. For instance, if VR funds equipment, then they retain ownership until the counselor determines the business is successful. Because the equipment still belongs to VR, the business owner cannot depreciate it on the tax return. By negotiating an early release of title to the equipment, the business owner reduces the tax burden by claiming depreciable assets.

Of course, the impact of earned income from the business is also of concern. SSA requires monthly reporting of NESE, and fluctuations in earnings should be planned for. Modifications to a PASS will also likely be required as the business launches and grows. In addition, an application detailing ongoing support needs will be required for states now implementing portable funding and individual budgets.

Business Roll-Out

Business roll-out can occur at many points along this nonlinear route. As illustrated with Evan's business, Evan started operations before solid funding and planning was complete because this was the best way to test his idea and his commitment. Running the business also presented Evan, staff, and family with hard data on support needs, training issues, the best suppliers to use, pricing parameters, and the best days and hours of operation.

Business roll-outs can vary from having a grand opening celebration to placing an advertisement in the newspaper. A strategy for a business roll-out should be developed in the business plan under the marketing section because this first impression can be critical to attracting long-term customers.

A mistake often made in retail operations is opening without sufficient inventory or without the proper pricing for the quality level of goods sold. Customers may not ever come back even if the inventory grows because the bad first impression taught them not to waste their time. It is often better to wait until better inventory is available through funders or loans or slowly and quietly roll out the business, the way Evan did with his hip hop clothing.

Refining business operations occurs and continues throughout the life of the enterprise. Changes in business climate, product improvements, customer requests, opportunities for collaboration and partnership, or just a change in the owner's focus affects businesses daily. The long-term survival of a business necessitates ongoing vigilance in customer service and operations management. It is a widely held belief that 80% of a company's business generally comes from 20% of its customers and that retaining repeat customers costs 80% less than attracting new ones (Kawasaki, 1995). Great customer service is essential for survival, and every effort to improve the business should be made.

Companies often make the mistake of arguing over minor losses and fail to consider the lifetime purchasing impact of a customer. Customers may not always be right, but they usually think they are. Weigh the options before alienating someone. For instance, a regular customer at an espresso stand may buy three lattes per week at $3.00 each. The customer also requests a free cup of water to go. Water is generally free, but the cup costs $.06. Charging the customer the additional $.06 might discourage that steady customer from ever returning, resulting in a gross loss of $468 annually. Of course, that customer will also tell, on average, 20 others of the mistreatment at the hands of the espresso stand (Gerson, 1994). So, be flexible, appreciate the customer, and think about more than the day's till.

Along these same lines, one way to keep customers is by improving product quality while keeping prices reasonable or stable. Keeping costs in line with the customer's perceived value is critical to growth and stability. Often, this means investments in new technology, training, processes, and personnel. The business owner and the team should consider long-term adaptations and expansion, both for survival's sake and in order to grow profits. Certainly the corner garage has invested in computer diagnostic equipment, and it will not be long before the corner drugstore will have a computer-based digital picture printer. Such advances in technology and process do not simply mean a cash threat to small business, they also represent growth and new customers.

CONCLUSION

It is important to reemphasize that the process of creating a small business is fluid and nonlinear. Many people already know what they want to do, and they know how to do it. Others will need extensive supports, a few job trials to clarify their career choices, and significant assistance in managing their money and operations. All of these can be planned for and accommodated, given the availability and affordability of supports and a spot in the marketplace. There is no doubt that anyone can own and operate a business. The challenge remains the mutual inventiveness in creating something legitimate that engages the individual's personal genius and simultaneously satisfies or creates a market niche.

REFERENCES

Access to Credit. (1998). *Small enterprise, big dreams* [Videotape]. Frederick, MD: Access to Credit Media Project.

Americans with Disabilities Act (ADA) of 1990, PL 101-336, 42 U.S.C. §§ 12101 *et seq.*

Arnold, N. (Ed). (1998). *Self employment in vocational rehabilitation: Building on lessons from rural America.* Missoula: University of Montana, Rural Institute.

Brodsky, N. (2002, February). *Street smarts: Opportunity knocks.* Available on-line at http://www.inc.com

Brown, L., Udvari-Solner, A., Frattura-Kampschroer, L., Davis, L., Ahlgren, C., Van Deventer, P., et al. (1987). The Madison strategy for evaluating the vocational milieu of a worker with severe intellectual disabilities. In L. Brown, A. Udvari-Solner, L. Frattura-Kampschroer, L. Davis, & J. Jorgensen (Eds.), *Educational programs for students with severe intellectual disabilities* (Vol. XVII, pp. 1–372). Madison, WI: Madison Metropolitan School District.

Brown v. Board of Education, 347 U.S. 483 (1954).

Callahan, M. (2003). *Customized employment Q & A.* Washington, DC: U.S. Department of Labor, Office of Disability & Employment Policy.

Callahan, M.J., & Garner, J.B. (1997). *Keys to the workplace: Skills and supports for people with disabilities.* Baltimore: Paul H. Brookes Publishing Co.

Callahan, M., & Nisbet, J. (1997). *The vocational profile: An alternative to traditional evaluation.* Gautier, MS: Marc Gold & Associates.

Civil Rights Act of 1964, PL 88-352, 20 U.S.C. §§ 241 *et seq.*

Condon, E., Moses, L., Brown, K., & Jurica, J. (2003). *Pass the bucks: Increasing choice and control in transition planning through the use of SSA work incentives.* Missoula: University of Montana, Rural Institute.

Couto, R. (1999). *Making democracy work better.* Chapel Hill: University of North Carolina Press.

Doyel, A.W. (2000). *No more job interviews: Self-employment strategies for people with disabilities.* St. Augustine, FL: Training Resource Network.

Fogel, R., & Engerman, S. (1994). *Time on the cross: The economics of American Negro slavery.* New York: W.W. Norton Company.

Forest, M., & Pearpoint, J. (1992). Family, friends, and circles. In J. Nisbet (Ed.), *Natural supports in school, at work, and in the community for people with severe disabilities* (pp. 65–86). Baltimore: Paul H. Brookes Publishing Co.

Friedman, S. (1996). *Forming your own limited liability company.* Chicago: Upstart Publishing.

Gerson, R.F. (1994). *Marketing strategies for small businesses.* Menlo Park, CA: Crisp Publications.

Griffin, C.C., & Hammis, D. (1996). *StreetWise guide to person-centered career planning.* Denver: Creative Training Accelerating Talent.

Griffin, C.C., & Hammis, D. (2002). Assistance not assessment: Getting to the heart of small business feasibility. *Rural Exchange, 2*(15), 1–4.

Griffin, C.C., & Hammis, D. (2003). *Making self employment work for people with disabilities.* Baltimore: Paul H. Brookes Publishing Co.

Griffin, C.C., & Hammis, D. (2004a). *Clarinda's custom card company: A financial management primer.* Florence, MT: Griffin-Hammis Associates.

Griffin, C.C., & Hammis, D. (2004b). *Self-employment and microenterprise: A customized employment option*. Washington, DC: U.S. Department of Labor, Office of Disability and Employment Policy.

Griffin, C., & Targett, P.S. (2000). Finding jobs for young people with disabilities. In P. Wehman (Ed.), *Life beyond the classroom: Transition strategies for young people with disabilities* (3rd ed., pp. 171–210). Baltimore: Paul H. Brookes Publishing Co.

Hammis, D., & Griffin, C.C. (2002). *Social Security considerations for entrepreneurs with significant disabilities*. Florence, MT: Griffin-Hammis Associates.

Jefferson, T. (2001). *Notes on the state of Virginia*. New York: St. Martin's Press.

Kawasaki, G. (1995). *How to drive your competition crazy*. New York: Hyperion.

Lewis, R.W.B. (1990). *The American Adam*. Chicago: University of Chicago Press.

Merk, F. (1995). *Manifest destiny and mission in American history*. Cambridge, MA: Harvard University Press.

Mount, B. (1987). *Personal futures planning: Finding directions for change*. Unpublished doctoral dissertation, University of Georgia, Athens.

Norris, F. (1994). *The Octopus*. New York: Penguin Classics.

O'Brien, J., & Mount, B. (1991). Telling new stories: The search for capacity among people with severe handicaps. In L.H. Meyer, C.A. Peck, & L. Brown (Eds.), *Critical issues in the lives of people with severe disabilities* (pp. 89–92). Baltimore: Paul H. Brookes Publishing Co.

Putnam, R. (2000). *Bowling alone*. New York: Simon and Schuster.

Rehabilitation Act of 1973, PL 93-112, 29 U.S.C. §§ 701 *et seq.*

Riis, J. (1985). *How the other half lives*. New York: Dover Publishers.

Schlesinger, A. (1945). *The age of Jackson*. New York: Little, Brown & Company.

Shapiro, J. (1993). *No pity: People with disabilities forging a new civil rights movement*. New York: Crown Publishing.

Sinclair, U. (2003). *The jungle*. New York: Barnes & Noble Classic Series.

Sirolli, E. (1999). *Ripples from the Zambezi*. British Columbia, Canada: New Society Publishers.

Smith, A. (2003). *An inquiry into the nature and causes of the wealth of nations*. New York: Bantam Books. (Original work published in 1776)

Steinbeck, J. (1992). *The grapes of wrath*. New York: Penguin Classics.

Thoreau, H.D. (1902). *Walden; a story of life in the woods*. Princeton, NJ: Princeton University Press.

Tocqueville, de A. (2001). *Democracy in America*. New York: Signet Classics.

Trent, J. (1995). *Inventing the feeble mind*. Los Angeles: University of California Press.

Turner, F.J. (1985). *The frontier in American history*. Melbourne, FL: Krieger Publishing.

Twain, M. (1996). *Roughing it*. Los Angeles: University of California Press.

Twain, M. (2001). *The gilded age*. New York: Penguin Classics.

U.S. Census Bureau. (2001). *Statistical abstract of the United States: 2001*. Available on-line at http://www.census.gov

U.S. Department of Commerce. (2000). *Report on small business success*. Retrieved August 1, 2000, from http://www.usdoc.gov

Wehman, P. (Ed.). (2000). *Life beyond the classroom: Transition strategies for young people with disabilities* (3rd ed.). Baltimore: Paul H. Brookes Publishing Co.

Wehman, P., & Kregel, J. (1998). *More than a job: Securing satisfying careers for people with disabilities*. Baltimore: Paul H. Brookes Publishing Co.

Workforce Investment Act (WIA) of 1998, PL 105-220, 29 U.S.C. §§ 2801 *et seq.*

Chapter 12

Alternative
Work Arrangements

Benefits and Limitations
for Individuals with Disabilities

Patrice A. Londoner and Michael D. West

The task of acquiring, developing, motivating, and maintaining a high quality work-force ... will present management with unparalleled human resource challenges. As managers grapple with new workplace complexities ... growing diversity, changing social forces, attention to work-family conflict, and alterations in worker lifestyles, they must reconsider traditional work arrangements. Alternative work arrangements ... have been used to deal with these increasingly complex human resource issues. (Hartman, Stoner, & Arora, 1992, p. 35)

The nature of work is changing dramatically in the world today; much of what transpires at work creates portable knowledge housed within the minds of employees. Employees take this information with them when they leave work in personal experiences, skills, attributes, and abilities (Gibson, Blackwell, Dominicis, & Demerath, 2002; Wiesenfeld, Raghuram, & Garud, 2001). With the rapid onslaught of technology, traditional work environments may no longer keep organizations competitive in their marketplace. Therefore, companies must proactively look for creative and innovative methods to recruit, develop, and retain high-performing individuals by meeting work-force expectations, needs, and desires (Gainey, Kelley, & Hill, 1999; Hartman et al., 1992; Wiesenfeld et al., 2001). In order to do this, businesses must look for alternative ways of working and surrogates to traditional employees.

The 21st century reflects a different structure than the American work force of the 1970s and 1980s. At one point, employees typically went to work Monday through Friday from 8:00 A.M. to 5:00 P.M., retiring from the same company where they started in their first position. Today, many workers desire more flexible work hours or the

Note: Preparation of this chapter was supported in part by Cooperative Agreement #H133G020158 from the National Institute on Disability and Rehabilitation Research, U.S. Department of Education, and Grant #EMP-02-01 from the Commonwealth of Virginia, Virginia Board for People with Disabilities. Official endorsement of chapter contents should not be inferred.

ability to operate from home when possible, allowing for a better balance between work and personal life demands. Yet, businesses today often find they do not need as many full-time employees on a regular basis but require a more adaptable way to meet fluctuating flows in the workload. By adopting a different approach to staffing, one geared toward variability in everyday work cycles, companies are implementing a more proactive attitude toward employment needs. Some nontraditional employees and supplementary sources of labor include people with disabilities, retired individuals, older workers, and part-time employees (Chemers, Oskamp, & Costanzo, 1995; Riccucci, 2002).

Telecommuting and the use of *temporary staffing* are two avenues employers are initiating to accommodate employee demands for more responsive accommodations and the negative effects of uneven workloads. These two alternative work arrangements open the door for organizations to be more flexible in meeting the changing expectations of employees as well as business needs. On one hand, companies realize that pursuing nontraditional employees increases the available labor pool for employers and does not restrict employers or employees to geographical locations when recruiting for positions. For example, if an employee experiences a lifestyle change while working for a company, telecommuting may offer the opportunity to continue working for the organization if the position is one of importance to the business.

On the other hand, organizations with flexible workloads may discover one day that they only need 50 people but the next day they may require 150 people to handle the incoming work. This type of environment is conducive to using temporary help to supplement the need for hiring full-time employees. Many businesses utilize temporary employees for strategic long-term assignments that will never become permanent positions yet are vital to the company. Quite often temporary help is used for providing relief for temporary loss of staff due to illness, vacations, and so forth. Businesses must face the idea that "lean and mean" is not only a saying but also a reality in order to stay competitive in today's marketplace.

How may these alternative work arrangements be used to benefit employees or job seekers with disabilities? Employment and underemployment remain serious issues for people with disabilities as a group. According to the American Community Survey conducted by the U.S. Census Bureau (2003), only about 34% of individuals with disabilities age 21–64 are employed. Significant numbers of those who are employed are working at less than their potential, often in an effort to retain disability benefits. Telecommuting and temporary staffing provide alternative routes for enabling more individuals with disabilities to enter the work force or to increase their level of involvement and earnings.

Alternative work arrangements can help the worker and the employer to mitigate the effects of his or her disability. For example, for many individuals with psychiatric disabilities, episodic symptoms, hospitalizations, and employer/co-worker fears typically contribute to poor employment histories. For those with mobility impairments, typical contributing factors include lack of affordable and reliable transportation, limited numbers of accessible businesses, and lack of personal assistance services in the workplace. A common barrier for individuals with chronic fatigue or pain is that employers may be unwilling or unable to accommodate needs for extended rest periods, alternative scheduling, or reallocation of work duties.

For many people with significant disabilities, the increasing prevalence of telecommuting and temporary staffing opportunities offer the possibility of an accessible, barrier-free workplace; flexible scheduling; and the elimination of disability-related bias or discrimination (Cassam, 1995; Cleaver, 1999; Hesse, 1995; Woelders, 1990). Many people with disabilities have the desire and capability to work from their homes. These individuals, many with good job skills and a strong work ethic, constitute a hidden labor pool. By one estimate, increasing the availability of telecommuting for unemployed individuals with disabilities in the United States alone would save employers between $48 billion and $96 billion dollars annually (Eaton, 1998) in reduced short- and long-term disability payments, workers compensation, and personnel replacement costs. This estimate does not include the potential benefits to American taxpayers in increased tax revenues and reduced public benefits, such as Social Security Disability Insurance (SSDI), Supplemental Security Income (SSI), Medicaid, Medicare, and housing and food supplements.

This chapter describes two commonly used alternative work arrangements, telecommuting and temporary staffing. It also presents the benefits and potential problems with these methods, with a focus on benefits and problems for workers with disabilities.

TELECOMMUTING

Multiple definitions exist for *telecommuting*. One definition is "a work arrangement where organizational employees regularly work at home or at a remote site one or more complete workdays a week in lieu of working in the office" (Hartman et al., 1992, p. 36). Another definition construes telecommuting as job-related functions performed in a work-at-home site as opposed to a worksite, even when work is not electronically transferred (DuBrin & Barnard, 1993). Craumer and Marshall (1997) preferred to draw distinctions between telecommuting and remote employment. Telecommuting is "working at home during business hours one or more days a week, using a combination of computing and communications technology to stay productive and connected to the office and client" (p. 94). These researchers argued remote employment encompasses any work arrangement in which a significant portion of work is performed and completed at a fixed location other than the employer's central office location. As can be seen in the previous definitions, Craumer and Marshall's idea of the difference between telecommuting and remote work conflicts with the definition proffered by DuBrin and Barnard (1993), which tends to combine the two domains.

Prevalence of Telecommuting

The differences in definitions of a telecommuter lead to discrepancies in an accurate nationwide number count for this work-force population. Apparently, the disparity results from numerous headcounts combining freelance creative workers, self-employed people with contracts, and contingent workers operating from home, many of whom perform defined telecommuter roles and responsibilities. This makes it difficult to grasp exactly how far reaching telecommuting currently is or how much impact telecommuters will have in the future on workplace employment.

In 1993, DuBrin and Barnard estimated that 26.6 million Americans worked from home, with 10 million categorized as telecommuters. Of those 10 million, 5.6 million were working for somebody other than themselves. In a 2002 report, the U.S. Bureau of Labor Statistics indicated that 1 in 10 Americans are self-employed (Goldsborough, 2002). The International Telework Association and Council (ITAC) claims the number of U.S. telecommuters in 2000 reached almost 24 million, with a 20% increase over the number in 1999, but with less than 3% of federal employees telecommuting in early 2001 due to limited access (West, 2001). This number indicates a low utilization rate by federal employees; however, the Office of Personnel Management had until 2004 to increase this availability to 100% for eligible workers. In projections from 2000, the U.S. Department of Labor estimated between 13 and 19 million full- and part-time telecommuters would be involved in telecommuting and remote work by 2003, whereas the Gartner Group estimated the worldwide number to be closer to 137 million workers (Mills, Wong-Ellison, Werner, & Clay, 2001).

Estimates of the number of telecommuters with disabilities are not available, but the number in the United States is thought to be relatively small (Eaton, 1998). There appear to be many more workers interested in telecommuting than are able to do so, in part because of the reluctance of employers to provide that option (Mokhtarian, Bagley, & Salomon, 1998). Among the reasons for employer reluctance have been concerns about unmonitored work, supervision and evaluation, network security concerns, and implementation costs (Korzeniowski, 1999; Nilles, 1997; Watad, 1999).

Characteristics of Telecommuters

In a survey conducted in 2000 by the Behavior Research Center, the general age of telecommuters was more than 25 years old, with a mean age around 45 (Gibson et al., 2002). Telecommuters tend to include diverse groups of people across a myriad of vocations. Typically, telecommuters live in urban areas, and, although some work in manufacturing, construction, and transportation, these individuals most commonly work in white-collar occupations. Telecommuters also work in industries such as business services, banking, transportation, communication, and insurance (DuBrin & Barnard, 1993). Some typical telecommuting occupations include sales representatives, claims adjusters, computer programmers, and customer service representatives. Characteristics such as race, age, ethnicity, and marital status do not appear to make a discernable difference in who pursues this type of employment (Fetto, 2002).

In a literature review included in a research study by Haines, St-Onge, and Archambault (2002), Ford and McLaughlin (1995) as well as Haddon and Lewis (1994) named self-discipline and effective organizational and personal time management skills as important to telecommuting success. Meanwhile, Robertson (1994) and Duxbury, Higgins, and Mills (1992) indicated self-control skills are imperative in telecommuters because this group of employees tends to overwork. Self-motivation is the ability to work with minimal supervision, and the need for minimal supervision is an indication of low affiliation or low social interaction needs. Self-motivation, flexibility due to changing demands, and a results-oriented focus are key features required in a successful telecommuter.

In considering employees for telecommuter positions, Edwards (2001) listed the ability to work with minimal supervision, minimal feedback, and limited social contact as imperative traits. In addition, being a self-motivated worker with good organizational skills proved of utmost importance. Edwards further advocated a successful telecommuter would consistently perform well and have a proven ability to follow policy and procedures. Successful telecommuters are also technologically literate and possess clear and consistent written and oral communication skills (see Table 12.1). The study conducted by Haines et al. (2002) supported the need for high self-management

Table 12.1.   Attributes of a successful telecommuter

Has the desire and ability to work independently with minimal
supervision, feedback, and social contact

Has proven time-management ability

Is flexible

Is results oriented

Has the proven ability to follow policy and procedures

Has consistently good performance

Is technologically literate

Possesses clear and consistent communication skills—written
and oral

Is dependable and honest

Possesses high self-management skills in the following areas:
self-discipline, self-control (does not overwork), self-
motivation, self-observation, goal setting, self-rewarding,
and self-punishing

Source: Edwards (2001).

skills (self-observation, self-goal-setting, self-reward, and self-punishment) as healthy indicators of telecommuting outcomes. Other high self-management skills included self-discipline, a desire to work independently, dependability, and honesty (Lomo-David & Griffin, 2001).

Barriers to Successful Telecommuting

Barriers do exist in the telecommuting realm. Conventional teamwork presents a number of challenges in the traditional work environment. The total number of people permitted to work on the team for face-to-face interaction time is limited for several reasons. Efficient and effective communication combined with rapid response time and workload distribution in traditional work environments all have an impact on conventional teams and their productivity (Eom & Lee, 1999). In an attempt to retain skilled workers, telecommuting programs reduce personal restraints while allowing more employee discretion over work relations. This structure results in greater autonomy and flexibility; however, it may also produce ambiguity on the part of organizations, which may lead to concerns for future career opportunities (see Table 12.2; Wellman et al., 1996). Supporting this notion, Wiesenfeld et al. (2001) reported that telecommuters fear an "out of sight, out of mind" situation may occur when working offsite. This mindset may result in decisions by their supervisors that may affect telecommuters' careers if they are not considered for key projects or promotions. In reverse, many telecommuters admit to ambiguity in their own attachment to their organizations for the same "out of sight, out of mind" situation.

These issues are likely to affect employees with disabilities more so than employees without disabilities. Loneliness and social isolation are common problems with

Table 12.2.   General barriers to successful telecommuting

Ambiguity by the organization and the employee

Concerns for future career opportunities—"out of sight out of mind"
fears by employee and employer

Feelings of isolation and alienation

Diminished feelings of organizational attachment, leading to lower
levels of motivation and job satisfaction

High levels of stress, anxiety, depression, and physiological
symptoms

Sources: Wellman et al. (1996); Wiesenfeld, Raghuram, and Garud (2001).

individuals with disabilities (Hopps, Pepin, Arseneau, Frechette, & Begin, 2001), and many individuals with disabilities value highly the social interaction they experience in the workplace. In addition, separation from the workplace may exacerbate problems with discrimination in career advancement that many employees with disabilities already face.

It is important to note that home-based distractions often jeopardize the level of investment by employees. Feelings of isolation may lead to perceptions of alienation and diminished attitudes toward organizational attachment, in turn affecting employee motivation, job satisfaction, and commitment. These factors may ultimately affect telecommuter–supervisor relations, co-worker communication, and the overall company (Allen & Renn, 2002).

One of the core issues concerning management and telecommuters alike is the physical and mental separation between telecommuters, co-workers, supervisors, and other organizational members (Haines et al., 2002). "Virtual work may alter organizational structures and systems, individuals' work roles and required skills, and even how individuals define themselves with respect to the organization" (Wiesenfeld et al., 2001, p. 214). Buss (1991), along with Baumeister and Leary (1995), argued that individuals have a strong need to associate and identify with other people in established long-term positive relationships. Without these frequent and stable interactions, people experience stress, anxiety, depression, and sometimes negative physiological results (Gainey et al., 1999). Aspinwall and Taylor (1992), Dormann and Zapf (1999), and Lim (1997) all suggested that work-based support comes through communication with individuals in close proximity to one another. Yet, for telecommuters, close proximity is not an option; however, the people with whom telecommuters interact on a regular basis may come to provide this same support structure.

Hoyt (2000) described four primary factors operating as barriers to successful telecommuting.

1. *Reality congruence* describes the relationship between what the organization professes to be true and what individual employees personally experience.

2. *Task identification* distinguishes the specific tasks required to perform successfully as a telecommuter; some telecommuters believe job-related tasks will miraculously turn more desirable once they move from a traditional office setting to the home.

3. *Role strain* connotes the amount of stress an employee experiences when attempting to fulfill work and family role expectations while operating at home.

4. *Investment* addresses the personal level of effort, expertise, and emotional reserves of telecommuters in the organization.

An individual's perception of belonging to an organization is known as organizational identification. In order for an organization to have meaning in a telecommuter's mind, the individual member must feel a part of the organization (Wiesenfeld et al., 2001). If the fit between telecommuting and the employee is good, then higher feelings of personal satisfaction and commitment should mitigate feelings of isolation. If the feelings of isolation are high and the personal satisfaction, motivation, and commitment levels are low, then misalignment exists between the person and his or her environment (Edwards, 1996, as cited in Haines et al., 2002). This misalignment may lead to telecommuters leaving the company in search of a better person–environment or person–organization fit, which leads the telecommuters to the attraction-selection-attrition (ASA) theory. ASA theory predicts the fit between a person's values and those of the organization, forecasting an individual's level of satisfaction, commitment, performance, and turnover (Schnider, Goldstein, & Smith, 1995).

Why Choose Telecommuting?

A trend exists in the present postindustrial society in which many well-educated, professional people are seeking the opportunity to return to the home-based work of earlier generations (Gibson et al., 2002). Telecommuting presents one way to meet this changing need in work-force expectations. Telecommuters are a fast-growing ensemble comprised of people from diverse backgrounds, cultures, religions, ethnicities, genders, races, and work-related experiences. Some telecommuters have disabilities and others do not, but either way, telecommuting opens the door of opportunity for a larger employment pool than what is available to traditional work environments and practices.

Lomo-David and Griffin (2001) delineated telecommuting differently depending on the perspective taken: the employer, the government, or the employee. As an employer, it represents a corporate strategy to reduce the cost of overhead, meet affirmative action requirements, improve productivity, and increase bottom line. The U.S. government interpretations construe telecommuting as an environmentally friendly strategy reducing pollution and demands for transportation. Employees, however, see telecommuting as a work agreement with myriad possibilities not necessarily considered by either employers or the U.S. government.

DuBrin and Barnard (1993) noted multiple advantages for telecommuters, including the opportunity to balance child care and family needs with work, as well as the ability to schedule one's own work hours. Some workers construe the arrangement as a monetary enticement by helping to save expenses on gas, child care, and clothing because telecommuters can wear whatever they want while working at home. Others see this agreement as mitigating daily commutes to central offices in congested metropolitan areas or as a way for employees who live great distances from the office location to stay employed by the company. Telecommuting also provides an important opportunity for employees with disabilities to continue working for a company when being in the work environment is not as conducive to the nature of the disability as the home environment. As more and more people telecommute, organizations limit the risk of losing the knowledge capital, abilities, and skills of the employee when other life situations necessitate a move from the area.

Expectancy theory (self-fulfilling prophecy theory) is an important concept for managers to keep in mind regarding traditional and alternative work arrangements. This theory implies that people make choices in behavior and will select the choice resulting in the more valuable output or reward when they see the reward as attainable (Quick, 1988). Impression cues, both verbal and nonverbal, connote the supervisor's expectation for the employee, prompting the employee to strive to attain the expected level of success (Nadler, Cammann, Jenkins, & Lawler, 1975; Pool, 1997; Solomon, 2002). Therefore, the amount of effort exerted by an employee toward performing a job well will result in success and gaining a valued reward.

Quick (1988) asserted five key steps managers must take in order to sustain high performance in telecommuters. First, managers must define expectations clearly through goal-setting sessions and objectively measured results in order to eliminate gaps in understanding between the telecommuter and the manager. Second, employees and managers should establish personal goals for the telecommuter that support organizational goals. Third, the workload must be doable and the assignments realistic in the eyes of the telecommuter and the manager. If an employee is concerned about not being able to meet the manager's expectations for completing his or her work, then the result is a lack of motivation. Fourth, managers must give regular, specific feedback with positive reinforcement to maintain a telecommuter's self-esteem and motivation level. Fifth, rewards for meeting expectations should be built into management–telecommuter work arrangements. Positive praise, organizational recognition, and training and development opportunities are motivational rewards that can be used by management.

Table 12.3 presents the benefits and limitations of telecommuting for employees with disabilities. For people who experience chronic or changing disabilities, telecommuting options may be excellent solutions for assisting individuals to not only find employment but also to remain employed because of enhanced personal control (Hesse, 1995).

As disability symptoms fluctuate, these individuals can better preserve their stamina, thus remaining healthier and more reliable employees (Hesse 1995; Mabilleau, Szlamkowicz, & Masse, 1997). By eliminating daily commutes and reducing fatigue issues, telecommuting also helps them to maintain their productivity and may serve as a long-term job retention strategy. These benefits, however, have to be weighed by

Table 12.3.   Benefits and limitations of telecommuting for employees with disabilities

Benefits	Limitations
Barrier-free workplace	Potential feelings of isolation and alienation
Improved productivity	Potential for lack of organizational identification and subsequent lack of promotion opportunities
Ability to manage work schedule, breaks, and so forth to accommodate the effects of a disability	
Opportunity to balance child care and family needs with work	Potential for poor person–environment fit in nontraditional workplaces
No daily commute, reduced personal costs, and improved financial well-being	Potential turnover due to attraction-selection-fit theory

Source: Hesse (1995).

the individual with disabilities against the potential undesirable effects of telecommuting, such as social isolation and career stagnation. For some individuals, working in isolation and an absence of promotional opportunities are not issues; for others, these factors will make telecommuting an undesirable option. Failure to create a well-thought-out, detailed, deliberate approach for communicating, as well as the design and development of team relationships, ensures the breakdown of successful telecommuting efforts (McCready, Lockhart, & Sieyes, 2001, as cited in Gibson et al., 2002).

It is also critical for the individual with disabilities and rehabilitation professionals to ensure that the prospective telecommuter has the necessary attributes to successfully work from home. If the telecommuter has difficulty self-managing time or effort, cannot effectively deal with both work and home responsibilities, or wants or needs regular face-to-face contact with supervisors and co-workers, then telecommuting may not be a viable option for that individual.

TEMPORARY STAFFING

Temporary staffing is one of several related and rapidly growing alternative employment situations known as *contingent work*. Contingent workers are employees who are hired only when there is an immediate and direct need for their services (Freedman, 1988). The term has been broadly used to refer to leased employees, temporary employees, seasonal positions, on-call workers, independent contractors, and outsourced work. In 1989, the U.S. Bureau of Labor Statistics defined *contingent work* as any job in which an individual does not have an explicit or implicit contract for long-term employment (Polivka & Nardone, 1989). Although any of the contingent work options are appropriate avenues for individuals with disabilities, this section focuses on temporary staffing because that option has been documented more thoroughly with members of this population.

Temporary staffing may not be the most descriptive or appropriate terminology for many individuals who are engaged in this type of work. For example, many temporary staffing companies have long-term contracts with businesses to provide particular services, and there may not be a specified endpoint for the work. In other cases, the worker may be a long-term employee of the temporary staffing company but only works on temporary assignments. In essence, though, the definition of a *temporary employee* is one who is directly employed by a temporary staffing agency, regardless of the type of work performed or the duration of a particular assignment.

Prevalence of Temporary Workers

The temporary staffing industry in the United States has enjoyed explosive growth since the 1970s, during which time the market for temporary labor has become increasingly complex and diverse (Theodore & Peck, 2002). From 1982 to 1998, the number of jobs in the temporary staffing industry grew by 577%, whereas the economy as a whole grew by 41% (U.S. General Accounting Office, 2000). In 2000, the number of temporary service workers numbered more than 3.6 million, or approximately 3% of the total U.S. work force.

Despite the growth of temporary employees since the mid-1970s, Mehta and Theodore (2001) described the cyclical nature of temporary employment. Businesses tend to use temporary staffing agencies during economic slowdowns to reduce their own need for employees. Temporary staffing agencies can provide sufficient workers to maintain the business's production while reducing or holding its personnel costs, and can eliminate the need for recruitment, hiring, and training.

Characteristics of Temporary Workers

According to a report for the U.S. Bureau of Labor Statistics, DiNatale (2001) noted that temporary workers are disproportionately young African American or Hispanic women who have lower average levels of education than the general work force and than workers in other types of contingency work. Almost 80% of temporary staff are employed full time, which is approximately equal to the general population. Although temporary workers perform many varied functions within businesses, the primary occupations are in manufacturing and office work, with men principally in the former and women the latter. These are also the occupational areas in which temporary staffing growth will occur in the future. Table 12.4 provides information from the U.S. Bureau of Labor Statistics on the primary growth occupations for temporary workers from 1996 to 2006. Certainly, temporary staffing is a booming industry that offers a diverse array of positions that individuals with disabilities could fill.

Barriers to Successful Temporary Employment

Temporary staffing can be beneficial to individuals with disabilities in obtaining job-skills training and a work history and often leads to permanent employment. Still, there are some issues for both workers with disabilities and for rehabilitation providers. As Wehman, Hewitt, Tipton, Brooke, and Green (2004) reported, one of the barriers consistently faced by Manpower and other staffing agencies is educating business clients. Some of their business clients understand the full potential of hiring individuals with disabilities; however, others still believe the myths and misconceptions of hiring individuals with disabilities. It must be remembered that although temporary staffing agencies hire and train the employees, the client business provides the workplace, which may not be hospitable or accessible to workers with disabilities.

Another substantial barrier to using this avenue for workers with disabilities is the cyclical nature of the temporary staffing industry. As noted previously, use of temporary staffing by businesses often varies inversely with the status of the local economy. The vagaries of the local labor market may force temporary staffing agencies to deactivate some of their workers.

Table 12.4. Projected growth in temporary service workers by occupation, 1996–2006

Occupation	Percent growth
Operators, fabricators, and laborers	77.4%
Machine setters, set-up operators, operators, and tenders	121.2%
Hand packers and packagers	99.8%
Administrative support, including clerical	36.0%
Typists	8.8%
General office clerks	8.0%

Data obtained from the U.S. Bureau of Labor and Statistics web site, http://stats.bls.gov/

A final barrier relates to temporary employment's effects on Social Security disability benefits. Cycles of active and inactive status with a temporary agency can affect the benefit status of workers with disabilities and possibly affect their continued involvement in temporary employment. Work incentives such as expedited reinstatement can alleviate this barrier, but fear of losing benefits during periods of inactivity may cause some to forego employment altogether.

Why Choose Temporary Employment?

Temporary staffing agencies have been recognized as appropriate and viable sources of employment for individuals with disabilities. In a seminal study by Blanck and Steele (1998), interviews were conducted with temporary workers with disabilities employed by Manpower, Inc., an international temporary staffing agency. Using qualitative methods, the Manpower study found that temporary employment was often used as a means of gaining experience and skills for making the transition from unemployment to full-time employment. Interviews of Manpower employees with a range of physical and mental disabilities suggested that the company's investment in individualized training, job-skills assessment, and career development was critical to the company's success in hiring and retaining workers with disabilities. The investment also proved critical for employees' success in attaining their employment goals.

Interviews with Manpower management and staff suggested a corporate culture that emphasizes every individual has job skills and aptitudes. Furthermore, the interviews showed every job can be broken down into essential tasks and that every individual can attain employment by matching the potential employee's skills or developing those skills to match essential tasks. Temporary and staffing agencies work with people with disabilities in the same way they work with people without disabilities. The focus on the job placement process for all applicants is on individual abilities, job skills, and interests. The temporary staffing industry uses job assessment services, temporary job assignments, and work-skills training to assist individuals with disabilities to find employment. Most temporary staffing agencies provide individualized applicant assessment and systematized skill assessments for a variety of job tasks. These agencies focus on matching employee skills to workplace demands, individualized training, and accommodations as part of the placement process.

A report by Wehman et al. (2004) described a model demonstration project to form a partnership between public rehabilitation programs and private temporary staffing agencies, using Manpower, Inc. The project tested the use of a staffing specialist knowledgeable in disabilities and accommodations for workers with disabilities, who served as a liaison between community rehabilitation providers, Manpower, and Manpower's clients. After 9 months of operation, the project had placed 14 individuals in competitive employment, and 10 were employed a minimum of 180 days.

CONCLUSION

The diverse work force and proliferation of alternative work arrangements may prove a blessing and a challenge to businesses and employees in the 21st century. There is no doubt that alternative work arrangements present a wider pool of prospective employees to organizations, including individuals with disabilities. For individuals choosing to work from home or for temporary staffing agencies, these alternative work approaches provide a plethora of opportunities. These opportunities include increased earnings, socialization, an improved level of job satisfaction, better opportunities for leisure time and personal goals, and a higher quality of life.

It is important to keep in mind, however, that alternative work arrangements are not a panacea for the problems of unemployment and underemployment of people with disabilities. Telecommuting and temporary employment may be attractive work options for many people, including those with disabilities, but these options must be balanced against each individual's goals, interests, life situation, and work personality. With these alternative work arrangements, as with more typical employment situations, individuals with disabilities need to be informed of the benefits and the possible disadvantages they may face so that they may make informed decisions.

REFERENCES

Allen, D.G., & Renn, R.W. (2002). Telecommuting: Understanding and managing remote workers. In G.R. Ferris, M.R. Buckley, & D.B. Fedor (Eds.), *Human resource management: Perspectives, context, function, and outcomes* (4th ed., pp. 145–164). Upper Saddle River, NJ: Prentice Hall.

Aspinwall, L.G., & Taylor, S.E. (1992). Modeling cognitive adaptation: A longitudinal investigation of the impact of individual differences and coping on college adjustment and performance. *Journal of Personality and Social Psychology, 63*(6), 989–1003.

Baumeister, R.F., & Leary, M.R. (1995). The need to belong: Desire for interpersonal attachments as a fundamental human motivation. *Psychological Bulletin, 117,* 497–529.

Blanck, P.D., & Steele, P. (1998). *The emerging role of the staffing industry in the employment of persons with disabilities: A case report on Manpower, Inc.* Iowa City: University of Iowa Law, Health Policy, and Disability Center.

Buss, D.M. (1991). Evolutional personality psychology. *Annual Review of Psychology, 42,* 459–491.

Cassam, D. (1995). Telework: Enabling the disabled. *Search, 26*(7), 201–202.

Chemers, M.M., Oskamp, S., & Costanzo, M.A. (Eds.). (1995). *Diversity in organizations: New perspectives for a changing workplace.* Thousand Oaks, CA: Sage Publications.

Cleaver, J. (1999). Willing and able: Telecommuters with physical impairments. *Home Office Computing, 17*(12), 112.

Craumer, P., & Marshall, L. (1997, November/December). Telecommuting from an electronic cottage: Negotiating potholes and toll booths. *Online, 21*(6), 94–102.

DiNatale, M. (2001). Characteristics of and preferences for alternative work arrangements, 1999. *Monthly Labor Review, 124*(3), 28–49.

Dormann, C., & Zapf, D. (1999). Volunteer participation and withdrawal: A psychological contract perspective on the role of expectations and organizational support. *Nonprofit Management and Leadership, 9*(4), 349–367.

DuBrin, A.J., & Barnard, J.C. (1993, Summer). What telecommuters like and dislike about their jobs. *Business Forum, 18*(3), 13–18.

Duxbury, L.E., Higgins, C.A., & Mills, S. (1992). After-hours telecommuting and work–family conflict: A comparative analysis. *Information Systems Research, 3*(2), 173–190.

Eaton, H. (1998, August). *Can telecommuting close disability-related employment gaps?* [On-line serial]. Available on-line at http://www.hightechcareers.com

Edwards, J.M.H. (2001, Fall). Assessing your organization's readiness for teleworking: Will telework work for us? How to determine if your organization is ready for telework. *Public Manager, 30*(3), 47–50.

Eom, S.B., & Lee, C.K. (1999, Spring). Virtual teams: An information age opportunity for mobilizing hidden manpower. *SAM Advanced Management Journal, 64*(2), 12–17.

Fetto, J. (2002, February). You can take it with you. *American Demographics, 24*(2), 10–11.

Ford, R.C., & McLaughlin, F. (1995, May/June). Questions and answers about telecommuting programs. *Business Horizons,* 66–72.

Freedman, A. (1988, May 19). Testimony before the Employment and Housing Subcommittee of the Committee on Government Operations, House of Representatives, Washington, DC.

Gainey, T.W., Kelley, D.E., & Hill, J.A. (1999, Autumn). Telecommuting's impact on corporate culture and individual workers: Examining the effect of employee isolation. *SAM Advanced Management Journal, 64*(4), 4.

Gibson, J.W., Blackwell, C.W., Dominicis, P., & Demerath, N. (2002, Spring). Telecommuting in the 21st century: Benefits, issues, and a leadership model which will work. *Journal of Leadership Studies, 8*(4), 75–87.

Goldsborough, R. (2002, June). Making working alone work for you. *Teacher Librarian, 29*(5), 45.

Haddon, L., & Lewis, A. (1994). The experience of telecommuting: An annotated review. *International Journal of Human Resource Management, 5*(1), 194–223.

Haines III, V.Y., St-Onge, S., & Archambault, M. (2002, July–September). Environmental and person antecedents of telecommuting outcomes. *Journal of End User Computing, 14*(3), 32–51.

Hartman, R.I., Stoner, C.R., & Arora, R. (1992). Developing successful organizational telecommuting arrangements: Worker perceptions and managerial prescriptions. *SAM Advanced Management Journal, 57*(3), 35–43.

Hesse, B.W. (1995). Curb cuts in the virtual community: Telework and persons with disabilities. *Proceedings of the 28th Annual Hawaii International Conference on Systems Sciences, IEEE, 36*(6), 418–425.

Hopps, S.L., Pepin, M., Arseneau, I., Frechette, M., & Begin, G. (2001, July–September). Disability related variables associated with loneliness among people with disabilities. *Journal of Rehabilitation, 67*(3), 42–48.

Hoyt, B.R. (2000, October). Techniques to manage participation and contribution of team members in virtual teams. *WebNet Journal, 2*(4), 16.

Korzeniowski, P. (1999). Build or buy: Enterprises weigh remote access options. *Business Communications Review, 29*(12), 22–24.

Lim, V.K.G. (1997). Moderating effects of work-based support on the relationship between job insecurity and its consequences. *Work and Stress, 11*, 251–266.

Lomo-David, E., & Griffin, F. (2001, May/June). Personality traits of white-collar telecommuters: Perceptions of graduating business students. *Journal of Education for Business, 76*(5), 257–262.

Mabilleau, P., Szlamkowicz, D., & Masse, D. (1997). Job-Access: Teleworking at home and keeping persons with disabilities in the workforce. *WORC report 1997: Second International Workshop on Telework Building Actions on Ideas*, 117–122.

Mehta, C., & Theodore, N. (2001, June 25–26). *The temporary staffing industry and U.S. labor markets: Implications for the unemployment insurance system.* Paper presented at the U.S. Department of Labor, America's Network Research Conference, Washington, DC.

Mills, J.E., Wong-Ellison, C., Werner, W., & Clay, J.M. (2001, October/November). Employer liability for telecommuting employees: Despite the many potential benefits of telecommuting, employees based in remote offices may cause unanticipated legal liability for employers. *Cornell Hotel and Restaurant Administration Quarterly, 42*(5), 48–60.

Mokhtarian, P.L., Bagley, M.N., & Salomon, I. (1998). The impact of gender, occupation, and the presence of children on telecommuting motivations and constraints. *Journal of the American Society for Information Science, 49*(12), 1115–1134.

Nadler, D.A., Cammann, C., Jenkins, G.D., & Lawler, E.E. (1975). *The Michigan organizational assessment package (Progress Report II).* Ann Arbor, MI: Survey Research Center.

Nilles, J. (1997). Telework: Enabling distributed organizations. *Information Systems Management, 14*(4), 7–14.

Polivka, A.E., & Nardone, T. (1989). On the definition of "contingent work." *Monthly Labor Review, 112*(12), 9–16.

Pool, S.W. (1997, May). The relationship of job satisfaction with substitutes of leadership, leadership behavior, and work motivation. *Journal of Psychology, 131*(3), 271–284.

Quick, T.L. (1988, July). Expectancy theory in five simple steps. *Training and Development Journal, 42*(7), 30–33.

Riccucci, N.M. (2002). *Managing diversity in public sector workforces.* Cambridge, MA: Westview Press.

Robertson, K. (1994). *Is telecommuting for your organization?* Unpublished master's thesis, Simon Fraser University, Burnaby, British Columbia, Canada.

Schnider, B., Goldstein, H.W., & Smith, D.B. (1995, Winter). The ASA framework: An update. *Personnel Psychology, 48*(4), 747–774.

Solomon, G.B. (2002, September). Sources of expectancy theory information among assistant coaches: The influence of performance and psychological cues. *Journal of Sport Behavior, 25*(3), 279–287.

Theodore, N., & Peck, J. (2002). The temporary staffing industry: Growth imperatives and limits to contingency. *Economic Geography, 78,* 463–494.

U.S. Census Bureau. (2003). *2003 American Community Survey.* Available on-line at http://www.census.gov

U.S. General Accounting Office. (2000). *Unemployment insurance: Role as safety net for low-wage workers is limited.* Washington, DC: Author.

Watad, M. (1999, August 13–15). Managing distributed workforce in a telework environment. In *Proceedings of the 1999 Americas Conference on Information Systems* (pp. 447–449). Pittsburgh: Association for Information Systems.

Wehman, P., Hewitt, M., Tipton, M., Brooke, V., & Green, H. (2004). *Business and the public sector working together to promote employment for persons with developmental disabilities: Preliminary results.* Manuscript submitted for publication.

Wellman, B., Salaff, J., Dimitrova, D., Garton, L., Gulia, M., & Haythornthwaite, C. (1996). Computer networks as social networks: Collaborative work, telework, and virtual community. *Annual Review of Sociology, 22,* 213–238.

West, H. (2001, Fall). Teleworking in the public sector: A four-part series to help federal managers implement new requirements by Congress for enabling 100 percent of eligible agency employees to telecommute by 2004. *Public Manager, 30*(3), 45–47.

Wiesenfeld, B.M., Raghuram, S., & Garud, R. (2001, March-April). Organizational identification among virtual workers: The role of need for affiliation and perceived work-based social support. *Journal of Management, 27*(2), 213–229.

Woelders, H.J. (1990). Telework: New opportunities for the handicapped unemployed workers. *International Journal of Sociology and Social Policy, 10*(4–6), 176–180.

Section III

Key Organization and Policy Issues

Chapter 13

Moving from Segregation to Integration

Organizational Change Strategies and Outcomes

Patricia M. Rogan

Sheltered facilities and day activity centers that serve adults with disabilities represent an outdated model of service delivery that congregates and segregates people. Under the rubric of "needs," "treatment," and/or "rehabilitation," people assigned to sheltered facilities become what Glasser (1978) termed *prisoners of benevolence* because they are deprived of the right to pursue meaningful work opportunities of their choice (Murphy & Rogan, 1995). Segregated facilities have proliferated as the primary day service option for adults with disabilities since the 1960s (Butterworth, Gilmore, Kiernan, & Schalock, 1999; McGaughey, Kiernan, McNally, Gilmore, & Keith, 1996), and access to integrated work in the community continues to be limited (Wehman, Revell, & Brooke, 2003; Yamaki & Fujiura, 2002).

Workshops and day activity centers claim to address three major needs—shelter, vocational readiness, and choice—but people are denied access to typical quality-of-life outcomes when they are sheltered from experiencing typical lifestyles. People do not need to get ready for the real world in artificial, simulated settings. True choice involves knowing one's options and gaining experiences on which to make informed choices. Sheltered facilities, in reality, offer few choices.

It is estimated that 75% of individuals served in rehabilitation programs are either in sheltered workshops or segregated nonwork day programs, and only 23% are in supported or competitive employment (Braddock, Hemp, & Rizzolo, 2004; McGaughey, Kiernan, McNally, Gilmore, & Keith, 1994; Metzel, Boeltzig, Butterworth, & Gilmore, 2004). The weight of federal and state funding remains largely devoted to segregated services, and, unfortunately, the number of individuals in facility-based programs has risen since the 1990s (Braddock et al., 2004; Butterworth, Gilmore, Kiernan, & Schalock, 1998; Dreilinger, Gilmore, & Butterworth, 2001). Only 37% of community

The author is grateful to W. Grant Revell, Jr., and Paul Wehman for their editorial assistance.

rehabilitation organizations that provided both sheltered and segregated work reported downsizing their segregated programs (West, Revell, & Wehman, 1998).

MOVEMENT TOWARD THE COMMUNITY

Americans are fortunate to have strong disability-related legislation that promotes and protects the civil rights of individuals with disabilities. For example, the Rehabilitation Act Amendments of 1998 (part of the Workforce Investment Act [WIA] of 1998 [PL 105-220]) stipulate that the intended outcome of vocational rehabilitation (VR) services is employment and includes the term *presumption of benefit*. This term means that all individuals can benefit from VR services unless the state unit can demonstrate by clear and convincing evidence that an individual is incapable of benefiting in terms of an employment outcome due to the severity of the disability of the individual (Section 102). Because VR is mandated to serve people with the most significant disabilities, people with high support needs should not experience difficulty gaining access to this funding source.

The Individuals with Disabilities Education Act (IDEA) of 1990 (PL 101-476) and its subsequent reauthorizations have promoted inclusive education for youth with disabilities. These former students and their families now want similar inclusive services in the adult world. They want to make the transition to meaningful, typical, integrated adult lifestyles, including postsecondary education and/or employment, community living, and social relationships and activities of their choice.

There has been an amazing array of employment-related legislation in the United States, including the Americans with Disabilities Act of 1990 (PL 101-336), the WIA (including amendments to the Rehabilitation Act), and the Ticket to Work and Work Incentives Improvement Act of 1999 (PL 106-170), all highlighting access, choice, community-based services, and employment. In January 2001, the Rehabilitation Services Administration made a very significant policy shift that affected state VR agencies. The decision stated that facility-based services could no longer be deemed a satisfactory employment outcome for VR. Instead, only integrated jobs in the community would meet their new criteria for an employment outcome (State Vocational Rehabilitation Services, 2001; Wehman et al., 2003). Many states have taken this federal directive to heart and are working to translate the spirit and intent of the law into practice. For example, Vermont no longer has state-funded sheltered workshops. Washington state has recently adopted a policy that all day services must be employment focused if they wish to receive state funding. Tennessee and Florida have set targets for reduction of numbers in sheltered facilities and concurrent increases in the percentage of people in integrated employment.

The Supreme Court's *Olmstead* decision mandated that services be provided in the most integrated setting. This decision has major implications for day services because segregated facilities cannot be considered the most integrated setting. Finally, the movement toward the community has been influenced by the growing voice of self-advocates. Self-advocates and other advocates have been promoting self-determination, including choice and control of services and funding (Nerny, 2000), and have often bypassed the traditional, entrenched service system.

There is no doubt that funding drives services, and a variety of approaches to tweak and reconstruct the way that dollars flow for services have emerged. Recent approaches include results-based funding, which focuses on specific desired outcomes; personal budgets (person-centered funding), which involve putting resources in the hands of people with disabilities to purchase desired services and supports (Novak,

Mank, Revell, & O'Brien, 1999; O'Brien, Ford, & Malloy, 2005; Wehman & Revell, 2002); and Medicaid waivers, which offer more flexibility and individualization in services than traditional Medicaid funding.

Many community rehabilitation programs have responded positively to federal and state initiatives to provide integrated employment services. As a result, since the 1980s nearly 140,000 people previously considered unemployable are now working and earning more money than people in other vocational options (Wehman, Revell, & Kregel, 1998). Research has shown that quality-of-life outcomes are better for those in supported employment compared with their counterparts in segregated day services (McCaughrin, Ellis, Rusch, & Heal, 1993; Rogan, Grossi, et al., 2001; Wehman et al., 1998). People in competitive employment earn more than four times as much as individuals in sheltered employment (Butterworth, Sullivan, & Smith, 2001). Earnings in competitive employment remain consistently 250%–300% higher than those in sheltered employment, even when accounting for severity of disability (Butterworth, Gilmore, & Kiernan, 2000). Individuals in competitive employment worked a mean of 32 hours per week at the time of VR case closure, compared with a mean of 26 hours per week for those in sheltered employment.

A growing number of organizations have completely shifted from facility-based to community-based services and supports. These organizations have demonstrated that the provision of "services without walls" is not only possible but also results in better outcomes for individuals, the organization itself, and the community.

The process of organizational change, sometimes referred to as *conversion*, is complex. Among its many challenging facets, organizational change involves a period of operating dual systems (the old and the new) simultaneously; changing staff attitudes and skills; marketing a new organizational image; partnering with businesses; shifting fiscal structures and priorities; and assisting people with disabilities to develop self-determination and employment and career opportunities and to pursue their dreams. Researchers have begun to discover why some organizations have chosen to undertake the changeover process, why only some succeed, what barriers organizations encounter, what strategies are most successful in helping them make the change, and what outcomes they achieve.

Murphy and Rogan (1995) described the experiences of four organizations that had completed the conversion process. Although each of the four organizations experienced unique barriers to changeover, common barriers included the following:

- *Funding issues*—It was difficult to operate dual programs and services (facility based and community based) within the organization's funding structures and funding streams. That is, funding may have been tied to programs, not people, and therefore could not follow individuals and be used for community services. For some organizations, uniform funding amounts (e.g., per diem rates) were not based on the amount of support each person needed and did not cover true costs.

- *Lack of staff competence*—Staff members who had worked in the facility were often averse to leaving it to work in the community with businesses and did not have the attitudes and skills to successfully assist individuals to get and keep employment.

- *Organizational structures and personnel roles that impeded a focus on employment and community services*—Typically, direct-services staff were at the bottom of the organizational hierarchy with little decision-making power about the individuals they served. Their job descriptions offered little guidance in terms of roles and expectations for providing community employment opportunities.

- *Negative attitudes among various stakeholders*—Every stakeholder group, including funding agencies, staff members, parents, and the individuals in the facility, had people who were opposed to closing the "shop." These individuals worked hard to impede progress toward organizational change, both covertly and overtly.

- *Lack of transportation*—People were transported to and from the facility, but it was often difficult to gain access to typical forms of transportation to and from community jobs.

- *Difficulty finding quality jobs, especially for people with the most significant disabilities*—The process of assisting individuals with high support needs to get and keep employment required knowledge and skills that were fairly sophisticated. Many organizations have struggled with each and every aspect of this process.

    This study identified multiple strategies considered key to the success of organizational change efforts. Organizations reported the importance of articulating a clear vision; involving key stakeholders from the start; using individualized, person-centered planning approaches; hiring and training quality staff; securing high-quality jobs; terminating facility admissions; gaining access to external consultants to help guide the change; working to flatten the organizational structure with most staff providing direct services; changing the agency's image through marketing; building business partnerships; divesting in buildings and equipment; and pursuing flexible funding and alternative sources of funds. Each of these factors will be discussed in depth in later sections of this chapter.

    Albin, Rhodes, and Mank (1994) studied the changeover process and consequent outcomes of eight organizations that had either converted or were in the conversion process. The decisions to change were primarily driven by values. A major barrier was associated with the difficulty in trying to operate the old and the new programs at the same time. Finding adequate resources and working through conflicting values also presented challenges. The majority of respondents said that trying to negotiate contradicting policies was a barrier, as well as the lack of staff with the needed skills. Negative attitudes regarding the abilities of the people being served, as well as the inadequacies of the funding systems, were also stated as primary obstacles to changeover.

    In-depth case studies of six organizations that have undertaken organizational change revealed similar themes to previous studies (Butterworth & Fesko, 1998). For these organizations, the changeover process led to confusion about roles and responsibilities. Some staff said that it was difficult to determine how to move from "taking care of" individuals with disabilities to supporting them to become more self-determined. Facilitating inclusion at work and in the community was also mentioned as an ongoing challenge for staff. More recently, the Institute for Community Inclusion completed a national study of 10 organizations, including six that successfully closed a facility-based program and four that were in the process of organizational change (Butterworth, Fesko, & Ma, 2000). Data from this study support research from other studies, indicating that internal factors (e.g., beliefs, organizational values) have the greatest impact on the development of integrated employment services. Among the six organizations that "converted," the following themes or organizational characteristics were consistent across each:

- Openness to risk taking

- Services driven by shared values

- Ongoing process of self-evaluation

- Linkages to external resources

- Holistic focus on the needs of individuals with disabilities

- Central roles for direct-services staff in developing organizational goals and making decisions that affect individuals with disabilities

- Emphasis on continuous improvement

Among numerous factors these organizations attributed to their success, all reported leadership as the single most important element. Other successful strategies included shared decision making, funding that provided an incentive to make the change, connecting with others undergoing changeover, adopting and abiding by a vision of community, and listening to and acting on the desires of people with disabilities and their families. Additional discussion of these strategies is presented later in the chapter.

It has been very interesting and informative to track organizational change efforts in order to understand who is doing what, where, and how. There are hundreds of organizations that have either fully shifted to totally community-based services or are at various stages of the changeover process. A great deal has been learned from these organizations that have pursued their vision, demonstrated success, and set a course for others to follow (Center on Disability and Employment, 2005). The purpose of this chapter is to summarize information about the organizational change process gleaned from multiple organizations throughout the country. Information about a national study of organizational change is provided. Also highlighted are outcomes of this challenging but rewarding change process and future directions.

NATIONAL STUDY OF ORGANIZATIONAL CHANGE

In an effort to better understand the scope and nature of organizational change efforts from sheltered facilities to community-based services, a national study was conducted (Rogan, Held, & Rinne, 2001) that focused on 41 organizations in 25 states. Of these organizations, 12 no longer ran facility-based services, whereas 13 were at various stages of change.

The survey gathered information about whom these organizations served, their staffing patterns, and the process that they undertook to make change happen. Key questions for investigation included why they undertook the process and what the catalyst was for this change. It was very instructive to learn that it was primarily those in leadership positions within each organization who drove the changeover process—the CEO, executive director, or top-level management personnel. Although this is not necessarily a surprise, it is still significant in that it points to the fact that future changeover efforts will likely be internally versus externally driven and will rely on the passion and commitment of top-level management to promote and sustain the change.

Barriers to Organizational Change

What were some of the major barriers to organizational change? What seemed to be getting in the way, both before the organization undertook the changeover process and as it proceeded through the change process? Interestingly, the highest rated impediment was negative attitudes among stakeholders. In other words, many staff, family members, board members, and business personnel held negative beliefs and attitudes about the employability of people with disabilities. Funding was rated as the second greatest barrier, followed by regulations that impeded integrated services. These factors are common, given the current funding orientation toward segregated day services and the outdated regulations related to traditional system services. Other barriers include a lack of expertise (because there is no road map for organizational change), lack of leadership, transportation issues, lack of personal care services, and safety net issues (i.e., the plan for what people will do if and when they lose their job). Organizations reported overcoming these barriers in the following ways.

Negative Attitudes

Negative attitudes among various stakeholders were addressed by providing a great deal of information, training, and opportunities for discussion, including parent-to-parent, customer-to-customer, and staff meetings. A "one person at a time" approach was suggested in order to address the unique interests and needs of each individual. A key question for hesitant family members and workshop participants was, "What would it take to make you feel comfortable?" For example, if a parent was reluctant to let his or her adult son or daughter ride the city bus, then this question might lead to plans for providing systematic instruction, gradually fading support, and building in natural supports and contingency plans.

Demonstrating success and showcasing success stories (e.g., in newsletters and the local media) also helped to shift attitudes. Person-centered planning approaches (e.g., PATH, Personal Futures Planning) helped families and individuals design desired services and supports, thereby easing fears. Agency staff worked first with individuals who wanted out and with supportive families. These individuals, in turn, influenced the next wave of people who were interested in community employment. Individuals with disabilities were invited to participate in job clubs, job shadowing, job tryouts, volunteer work, and other community activities in order to gain experience, ease their fears, and assist with decision making.

Funding Issues

Strategies for addressing funding issues included developing better working relationships with funding agencies and policy makers in order to negotiate appropriate funding for desired outcomes and demonstrating success as a provider agency. For many, it meant negotiating alternative funding mechanisms (e.g., block funding, hourly rates), diversifying funding sources (e.g., VR, Medicaid waiver, Title XX, Workforce Development, Temporary Assistance for Needy Families [TANF], grants), seeking "bridge" funding (e.g., from the state Developmental Disabilities Council, grants, fundraising), cutting expenses (e.g., selling, leasing, or renting the facility and equipment), and redirecting excess earnings to community-based services.

Incompatible Regulations

Changing state regulations involved ongoing discussions with policymakers and legislators. Partnering with other agencies with similar interests was also helpful in building a stronger voice and lobbying effort. Some organizations were able to negotiate waivers of, or changes to, problematic regulations.

Lack of Expertise

Training, attending conferences, becoming members in professional organizations, and networking with other agencies were all used to build expertise within these organizations. For some, experience in the field, along with "figuring it out as you go," proved helpful. Finally, hiring staff with desired skills and increasing participatory management were successful strategies.

Lack of Leadership

To address a lack of leadership, organizations hired new leaders, brought in expert consultants, and formed change-management teams to guide changeover activities. These teams were comprised of representatives of major stakeholder groups and were charged with guiding the changeover process and communicating with their respective constituents in order to have a continuous feedback loop. Agencies also partnered with and/or visited organizations that were further along in the changeover process. To support staff development and collaboration, some agencies reorganized staff into teams and provided cross-training in order to learn about one another's areas of expertise. This strategy proved to build leadership within the staff ranks by moving more decision-making power to the "front lines."

Transportation Issues

Transportation barriers were addressed via local and state efforts. Organizations became involved with their local transit authority and/or state transportation coalition to advocate for flexible and inexpensive options. Several organizations joined with aging coalitions and other community groups that needed affordable and accessible transportation to develop a van service. Still others became creative by using Social Security Work Incentives (i.e., Plan for Achieving Self-Support, Impairment-Related Work Expense).

The key point here is that despite many and varied barriers, these organizations found a way to work around or through them and make positive changes. A critical strategy was to articulate the mission, vision, and values of the organization early in the changeover process. Key questions for discussion with staff and other stakeholders included:

- What is our purpose? What services will we provide?

- Who are our primary and secondary customers?

- What outcomes do we want to achieve?

- What is the best process or path to get there?

- How will we measure success?

Role Redefinition

Another strategy that organizations used included flattening the organizational structure in order to increase the number of positions that focus on helping people get and keep jobs. Many agencies redefined some of the position descriptions to more effectively deliver community-based services and achieve desired outcomes. For example, the position description of an employment specialist might include 1) overall organizational expectations (e.g., receptivity to change, teamwork, commitment to the organization's vision, efficiency/accountability, customer service); 2) specific job duties (e.g., person-centered assessment and planning, job development, training and support, advocacy); and 3) enhanced job functions (nonessentials) that add value to themselves, their team, and the organization.

Teamwork was identified as a critical element in the changeover process. Staff were being redeployed from traditional roles and practices to new expectations. They ventured out into the community, often working alone and having to make more decisions on their own. Staff interacted with the business community, which for most was new and somewhat intimidating. Some organizations restructured staff into teams so that they could support and learn from each other and capitalize on the expertise of the various team members.

Person-Centered Planning

As agencies began to expand integrated employment services, they indicated that person-centered planning approaches were a critical element of all individualized services. Regardless of the version of person-centered planning used, the objective was to learn about the person's interests, dreams, and needs. From that knowledge came the development of an individualized plan for their daily activities and the types of supports each person might need.

Results

What were the outcomes that these organizations achieved? The majority (90.5%) of people with disabilities were reported to be happier. People experienced growth in their self-esteem and their feelings of self-worth. People repeatedly talked about the increase in their wages, their greater independence, and the relationships that they had built in the community. In all of its various shapes and forms, people were saying, "I like it better here in the community." Very few expressed an interest in returning to the sheltered facility.

Staff and organizations reported better-quality services. They felt more focused on a unified vision and outcome. They felt that they were more streamlined, more directive in what they wanted to accomplish, and better aligned in their practices. About 70% of the staff said that they had better community/employer relations because they now had to be out in, and of, the community. Staff members joined their local Chamber of Commerce and other business organizations. They developed business relationships and partnerships. Although not all staff members thought the changeover process was a good thing for them personally (especially those who quit or were asked to leave), the majority of staff did come away feeling a sense of satisfaction and accomplishment, feeling a strong purpose and direction in their work, and being very excited about the many positive and varied changes in people's lives of which they were a part.

Lastly, about a third of the organizations reported being more cost efficient in their services as a result of the organizational change process (Butterworth, Ghiloni, Revell, & Brooks-Lane, 2004). This outcome was achieved through streamlining (e.g., eliminating some mid-management positions), shrewdness about the way that they allocated their dollars (e.g., focusing on expenditures directly related to employment outcomes), unloading sunk costs (e.g., selling, leasing, or renting their building and equipment), and acquiring additional sources of revenue (e.g., grants, funding for serving new populations, fundraising). Despite a more effective and efficient use of public dollars, however, it is important that organizational change is not sold solely on the basis of cost savings.

MAKING A PARADIGM SHIFT:
FROM FACILITIES TO THE COMMUNITY

As stated previously, it is essential that organizations examine and establish their mission, vision, and values as they undertake the organizational change process. This section highlights some of the principles and practices that have been established as guideposts for service delivery among exemplary provider agencies.

Zero Rejection

Zero rejection reflects a principle that no one will be rejected for services for having disabilities that are too severe. In other words, the burden for proving that a person can work should fall on the agency, rather than the individual with disabilities. Zero rejection also implies that individuals do not need to get ready for living and working in the community by being in a segregated facility. In reality, organizations that welcome people with the most significant disabilities also served individuals with less intense support needs out of necessity, due to funding constraints. It is important for such organizations to avoid the pitfall of serving all of the "easy" people first and never quite getting to those who present significant challenges.

Individualized Planning

Individualized planning and services designed around each and every person reflects a "one person at a time" approach. Group enclaves and work crews violate this principle. John O'Brien (1989) provided a wonderful framework for guiding lifestyle planning with each person. He described five accomplishments essential to quality of life: 1) community presence (being in typical community settings shared by others without disabilities); 2) choice (having ample opportunities to experience decision making about one's life); 3) community participation (being part of a growing number of personal relationships that can occur through regular presence in everyday settings); 4) respect (having a valued place among a network of people and valued roles in daily life); and 5) competence (having the opportunity to engage in activities that are meaningful in order to build useful skills and experiences). If providers adhere closely to this framework, it is more likely that people will achieve meaningful lives that are designed to meet the needs and interests of each person.

Individualized, person-centered planning addresses not only work tasks at a particular workplace, but also the work environment, the nature of supports therein, and how to facilitate and support personal relationships. Community rehabilitation programs have been negligent in supporting old and new friendships when people leave sheltered facilities. As a result, people in community jobs sometimes lament the fact that they miss their friends in the sheltered workshop. It is important to be very thoughtful and purposeful about supporting people to maintain friendships and build new relationships in the community. Regular social activities need to be built into people's daily and weekly schedules so that the necessary supports are available.

Appropriate Supports

Appropriate supports are the backbone of community integration and success. Too often people lose their jobs because the type and degree of needed support was lacking. It is an art to balance too much versus too little support for each individual in the community. The principle "as little as possible, as much as necessary" is relevant to guiding decisions about individual supports. A great deal has been learned about the importance of abiding by typical workplace features and facilitating natural supports in the workplace (Mank, Cioffi & Yovanoff, 1997, 1999; Rogan, Banks, & Howard, 2000, 2003). Thus, support should come from "natural" sources (the people, processes, and environmental features that are present in various community settings) as much as possible, with human services personnel acting to supplement and complement these supports.

Organizational Responsiveness

Traditionally, organizations have offered programs into which people must fit, whether individuals needed or wanted the services and activities. Organizational responsiveness requires that service providers be flexible versus rigid and be able to adapt and accommodate the needs of each person to the maximum extent possible (Butterworth & Fesko, 2004).

Cost Effectiveness

Whereas traditional facility-based programs have been funded ad infinitum without any attention to benefits and outcomes, community-based services have been closely scrutinized, especially during times of fiscal constraints. It is essential that organizations be responsible with the public dollars at their disposal by focusing on cost-effectiveness and desired outcomes. Results-based funding can serve to focus the organization on cost-effective and outcome-based services, but it must allow for individualization and must cover costs for people with high support needs.

It is clear that organizational change is a complex process that affects all aspects of an organization. It does not entail a band-aid tweaking of one aspect of the organization. It requires major surgery because all aspects of the organization are interrelated. It does not mean tacking on supported employment to an organization's continuum of services. It requires addressing the following hard questions simultaneously: How will we involve our various stakeholders from the beginning? How will we accommodate staff who may have been with the organization for many years as well as hire new talent for our future direction? How do we shift our organization's image in the community from a "special" place where people with disabilities go to a viable source of employees for the business community?

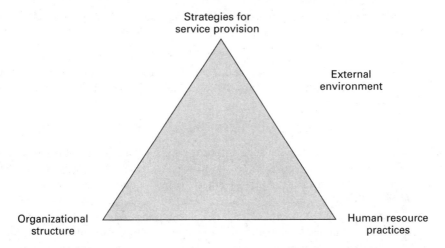

Figure 13.1. Organizational change triangle. (From Rogan, P., Held, M., & Rinne, S. [2001]. Organizational change from sheltered to integrated employment for adults with disabilities. In P. Wehman [Ed.], *Supported employment in business: Expanding the capacity of workers with disabilities* [p. 199]. St. Augustine, FL: Training Resource Network; reprinted by permission.)

FRAMEWORK FOR ORGANIZATIONAL CHANGE

Key elements of the changeover process are represented in the organization change triangle depicted in Figure 13.1. Each corner of the triangle represents a major area needing attention during changeover: human resource practices, the organizational structure, and strategies for service provision. Organizations do not operate in isolation. They influence and are influenced by an external environment that includes the board of directors, funders, businesses, families, community members, and other stakeholders and organizations.

One point of the triangle represents the services that agencies currently provide and those they are moving toward—from facility-based to individualized and integrated employment and community supports. Another point of the triangle represents human resource practices. How should staff be recruited, hired, oriented, trained, and supported? The third corner of the triangle represents the organizational structure. How are staff roles and responsibilities aligned with the mission, vision, and values of the organization? How does the current flow chart, or organizational hierarchy, support or impede a focus on integrated employment and community supports? These aspects of the changeover process are often viewed as the most difficult and controversial, and yet are very exciting as the basis for organizational transformation.

Current literature provides extensive information about strategies for job development, training, and supports. This information will not be discussed here. The following section focuses on two major components of the framework for change: organizational structure (or restructuring) and human resource practices.

Organizational Restructuring

Organizational restructuring involves staff roles and responsibilities and the general organization of the agency. Consider these questions:

1. What are the roles of staff members? What are their job descriptions? Do the job descriptions delineate specific responsibilities that support integrated employment and community integration?

2. How are staff organized? What are their lines of authority and decision-making powers? What does the organizational flow chart look like? How do staff collaborate to better serve individuals?

3. How are staff classified? What is their status within the organization?

Many traditional community rehabilitation programs have an organizational structure similar to that depicted in Figure 13.2. The flow chart looks like a pyramid, with the CEO or executive director at the top—farthest from the clientele, yet with the most decision-making power. There is typically a fiscal officer, a human resource person, possibly a marketing position, and often a vice president and tiers of managerial staff. Underneath the formal leadership and mid-management positions are frontline workers assigned to various programs: residential, sheltered work, day activity, supported employment, and so forth. People who receive services are often served in programs that are segmented, with little alignment and coordination. As a result, programs slice individuals into different parts and pieces of their day and their lives, with different staff for each piece, who rarely communicate with each other. In some organizations, there are up to 20 different job descriptions (Rogan, Held, et al., 2001).

Restructuring often involves flattening the organizational structure by taking a hard look at management positions and other extraneous roles that have little or no connection to the provision of community-based services. Discussions about eliminating or revising people's jobs can cause anxiety and anger and can be highly controversial. It is extremely important to be very thoughtful about who is needed in what roles and at what pace the role changes will occur. There will be fallout during the restructuring process. Staff will leave. In some cases, more than half of the facility staff have left or been asked to leave during the changeover process (Fesko & Butterworth, 1999; Hutcheson, 2003).

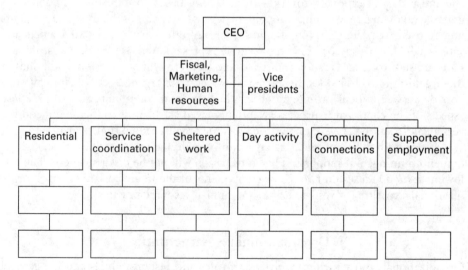

Figure 13.2. Traditional organizational structures. (*Source:* Unpublished document by Susan Rinne and Michelle Howard Herbein, 1996.)

As organizations begin to move away from facility-based services toward individualized services designed around each person, it makes sense to align staff with people instead of programs (Inge & Targett, 2004). Many organizations have endeavored to move most staff to direct-service positions and to develop a more generic job description that better describes the community support role of staff. The effort to expand staff roles from specialists to generalists, known as *broad banding*, allows them to learn and share the job duties of others for more holistic service delivery. An example of a generic "employment specialist" job description might include the following components: roles and responsibilities (including teamwork), performance expectations (e.g., number of job placements per month, membership in community/business organizations), percentage of time people might spend in various job-related activities (e.g., time in the community versus time at the office), and professional developmental expectations (in order to communicate that ongoing skill development is required) along with undertaking leadership roles and responsibilities.

What is the rationale behind a generalist job description? A generalist provides the array of supports needed by the individual, whatever they are and whenever they may be needed. In supported employment, a generalist is involved in all aspects of the job development process. This staff member would get to know the individual seeking employment and services, make contact with community businesses, and assist in the training and support of that individual over time. Some agencies that provide both day and residential services use "community support specialist" positions that support an individual in any aspect of the day or night. This approach promotes continuity and seamless services. It helps staff get to know the whole person. Staff become well rounded in their skills and experiences and ultimately more valuable and flexible. This approach, however, requires a great deal of investment in staff training, and not all staff are able to develop the array of desired skills. Each organization must decide what works best for them based on their current staff's experience, expertise, and interests (Gandolfo, Butterworth, Lavin, & Elwood, 2004). Some organizations not only use a generalist job description but also have some staff on each team who focus primarily on job development. This approach has served to reduce the bottleneck of people waiting for jobs.

In addition to changing job descriptions, many organizations have used a team approach to service delivery. Figure 13.3 depicts an interim, or Phase One, strategy for organizational restructuring. In this chart, staff have moved into teams but continue to carry their specialist roles and responsibilities. That is, initially, staff positions on the team may include someone from the sheltered workshop, residential services, supported-employment services, and community-participation program. This interim phase allows staff to begin working together to serve a set group of individuals, to begin to share information about their various roles and responsibilities, and to gradually move toward more generic roles and responsibilities (i.e., supporting individuals in employment and community living). Phase Two (Figure 13.4) shows an organizational structure comprised of generalist staff who all share the same job description (in this example, a Community Resource Consultant) and who work in teams.

Staff caseloads have often been assigned according to disability labels and levels. For example, staff may be assigned to a program that serves a particular population, such as people with the highest support needs, people with behavioral issues, people with physical or psychiatric disabilities, or people who are older. Many agencies that provide community-based services have shifted to a totally different approach to assigning caseloads based on personal relationships and geographic location. In other

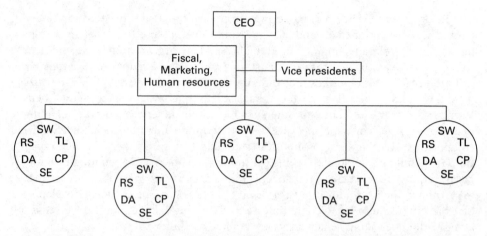

Figure 13.3. Phase One—Deprogramming. (*Source:* Unpublished document by Susan Rinne and Michelle Howard Herbein, 1996.) (*Key:* CP, community participation staff; DA, day activity staff; RS, residential staff; SE, supported employment staff; SW, sheltered workshop staff; TL, team leader.)

words, individuals and staff members who know and like each other may be connected. Ideally, individuals are given a choice of their support provider. Another dimension to consider is where staff live in relation to the individual receiving services. Staff who are from the same community as a service recipient are more likely to be familiar with local businesses and have established networks of contact people, making them more effective at job development and community connections and more efficient in terms of drive time.

Human Resource Practices

In addition to restructuring, the organizational change process requires revisions to human resource practices, including staff recruitment, hiring, orientation, training, support, feedback systems, and pay and compensation. Let's start with recruitment and hiring. After organizations have reviewed and revised their job descriptions, as

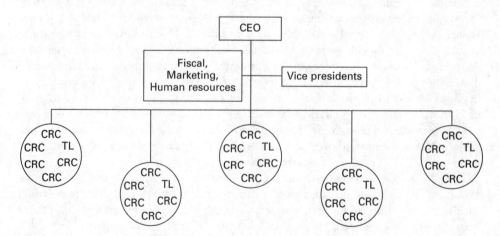

Figure 13.4. Phase Two—Deprogramming. (*Source:* Unpublished document by Susan Rinne and Michelle Howard Herbein, 1996.) (*Key:* CRC, community resource consultant; TL, team leader.)

discussed previously, they are in a better position to articulate the roles and expectations for veteran and new staff. Some agencies have required all existing staff in their
facility to reapply for the new job description. This process of redeployment allows
management to better understand the attitudes and skills that staff members bring to
their new roles and allows staff to better understand the nature and extent of their role
change.

When recruiting and hiring new staff, it is important to examine the organization's strengths and needs for expertise. Hiring for the future involves looking ahead
and projecting the staffing needs. It is not easy to find people who have needed experiences and expertise. Many organizations look for desired attitudes and people skills,
knowing that they can develop desired employment-related skills. Some organizations
have elevated the status and pay for community-support positions in order to attract
and keep quality personnel and to reinforce the significance of these positions to the
organization (Murphy, Rogan, Handley, Kincaid, & Royce-Davis, 2002).

Once staff assume their new roles, it is important to invest heavily in their learning. Staff need to be oriented to the mission and values of the organization. They need
"classroom" time as well as job shadowing time with a mentor in the community. An
inventory can be used to identify the skills people already have in their repertoire.
Such a tool can help staff shape an individual professional development plan.

If staff will be assuming new roles, then some cross-training is probably necessary. As indicated in Figure 13.3, people may initially keep their specialized roles on
their team, but through cross-training, they may eventually move into generalist roles.
Training and support must be ongoing and "just on time," as staff are required to
demonstrate new competencies.

Organizations that establish a learning culture expect support staff to continually
grow and develop professionally. It is also helpful to bring in external expertise and
consultants to provide both incidental and ongoing training for staff. For example, an
agency interested in pursuing self-employment opportunities might invite a nationally
recognized expert to provide training and ongoing consultation.

Another important aspect of human resource practices involves feedback systems.
In other words, how will staff be evaluated? Too often organizations use a once-per-
year, one-way annual review by the supervisor to the staff, a practice that has proven
to be largely ineffective. Some organizations are being thoughtful about the way that
staff can take charge of the evaluation process. Each staff member can be actively involved in soliciting and utilizing feedback from those with whom he or she interacts
most directly. For example, staff may solicit feedback from individuals with disabilities, employers, parents, and other team members on a regular basis. They can also
conduct a self-evaluation. This approach, known as a *360-degree evaluation*, allows staff
to identify areas of strengths and needs and to develop specific professional development and career growth plans with their supervisor. Ideally, staff are rewarded or compensated for acquiring some of the additional skills because they add value to the
agency. It is a win-win situation for the organization and the individual. In addition to
self-evaluation and career plans, agencies should implement a system for team evaluations. It is important for team members to reflect on how well they are working together to achieve desired goals and outcomes.

Next, rewards and compensation are discussed. In the current climate of tight
budgets, many organizations struggle to pay staff respectable salaries. This situation, in
part, results in high staff turnover. How do agencies attract and keep good workers?
First, agencies need to pay attention to the salary and benefits schedule of their fellow

agencies and should try to offer a higher pay rate and better benefits package. One organization reported reducing its staff turnover from 70% to less than 40% when it offered a better benefits package than its competitors did (Rinne, personal communication, May 2005). Although a decent salary is important, there are other ways that organizations can help staff feel valued and recognized for their efforts. In addition to longevity on the job, staff performance should be a key factor in determining raises and perks. As mentioned previously, staff should be compensated for the "added value" they have acquired in terms of skills, leadership roles, and other responsibilities.

What are some other rewards that staff appreciate in addition to salary? Some people relish the opportunity to increase their status or leadership roles within an organization. It is difficult to establish a lot of career pathways within a flat organization, but roles such as team leaders or mentors can be established. Others appreciate being recognized for their contributions. Even the most simple recognition, such as being selected employee of the month, pictured on the "wall of fame," or featured in agency newsletters, goes a long way. Others appreciate receiving funding to attend conferences or taking courses toward college degrees. Job flexibility and time off are also rewards for good performance. Some organizations provide a cash bonus for such things as job placements and longevity on the job. The key is to help staff feel valued within the organization.

GETTING STARTED IN THE CHANGE PROCESS

The importance of getting stakeholder involvement and buy-in from the start was mentioned previously. This is a key beginning point in the changeover process. Undertaking a *stakeholder analysis* is one way that organizations can better understand stakeholder attitudes toward community services and how best to pull stakeholders into the change process. This simple process involves finding answers to the following questions:

- Who are your primary constituents?

- What do they think about a shift to community services? Who is supportive, and who is resistant?

- What influence do they have on the change process?

- How can they be proactively involved in changeover efforts?

- What information do they have that might facilitate the change process?

- What information might they need to better understand the vision, direction, and challenges?

It is important to consider the array of people who provide support to individuals in the facility, including family members, residential services providers, and service coordinators. A stakeholder analysis is used as a first step to build stakeholder buy-in. As mentioned previously, it is critical to get people to commit to and feel a sense of ownership about the change process. Some organizations actually send stakeholders to visit one or more organizations that have "converted." This helps people see, feel, and hopefully understand what it is all about. They can see the impact that the change process has had on individual lives, talk to those involved, and begin to envision the possibilities for those they love and support.

Various *strategic planning* tools have been used to help organizations document where they are, where they want to be, and how to get there. PATH (Parent, Unger, & Inge, 1997; Pearpoint, O'Brien, & Forest, 1993) is one such tool that has been used effectively to pull stakeholders together to envision and plan for a desired future. PATH is a visual tool that uses graphics to depict the focus person's dreams and goals. The planning process involves the following steps:

1. Identify the vision and dream of the pathfinder.

2. Set goals for a specific time frame—anywhere from 6 months to 5 years.

3. Look at what is in place *now*.

4. Determine who should be enrolled to work toward the goals set in Step 2.

5. Identify the things that get in the way of achieving desired goals.

6. What needs to be done for the team to remain strong and focused on achieving their goals?

7. Envision time traveling to the future and seeing what you have achieved in a shorter time frame (i.e., a few months to a year).

8. Identify the first things you need to accomplish the future you envisioned in Step 7.

Plans should be shared widely and displayed prominently within the agency. In addition, strategic plans must be revisited and revised on a regular basis to keep momentum and progress moving ahead. The strategic planning process can be used to continually energize team members as they celebrate accomplishments and realize that positive changes are taking place.

Forming a *change-management team* comprised of key stakeholders has proven very beneficial. Such a group meets regularly to plan, raise questions and issues, and evaluate progress. This team should constantly communicate with "the ranks" by soliciting issues and questions and sharing information in order to ensure that the change process is fully transparent. Thus, a change management team can be used as a sounding board throughout the changeover process in which the voices of all constituents can be heard. Such teams have facilitated stakeholder buy-in and have instilled confidence and positive attitudes both inside and outside of the organization.

It is essential that agencies *demonstrate* success early in the organizational change process in order to help people, especially those who are resistant, to *see* what it looks like. Agencies should *do it right the first time* by using a "one person at a time" approach. For example, organizations should try to avoid enclaves and work crews as a fast way to move people into the community. There will always be compromises, which should be recognized as such and minimized.

Finally, agencies must find ways to *celebrate* their successes. The change process can be exhausting and exhilarating. There will likely be barriers and setbacks. Some will tire of the constant change and uncertainty. Thus, stepping back periodically to celebrate successes will ultimately boost morale and a sense of accomplishment. There are many ways to celebrate individually, in teams, as an organization, and as a community when good things have been accomplished.

CONCLUSION

Although every organization is unique, common themes have emerged from the changeover efforts of many agencies. This chapter has identified common barriers and strategies for organizational change. *All* of the organizations that have been studied feel that their changeover process was the right thing to do. They had to balance the tension between moving too fast and moving too slow. In order to evaluate progress and develop future directions, many organizations have utilized external expertise to "hold a mirror" up to their agency. External expertise can offer fresh eyes and new perspectives and can play the "heavy" as needed. Sustaining quality community-based services and supports can be as challenging as the changeover process, so organizations must continue to learn and change.

In the end, it's about leadership. The leaders within the organization must have a "fire in their belly" about the necessity of change. They must truly believe it is the right thing to do. Leaders must be willing to take risks and make a commitment to follow through, even when the changeover process is rough and lasts years. A great deal of gratitude is owed to those leaders who have stepped forward when others maintained the status quo and who have demonstrated success while others have settled for mediocrity. As the saying goes, "Those who say it can't be done should get out of the way of those who are doing it!"

REFERENCES

Albin, J.M., Rhodes, L., & Mank, D. (1994). Changeover to community employment: The problem of realigning organizational culture, resources, and community roles. *Journal of The Association for Persons with Severe Handicaps, 19*(2), 105–115.

Americans with Disabilities Act (ADA) of 1990, PL 101-336, 42 U.S.C §§ 12101 *et seq.*

Braddock, D., Hemp, R., & Rizzolo, M. (2004). State of the states in developmental disabilities: 2004. *Mental Retardation, 42*(5), 356–370.

Butterworth, J., & Fesko, S. (1998). *Conversion to integrated employment: Case studies of organizational change.* Boston: Children's Hospital Boston, Institute for Community Inclusion.

Butterworth, J., & Fesko, S. (2004). *Successful organizational change.* Richmond: Virginia Commonwealth University, Training and Technical Assistance for Providers. Available on-line at http://www.t-tap.org/strategies/factsheet/successchange.htm

Butterworth, J., Fesko, S., & Ma, V. (2000). Because it was the right thing to do: Changeover from facility based services to community employment. *Journal of Vocational Rehabilitation, 14*(1), 23–35.

Butterworth, J., Ghiloni, C., Revell, G., & Brooks-Lane, N. (2004). *Creating a diversified funding base.* Richmond: Virginia Commonwealth University, Training and Technical Assistance for Providers. Available on-line at http://www.t-tap.org/strategies/factsheet/diversifiedfunding.html

Butterworth, J., Gilmore, D., & Kiernan, W. (2000, August). *Trends and issues in sheltered employment services.* Briefing paper submitted to the National Institute on Disability and Rehabilitation Research for the Government Accountability Office study of sheltered workshops, Children's Hospital Boston, Institute for Community Inclusion.

Butterworth, J., Gilmore, D., Kiernan, W., & Schalock, R. (1998). *Day and employment services in developmental disabilities: State and national trends.* Boston: Children's Hospital Boston, Institute on Community Inclusion.

Butterworth, J., Gilmore, D., Kiernan, W., & Schalock, R. (1999). *State trends in employment services for people with developmental disabilities: Multiyear comparisons based on state MR/DD agency and vocational rehabilitation (RSA) data.* Boston: Children's Hospital Boston, Institute for Community Inclusion.

Butterworth, J., Sullivan, J., & Smith, C. (2001). *The impact of organizational change on individual outcomes: Transition from facility-based services to integrated employment.* Boston: Children's Hospital Boston, Institute for Community Inclusion.

Center on Disability and Employment. (2005). *Organizational change mentoring.* Knoxville: University of Tennessee, College of Education, Health, and Human Services.

Dreilinger, D., Gilmore, D., & Butterworth, J. (2001). *National day and employment service trends in MR/DD agencies.* Boston: Children's Hospital Boston, Institute for Community Inclusion.

Fesko, S., & Butterworth, J. (1999). *Conversion to integrated employment: Case studies of organizational change.* Boston: Children's Hospital Boston, Institute for Community Inclusion.

Gandolfo, C., Butterworth, J., Lavin, D., & Elwood, L. (2004). *Staff development.* Richmond: Virginia Commonwealth University, Training and Technical Assistance for Providers. Available on-line at http://www.t-tap.org/strategies/factsheet/staffdev.htm

Glasser, I. (1978). Prisoners of benevolence. In W. Gaylin, I. Glasser, S. Marcus, & D. Rothman (Eds.), *Doing good: The limits of benevolence* (pp. 97–170). New York: Pantheon Books.

Hutcheson, S. (2003, March 10). *Dispelling the myths of conversion* [Web cast]. Richmond: Virginia Commonwealth University, Training and Technical Assistance for Providers.

Individuals with Disabilities Education Act (IDEA) of 1990, PL 101-476, 20 U.S.C. §§ 1400 *et seq.*

Inge, K., & Targett, P. (2004). *Changing staff roles.* Richmond: Virginia Commonwealth University, Training and Technical Assistance for Providers. Available on-line at http://www.t-tap.org/strategies/factsheet/changingstaffroles.html

Mank, D., Cioffi, A., & Yovanoff, P. (1997). Analysis of the typicalness of supported employment jobs, natural supports, and wage and integration outcomes. *Mental Retardation, 35*(3), 185–197.

Mank, D., Cioffi, A., & Yovanoff, P. (1999). Impact of coworker involvement with supported employees on wage and integration outcomes. *Mental Retardation, 37*(5), 383–394.

McCaughrin, W., Ellis, W., Rusch, F., & Heal, L. (1993). Cost-effectiveness of supported employment. *Mental Retardation, 31*(1), 41–48.

McGaughey, M.J., Kiernan, W.E., McNally, L.C., Gilmore, D.S., & Keith, G.R. (1994). *Beyond the workshop: National perspectives on integrated employment.* Boston: Children's Hospital Boston, Institute for Community Inclusion.

McGaughey, M.J., Kiernan, W.E., McNally, L.C., Gilmore, D.S., & Keith, G.R. (1996). Beyond the workshop: National trends in integrated and segregated day and employment services. *Journal of The Association for Persons with Severe Handicaps, 20*(4), 270–285.

Metzel, D., Boeltzig, H., Butterworth, J., & Gilmore, D. (2004). *The national survey of community rehabilitation providers, FY 2002–2003, Report 1: Overview of services and provider characteristics.* Boston: Children's Hospital Boston, Institute for Community Inclusion.

Murphy, S.T., & Rogan, P.M. (1995). *Closing the shop: Conversion from sheltered to integrated work.* Baltimore: Paul H. Brookes Publishing Co.

Murphy, S., Rogan, P., Handley, M., Kincaid, C., & Royce-Davis, J. (2002). People's situations and perspectives eight years after workshop conversion. *Mental Retardation, 40*, 30–40.

Nerny, T. (2000). *Tools of self-determination: Communicating self-determination: Freedom, authority, support, and responsibility.* Ann Arbor, MI: Center for Self-Determination.

Novak, J., Mank, D., Revell, G., & O'Brien, D. (1999). Paying for success: Results-based approaches to funding supported employment. In G. Revell, K. Inge, D. Mank, & P. Wehman (Eds.), *The impact of supported employment for people with significant disabilities: Preliminary findings from the National Supported Employment Consortium.* Richmond: Virginia Commonwealth University Rehabilitation Research and Training Center on Workplace Supports and Job Retention.

O'Brien, D., Ford, L., & Malloy, J. (2005). Person-centered funding. Using vouchers and personal budgets to support recovery and employment for people with psychiatric disabilities. *Journal of Vocational Rehabilitation, 23*(2), 71–79.

O'Brien, J. (1989). *What's worth working for? Leadership for better quality human services.* Syracuse, NY: Center on Human Policy.

Parent, W., Unger, D., & Inge, K. (1997). Customer profile. In V. Brooke, K. Inge, A. Armstrong, & P. Wehman (Eds.), *Supported employment handbook: A customer-driven approach for persons with significant disabilities.* Richmond: Virginia Commonwealth University Rehabilitation Research and Training Center on Workplace Supports and Job Retention.

Pearpoint, J., O'Brien, J., & Forest, M. (1993). *PATH: A workbook for planning positive personal futures*. Toronto: Inclusion Press.

Rogan, P., Banks, B., & Howard, M. (2000). Workplace supports in practice: As little as possible, as much as necessary. *Focus on Autism and Other Developmental Disabilities, 15*(1), 2–11.

Rogan, P., Banks, B., & Howard, M. (2003). Supported employment and workplace supports: A qualitative study. *Journal of Vocational Rehabilitation, 19*(1), 5–18

Rogan, P., Grossi, T., Mank, D., Haynes, D., Thomas, F., & Majd, C. (2001). *Changes in wages, hours, benefits, and integration outcomes of former sheltered workshop participants who are in supported employment*. Report for the President's Task Force on the Employment of Adults with Disabilities, Indiana University, Institute on Disability and Community, Bloomington.

Rogan, P., Held, M., & Rinne, S. (2001). Organizational change from sheltered to integrated employment for adults with disabilities. In P. Wehman (Ed.), *Supported employment in business: Expanding the capacity of workers with disabilities* (pp. 195–214). St. Augustine, FL: Training Resource Network.

State Vocational Rehabilitation Services Program: Final Rule, 66(14) Fed. Reg. 7,249–7,258 (January 22, 2001) (to be codified at 34 C.F.R. pt. 361).

Ticket to Work and Work Incentives Improvement Act of 1999, PL 106-170, 42 U.S.C. §§ 1305 *et seq.*

Wehman, P., & Revell, G. (2002). Lessons learned from the provision and funding of employment services for the MR/DD population: Implications for assessing the adequacy of the SSA Ticket to Work. In S. Bell & K. Rupp (Eds.), *Paying for results in a vocational rehabilitation: Will provider incentives work for Ticket to Work?* (pp. 355–393). Washington, DC: Urban Institute.

Wehman, P., Revell, G., & Brooke, V. (2003). Competitive employment: Has it become the first choice yet? *Journal of Disability Policy Studies, 14*(3), 163–173.

Wehman, P., Revell, G., & Kregel, J. (1998). Supported employment: A decade of rapid growth and impact. *American Rehabilitation, 24*(1), 31–43.

West, M., Revell, G., & Wehman, P. (1998). Conversion from segregated services to supported employment: A continuing challenge to the VR service system. *Education and Training in Mental Retardation and Developmental Disabilities, 33*(3), 239–247.

Workforce Investment Act (WIA) of 1998, PL 105-220, 29 U.S.C. §§ 2801 *et seq.*

Yamaki, K., & Fujiura, G.T. (2002). Employment and income status of adults with developmental disabilities living in the community. *Mental Retardation, 40*(2), 132–141.

Chapter 14

Current Trends on Partnerships with Private Enterprises

J. Howard Green, Paul Wehman, John W. Luna, and Allyson J. Merkle

For years, public rehabilitation agencies, service providers, and educational organizations seeking to secure employment for people with disabilities have attempted to do this by using a one-to-one approach. Since the mid-1990s, there has been an increased awareness of the need to broaden this approach and begin to build long-term relationships and partnerships with private businesses. In order to address the issue of long-term unemployment for people with disabilities, strong partnerships are going to be necessary.

In the spring of 2003, the U.S. Chamber of Commerce, Center for Workforce Preparation, hosted a summit titled, *Creating a 21st Century Workforce for Business*. Wes Jurey, President and CEO of the Arlington, Texas, Chamber of Commerce, told the audience that he had more "ships" than anyone in the room and his "ships" were bigger and better than most people's. Jurey was speaking directly about his many business relationships and partnerships.

Partnerships and strong relationships are needed to build a new strategy for addressing the large unemployment rate of people with disabilities in America. It is important to note that partnerships and relationships are not created over a short period of time. A strong and successful relationship is created first by the recognition of a need and then by the ability of the parties to build a trust level with each other. Partnerships and relationships with businesses are dependent on the idea that each partner brings certain components to the relationship that will be beneficial to the other partner (Luecking, Fabian, & Tilson, 2004). The following case study demonstrates a successful partnership/relationship that has resulted in many individuals with disabilities working successfully.

UNIVERSITY OF ALABAMA AT BIRMINGHAM AND ALABAMA DEPARTMENT OF REHABILITATION SERVICES

In the late 1970s, the Alabama vocational rehabilitation (VR) agency first approached the University of Alabama at Birmingham (UAB) to develop the university as an employer account for securing employment opportunities for the people with disabilities that it served. VR recognized UAB as a customer in the VR process and realized that the needs of the employer must be met as well as the needs of the people with disabilities being placed into employment. Instead of VR staff approaching UAB on a case-by-case basis, the employer account system allowed VR to do this in a coordinated manner, thereby reducing the number of VR staff contacting various human resource and supervisory personnel within UAB on behalf of individual applicants.

Over time, both Alabama VR and UAB designed a staff member to serve as a single point of contact between organizations. Peggy Anderson, Coordinator of Employer Development for VR, explained that this arrangement allows the VR staff to function more as "insiders," becoming familiar with the jobs, supervisors, and the hiring process at UAB. This system improved the prescreening and matching of applicants with jobs, made VR more accountable to UAB after placements, and gave VR more timely access to hiring opportunities for its clients.

The relationship has been supported at top management levels through direct involvement of an assistant vice president in human resources on the VR agency's governing board. In turn, the agency has cultivated its role as a trusted partner by providing a growing scope of disability employment services in response to needs that are identified by being on site. This win-win partnership for recruitment and retention has enabled both partners to fulfill their missions more effectively and achieve greater benefits from their investments while securing the employment of people with disabilities. The success of this partnership—what has driven its endurance, evolution, and growth—is a working relationship based on need, trust, mutual benefits, and effective business practices. By helping to meet each other's needs, UAB and the Alabama Department of Rehabilitation Services have developed a highly successful partnership that can be replicated by others (Wehman, Brooke, & Green, 2004).

Since the passage of the Americans with Disabilities Act (ADA) of 1990 (PL 101-336), there have been tremendous changes in the way businesses perceive hiring individuals with disabilities. As a whole, the business community appears to have increasingly embraced the employment of individuals with disabilities as a sound business strategy, with many corporations investing substantially in appropriate supports (e.g., Unger, Kregel, Wehman, & Brooke, 2002). For example, the Society for Human Resource Management (1997) reported that, of 813 human resource executives, 75% had changed their procedures for hiring new employees since the passage of the ADA to better accommodate job applicants and new hires with disabilities.

Further evidence of increasing employer support for hiring workers with disabilities is found in a 1998 survey of human resource professionals at 35 companies, conducted jointly by the UnumProvident insurance company and the Washington Business Group on Health. The vast majority of the survey respondents (78%) reported that their efforts to accommodate workers with disabilities were greater than in the past. The survey also found a 5% increase in written return-to-work policies for workers with disabilities since the previous year's survey. This is significant because return-to-work policies and other disability-related policies have been linked to better work environments for workers with disabilities (Habeck, Leahy, Hunt, Chan, & Welch, 1991).

Finally, Unger et al. (2002) investigated the attitudes of 255 supervisors within 43 large businesses toward people with disabilities. The participating businesses were diverse in terms of types of industry. The supervisors were asked to rate the employee with a disability on a scale from 1 (extremely dissatisfied) to 5 (extremely satisfied) on items such as timeliness of arrival and departure, punctuality, attendance, task consistency, and work speed. The 255 supervisors indicated that they were satisfied with the performance of the worker with disabilities in the areas of timeliness of arrival and departure, punctuality, attendance, and consistency in task. The supervisors then ranked the employee's work performance in relation to their co-workers without disabilities. Unger et al. (2002) found that supervisors rated the work performance of employees with disabilities the same or better than co-workers in the areas of punctuality, attendance, work quality, task consistency, and overall proficiency. This research is significant because it helps to dispel the myths and misconceptions many employers have of hiring employees with disabilities.

ROLE OF BUSINESSES IN PROVIDING WORKPLACE SUPPORTS

As noted previously, it appears that the business community is increasingly receptive to hiring people with disabilities. Clearly, the role of businesses in providing workplace supports for individuals with disabilities is much expanded today. Employers have emerged as an increasingly visible initiator of work supports, not only in terms of more traditional accommodations such as job carving, but also in terms of assistive technologies and new work arrangements (Hanley-Maxwell & Millington, 1992; Sandow, Olson, & Yan, 1993; Shoemaker, Robin, & Robin, 1992; Sowers, Kouwenhoven, Sousa, & Milliken, 1997; Tilson, Luecking, & West, 1996).

In addition to providing financial and human resources for workplace supports, businesses have also turned to other entities for the means to provide needed supports. For example, businesses have utilized external resources from both government-sponsored (e.g., Sections 44 and 190 of the IRS Code–The Disabled Access Tax Credit) and nongovernmental organization-sponsored funds (e.g., the Arc's wage reimbursement program) to expand their hiring, training, and accommodation of workers with disabilities (Golden, 1995). These funds flow through businesses and require businesses to be knowledgeable about such financial resources and committed to getting them. Thus, these financial supports, like workplace accommodations, are mediated by the business "hosts." The vital role played by businesses in providing supports can thus be conceptualized in terms of "mediating" workplace supports that businesses administer, implement, and evaluate, either solely or in conjunction with other parties (e.g., government, VR, human service, or supported employment agencies). The critical aspect of "business-mediated" workplace supports is that they would not be possible without the active, ongoing participation of the employer or business.

Business-mediated workplace supports refer specifically to work arrangements, programs, and policies that permit a qualified worker with disabilities to meet essential job functions (Wehman, Bricout, & Kregel, 2000). These supports may include accommodations (i.e., adaptations for workers with disabilities), such as job restructuring and schedule modifications, but are not limited to accommodations only. Also included in business-mediated workplace supports are work arrangements and programs that are also available to workers without disabilities and may therefore not constitute "accommodations" as such (e.g., transitional work, telework). Whether businesses enter into partnerships with rehabilitation programs or contract with rehabilitation programs to provide workplace supports, they "mediate" the support programs, practices, policies, and procedures for workers with disabilities. Thus, businesses become invaluable allies to supported-employment providers in designing, mounting, and assessing workplace supports for individuals with disabilities.

It is important to expand the role of businesses in creating appropriate workplace supports because it is ultimately the employer who evaluates and establishes a worker's performance, individually and in the context of his or her contribution to the efforts of a workgroup or team. The employer establishes performance standards and the criteria by which those standards are assessed. One clear advantage of business-mediated supports in this regard is that the employer incorporates workplace supports into the strategic planning for the workgroup and thus becomes invested in the efficacy and, ultimately, success of such supports. Business-mediated supports thus create a partnership between the worker with disabilities and the employer.

There is relatively little published information available on how public–private sector partnerships with collaboration specifically work. Therefore, the purpose of this chapter is to look briefly at the literature in this area and then describe a model project in progress that begins to validate the utility of a public–private sector business model.

DETERMINING A BUSINESS'S NEEDS

A study by Hagner and Daning (1993) revealed that job developers who focused on establishing personal, trusting relations with employers were more successful. Businesses have been asked many times about the best ways to get jobs for people with disabilities. The answer is always the same: Get to know the business and find out its needs. If partnerships and relationships are going to be formed, then the rehabilitation community has to do a better job of identifying business needs as well as understanding corporate culture.

Taking a marketing approach requires a rehabilitation program to understand the needs of its customers, and, by meeting the needs of its customers, its needs will be met as well (Anderson, 2001). A program can achieve a proactive approach to determining business needs and culture by adhering to the following four steps.

1. Research

2. Conduct focus groups

3. Conduct business interviews and schedule business tours

4. Build a business database

Research

A critical aspect of establishing relationships is becoming knowledgeable about the business world and getting to know the business community as customers (Luecking, Fabian, & Tilson, 2004). The business community and the make up of the 21st century work force are forever changing, and in order to learn about the needs of businesses, it is important for rehabilitation programs to do the required homework. There are many avenues available where important information about businesses can be found. In order to begin to think about developing partnerships/relationships with businesses, rehabilitation programs should develop a strong informational base about the business community. It will be important to glean information about specific business issues that will be used later as business contacts are initiated.

The research activity should yield information regarding the size of the business, type of business, decision makers, trends, growth potential, profits and/or losses in the past year, experience in working with people with disabilities, company culture, dress code, community involvement activities, and skills needed in the work environment. By doing this research, the rehabilitation program demonstrates a level of knowledge and commitment to the company (Green & Brooke, 2001). When initiating their research of the business community, rehabilitation programs should

- Utilize the computer, and surf the Internet
- Contact and secure information from local economic development offices
- Subscribe to business journals and newspapers such as *Business Week* and the *Wall Street Journal*
- Read and maintain a file of the business section in the local paper
- Join organizations, and serve on committees that allow for access to businesses' information

Conduct Focus Groups

Focus groups are an excellent way to gather pertinent information to assist with identifying business needs. It is important for rehabilitation programs to choose the group carefully and create an environment that will get the best results. This process of collecting business needs will give a broad perspective regarding the businesses in the community and will save valuable time.

If possible, rehabilitation programs should conduct several of these focus-group sessions so that information can be obtained on a variety of businesses. For example, it would be preferable to do a focus-group session with businesses of various sizes because the needs probably will be different. Also, it would be advisable to conduct a focus group based on the type of business, such as retail, hospitality, manufacturing, financial, and other segments in the community.

Programs that generate the most success in their efforts to establish relationships with businesses are the ones that listen to input from business focus groups and design their services based on the information received (Green & Brooke, 2001). Table 14.1 presents steps to arrange and conduct business focus groups.

Conduct Business Interviews and Schedule Business Tours

Rehabilitation programs that try to establish a relationship with a specific business without having detailed information about the business are like doctors who prescribe medical treatment without diagnosing an illness (Bissonnette, 1994). The best way to identify the needs of a business is to make an appointment with the business to inquire about its needs. Prior to the site visit, rehabilitation programs should prepare specific questions that will assist in identifying the business's needs and learn about the busi-

Table 14.1.   Steps for arranging and conducting business focus groups

---

Identify and select specific target business groups.

Select 5–10 representatives from a specific target area.

Prepare a list of questions for which business input is desired.
- What is your biggest need at this time?
- Are you familiar with our program?
- Has your organization hired people with disabilities?
- Do you have concerns regarding cost or other issues with hiring people with disabilities?
- Are you satisfied with your current labor pool recruitment process?
- How can our program help you with your business needs?

Schedule and conduct a short meeting (1 hour or less) with businesses to gather information.
- Send a letter to confirm the date, place, and time.
- Call 1 day prior to confirm attendance.

Provide businesses attending the focus group with appropriate feedback.
- Send thank-you notes and small tokens of appreciation.
- Send a summary of the meeting.

Analyze the data received from the businesses, and make decisions on how it will be used.

---

ness's culture. Information such as the name of the company, the name and title of the person to be interviewed, the address, the telephone and fax numbers, and the e-mail address are just the basics. To help build more in-depth knowledge of the business, rehabilitation programs should get a description of the company and what it does as well as its production and quality needs and expectations. It will be important to gain information regarding the company's hiring needs, now and in the future. In addition, programs should try to identify the company's experiences and comfort level in working with people with disabilities.

The mission of the business interview is to find out as much about the company as possible. During the Public Private Partnership Summit conducted in Atlanta, Georgia, a representative with CVS Pharmacy provided the following statement in discussing building partnerships and relationships with the rehabilitation community. "A vocational rehabilitation representative worked directly with our store managers to find out what positions we recruit for and what new workers need to know. Then they found us the right person to join our team" (U.S. Chamber of Commerce, 2003, p 11).

As a follow-up to conducting business interviews, rehabilitation programs should see the operation of the business. This is a great way to gather information that could

Table 14.2.   Steps in arranging a business interview and tour

Design informational interview and business tour forms to collect the data.

Identify the businesses to be interviewed.

Schedule an appointment for a face-to-face meeting, and allow at least 1 hour for the initial interview and tour.

Conduct the interview and tour.

Send a thank-you note and token of appreciation.

Organize, analyze, and enter the data into a business database file.

Create a plan to utilize the data for building a relationship.

be of assistance to the business. For example, a job developer who has been trained to do worksite evaluations will be able to identify problem areas for an employee who is working in an office environment. The job developer can easily look at the individual's workstation and assess the work-area layout, seating, positioning of equipment, lighting, and noise. Businesses should be very interested in this assessment, especially when they realize the possible cost factors that may arise if the conditions create medical problems for the employee (e.g., carpel tunnel syndrome), requiring the person to take extended medical leave and possibly leading to worker's compensation claims as well as lost days of work.

Conducting business tours will provide more detailed information that will assist in making better job matches as well as coordinating services for the business. Manpower, Inc., the world's largest private employer, collects labor-market information from businesses through its services representatives. Staff from Manpower tour a business and complete a Work Environment Survey in order to assess the business's expectations, physical details of the work area, work pace, dress requirements, work hours, breaks, safety issues, parking, accessibility issues, required equipment, software, and machinery tasks (Blanck, 1998). Rehabilitation programs and job developers can create similar mechanisms to gather information needed about a business that helps to validate a relationship. Table 14.2 outlines the steps for a business interview and tour.

Build a Database

Once research efforts have been completed, it will be important to create a system that organizes the business data and information. A business database will help the rehabilitation program build solid employer relationships (DiLeo & Langton, 1993). Rehabilitation programs are good and efficient at keeping records and information on individuals with disabilities; however, they rarely keep track of business information. If employer files are maintained, usually the only information captured relates to job openings, salary, benefits, and whether an individual with disabilities got a job, but there is so much more information that could assist rehabilitation programs.

Creating a tracking system will give the capability to prove the success gained from business partnerships/relationships. A question often asked is: "Is our relationship with the business successful, and how do we know?" An ongoing data system will establish a clear picture of the business needs in the community, but, more important,

Table 14.3.   Business data needed for a database system

General business demographic information

- Name of company
- Address, telephone number, fax number, e-mail address
- Contact person's name and title
- Date interview was completed

Specific business information

- Total number of employees
- Type of workers, shifts, full time or part time
- Types of positions outsourced to employment agencies
- Turnover rate
- Description of products/services
- Production needs
- Hiring needs (short term and long term)
- Recruitment process
- Benefit packages
- Specific job requirements
- Advancement opportunities
- Environmental/worksite issues (physical barriers, temperature extremes)

Disability-related information

- Experience with employees with disabilities
- Experience with job accommodations
- Experience with community rehabilitation programs

Partnership-related information

- Contact information (date, contact person, reasons, and outcome)
- Type and number of disability-related services offered to the company (e.g., awareness training, recruitment and job screening, retention program, worksite evaluations)
- Type and number of disability-related services utilized by the company (e.g., number of training sessions requested, number of candidates referred and screened, number of worksite and workstation evaluations completed, other specific requests by the company)

Business satisfaction surveys about the partnership

services being provided to the business can be tracked. Table 14.3 provides an example of the data needed from a business relationship.

A rehabilitation professional can use the information collected to demonstrate tangible evidence to management about the success of the business relationship/

partnership. In addition, the data can also be used to show the business how the relationship benefited the business's bottom line.

UNDERSTANDING THE VALUE
OF PARTNERSHIPS FOR BUSINESSES

In building business relationships/partnerships, the rehabilitation community has to move away from the old way of conducting business with employers. Given the growing demands for labor in this country and the dwindling number of available workers, rehabilitation programs must take a new approach. The Herman Group reported that the private sector is facing an estimated 10 million–employee labor shortage by 2010, and there is a need to actively recruit from untapped labor pools (Herman, Olivo, & Gioia, 2002) such as people with disabilities. A marketing approach requires the collection of data about the business needs and then use of that information to satisfy the demands of the business (Green & Brooke, 2001).

The key to the marketing approach is satisfying the needs of the business through an exchange process in which each party receives some value from the relationship. Often, rehabilitation programs do not see themselves as having any value to the business community; however, businesses have many needs and are looking to rehabilitation programs for assistance. Businesses want to know more about issues facing people with disabilities as they relate to employment and would like to know how rehabilitation programs can benefit their business operation (Green & Brooke, 2001). They want to know the value rehabilitation programs bring to the relationship and how that will help affect the bottom line for the business.

Rehabilitation programs need to develop a clear and simple message to businesses regarding the value they bring to a relationship. They need to understand the services that can be provided and how they benefit the business community. Examples of possible services include prescreening applicants, assisting to retain workers on the job, worksite assessments, and training of staff on disability awareness and etiquette.

Manpower, for example, does an excellent job of matching (exchanging) worker skills to workplace demands. It routinely conducts labor-market surveys and follows economic trends. Manpower is an expert in understanding business needs and developing business relationships to supply companies with their labor needs. Manpower uses a "reverse-funnel" approach to make the exchange. In a typical situation, many job applicants are put in the large end of the funnel, and one emerges as the best candidate for a specific job; however, the reverse-funnel approach allows each job seeker to be treated as an individual and come out of the funnel with many opportunities with a number of potential employers and job possibilities (Blanck, 1998).

This reverse-funnel approach should be considered by rehabilitation programs instead of the rehabilitation professional working with one employer at a time and trying to match that employer to one individual with disabilities. It is important for rehabilitation programs to audit their business databases and determine the status of their business relationships (DiLeo & Langton, 1993). For example, a rehabilitation program should have a business strategy to develop 20 or more business partnerships with companies in the community. Then, individuals seeking employment could be screened and assessed for their skills and abilities with possible placement opportunities in at least 20 employment sites. What a difference this could make in the employment approach for people with disabilities! Figure 14.1 illustrates the reverse funnel approach for public–private sector partnerships.

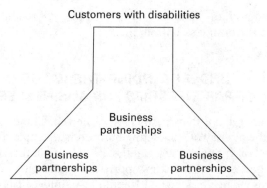

Figure 14.1.   Reverse funnel approach for public–private partnerships.

ROLE OF REHABILITATION PROGRAMS

As previously noted, the connection between businesses and rehabilitation programs is not always clear. People with disabilities are customers of rehabilitation programs, and their ultimate outcome is securing a job of choice in the community (Luecking et al., 2004). In achieving this goal, rehabilitation professionals must be keenly aware of general marketing and networking principles in order to be able to meet and open up discussions with a variety of employers. Rehabilitation programs must be able to satisfy all of their customers and the business sector; this requires new skills and knowledge.

To ensure that rehabilitation professionals are properly trained in this area, rehabilitation programs must concentrate on providing adequate training in understanding basic marketing and sales techniques (e.g., how to deliver the message, who should be hearing the message, identifying the venues to spread the message), business and labor trends of the community, and appropriate business attire and etiquette (e.g., greeting people, writing professional e-mails and letters, telephone etiquette). Rehabilitation professionals must be trained in identifying the goals of employers to ensure that appropriate matches can be made. They must believe in the product and the service they are providing and gain the trust of the employer. To do this, rehabilitation professionals must be honest, trustworthy, and have excellent follow-up services. They must be reliable, keep a positive attitude, and be able to recommit themselves to their mission, even when faced with negative outcomes.

Over the years, businesses have continually stressed the need for rehabilitation programs to work together in order to avoid duplication of effort. It is not unusual for as many as five or more different rehabilitation programs to approach an employer in one day. Personnel training for rehabilitation professionals should emphasize that employers expect the public agencies to share business contact information, reveal job leads, assign a primary contact person, and develop a seamless system to get job candidates to the business (Anderson, 2001).

Integrity and Enthusiasm

A business partnership needs to be nurtured in order to grow and stay healthy. The qualities that make most relationships successful would apply to any business partnership that a rehabilitation program forms, including trustworthiness, honesty, commitment, perseverance, and reliability. It is in the best interest for all involved (e.g., agency, employer, the individuals served) that promises are lived up to and commitments are made. Rehabilitation professionals should not promise an employer a qualified worker if no one is available who can meet the employer's needs. They should not promise an individual with disabilities a job with a specific employer if one does not exist. The sole object is not to place someone in just any job but that the person placed in the job actually fits the job and vice versa.

Rehabilitation professionals should always follow through on commitments. If they promise to make a telephone call at a certain time, they should make it. If they promise to give information to someone, they should give it. If rehabilitation professionals make a promise that they cannot keep, then they should acknowledge their limitations immediately, not ignore the promise or make up an excuse. Following through also includes sending thank-you notes for the time someone has given to listen to a pitch or thanking someone for any assistance that he or she may have provided. Good business sense also includes sending follow-up letters acknowledging meeting new contacts at functions attended.

Rehabilitation professionals cannot be complacent. They must always seek to learn more about current trends in employment, about the latest assistive technology, about changes in laws, and about new employers in the community. They must be willing to try something new or different from the status quo. It is easy to overutilize or saturate a type of employment for individuals with disabilities because those doors have been open in the past and it makes job placement easier. Rehabilitation professionals, however, must remember not to limit the potential of individuals with disabilities by pigeonholing them into certain types of work. Employers and individuals with disabilities must have faith in the rehabilitation professional's ability to follow through with his or her mission—a belief that people with disabilities can work and establish themselves as independent and valued employees, as well as be active members of their communities.

Join Business Associations

In order to understand the community, rehabilitation programs must be a part of and belong to the community. The most basic way to belong is to join civic groups and business associations. Valuable information can be learned that will assist in building successful relationships. Over time, these relationships will result in more employers gaining greater knowledge about the benefits of recruiting and hiring people with disabilities. Table 14.4 provides a list of potential groups to join or attend.

Simply being a member is not enough, though—rehabilitation professionals must be active participants of the group. They should plan to attend several consecutive

Table 14.4.   List of business organizations and civic groups

Local Chamber of Commerce
Local, state, and national Society for Human Resource Management
Local, state, and national American Staffing Association
Lions Clubs
Rotary Clubs
Jaycees
Local community economic and business development groups

meetings of the group in order to become a familiar face (Bissonnette, 1994). Once a rehabilitation professional is involved with an organization, he or she should look for ways to become more active—volunteer to greet members at a function, offer to be a presenter, volunteer for specific committees, and attend the functions that the organization plans (e.g., luncheons, happy hours, golf tournaments). A message would reach 6 billion people in 33 days (Jones, 2002) if the only "recruiting" method was telling two people and asking them to tell two more people and then asking those people to tell two more people. That is an astounding accomplishment to achieve for any employer wishing to draw attention to its product, service, and mission.

EXAMPLES OF SUCCESSFUL PARTNERSHIPS

There are many examples of excellent successful public–private sector partnerships throughout the country. Businesses such as Manpower, Bank of America, Medtronic, Pitney Bowes, Marriott International, CVS, Lowes, Alaska Airlines, Safeway, SunTrust, Home Depot, IBM, Wells Fargo, Hyatt, Philip Morris, MBNA, and Cincinnati Children's Hospital Medical Center are all part of successful partnerships to increase the employment of people with disabilities. These partnerships/relationships have been established because both parties were able to build trust with each other. The rehabilitation programs did their research and were able to identify needs and then provide targeted quality services.

CINCINNATI CHILDREN'S HOSPITAL MEDICAL CENTER

Cincinnati Children's Hospital Medical Center is dedicated to providing the highest level of pediatric care to meet the medical needs of infants, children, and adolescents. In the late 1990s, Erin Riehle, clinical director of the emergency department at Children's Hospital, had a revelation. She had been struggling to solve a performance problem that plagued the efficient operation of the emergency department that involved restocking supplies in a timely and dependable manner. It was no problem to fill these entry-level jobs with students and other part-time workers hoping to pursue careers in health care professions; however, their turnover was continuous due to the repetitious nature of this task. Though critically important, restocking of emergency department supplies was not valued nor reliably performed.

Riehle saw that Children's Hospital had adopted a policy statement from the American College of Healthcare Executives that read, "Healthcare organizations must lead their communities in increasing employment opportunities for qualified people with disabilities and advocate on behalf of their employment to other organizations." She recognized that virtually every child with disabilities in Cincinnati is a customer at Children's Hospital at some point in his or her growing years, yet such children encounter almost no role models with disabilities among the staff.

Putting these factors together, she realized that the solution to her staffing problem could also help fulfill the diversity mission of her hospital in a more complete way. So, the idea for Project SEARCH was born—a program that would provide employment for individuals whose disabilities had been a significant barrier to employment.

Riehle realized that the hospital would need community partners to achieve her goal of bringing people with significant developmental disabilities, such as intellectual disabilities, into the emergency department to fill these jobs as productive employees. The two collaborating partners were Great Oaks Institute of Technology and Career Development, a public human services agency that serves people with disabilities, and Hamilton County Board of Mental Retardation and Developmental Disabilities (MR/DD). Great Oaks is a large career and technical school serving 36 school districts and preparing more than 6,000 youth in full- and part-time programs per year. The Hamilton County Board of MR/DD provides educational, vocational coordination, and residential services to adults and children with intellectual and developmental disabilities. More than 10,000 participants are currently involved with the Hamilton County Board of MR/DD.

These partners recognized Children's Hospital as a highly desirable, large local employer with good jobs in a wide array of vocational areas that would result in a win-win situation for all. The partners committed themselves to providing staff who would be devoted to this employer and become truly knowledgeable about the worksite. In addition, there was a commitment to provide training and support services that would enable carefully selected and motivated candidates to successfully and reliably perform the necessary functions of identified jobs.

Project SEARCH is located at Children's Hospital. Employees are provided by each organization, with Riehle directing the overall program as Director of Disability Services. There are now several pathways for young people with disabilities in this program, including training programs in health care occupations and a transition-to-work program for high school students, but the payoff for the hospital is the employment program that started it all.

The partner agencies assist in preparing and screening their participants to meet several eligibility requirements (e.g., social and communication skills, independent in self-care, able to take direction, desire to work) to enter the program. Program staff members identify open positions and analyze the tasks and demands of these jobs to match with program participants who are qualified to perform them. After coordinating the hiring process, program staff members provide on-the-job support to these new employees.

"The key to our program is having the professionals from the Great Oaks Institute of Technical and Career Development and Hamilton County Board of Mental Retardation and Developmental Disabilities working on site," Riehle explained. "All the managers know them, and they know the jobs and what it takes to succeed in them."

All of the employed individuals with disabilities report to their department supervisors, like traditional employees. In addition, follow-along services assist workers in resolving problems and adapting to changes that may seem minor or embarrassing for supervisors to address (scheduling special transportation, dealing with co-worker requests, hygiene), yet can lead to termination for these workers if effective and knowledgeable support is not provided.

Each participant receives up to 8 hours of follow-along services per month of employment from program staff dedicated to the program site. Thus, the amount of staff members allocated to the site increases with the number of people placed in employment. This keeps the program cost-effective for the agencies and adequately staffed to meet the needs of the employer and the workers.

Currently, more than 70 people with significant developmental disabilities are working as employees of Children's Hospital through this program, with two staff members providing on-the-job support services to these individuals. On average, these individuals have been employed for 5 years and earn a wage of more than $8 per hour. Most are working approximately 32 hours per week and receiving full benefits. These employees work in a wide range of positions that are often overlooked for people with developmental disabilities. Many of these require mastering complex functions, yet they are routine in nature (e.g., sterilization technician, lab courier).

From the employer's point of view, the program has been enormously successful by improving performance in high-turnover, entry-level positions. The Project SEARCH employees have also had a low rate of absenteeism and been rated highly for their work ethic, accuracy, and enthusiastic attitude. The program has helped the hospital achieve its diversity objectives and has resulted in extensive local and national acclaim for its efforts. The collaborative model has benefited its community partners and their participants in achieving their objectives, as well.

"Our program uses a business model," explained Riehle. "We provide a single conduit for organizing and delivering employment services, in collaboration with the community, and deliver them in an effective and accountable way as an integrated part of the worksite. It is an appealing model to employers, and it works."

BANK OF AMERICA CARD SERVICES

More than 20 years ago, a small credit card company opened for business with 150 people working in an abandoned supermarket in Newark, Delaware. Today, after years of spectacular growth fueled by the imagination and innovation of its associates and leaders, Bank of America Card Services is the largest credit card operation in the United States.

Card Services, which operated formerly as MBNA Corp. until its January 2006 merger with the Bank of America Corp., provides retail deposits, consumer loans, and insurance products to its customers in the United States, Canada, Ireland, Spain, and the United Kingdom. It is the leading affinity marketing company in the credit card industry, with endorsements from more than 5,000 organizations.

The company's diverse work force and commitment to equal opportunities for all have been both sound business practices and a reflection of the values of the 20,000 Card Services associates. Educational programs help the associates of the company to understand and value differences among co-workers and customers, making associates more effective as teammates and more empathetic in interacting with customers.

The company has benefited from the insights of associates from a variety of backgrounds. Card Services insists on an inclusive work environment where each associate is given the encouragement, support, and opportunity to be successful. It ensures that its employees have meaningful work to do and the education, equipment, and support to do it. Within this context, the company's Support Services department arose and thrives, offering opportunities for associates with intellectual and developmental disabilities in Maine, Delaware, Ohio, Georgia, Texas, and Canada.

Launched in 1990 with 4 associates, Support Services now employs more than 335 associates, who provide integral business services such as packaging and mailing, premium fulfillment, collating, data entry, and courier services to other Card Services departments. Support Services associates earn salaries that are commensurate with other Card Services associates at the same level. They receive the same benefits package, including contributions to a 401K. The average tenure attained by Support Services representatives is 7 years and by managers is 8.5 years.

In its first years, Support Services worked in partnership with a residential program for people with intellectual and developmental disabilities, providing employee mentors on site. It assisted employees with disabilities in obtaining group home living in the community and brought on professional help from community organizations. Card Services now provides all job support internally through Support Services managers, thereby improving program efficiency and effectiveness.

Support Services has evolved into an effective business model, explained Mark Feinour, Director of Support Services. "We found that we can capture business processes, procedures, and needs that have been completed by outside vendors by doing a better job internally. We kept moving downstream to address internal customer needs, such as on-line inventory management and ordering for marketing functions. We benchmark against the market for the cost to the business unit. We charge the same but improve the quality and response time. We are able to provide the customer—the Bank of America associates—with total control over the product, a wider span of control over the process, no invoicing, and rapid turnaround for urgent needs. All this work happens to be done by associates with cognitive and developmental disabilities, helping our company fulfill the philosophical commitment expressed by leadership."

Individuals in Support Services' competitive employment program are placed in business areas throughout Card Services (rather than in the Support Services department). Competitive employment managers from Support Services support the associates placed in these business areas. To secure competitive employment opportunities, these managers seek out opportunities in the company. After developing these jobs, they recruit individuals with intellectual and developmental disabilities through nonprofit agencies in the surrounding community as well as from within Support Services. As associates of Card Services, the managers are able to explain the job requirements and the skills required.

Nonprofit agencies select and refer participants who appear to be good matches for the jobs. Competitive employment managers screen these candidates and refer only the ones who qualify for interviews and final selection. After an associate is hired, the community agency and/or rehabilitation program retains responsibility for managing the personal efforts and needs of the individual outside of work, such as transportation, housing, finances, and health care. Card Services provides job coaching and other support through competitive employment managers.

Card Services maintains regular communication with sponsoring agencies to collaborate as needed to help individuals retain employment. In addition, because Card Services is a major employer and employs so many individuals with intellectual and developmental disabilities, the company plays an important role in advocating for improvements in services and resources that benefit all customers, such as the paratransit system.

Card Services has developed a remarkably successful program that has led to long tenure and high-quality employment outcomes for many people with significant disabilities, with equally favorable outcomes for the company. The business model has established a program where associates with intellectual and developmental disabilities perform meaningful work that contributes to company operations.

"This has not been hard," Feinour said. "These are good people who like people, and they demonstrate each and every day they have the desire and ability to be very successful in a corporate environment like Card Services."

PITNEY BOWES

Pitney Bowes is the world's leading provider of integrated mail and document management systems, services, and solutions. More than 35,000 individuals are employed by Pitney Bowes and serve more than 2 million customers in 130 countries worldwide. In 2005, Pitney Bowes was ranked nineteenth nationally by *DiversityInc.* for the diversity of its work force and was cited for recruitment of qualified individuals with disabilities (Top 50 Companies, 2005).

In the Spokane, Washington area, the company has hired 400 people in the last 12 years at its North Atlantic Street site to handle billing issues, customer equipment consultation, and customer retention. The site handles 12,000–14,000 calls daily that include all customer calls west of the Mississippi.

Pitney Bowes made a commitment to establish 2% of its work force as qualified individuals with disabilities. The company has more than exceeded this goal, and now 6% of the employees on site (24 individuals) have diverse disabilities. Terry Besenyody, human resources manager, was recruited to serve on the project with Industry's advisory board, and Pitney Bowes has become a leader in the establishment of the area's Business Leadership Network (BLN). Pitney Bowes, along with other are companies, has led the effort to secure State Division of Vocational Rehabilitation funding for part of the BLN infrastructure and job placement center.

Of particular interest is the company's effort to engage in reasonable accommodation. The company has hired individuals with disabilities such as deafness, diabetes, blindness, mental illness, and back injuries. Adaptations have included such items as a headset with magnified sound (employee with legal deafness), computer screen magnifications (employee with legal blindness), screen magnifier on eyeglasses (employee with visual field cut), and chair adaptation and risers allowing an individual to be supported while standing (for individuals with back injuries who require changes in positions).

Besenyody indicates that prevailing employer attitudes about individuals with disabilities can be "ridiculous." She describes her employees with disabilities as "role models" relative to both work productivity and attendance. In relation to other employees, these individuals have above-average productivity and almost optimal attendance. In addition to outreach activities, Besenyody assisted the state VR agency in developing a job seeking skills program and developed program segments related to optimal interviewing techniques.

Pitney Bowes has also made a commitment to mentor high school students with disabilities. It has provided internships to students with disabilities from the Goodwill's High School/High Tech Program. In addition to its efforts to outreach to these individuals, the company has also made exemplary efforts to engage new employees through the Work First Program for those subsisting on welfare funding. In recent years, Pitney Bowes has hired 80 new employees through the Work First Program.

Besenyody is curious why more companies don't make efforts to hire people with disabilities. She stated, "The company is very willing to spend funds on accommodations, generally with some state rehabilitation agency match. Most of the accommodations at the Spokane site have been under $500 per employee with a disability, a very reasonable expenditure."

BARRIERS TO SUCCESSFUL PARTNERSHIPS

In order to understand the full development of successful partnerships, it is important to investigate barriers that have been faced and barriers that remain. For example, one of the barriers that has been consistently faced by Manpower is educating business clients (Wehman, McLaughlin, & Wehman, 2005). Some of the company's business clients understand the full potential of hiring individuals with disabilities; however, others still believe the myths and misconceptions of hiring individuals with disabilities. This barrier is faced one day at a time, and Manpower, along with the help of the university, has been very successful in breaking down this barrier.

An unstable job market is one of the most substantial barriers currently facing businesses. Hiring levels are stagnant around the country's largest companies, reflecting the weakness in the economy. It is also significant to understand that these reflections are true for companies still being developed. People used to look to large corporations for employment, but now they are going to smaller businesses. This is evident in the number of placements related to the number of referrals. Manpower conducts an Employment Outlook Survey every quarter to measure employers' intentions to increase or decrease the number of employees in their work force during the next quarter. It is the only forward-looking survey of its kind, unparalleled in size, scope, longevity, and area of focus. The survey has been running for more than 40 years and is one of the most trusted surveys of employment activity in the world. The Manpower Employment Outlook Survey in the United States is based on interviews with nearly 16,000 public and private employers in 470 markets across the country and is considered a highly respected economic indicator.

The national results of the Manpower Employment Outlook Survey revealed that U.S. employers remain cautious in their hiring intentions for the third quarter. Even though companies across the country anticipate some job opportunities in the July to September period, their hiring forecast has decreased since the second quarter survey and has dropped lower than it was a year ago at this time. The national employment outlook reveals that of the 16,000 employers surveyed, 20% plan to increase hiring activity for the third quarter, whereas 9% expect a decrease in job prospects. A solid 65% of the companies surveyed expect no change in hiring, and 6% are uncertain of their employment plans. It is important to note that the job market is poised to improve. Once the job market improves, there will be more placements of people with disabilities through Manpower.

Critical Forces in the Public Sector

During the late 1990s when the United States was facing severe labor market shortages, it was anticipated that there would be a rise in the employment of people with disabilities; however, this has not been the case (Green & Brooke, 2001). The Virginia Commonwealth University Rehabilitation Research and Training Center (VCU-RRTC) on Workplace Supports and Job Retention has been interested in finding out why businesses who faced a labor shortage did not recruit and hire people with disabilities. It has been the mission of the VCU-RRTC on Workplace Supports and Job Retention's Charter Business Roundtable to identify and address the factors that inhibit or deter industries from hiring people with disabilities. Through a collaborative relationship with the members of the business roundtable, a number of new and different business strategies have been identified to address the range of issues facing individuals with disabilities attempting to enter the work force.

Another noteworthy advancement in the development of public–private sector partnerships occurred in October 2001 when the American Association of People with Disabilities (AAPD) served as the first national host of National Disability Mentoring Day (NDMD): Career Development for the 21st Century. NDMD began as a White House initiative to promote the employment of individuals with disabilities and increase appreciation of National Disability Employment Awareness Month. The initial purpose of the mentoring day was to draw national attention to the importance of encouraging young people with disabilities to develop the skills and obtain the experiences necessary to compete in today's economy. The most important development for NDMD 2001 was its emergence as a true community-based, public–private sector partnership (NDMD Year-End Report, 2002).

AAPD immediately began to invite major corporations to sponsor the NDMD. The response was enthusiastic, and in just 1 month, 13 corporations joined as National Corporate Sponsors (NDMD Year-End Report, 2002). The NDMD Year-End Report documented that the strong collaboration between National Public Sponsors and National Corporate Sponsors to launch NDMD sent a powerful message that long-term employment gains for people with disabilities can best be achieved through engaging partnerships between public agencies, nonprofit disability organizations, and private employers.

Critical Forces in the Private Sector

One of the leading organizations promoting public–private sector partnerships is the BLN consisting of employers, corporate representatives, state and federal agencies, and community rehabilitation providers. The President's Committee on Employment of People with Disabilities established the BLN as an employer-lead coalition promoting opportunities that benefit businesses and people with disabilities (Lieshout, 2001).

In order for the BLN to exist effectively, it must have the participation of employers and businesses. Therefore, the BLN focuses primarily on meeting the interests and needs of the employer. With the business-led focus, the payoff to the public sector, and specifically people with disabilities, comes when corporations are able to achieve greater outcomes with their resources (Lieshout, 2001). The BLN understands that partnerships between the public and private sector can expand opportunities and resources for both sectors, and it works on demonstrating the benefits of a partnership to its members. People with disabilities are recognized by the BLN as the largest source of untapped talent, and the BLN is confident that it can help businesses effectively gain access to this talent pool through introduction and education. The BLN has proven to be a prosperous partnership organization because of the success that job seekers and employers have attained.

Another leading force in the development of public–private sector partnerships is supplemental staffing companies. Staffing companies have immense job opportunities for their applicants because they fill 80% of all information technology positions and 50% of all other positions (Egan, 2001). HirePotential, a regional supplemental staffing organization, realized their capacity to place people with disabilities into high-quality jobs. Staffing companies must discover the talents that people with disabilities have to offer an employer, and if pre-employment training is key to the future success of an applicant, then a high-quality staffing company can coordinate it with an outside facility or do it themselves in-house.

Egan stated that a quality service requires establishing a relationship between a staffing company such as HirePotential and agencies that specialize in assisting people with returning to work. The people and agencies that specialize in helping individuals with disabilities find employment also bring a key component of awareness training to the client-employers of the staffing company. HirePotential found that the hardest part of employing people with disabilities was selling the concept to their client-employers because of the fears and misconceptions of how an individual with disabilities might fit into their corporate environment.

The training and information from agencies that support individuals with disabilities can help staffing companies dispel the myths and fears of their client-employers. Egan recognized that HirePotential and other staffing companies interested in employing people with disabilities needed to receive additional training on reasonable accommodations so that they can inform and recommend accommodations and potential costs to their client-employers. Favorable outcomes have occurred because of HirePotential's willingness to collaborate with VR providers, social services agencies, and other state and local programs that specialize in the employment of people with disabilities. HirePotential now experiences approximately a 30% success rate for assisting individuals from this untapped work force in obtaining permanent positions with client-employers (Egan, 2001).

Finally, a number of businesses are getting involved with local schools and special education and vocational programs to bring students with disabilities into the workplace, where they can learn firsthand about career opportunities. These companies are recognizing that, not only do they need to focus on recruiting from adult untapped talent pools, but they also need to begin recruiting with youth who represent the future of the work force. A partnership was developed between Bergen County Vocational-Technical Schools in New Jersey, the Wakefern Food Corporation/Shoprite, and Cornell University to implement supermarket skills training programs.

The ultimate goals of the program included preparing students with learning disabilities for career alternatives in the supermarket industry, placing them in unsubsidized employment, and heightening public and corporate awareness of the value of individuals with disabilities as reliable, stable employees. A final report documented a partnership between San Marcos, California–area employers, Disabled Student Programs and Services, and Student Placement Offices of Palomar College that enabled students with disabilities to enter the employment mainstream and establish a safety-net support system within the work environment. The active 35-member advisory board included representatives from the college and business community and has stimulated a true partnership between the project and business community. As a result of the partnership in San Marcos, California, 21 students have been placed.

CONCLUSION

Clearly, public–private sector partnerships are developing and have proven beneficial to all parties involved. Rehabilitation professionals are strengthening their relationships with businesses, which in turn is increasing the number of competitive job opportunities for individuals with disabilities. Finally, companies are realizing that rehabilitation is an extremely valuable resource, and employing individuals with disabilities has positive effects on their bottom line. The literature demonstrates that there has never been a better time than the present to develop these mutually beneficial public–private sector partnerships.

REFERENCES

Americans with Disabilities Act (ADA) of 1990, PL 101-336, 42 U.S.C. §§ 12101 *et seq.*

Anderson, P. (2001). The rehabilitation and employer partnership: Walking the walk. *Journal of Vocational Rehabilitation, 16*(4), 105–109.

Bissonnette, D. (1994). *Beyond traditional job development.* Washington, DC: Milt Wright & Associates.

Blanck, P. (1998). *The emerging role of the staffing industry in the employment of persons with disabilities: A case report on Manpower, Inc.* Iowa City, IA: University of Iowa.

Dileo, D., & Langton, D. (1993). *Get the marketing edge: A job developer's toolkit for people with disabilities.* St Augustine, FL: Training Resource Network.

Egan, K. (2001). Staffing companies opening new doors to people with disabilities. *Journal of Vocational Rehabilitation, 16,* 93–96.

Golden, T.P. (1995). *Employer incentives for hiring workers with disabilities: How job developers can consult with business to access supports for employees with disabilities.* St. Augustine, FL: Training Resource Network.

Green, J.H., & Brooke, V. (2001). Recruiting and retaining the best from America's largest untapped talent pool. *Journal of Vocational Rehabilitation, 16,* 83–88.

Habeck, R.V., Leahy, M.J., Hunt, H.A., Chan, F., & Welch, E.M. (1991). Employer factors related to workers' compensation claims and disability management. *Rehabilitation Counseling, 34*(3), 210–226.

Hagner, D., & Daning, R. (1993). *Opening lines: How job developers talk to employers.* Syracuse, NY: Syracuse University, Department of Special Education and Rehabilitation.

Hanley-Mawell, C., & Millington, M. (1992). Enhancing independence in supported employment: Natural supports in business and industry. *Journal of Vocational Rehabilitation, 2*(40), 51–58.

Herman, R., Olivo, T., & Gioia, J. (2002). *Impending crisis: Too many jobs, too few people.* Winchester, VA: Oak Hill Press.

Jones, L.B. (2002). *Teach your team to fish.* New York: Crown Business.

Lieshout, R. (2001). Increasing the employment of people with disabilities through the business leadership network. *Journal of Vocational Rehabilitation, 16,* 77–81.

Luecking, R.G., Fabian, E.S., & Tilson, G.P. (2004). *Working relationships: Creating career opportunities for job seekers with disabilities through employer partnerships.* Baltimore: Paul H. Brookes Publishing Co.

National Disability Mentoring Day Year-End Report. (2002). *National disability mentoring day: Career development for the 21st century.* Washington, DC: American Association of People with Disabilities.

Sandow, D., Olson, D., & Yan, X. (1993). The evolution of supports in the workplace. *Journal of Vocational Rehabilitation, 3*(4) 30–37.

Shoemaker, R.J., Robin, S.S., & Robin, H.S. (1992). Reaction to disability through organizational policy: Early return to work policy. *Journal of Rehabilitation, 58*(3), 18–24.

Society for Human Resource Management. (1997). *The ADA at work: Implementation of the employment provisions of the Americans with Disabilities Act.* Washington, DC: Author.

Sowers, P.C., Kouwenhoven, K., Sousa, F., & Milliken, K. (1997). *Community-based employment for people with the most severe disabilities: New perspectives and strategies.* Durham: University of New Hampshire, Institute on Disability.

Tilson, G.P., Luecking, R., & West, L.L. (1996). The employer partnership in transition for youth with disabilities. *Journal for Vocational Special Needs Education, 18*(3), 88–92.

Top 50 Companies for Diversity List. (2005, June). *DiversityInc.,* 72.

Unger, D., Kregel, J., Wehman, P., & Brooke, V. (2002). *Employers' views of workplace supports: Virginia Commonwealth University Charter Business Roundtable's National Study of Employers' Experiences with Workers with Disabilities.* Richmond: Virginia Commonwealth University Rehabilitation Research and Training Center on Workplace Supports and Job Retention.

U.S. Chamber of Commerce, Center for Workforce Preparation. (2003). *Creating a 21st century workforce for business.* Washington, DC: Author.

Wehman, P., Bricout, J., & Kregel, J. (2000). Supported employment in 2000: Changing the locus of control from agency to consumer. In M. Wehmeyer & R.J. Patton (Eds.), *Mental retardation in the year 2000* (pp. 115–150). Austin, TX: PRO-ED.

Wehman, P., Brooke, V., & Green, J.H. (2004). *Public/private partnerships: A model for success.* Richmond: Virginia Commonwealth University Rehabilitation Research and Training Center on Workplace Supports and Job Retention.

Wehman, P., McLaughlin, J., & Wehman, T. (2005). *Intellectual and developmental disabilities: Toward full community inclusion.* Austin, TX: PRO-ED.

Zadny, J., & James, L. (1979). Job placement in state vocational rehabilitation agencies: A survey of techniques. *Rehabilitation Counseling Bulletin, 22,* 361–378.

Chapter 15

Interagency Partnerships

Their Critical Role
in Enhancing Services

PAUL WEHMAN AND W. GRANT REVELL, JR.

The formation of meaningful agreements of collaborators between different public agencies is an essential way to maximize resources. Skilled professionals know that few agencies can undertake the employment mission alone. The sharing of targeted resources to different tasks is an extraordinary way to leverage existing dollars to create a larger pool of potential resources than any one agency may be able to amass on its own. Inevitably, any successful inclusive employment program will reflect shared interagency partnerships.

IMPORTANCE OF INTERAGENCY PARTNERSHIPS

Interagency partnerships that target improved employment outcomes for individuals with significant disabilities are important for a number of reasons. First, individuals with significant disabilities face multiple challenges when pursuing employment. These challenges are related in part to the impact of having to deal with varying obstacles in the job search. For example, individuals with significant disabilities are often not well understood by the community, particularly by employers (Wehman, Brooke, & Green, 2004). This misunderstanding leads to myths and stereotypes that can limit vocational opportunities. The challenges faced by individuals with significant disabilities are also related to a frequently complex, sometimes splintered, and often overextended service network in the community (exemplified by multiple service providers trying to help an individual with disabilities without clear lines of responsibility).

Interagency partnerships can move professionals from offering a series of discrete services to an integrated approach to service coordination and delivery. What is meant by an integrated approach? There are multiple agencies and points of contacts that can be involved in employment efforts for individuals with significant disabilities. This mix of service providers can follow different philosophies and selection criteria; use various models of treatment and recovery; and have staff with different backgrounds and experiences.

When an individual with disabilities is dealing with a series of discrete, noninte-grated programs, these differences can at times become roadblocks to services. When this person is working with an integrated service system, these differences are worked out within the partnership, and the service flow is fluid among the partners. The over-arching goal of an interagency partnership is to create an integrated, seamless service process in which the individual can move from partner to partner as needed to suc-cessfully obtain, retain, and advance in employment (Revell, Brooks-Lane, & Durkee, 2005; West, Wehman, & Wehman, 2005).

Let's walk through a typical service scenario with a person with *mental illness* to il-lustrate why many individuals with significant disabilities seeking employment can have difficulty gaining access to and coordinating the variety of services and agencies that can be involved in this process. The mental health day treatment center provides therapeutic and service-coordination services, but it does not provide employment sup-ports and does not have funds to pay for employment services. To gain access to em-ployment services, the mental health center refers the person to the vocational rehabil-itation (VR) agency. This agency goes through its eligibility process and sets up a plan for employment involving referral to a community rehabilitation program that will ac-tually assist the person in getting a job. One step in the job search process might in-volve the job seeker going to the local One Stop Career Center to review existing job opening information. If the person is a recipient of Social Security disability benefits, such as Supplemental Security Income (SSI), then it is critically important that he or she be well informed on the potential impact of earnings through employment on ben-efits. Therefore, referral to a benefits planning specialist is now added to the service mix. The individual now has multiple points of contact in his or her service plan. It is very easy to see the challenge faced by this person in self-managing this array of ser-vices and contacts, particularly in situations where the agencies themselves have not worked out an integrated approach to sharing information and coordinating services.

MAJOR CHALLENGES IN ESTABLISHING INTERAGENCY PARTNERSHIPS

What are the major challenges faced in establishing interagency partnerships focused on achieving employment outcomes for individuals with significant disabilities? The first is identifying the service coordinator, employment, and workplace supports that may be needed, including the different funding sources that will be required. Identi-fication of these supports and funds is a uniquely challenging part of implementing supported employment programs.

The second challenge to forming effective interagency partnerships is addressing potential "turf" issues that exist among partnering agencies. Is there an agency in the partnership that is designated by law (or maybe even by traditional practices) as the lead agency for employment services for individuals with significant disabilities? If this partnership is being formed because current employment practices are not generating employment outcomes, then the designated lead agency could approach the partner-ship with a defensive, protective attitude. A positive strategy for defusing turf issues is involving customer and advocacy representatives in sufficient numbers so that they are not token participants. Another strategy is to disperse leadership responsibility among the partners so that it is not centered with any one agency. The partnership can also agree to the completion of a strategic plan as the first step. An agreed-on strategic plan that has the full participation of the partners and other stakeholders can guide the partnership through the implementation phase.

The third challenge is recognizing what has come before in the provision of employment services and what tensions currently exist among the key partners and stakeholders. For example, have key advocate groups gone public in their dissatisfaction with public agencies over perceived failures in the current employment service process? Are community service providers resistant to participating in the employment partnership because they perceive that current funding levels are insufficient to provide needed services? Have multiple efforts been tried without success in the past to develop viable employment partnerships, leaving stakeholders skeptical about current efforts? Again, an effective strategic planning process can provide an opportunity for stakeholders to voice their concerns and doubts and to clear the air of tensions.

The final challenge is to build a strong knowledge base of the various missions, policies, production standards, and timetables for each of the partnering agencies. Among public agencies, there can be differences over eligibility-determination practices, fiscal responsibilities, and duration of services. These differences can be particularly problematic for the partnership when it goes to fill existing gaps in services, such as maintaining employment supports for an extended period after employment. There can be different views on service-delivery models, a particularly critical concern when a key partner will not endorse a service model, such as one based on evidence-based principles of supported employment (Bond, 2004). There can also be differences in performance goals in which, for example, employment outcomes are not a driving force in the performance standards of a key stakeholder. Finally, there can be overlaps in perceived authority. Bureaucratic forces can cause havoc in interagency efforts and must be addressed early on in the partnership by keeping a clear focus on the intended outcomes of the partnership and the proven strategies that can help achieve those outcomes.

WHAT ARE PRIMARY FOCAL POINTS IN ESTABLISHING INTERAGENCY PARTNERSHIPS?

Wehman, Revell, and Brooke (2003) described supported-employment quality indicators associated with effective inclusive outcomes. These practices, detailed in Chapter 6, include such factors as presumption of employment, competitive employment, self-determination and control, commensurate wages, power of supports, and the importance of community. These quality indicators should serve as the primary service-related focal points for establishing an interagency partnership targeting employment outcomes for individuals with significant disabilities. Gowdy, Carlson, and Rapp (2003) studied the practices differentiating high-performing and low-performing supported-employment programs in Kansas specifically related to people with mental illness. High-performing sites had an employment outcome rate with their customers above the state norm for comparable programs; their rate was also at least twice the employment-outcome rate of low-performing providers. The results of this study provide very helpful practitioner-level examples of how the evidence-based principles for supported employment are put into practice. For example, five evidence-based practices of providing supported employment services for individuals with significant disabilities cited by Bond (2004) are as follows:

1. A clear focus on competitive employment outcomes exists.

2. Individualized job goals are established.

3. Individuals with disabilities move rapidly to employment.

4. Service coordination, employment, and clinical services are integrated.

5. Employment supports are continuous after employment.

How can an interagency partnership determine whether its services are in fact representative of the evidenced-based principles? Let's look at practical examples of some of these principles being put into practice (Gowdy et al., 2003).

A clear focus on competitive employment exists when the staff members inform the individual with disabilities about employment services during the intake process. This information does not come just from a service coordinator and/or a job counselor. Instead, therapeutic staff members also incorporate discussions about work early on in their meetings with the individual. A service coordinator in one of the high-performing sites in the Gowdy et al. study said,

> You just go over work and keep talking about it and at one point in time, they begin to realize, well, maybe I could do this. That's how I found work. I remember very specifically talking about it frequently and long. (2003, p. 234)

Contrast the positive employment focus of the preceding statement with the very different message drawn from the following quote from a service coordinator from a low-performing site about working with individuals with disabilities: "With [my customers], they basically come to me. I let them; I don't pressure them about getting a job. It just adds more to their stress." (Gowdy et al., 2003, p. 234)

These are two very different staff attitudes. In the high-performing program, work is valued and emphasized from intake. In the low-performing program, work is seen as a potential stressor, although there is a clear body of research indicating that employment does not heighten symptoms of significant disabilities (Bond et al., 2001). The employment focuses of these two programs, as represented by staff attitude and practice, are clearly different, and as a result, the employment outcomes achieved vary substantially.

What are practical examples of a program focus on rapid movement to employment? High-performing programs de-emphasize prevocational programming. Vocational assessments occur rapidly. Interagency arrangements, such as getting funding approval from VR, also occur rapidly, usually in 2–4 weeks. These programs are more comfortable in encouraging people with disabilities to use informed choice about disclosing the presence of a significant disability to employers. High-performing programs had more direct contact with employers about a specific individual with disabilities at the time the individual was seeking employment. In contrast, the low-performing programs emphasized prevocational programs, took longer completing vocational assessments, and took 9–12 weeks to obtain VR approval. Individuals receiving services at low-performing sites voiced fear about disclosure to employers and indicated that staff did not assist them in working with employers on disclosure (Gowdy et al., 2003).

These examples differentiate the practices of programs that are focused on employment and those that are not. The evidence is clear: Employment outcomes are much stronger in programs that utilize practices based on the evidence-based practices of supported employment. Interagency partnerships emphasizing employment outcomes have available a clear and proven set of programming guidelines to follow.

IMPORTANCE OF CONTINUED SUPPORTS

Continuity of employment supports must be a primary focal point of a partnership targeting improved employment outcomes for individuals with significant disabilities. This finding is drawn from a study on the durability of supported-employment effects (McHugo, Drake, & Becker, 1998). The study was conducted following the completion of the experimental phase of a research project in New Hampshire that compared the employment outcomes achieved through use of the Individualized Placement and Support (IPS) model (Corbière, Bond, Goldner, & Ptasinski, 2005) of supported employment with an alternative form of employment programming using a group skills training approach.

The IPS approach assisted people with psychiatric disabilities to find and maintain competitive employment using a person-centered, rapid job search process that integrated clinical and mental health services within the mental health center (Drake, McHugo, Becker, Anthony, & Clark, 1996). At the conclusion of the 18-month experimental period, consenting participants were offered access to continued employment supports extended for up to 2 additional years. Study participants in the IPS model who received the continued employment support during the extension phase of the study worked almost twice as many hours as those participants in the IPS model who did not receive the extended supports. The study concluded that receiving services during the extension phase was positively related to the amount of employment for participants served in the IPS model.

There are numerous implications of this study for interagency partnerships targeting improved employment outcomes for individuals with significant disabilities. The first is service design. The employment support strategy must include a continuous support strategy. Maintaining employment supports over time is clearly a staff resource issue. When partnerships are working with limited resources and potential waiting lists of individuals who are seeking entry into the job market, maintaining supports for individuals with disabilities who are already working can be challenging. By setting up continuous support as a clear defined value of the employment partnership, a priority can be placed on allotting resources to this crucial component of the service design.

The second implication is assuring continuity of service access. Frequently, individual employment programs have limited time frames for their services. VR agencies, for example, work with a mandated case closure system following successful employment (Revell, West, & Cheng, 1998). Services from a VR agency frequently end 90 days after job placement if the individual is stable in employment. A community rehabilitation program providing employment supports might have contracts or service authorizations that limit support service to a certain period after placement. To maintain continuity of supports, the partnership will need to break down the support service into its component parts and identify who provides the support services and how these services can be continued over time. It is very possible that responsibility for continued supports will need to move from one partner agency to another over time. Coordinated planning and communication among the partners can enhance continuity of service access during these transition periods.

The final implication is assuring continuity of funding. VR agencies are considered to be time-limited funding sources because of their case closure requirements. Financial resources beyond VR are needed for supports to be continued. Pooling of funds across agencies is an effective strategy for funding ongoing support services because it shares the expense. Potential funding resources beyond VR include the Home and Community-Based Medicaid Waiver through the developmental disabilities service resource; Individual Training Accounts through One Stop Career Centers; and Plans for Achieving Self-Support (PASS) through the Social Security Administration (Butterworth, Ghiloni, Revell, & Brooks-Lane, 2004; see Chapter 2). Identifying, pooling, and managing the funds to provide continued supports can be a multiagency partnership's most testing challenge. Successfully crossing the continued-supports funding barrier can also be the partnership's most satisfying accomplishment.

FOCAL POINTS FOR CONTINUED SUPPORTS

What are the continuous supports that are so important to successful employment outcomes? Ridgway and Rapp (1998) provided a synthesis of research on effective employment supports for individuals with significant disabilities. Consistent with the evidence-based principles for implementing employment services for people with significant disabilities, the employment supports identified in this report emphasized commitment to competitive work, rapid movement to employment, individualized job exploration, and ongoing support. Table 15.1 outlines these supports for people with mental illness. Here is a brief summary of primary examples of the continuous supports.

The first support is ongoing advocacy and support focused on work. This support comes in part from setting an organizational climate and culture that clearly advocates for work. Competitive employment outcomes must be seen as the focal point of the employment service. Success at work is encouraged, and job-threatening issues are addressed aggressively.

The second support is facilitation of employment. Practical assistance is provided focused specifically on employment. Employment is a key part of the integrated approach to rehabilitation and mental health services, meaning that the same workers, the same team, and the same agencies work together to help the person to succeed at work.

The third support is a clear emphasis on individual preferences and strengths. Rapid assistance is provided when an individual with disabilities is interested in working. Supports respond to the person's personal interests, goals, and preferences. If jobs do not exist that match preferences, then the supports include working with employers to develop customized job opportunities.

The fourth support is ongoing, flexible, and individualized supports. These supports include workplace accommodations, job coaching, supportive counseling, off-site assistance, support groups linked to other community supports such as medication monitoring, service coordination, and housing (MacDonald-Wilson, 2005). Ongoing assessment of support needs is conducted after the person is on the job. Ongoing assessment of the workplace environment takes place, and modifications of the workplace environment occur as needed.

Table 15.1.   Focal points for continued supports

First support	Ongoing advocacy and support focused on work
Second support	Facilitating employment
Third support	Emphasis on individual preferences and strengths
Fourth support	Ongoing, flexible, and individualized supports
Fifth support	Job replacement assistance

Source: Ridgway and Rapp (1998).

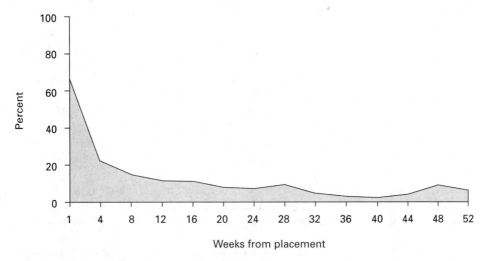

Figure 15.1. Average job coach intervention time for people with chronic mental illness for 52 weeks. (From MacDonald-Wilson, K., Revel, G., Nguyen, N., & Peterson, M. [1991]. Supported employment outcomes for people with psychiatric disabilities: A comparative analysis. *Journal of Vocational Rehabilitation, 1*[3], 36; reprinted by permission.)

The final support example is job replacement assistance. Working in jobs in the competitive labor market helps an individual with disabilities learn more about what he or she wants from employment. Replacement assistance encourages building toward a better match between the person's strengths and desires compared with the job characteristics. A key characteristic of continuous support for individuals with significant disabilities is assistance in planned moves to better, more fulfilling jobs.

The intervention chart represented in Figure 15.1 is a graphic representation of continuous supports for individuals with a primary disability of mental illness for 52 weeks from the point of job placement. These supports will vary substantially in type and intensity from person to person. The critical focal point for the partnership is to assure that individualized and continuous supports are available. Figure 15.1 provides an example of the intervention pattern of a job coach/employment specialist over the first 52 weeks of employment.

The graph represents the mean intervention time of the job coach as a percentage of the hours for which an individual was employed. For example, for week 1 of employment, the job coach provided assistance to the individual worker at an average of about 65% of the hours of employment during that first workweek. This assistance could involve, for example, jobsite training of the worker with disabilities or training for co-workers. It could also involve assistance away from the jobsite.

The graph demonstrates that the highest level of intervention occurs during the first 6–8 weeks of employment. At about 8 weeks, the intervention time reduces to about 15% of the hours of employment. The point where the graph line levels off is the point at which the interventions are moving from a primary focus on helping the individual worker acquire the skills and supports needed for that person to be effective. The focus now becomes using workplace and related supports to help the worker remain stable in employment. It is important to note that a level of support in the 10%–15% range of hours worked continues throughout the 52 weeks of employment.

This graph is an example of an intervention pattern that reflects the research finding discussed previously that the strongest predictor of an employment outcome is the availability of continued support. Note the increases in the intervention time that begin at about the twenty-fourth and forty-eighth weeks on the graph. Without the availability of continuous supports, the issues that precipitated these increased intervention levels could result in job loss if left unattended.

Each person with significant disabilities receiving employment supports will need different levels and types of supports. Some individuals will prefer supports away from the workplace; others will receive a mix of supports at and away from the workplace. See Chapter 6 for detailed examples of a variety of workplace and related supports. The key focal point for the interagency partnership is to assure that the continuous supports are available at the place and time needed by the individual participants.

Effective interagency partnerships promote actions that both improve personal outcomes for those receiving services and foster positive change in the systems that influence these services. The Institute for Community Inclusion at the University of Massachusetts Boston completed a research study on interagency partnerships (Butterworth, Foley, & Metzel, 2001). This study identified a series of quality indicators of effective interagency partnerships. For each of these quality indicators, there are a series of self-evaluation questions a partnership can use to identify its areas of strength and needed improvement. The questions focus on determining the extent to which each indicator is fully or partially in place. For those indicators that are not fully in place, follow-up actions can be identified and initiated. This self-evaluation can be used as a planning tool during the development of the partnership and for periodic reviews in monitoring the partnership's role and effectiveness. Let's review examples of self-evaluation for each of the indicators.

Indicator 1: The partnership has a clearly defined purpose. Purpose is operationally defined by having clearly identified outcomes and a data collection system in place to measure the intended outcomes. The outcome measures should emphasize quality of services and results. There should be clear details as to the number of outcome measures for the employment-focused partnership.

Indicator 2: Allies to the partnership are identified and involved with the collaborative effort. Allies to a partnership are both internal and external. Internal allies within the partnership must be identified and should include stakeholders in the planning and implementation of the partnership. Support is also needed from external allies, who need to ensure political support for the partnership. Allies to the partnership have a common interest in its purpose and a commitment to its success. Successful partnerships frequently have champions among their external allies who serve as key sponsors and advocates.

Indicator 3: The collaborators are committed to the partnership and exercise ownership in carrying out its activities. Ownership comes in part from identifying an individual from each partnering agency or program who is responsible for the implementation and success of the partnership. Inconsistent and/or rotating participation from partnering agencies will damage the development of any real sense of ownership.

Indicator 4: The partnership leads to actions and outcomes consistent with the defined purpose. Having specific action plans in place in which tasks are well defined drives action-oriented partnerships. Action-oriented partnerships also have needed resources committed to ensure that the desired results are achieved. These resources include both time from partners, particularly among the designated representatives, and monetary support.

Indicator 5: Mechanisms are in place to communicate values and resolve differences. Effective partnerships have organizational values that are identified and incorporated into action plans. For example, an organizational value for a partnership focused on employment outcomes for individuals with significant disabilities could be a zero-reject approach, meaning that any person who expresses any interest in employment is given an opportunity. Effective partnerships also have mechanisms in place to resolve disagreements.

These five quality indicators can be extremely useful both in forming a partnership and in monitoring and continually improving an existing partnership. Conscientious use of these indicators helps keep a partnership goal and action oriented.

POTENTIAL BENEFITS
OF SUCCESSFUL PARTNERSHIPS

At the customer level, what are the potential benefits of a successful interagency partnership targeting employment of individuals with significant disabilities? The first benefit is improvement in the timeliness and quality of the services provided, with individuals with disabilities having access to employment quickly, with supports in place. The second benefit is improved employment outcomes (O'Brien, Revell, & West, 2003).

Dependable and timely information on service and employment outcomes allows partners to accurately identify the strengths of the collaborative effort and the continuing issues that need to be addressed. The following are a series of example data measures that give important customer-level information on services and outcomes.

1. *Time waiting for services*—An individual with disabilities seeking services who is stuck on a waiting list or given delayed appointments for services will quickly lose interest. Waiting lists are sometimes used because of funding and/or staff shortfalls. Reducing waiting lists and time delays in gaining access to services are critical initial focal points of a partnership targeting improved employment outcomes.

2. *Time between intake and job placement*—Rapid movement to employment is one of the evidence-based practices identified previously in this chapter that can lead to improved employment outcomes for individuals with significant disabilities. Movement to employment can be delayed by a variety of factors, such as overemphasis on temporary work experiences or staff difficulties in helping individuals with disabilities match to an appropriate job. Just like time delays in initiating services, time delays between intake and job placement can cause frustration for the individual and can lead to high dropout rates. Partners need to regularly measure the time between intake and placement and take action if that time regularly exceeds 30–45 days.

3. *Number of people assessed but not placed*—Programs can sometimes find themselves providing assessment services with a much higher number of people than those who actually start working. Assessments are important, but assessments without job outcomes are a waste of resource and symptomatic of a problem the partners need to address (Wehman & Revell, 2002). Maybe there are staff development issues in which staff members are unsure about approaching employers; maybe the job placement service is understaffed. Tracking the number of people who are assessed but not placed is critically important in assessing the quality of an employment-focused partnership.

4. *Number of people achieving employment outcomes*—An increase in the number of people achieving the targeted employment outcomes is the primary indicator of a successful partnership. It is the most critical outcome measure and must be tracked closely if the partnership is truly committed to measuring its success.

5. *Number of people successful in first job placement*—Movement from a first to subsequent job placements is not a sign of failure in the first job. For many individuals who are either new to the job market or who are working on reentering the job market, the first job experience can be a trial work experience. The lessons learned from that first placement can help in improving subsequent job matches and support plans; however, a constant turnover in first jobs can also be a sign that staff is struggling with the job development process. It is important for partners to know the success rate in first job placements so that fact-based decisions can be made about staff development activities and allotment of staff resources.

CONCLUSION

A final comment on interagency partnerships: Successful partnerships have a clear mission, focus on actions that produce intended outcomes, and consistently track and evaluate their impact. Partnerships with an employment mission for individuals with significant disabilities must focus their attention on the timeliness and quality of both services delivered and job outcomes achieved. Employment service and outcome data are critical to the partnership in determining the extent it is successfully fulfilling its mission.

REFERENCES

Bond, G. (2004). Supported employment: Evidence for an evidenced-based practice. *Psychiatric Rehabilitation Journal*, 27(4), 345–359.

Bond, G.B., Becker, D.R., Drake, R.E., Rapp, C.A., Meisler, N., Lehman, A.F., et al. (2001). Implementing supported employment as an evidenced-based practice. *Psychiatric Services*, 52, 313–322.

Butterworth, J., Foley, S., & Metzel, D. (2001). *Developing interagency agreements: Four questions to consider.* Boston: University of Massachusetts Boston, Institute for Community Inclusion.

Butterworth, J., Ghiloni, C., Revell, G., & Brooks-Lane, N. (2004). *Creating a diversified funding base.* Richmond: Virginia Commonwealth University, Training and Technical Assistance for Providers. Available on-line at http://www.t-tap.org/strategies/factsheet/diversifiedfunding.html

Corbière, M., Bond, G., Goldner, E., & Ptasinski, T. (2005). The fidelity of supported employment implementation in Canada and the United States. *Psychiatric Services*, 56(11), 1444–1447.

Drake, R., McHugo, G., Becker, D., Anthony, W., & Clark, R. (1996). The New Hampshire study of supported employment for people with severe mental illness. *Journal of Consulting and Clinical Psychology*, 64(2), 391–399.

Gowdy, E.A., Carlson, L.S., & Rapp, C.A. (2003). Practices differentiating high-performing from low-performing supported employment programs. *Psychiatric Rehabilitation Journal*, 26, 232–239.

MacDonald-Wilson, K. (2005). Managing disclosure of psychiatric disabilities to employers. *Journal of Applied Rehabilitation Counseling*, 36(4), 11–21.

MacDonald-Wilson, K., Revel, G., Nguyen, N., & Peterson, M. (1991). Supported employment outcomes for people with psychiatric disabilities: A comparative analysis. *Journal of Vocational Rehabilitation*, 1(3), 30–44.

McHugo, G., Drake, R., & Becker, D. (1998). The durability of supported employment effects. *Psychiatric Rehabilitation Journal*, 22(1), 55–61.

O'Brien, D., Revell, G., & West, M. (2003). The impact of the current employment policy environment on self-determination of individuals with disabilities. *Journal of Vocational Rehabilitation, 19*(2), 105–118.

Revell, G., Brooks-Lane, N., & Durkee, B. (2005). *Developing collaborative community partnerships.* Richmond: Virginia Commonwealth University, Training and Technical Assistance for Providers. Available on-line at http://www.t-tap.org/strategies/factsheet/ceqa.html

Revell, G., West, M., & Cheng, Y. (1998). Funding supported employment: Are there better ways? *Journal of Disability Policy Studies, 9*(1), 60–79.

Ridgway, P., & Rapp, C. (1998). *The active ingredients in achieving competitive employment for people with psychiatric disabilities: A research synthesis.* Lawrence: University of Kansas, School of Welfare.

Wehman, P., Brooke, V., & Green, H. (2004). *Public/private partnerships: A model for success.* Richmond: Virginia Commonwealth University Rehabilitation Research and Training Center on Workplace Supports and Job Retention.

Wehman, P., & Revell, G. (2002). Lessons learned from the provision and funding of employment services for the MR/DD population: Implications for assessing the adequacy of the SSA Ticket to Work. In S. Bell & K. Rupp (Eds.), *Paying for results in vocational rehabilitation: Will provider incentives work for Ticket to Work?* (pp. 355–393) Washington, DC: The Urban Institute.

Wehman, P., Revell, W.G., & Brooke, V. (2003). Competitive employment: Has it become the "first choice" yet? *Journal of Disability Policy Studies, 14*(3), 163–173.

West, M., Wehman, B., & Wehman, P. (2005). Competitive employment outcomes for persons with intellectual and developmental disabilities: The national impact of the Best Buddies Job Program. *Journal of Vocational Rehabilitation, 23*(1), 51–63.

Chapter 16

Current Trends in Funding Employment Outcomes

DANIEL E. O'BRIEN AND W. GRANT REVELL, JR.

This chapter describes current trends in the purchase of employment services. Performance-based funding that focuses on outcomes, rather than the delivery of services, is a key compensation trend that has emerged recently in the purchase of employment services. The distinguishing feature of performance-based funding arrangements is that at least a portion of a provider's compensation is contingent on the achievement of specified outcome performance measures. In contrast, more process-oriented funding approaches, such as fee-for-service, base payment on units of service delivered rather than on specific outcomes achieved (Novak, Mank, Revell, & O'Brien, 1999). Vocational rehabilitation (VR) and other funding agencies are using performance-based funding strategies with increasing frequency to acquire employment services for people with significant disabilities. The following detailed analysis of the use of performance-based funding for the purchase of employment services emphasizes the outcomes achieved for service recipients with a variety of significant disabilities.

EVOLUTION OF THE USE OF PERFORMANCE-BASED FUNDING

The move toward using performance-based funding of employment services is a natural evolution from the original, more process-oriented, funding methods. The hourly unit of service funding method, which is most frequently used for supported employment, pays the provider agency based on the specific units of services received by each supported-employment participant (Wehman, Revell, & Kregel, 1998). The original intent of the hour-based purchase-of-service approach was to respond proactively to the service needs of people with significant disabilities by compensating a provider for the costs involved in implementing an individualized service plan (Revell, West, & Cheng, 1998). This plan for a particular individual could involve 75 hours of services; for another person, 150 hours of service might be involved. As long as a funding agency representative, such as a VR counselor, authorizes the funding for these services, the provider agency would be paid according to the total number of hours of service delivered.

For example, a provider agency may be paid a contracted fee of $35 for each hour of job development, job coaching, or related employment support service it provides to an eligible program participant. Ideally, this provides the employment-service participant the degree of service intensity prescriptively needed for job success. The funding agency has access to individualized information on the specific services being provided and the impact of funds being spent. For these reasons, the hour-based fee-for-service approach evolved as the predominant purchase-of-service method for individual job placements in supported employment (Wehman et al., 1998).

Despite its continued prevalence, there are a number of concerns with perceived breakdowns in the benefits obtained from the hourly unit of service approach in comparison to its costs. First, the hourly approach does not readily encourage quality assessment and quality control by service providers because hours of services are paid for without regard to the success/outcomes of those services. Second, there are limited incentives to encourage a movement toward a valued employment outcome. The focus of the hourly intervention funding approach is more on the service process and less on the service outcome. The process of providing hourly service may unintentionally become the operational goal of frontline staff members who are required to bill a set number of hours of service per day to justify their continued employment.

Performance-based funding approaches have emerged that compensate providers for the outcomes of services, rather than the process of service delivery. Movement to performance-based strategies is based both on the general concern that public funds ought to pay for valued outcomes and the specific concern that individuals receiving competitive employment services would benefit from a greater emphasis on outcomes within the funding system. A number of questions, however, should be raised during the design of a performance-based funding approach to address potential issues around adequacy of access to services for individuals viewed by employment services programs as being highly challenged or hard to serve in terms of their achieving an employment outcome. These questions have direct implications for structuring the performance-based funding components of state or national programs that are seeking more efficient methods for paying for human services.

- Will service providers limit use to a select sample of recipients who are viewed as the best candidates for success in employment? This is known as the "creaming" or "cherry picking" problem in which those who need help the least get more than they need and those who need help the most get nothing.

- Will funding be adequate to secure services for individuals who need ongoing support while in employment and for those individuals who need high-cost accommodations in the workplace?

- Will the reimbursements encourage provider agencies to consistently spend the time needed for quality job matches and job retention that will lead to significant earnings?

These concerns are faced by every funding agency in the design of funding strategies and can be addressed effectively in a well-designed performance-based funding approach. The next section of this chapter summarizes the potential benefits of performance-based funding.

BENEFITS OF PERFORMANCE-BASED FUNDING

Performance-based funding strategies offer a number of anticipated benefits over traditional funding strategies, including increased emphasis on valued outcomes; increased cost efficiency, effectiveness, and accountability; and increased customer choice and satisfaction. These benefits were discussed extensively in a report by Novak et al. (1999). A brief summary of the benefits of performance-based funding in the purchase of employment services follows.

Increased Emphasis on Valued Outcomes

The goal of employment services is to deliver valued participant outcomes. Performance-based funding strategies compensate the provider when program participants attain successful employment outcomes, rather than reimbursing the provider for the amount of services it delivers. The ultimate measure of a program's success is not the array or number of services it provides; success is measured by the extent to which it produces results valued by those being served, the funding agency, and society. Fee-for-service arrangements may have the unintended consequence of producing disincentives to customer independence. At a basic level, hourly billing tends to bear an inverse relationship to customer independence: the more independent the individual, the fewer units the provider can bill. It may often be in the provider's best fiscal interest to emphasize billable hours rather than working toward the successful, long-term employment of the individual (O'Brien & Cook, 1998). This creates a dilemma between the philosophy of decreasing dependence on the provider and the very real financial pressures to maintain billable hours. Performance-based funding helps to resolve this inherent paradox by tying payment to successful employment outcomes.

Increased Cost Efficiency, Effectiveness, and Accountability

One promise of performance-based funding is less emphasis on bureaucracy. Performance-based funding de-emphasizes regulations, accounting for time, and micromanagement of provider operations. Providers are granted greater flexibility in program administration in return for greater accountability for program performance. Provider efficiency is improved by reducing the paperwork load required of the direct-service provider. When hourly rates are the basis for payment, increments and categories of services provided must be meticulously tracked. Performance-based funding takes time formerly devoted to detailed documentation and redirects that staff time toward accomplishing the employment outcome for the individual with disabilities. Instead of documenting every minute and activity, the only information that must be recorded by the provider is that the quality/outcome indicators were accomplished and the outcome was achieved.

Effectiveness is improved by linking payment for the final milestone to the achievement of outcomes that have real meaning for the customer. For example, goal planning is reinforced by the requirement that the job achieved matches the customer's career goal. One of the best measures of effectiveness is whether the employer and the customer are satisfied with the job placement and service. Many performance-based funding systems require employer and/or customer satisfaction with the results before the final payments are made. This shifts accountability from process (i.e., hours of service) to results (i.e., milestone or benchmark payments tied to valued customer outcomes).

Increased Customer Choice and Satisfaction

Performance-based funding can result in a stronger focus on participant outcomes and more effective service delivery. In all likelihood, these factors will lead to the achievement of more timely outcomes for program participants and, hence, increased satisfaction with the system. It is important to note, however, that increased satisfaction and choice are only possible if 1) there is an individualized planning process in place that thoroughly involves the person with disabilities (with his or her circle of family and friends); 2) the individual is supported to explore a range of job opportunities and career options; and 3) the outcome indicators defined by the funding agency accurately measure the individual's satisfaction with the job, the services and supports received, and the ongoing support plan.

A study of the Milestone Results Based Funding (RBF) payment system in Indiana (McGrew, Johannesen, Griss, Born, & Katuin, 2005) concluded that those randomly assigned to the RBF payment system had significantly higher rates of completing the person-centered plan and retaining employment for 9 months. The person-centered plan is an essential vehicle for customer choice, and the employment goal set in the plan is the outcome most systems use to test customer satisfaction. Retention of employment for 9 months can also be a proxy for customer satisfaction because an unsatisfactory job will not likely be retained for that length of time. Collins concluded that outcome-based funding "when carefully constructed, appears to be an effective tool for creating a climate where consumer choice of jobs, careers and support services can occur" (2002, p. 17).

SIX COMMON ELEMENTS IN THE DESIGN OF PERFORMANCE-BASED FUNDING STRATEGIES

Performance-based funding includes any purchase-of-service arrangement that ties at least a portion of provider compensation to the achievement of outcome performance measures by linking provider payments to predefined participant outcomes. The provider receives payment only if the service recipient successfully achieves an outcome and the provider addresses the quality indicators defined as part of each incremental outcome (i.e., milestone, benchmark).

For example, the provider may be reimbursed $1,000 when the vocational assessment is completed, $2,000 when the service recipient begins working, and $3,000 when this individual reaches stabilization on the job. Stabilization on the job typically requires the provider to meet several quality indicators before payment is made; for example, satisfaction of the individual with disabilities and employer as well as job retention for a specified number of weeks beyond the completion of job training or completion of the probationary period.

Developing a performance-based funding strategy for the purchase of employment services involves six common, sequential elements:

1. Define the overall performance goal in a sequential series of clearly defined intermediate outcomes leading to a terminal outcome followed by a maintenance phase.

2. Identify benchmarks/milestones for the desired intermediate outcomes.

3. Define quality indicators for the benchmarks/milestones.

4. Assign a dollar value to the benchmarks/milestones.

5. Consider incentive payments and/or add-on provisions that fill services.

6. Define and establish funding for services that maintain the terminal outcome once achieved.

The six-step sequence for developing a performance-based funding strategy is critically important. Performance-based funding is a mechanism to distribute funds to achieve a desired outcome. The first three steps in the sequence concentrate on the desired employment outcomes that measure the success of employment services. Steps 4 and 5 incorporate cost information into the construction of the performance-based service strategy. Step 6 ensures that once achieved, the progress paid for is maintained so that the expensive initial services are less likely to have to be repeated. Effective performance-based funding strategies are linked inseparably both to the services and supports that produce a desired employment outcome and to the costs of these services.

The following description of each of these six steps draws examples from existing performance-based strategies used by state funding agencies to purchase employment services. Three state examples that this report draws on heavily are the Massachusetts Rehabilitation Commission's Community Based Employment Services (CBES), the New York State Office of Mental Health (NYOMH), and the Milestones System of the Oklahoma Department of Rehabilitative Services (DRS), which are described in detail later in this chapter.

Define the Overall Performance Goal in Terms of a Sequential Series of Clearly Defined Outcomes

Employment services for individuals with significant disabilities commonly proceed in several phases that involve community-based assessment and planning for a job goal; job development and job placement services leading to employment; initial jobsite and related training leading to stabilization in employment; and ongoing support at and away from the jobsite to facilitate retention of employment. The overall performance goal of the funding agency is that the individual receiving services remains employed for an extended period.

Identify Benchmarks/Milestones for the Desired Intermediate Outcomes

Once service outcomes are defined, the next step is to define the specific benchmarks/milestones that support these outcomes. Each desired outcome may be defined by one or more milestones. For example, the assessment component of the Massachusetts Rehabilitation Commission's CBES approach is reimbursed at two benchmarks (O'Brien & Revell, 2004). Providers receive one payment when a plan for assessment is submitted and a second payment when the final assessment report is completed. Performance-based outcomes might be designed as follows to achieve employment retention for 1 year after initial employment:

Desired outcomes	*Example payment points*
1. Establish job goal	1a. Completion of assessment
	1b. Assessment report
2. Become employed	2. Employed for 5 days
3. Stabilize in employment	3a. Employed for 30 days
	3b. Employed for 90 days
4. Continue in employment	4a. Employed for 6 months
	4b. Employed for 9 months
	4c. Employed for 12 months

Define Quality Indicators for the Benchmarks/Milestones

A critical step in defining payment points is to identify the criteria that represent successful attainment of each payment milestone. For example, in a performance-based supported employment system developed by NYOMH, *all* of the following criteria had to be met before a provider would be paid the job skills acquisition payment (Gates & Klein, 2003):

1. The individual is employed for a minimum of 4 weeks in a job consistent with the person's work plan.

2. The individual has mastered the core skills defined in the job analysis.

3. The individual has completed core skill evaluation and adjustments.

4. The individual has completed the work performance intervention plan.

These quality indicators in the NYOMH example emphasize the control of the individual with disabilities in the definition of outcomes. For the funding agency to make payment, the employment service agency must develop and provide supports for a job that are satisfactory to the individual. For example, for the job planning and placement payment to be made, the following quality indicators and services must be complete:

1. Career plan collaboratively developed and approved by customer

2. Job club/job search skills training provided

3. Accommodation planning, counseling, and negotiation with employer provided

4. Identification of job support needs, including natural supports, completed

5. Job placement achieved that meets the goal in the career plan and initial (3 days) training on the job provided

This final requirement—that the job meet the goal in the career plan—puts the individual with disabilities in the driver's seat like never before. Much has been made of customer-driven services, but services are truly customer driven only when customers have some control over resources. By withholding payment for the job placement milestone until individuals with disabilities approve that their career goals are met, customers are truly driving services. This fiscal/buying power of the individual with disabilities shifts the control of expenditures from the funding agency to one based on a service contract and involves negotiation by two equal parties. Individuals with disabilities are listened to and respected; if they are not, then there are financial consequences to the service provider.

Typical quality indicators for key job retention payment points, such as 90 days of employment, consist of documentation of both the satisfaction of the worker with the job and the employer with the performance of the worker with disabilities. Worker and employer satisfaction are positive indicators of long-term job retention. Typically, it is best if these measures are not taken until after the initial job training is complete. The results of testing the satisfaction of either party are not definitive until the stability/retention phase; prior to that point, testing is done only to identify problems that need addressing in order for the employee with disabilities to reach job stability.

Assign a Dollar Value to the Benchmarks/Milestones

The next step in the development of a performance-based funding strategy is assigning a dollar value to each payment point. Well-designed performance-based funding strategies recognize that all participants will not be successful. A provider agency will expend more resources in providing services than it will recoup for an individual who, for example, gets job development assistance but does not go to work or who works but loses employment before achieving a job retention payment point. Therefore, performance-based funding systems must allow service agencies to recoup lost revenue through payments for successful participants.

Performance-based funding systems that have been able to maintain provider participation over time have all included cost analysis methods that factor in the people who drop out of services between payment points. In order to adjust rates for risk, a methodology was developed by one of the authors based on a business technique known as *stochastic* or *probability modeling* (O'Brien & Revell, 2005). Stochastic models use a reasonable, probability projection of the likelihood of nonpayment. Specifically, databased projections of the likelihood of customers dropping out or stopping out (because of service interruptions) can help funders develop realistic rates. This methodology allows funders to develop rate structures that support the maintenance of the service-system capacity, as well as cover the cost of services to a particular individual. This true cost methodology uses a risk weighted formula to determine the full cost of providing services to a population that is at high risk for service interruption or dropping out before the stabilization/retention phase of the program.

Typically, performance-based systems increase payments as the customer retains employment for longer periods of time, achieving long-term attachment to the work force. The highest payments are made at a terminal milestone such as 6–12 months job retention, which marks the beginning of a lower payment maintenance phase. The actual cost of invested service hours frequently has an inverse relationship with success (i.e., the highest success rates are accomplished with individuals who need the lowest levels of intervention). Conversely, those most likely to drop out or stop out frequently use more hours of intervention and therefore cost the vendor more to serve. If there is not an opportunity to recoup this lost revenue through higher overall payment levels for successful cases combined with higher rates for more difficult cases, then the provider agency will limit access to its services. This presents an ethical dilemma to providers by tying the organization's survival to limiting access for those most in need. If they do not limit access to services for individuals who are high risk, then they will be unable to maintain their capacity to provide the service and will

cease taking referrals altogether. Those individuals who will be most adversely affected are those who are viewed as needing more intense services and/or as being a
higher risk for failure to achieve employment outcomes.

The primary strategy for creating the opportunity to recoup lost revenues is to
establish a unit of service rate that takes into consideration the inevitable lack of success of some participants. In other words, rates are set so as to overpay for successful
cases in order to compensate for the underpayment on unsuccessful cases. A compan-
ion strategy to address the access issue is to risk-adjust rates by creating multiple tiers
of payment with rates increasing as the risk of failure increases. These two strategies
work in conjunction with a requirement that providers have a no-reject policy or limit
access to services only in cases in which safety or security are documented issues.

The example in Figure 16.1 describes a rate-setting exercise for a performance-
based funding strategy. This example uses a simple stochastic budgeting approach
based on projected participation and success levels. In an actual rate-setting situation,
the projections are based on the experience of the provider agency with its targeted
population. The funding agency will also have its own projected success rates based
on experience and desired cost efficiencies. In rate setting, the final unit cost assigned
will usually be based on a combination of the provider's experience and the funding
agency's expectations (O'Brien & Revell, 2005).

The provider in the example needs to achieve 90 outcomes payments at the
agreed-on payment of $1,300 per successful outcome to meet its budget of $117,000.
Thus, the payment per milestone does not represent the direct cost for that particular successful case but includes the cost of maintaining the capacity to provide the program. Without the use of the probability model to factor in the cost of maintaining
program capacity, any experiments with performance-based funding will be short
lived (O'Brien & Revell, 2005).

Actual experience running an employment program rarely matches projections.
For example, if the provider receives only 75 outcome payments, then it will experience a budget shortfall of approximately 15 payments of $1,300 ($19,500). This shortfall can occur because the number of referrals is below projections or because the individuals being served do not move through the outcomes payment points with the
projected success rate. If the provider receives 105 payments and holds costs as budgeted, then it will exceed the budget total by $19,500. The higher-than-projected
number of payments can result from serving more people than projected. It can also
occur from a higher-than-projected success rate, an outcome of potential advantage to
the funding agency and the individuals being served if the success reflects more people getting and keeping jobs than was projected. In performance-based funding, employment success is rewarded financially.

Consider Incentive Payments
and/or Add-on Provisions that Fill Services

Incentive payments are premiums paid for achievement of outcomes over and above the
core outcome criteria. Incentive payments can also reflect monetary rewards for serving
individuals with the most significant disabilities who will potentially require a higher
level of support. For example, the Milestones System of the Oklahoma DRS (O'Brien
& Revell, 2004) and the NYOMH system (Gates & Klein, 2003) set up two-tiered payment systems. Provider agencies receive a higher rate of reimbursement for serving in-

Create a budget: For an employment service agency with two full-time job coaches with an average salary of $27,500 each and a part-time hourly back-up job coach, the total employment service budget is $117,000. This budget includes all direct-service costs of salary, fringe benefits, travel, and training. It also includes the indirect costs for administration, housing, payroll, and so forth.

Project outcomes for target group of individuals to be served: The agency is staffed to serve 25 candidates for employment. The funding agency is using a performance-based funding system with five payment points. In projecting outcomes for the individuals to be served, the provider agency uses its experience in providing employment services. Here is its projected success rate.

Payment milestone	Number of people projected to achieve milestone
Set employment goal	25
Become employed	20
Work for 30 days	17
Work for 90 days	15
Work for 180 days	13
Total number of potential payments	90

Establish unit costs: If the provider agency is accurate in its projections, it will receive a total of 90 payments from the funding agency. With a budget of $117,000 and expectation of 90 payments to cover this budget, the unit cost per milestone outcome for this provider is $1,300 ($117,000 divided by 90 payments). If the milestones are weighted equally and if the budget calculations are agreed to by the funding agency, then payments will be made to this provider at the rate of $1,300 per successful outcome. For each person in this example who completed all five milestones, the provider agency will collect a total of $6,500. Using the projected completion rate, here are the funding reimbursements to the agency, based on an agreed-on unit cost if $1,300, in a performance-based funding system in which the payment points are weighted equally.

Payment milestone	Number of individuals projected	Amount to be collected to complete each milestone
Set employment goal	25	$32,500 (25 × $1,300)
Become employed	20	$26,000
Work for 30 days	17	$22,100
Work for 90 days	15	$19,500
Work for 180 days	13	$16,900
Total amount to be collected		$117,000

Assign dollar values to each payment point: If milestones are weighted differently by the funding agency, then the unit payment must be adjusted to the various weights. For example, the later job retention outcomes can be assigned a higher value than the earlier assessment outcomes. The Oklahoma Milestones payment system places higher weights on its later milestones. The milestones component of the Ticket to Work and Work Incentives Improvement Act of 1999 (PL 106-170) places increasingly higher values on the payments made at the third, seventh, and twelfth months of employment at substantial gainful activity. Weighted payments are a means for the funding agency to create financial incentives for the provider agency around achievement of the most highly valued outcome.

Figure 16.1. Steps in establishing a rate based on a stochastic/probability model for a performance-based funding strategy

dividuals who are considered to have more challenges based on level of disability and other factors that create substantial employment difficulties (Frumkin, 2001).

Incentive payments can also be made for a variety of outcomes, such as earnings above a set goal (e.g., substantial gainful activity [SGA] level for recipients of Social Security Administration [SSA] disability benefits), jobs with benefits, and workweeks of 35 or more hours. NYOMH's highest payment level is for individuals who are incentive-payment eligible. Their stakeholder-planning group established four criteria for use with individuals experiencing a severe mental illness (Gates & Klein, 2003). When any one of the criteria is met, the provider qualifies for an additional 20% incentive payment on top of the established milestone payment rates. The four criteria are 1) no competitive work in the past 60 months; 2) three or more psychiatric hospitalizations in the past 2 years; 3) 12 or more weeks in the hospital in the past 2 years; or 4) 4 or more job failures in the past year.

Without this additional incentive to serve the most difficult cases, accepting only the easiest cases would be a pervasive problem. Data from NYOMH and Oklahoma DRS indicate that this method has worked to counteract the tendency of performance-based funding systems to serve individuals who are perceived as having a high likelihood for achieving a successful employment outcome while limiting access to more difficult cases, thus generating a full set of outcome payments.

The key to assuring full access to services regardless of severity is to develop clear definitions of those most likely to be rejected as too difficult to serve and to create financial incentives that encourage providers to serve those individuals. NYOMH incentive payment criteria and "highly challenged" criteria from the Milestones System of the Oklahoma DRS are presented in Table 16.1.

Table 16.1.   Criteria used to pay incentive payments

New York State Office of Mental Health criteria for "incentive payment eligible"

Individual must meet at least one of the following conditions:

- No competitive work in the past 60 months
- Three or more psychiatric hospitalizations in the past 2 years
- 12 or more weeks in the hospital in the past 2 years
- Four or more job failures in the past year

Oklahoma Department of Rehabilitative Services' Milestones System criteria for "highly challenged"

Individual must meet at least two of the following conditions:

- Need for a personal care attendant at the jobsite
- Three or more events (e.g., hospitalization, incarceration or other institutionalization, recurring health or mental health issues) during the last 2 years that interrupted work or the ability to live independently
- Ongoing, documented pattern of explosive behavior, physical aggression, self-abuse, or destruction of property that would jeopardize him- or herself or others at the worksite
- Evidence of rejection of the individual by other providers (e.g., vocational rehabilitation, schools) because of being too difficult to serve
- Membership in the Hissom Lawsuit class or fulfillment of eligibility criteria for the Assertive Community Treatment program
- Alcohol and/or substance abuse as a secondary disability that has resulted in loss of employment
- Borderline personality disorder, autism, or deafblindness as a primary or secondary disability
- Three or more changes of antipsychotic medications in the past year
- Need for specialized assistive technology such as sensory aids, telecommunication devices, adaptive equipment, and/or augmentative communication devices to succeed in employment

---

Source: O'Brien and Revell (2005).

Define and Establish Funding for Services
that Maintain the Terminal Outcome Once Achieved

State VR agencies such as the Oklahoma DRS and the Massachusetts Rehabilitation Commission have been leaders in developing performance-based funding for employment services targeted to people with significant disabilities. The challenge for VR agencies is that, by law, funding through VR is time limited (Rehabilitation Act Amendments of 1992 [PL 102-569]). VR agencies can be the primary funding source for supports needed to help achieve employment outcomes and maintain that outcome for a period of 90–180 days; however, to fund supports that help individuals maintain employment for more extended periods, VR agencies need to establish interagency funding arrangements that provide for the ongoing supports critical to job retention (McHugo, Drake, & Becker, 1998).

The Massachusetts Rehabilitation Commission's CBES approach is an excellent example of how to arrange funding for ongoing supports to maintain employment outcomes over time. Additional support services (e.g., car hand controls, adaptive workstations) are provided at a specified rate for specific support needs that are not covered in the CBES service definitions. Total payments for additional support services vary based on individual need. Extended ongoing support services to help maintain employment long term are provided at a fixed rate of $26 per hour. Interagency arrangements establish a variety of funding resources that can be used for extended ongoing supports (Inge, 2001).

ADDITIONAL CONSIDERATIONS FOR DESIGNING
EFFECTIVE PERFORMANCE-BASED FUNDING STRATEGIES

A well-designed performance-based funding strategy should take the five Cs of a sound design strategy into consideration. The system should be *customer centric*, include mechanisms for *choice*, be *collaboratively designed, contain countermeasures* to limiting services to individuals who are less challenged among the eligible population, and be based on proven *concepts*.

Customer centric payment points should be based on valued outcomes identified by the person receiving employment support, instead of funder- or system-centric outputs. Outcomes are results that an average customer would recognize as the goal or an intermediate step toward the goal that he or she engaged the service to provide. All too frequently, outputs focus on the funder and provider agencies (i.e., hours of service, costs/revenues).

Customer choice/control must be built in from the start. Customers should be involved in the design of the system and have mechanisms such as vouchers and/or performance report cards with choice of service provider (O'Brien, Revell, & West, 2003). Through informed customer choice, customers can reallocate funds to providers who get more outcomes for them.

Collaborative stakeholder planning and evaluation occurs when customers, vendors, and service-funding agencies have equal voices in the design of the performance-based funding system. A balanced stakeholder-planning group should be charged with addressing the six critical elements of a performance-based funding system that are described later in this chapter.

Countermeasures to limiting services to individuals who have fewer challenges among the eligible population involve creating financial incentives to serve those individuals who experience the most challenges. Without this added incentive, the most difficult cases will get little or no attention. A second strategy is what economists call risk-adjusted rates. Subgroups of the service populations may present a higher risk of dropping out and/or represent a higher cost to the provider. Several risk levels can be established and rates set for each risk subgroup.

Use of proven concepts involves basing the service requirements on proven best practices. Research findings in the area of evidence-based practices in supported employment give clear guidance on effective employment service designs (Bond, 2004). This research clearly points to the importance of basing employment services on individual preferences, focusing specifically on job outcomes, moving rapidly into employment, and providing ongoing support services. All of these critical practices are consistent with the performance-based funding designs described in this chapter.

These five considerations can be effectively addressed in the design of a performance-based funding strategy. The next section of this chapter describes two current performance-based funding initiatives. Although each is very different in its approach to structuring payments for employment outcomes, both share the common goal of ensuring access and support for individuals with the most significant disabilities.

DIVERSITY IN THE APPLICATIONS
OF PERFORMANCE-BASED FUNDING

Performance-based funding strategies can be designed to accommodate variations in service costs so that providers receive the compensation needed to provide quality services. Assisting a diverse range of individuals with significant disabilities to achieve successful employment outcomes requires the provision of a variety of services and supports. Employment services are individually driven. Performance-based funding strategies that establish costs across a wide population are challenged in providing adequate access and support to individuals whose costs of services substantially exceed the norms. Here are two examples from Oklahoma and New York that demonstrate diversity in the design of a performance-based funding approach.

MILESTONES SYSTEM OF THE
OKLAHOMA DEPARTMENT OF REHABILITATIVE SERVICES

The Oklahoma DRS moved to a performance-based funding design in the early 1990s with the initiation of the Milestones System (O'Brien & Revell, 2004). The Milestones System addresses the issue of adequacy of access by setting up two payment tiers. When a provider serves an individual who meets two or more of the criteria defined for "highly challenged," a higher payment is received for all successful outcomes except for determination of need and career planning. The total "highly challenged" rate for completion of all six outcomes is 22% more than the regular rate. Milestones System payment levels in place for Fiscal Years 2002–2005 are as follows:

Milestones for regular rate payment	Milestone
Determination of need and career planning	$500
Job placement	$1,350
4 weeks job retention	$1,800
8 weeks job retention	$1,350
Stabilization 12 weeks work	$1,700
Rehabilitated (90 days beyond stabilization)	$2,300
Total	$9,000

Milestones for "highly challenged" rate	Milestone
Determination of need and career planning	$500
Job placement	$2,500
4 weeks job retention	$1,500
8 weeks job retention	$1,500
Stabilization 17 weeks work	$1,700
Rehabilitated (90 days beyond stabilization)	$3,300
Total	$11,000

The statewide fixed rates presented here became effective July 1, 2001. Previously, rates were set at an individual provider level based on a negotiated bidding system (Oklahoma DRS, 2001). The Oklahoma DRS has consistently reported improved outcomes through the Milestones System. Since DRS moved from the previous hourly fee-based payment system to the Milestones System, more individuals with significant disabilities have gone to work more quickly at less cost per employment outcome (Inge, 2001).

The Milestones System also extends the period of potential VR support to a period of at least 6 months of employment, with an even longer period for those individuals who meet the "highly challenged" criteria. Research has documented that, nationally, there are often substantial problems in securing funds for extended services, the services that continue in supported employment after VR funding is completed (West, Wehman, & Revell, 2002). Research findings also point to the critical importance of maintaining ongoing supports for employment outcomes to be maintained among individuals with significant disabilities (McHugo et al., 1998). The Oklahoma Milestones timeline of at least 6 months of VR-sponsored support after employment helps assure a solid stabilization in employment at the time of movement to extended services funding.

NEW YORK STATE OFFICE OF MENTAL HEALTH

The NYOMH moved to a performance-based funding design in 2000 after a year-long stakeholder-design exercise (Gates & Klein, 2003). The stakeholder group was made up of one third customers, one third vendors, and one third funder-agency representatives. The charge of the group was to take the best practices in supported employment as embodied in the individual placement and support (IPS) and supported-employment evidence-based practices model as described by Bond (2004) and embed them within a milestone funding system based on the successful Milestones System of the Oklahoma DRS.

The group developed a consensus model that represented the collective best interests of all three parties. The group renamed Oklahoma's "highly challenged" concept to "incentive payment eligible," or just IPE, because group members felt the term might be stigmatizing. The criteria were simplified and reduced to four conditions (see Table 16.1), any one of which would qualify the individual for the 20% higher rate for completion of all six outcomes, which is roughly the same incentive represented in the Milestones System. (*Note:* the 20% increase also applies to each milestone in the NYOMH model but not in the Milestones System.). Here are the milestone payment levels in place for Fiscal Year 2002. *Long-term job supports* refers to the continuous supports provided after the completion of the milestones system. These continuous supports focus on job retention over time.

Milestones for supported-employment standard rate	*Milestone*
Life skills assessment (10% of the total)	$750
Career planning and initial job placement (10%)	$750
Job skill acquisition for 4 weeks (20%)	$1,500
Job retention at 3 months (20%)	$1,500
Job retention at 6 months (25%)	$1,875
Job retention at 9 months (15%)	$1,125
Total	$7,500
Long-term job supports	$1,300/year

Milestones for incentive eligible	*Milestone*
Life skills assessment (10%)	$900
Career planning and initial job placement (10%)	$900
Job skill acquisition for 4 weeks (20%)	$1,800
Job retention at 3 months (20%)	$1,800
Job retention at 6 months (25%)	$2,250
Job retention at 9 months (15%)	$1,350
Total	$9,000
Long-term job supports	$1,300/year

The NYOMH Milestone pilot ran for 2 years and is being evaluated for inclusion in a Medicaid-funded employment initiative. During the 2 years, a study was done by the Columbia University School of Social Work, Workplace Center (Gates & Klein, 2003). Results show that the milestone funding approach to performance-based funding was very effective. During the 2-year pilot, 92 individuals completed the 6-month retention milestone out of 146 who were placed in jobs. This compares favorably with the national benchmark studies done on the IPS model (Bond et al., 2001). The average hourly wage for these individuals was $7.50, and the individuals worked an average of 22 hours per week. The data also indicate that the incentive payments appear to have counteracted the problem of limiting services to individuals perceived as being more likely to achieve a successful employment outcome. Although the incentive-eligible individuals did seem to drop out at a higher rate and took more service hours to complete each milestone, they were not screened out and did accomplish the terminal outcomes of 6 months and 9 months job retention at a comparable rate.

CRITICAL ELEMENTS IN ASSURING ADEQUACY OF ACCESS TO PERFORMANCE-BASED FUNDING

There is a need to find a balance among the interests of individuals with disabilities requiring employment-related supports, the service provider agencies, and the funding agencies. Customers, regardless of the degree of challenge they face in obtaining an employment outcome, seek a design that allows them choice in employment goals and service providers. Provider agencies seek to cover the true cost of providing services. Funding agencies seek to purchase services from providers that achieve desired participant outcomes in a cost-efficient and effective manner.

Clearly, each party has a valuable perspective and must be accommodated to some extent if the design is to work. Funding systems that are unbalanced result in people being excluded from services, poor-quality services that fail to consistently achieve desired outcomes, and/or inflated costs for services. For example, a funding design that underfunds (i.e., sets payment levels that do not cover the actual costs associated with serving people with more intensive support needs) and provides no mechanism for a provider to recoup costs for needed services will leave certain individuals unserved or poorly served. As discussed in the Oklahoma and New York examples earlier, if there is to be a balance among the interests of key stakeholders, performance-based funding approaches must effectively address a number of key concerns.

Based on the lessons learned from existing performance-based funding examples, there are a number of factors that should be considered when assessing the adequacy of a performance-based funding system. The criteria that define an "adequate" performance-based funding system are as follows.

First, payment points in a performance-based system must be weighted and spaced effectively. Performance-based funding strategies must balance the funding agency's desire to weight pay schedules toward the final desired outcomes and the desire of the provider agency to maintain a steady cash flow. For example, if 75% of funds are held until an individual achieves a final outcome (e.g., 6–12 months of employment), then provider agencies may find it difficult to meet their ongoing financial commitments. Balancing of funding risks is particularly relevant to smaller specialty employment agencies that have a limited funding flow. These agencies need early payments for outcomes such as completion of assessments and successful job placement. Performance-based funding systems should ensure that competent providers of service are fairly compensated for quality services so that they can cover their costs.

Second, the performance-based funding strategy must reimburse at amounts consistent with the resource expenditure risks of providers. If an inadequate overall payment level is assigned, then the balance of risks in assisting individuals who are hard to serve falls heavily on the provider. Assigning adequate funds involves costing out the desired services accurately. It also involves accommodating the costs involved in the inevitable failure of some participants to reach key outcomes. The outcome payments made for successful participants must incorporate the expenses involved in serving those individuals for whom payments are not received.

Third, the performance-based funding strategy should provide support for proactive assessment and job placement activities. The better the information used for establishing a job goal, the better the chance for a quality job match. The goal of employment services is not just to help get jobs; the goal is to support long-term job retention. People stay in jobs that match their interests. Good funding strategies pay for sound assessments and person-centered planning processes that lead to realistic career goals to which job placement payments can be tied. The Louisiana VR agency is implementing a milestone payment system based on the Oklahoma model that uses the person-centered planning process to establish job placement payment criteria. The Ticket to Work Program of the SSA, however, pays nothing for assessment. The provider is expected to make a risk assessment as an unreimbursed business expense and only accept the candidates most likely to go off of benefits (Wehman & Revell, 2003).

Fourth, the performance-based funding strategy should support replacement activities and provide adequate funding for ongoing support needs. Individuals with significant disabilities frequently need replacement assistance to be successful in employment. Given the limited competitive employment history of many individuals with significant disabilities, there will be for some two, maybe three or more, job placements occurring before longer-term job stability occurs. The need for replacement assistance is not just a result of job loss—replacement can actually result from taking advantage of job improvement opportunities and from fulfilling career interests. The Oklahoma Milestones System, for example, allows for replacement by paying for cumulative weeks of employment, which can be on more than one job.

Lastly, the performance-based funding strategy must address the need of participants for access to a full range of additional support services. The core interventions addressed in most performance-based funding designs are the workplace and related supports that are critical to success in employment; however, there are additional support services (e.g., access to assistive technology, interpreter services and/or communication aides, complementary training services) that are also required by some individuals to be successful in employment.

The SSA's Ticket to Work Program is a notable example of a performance-based funding approach that did not follow a number of the design guidelines described in this chapter (Wehman & Revell, 2003). The Ticket to Work did not take the cost of dropouts and stopouts into consideration in its funding formula. As a result, vendor participation rates have been very low and customer choice and access to services has been minimal (Ticket to Work and Work Incentives Advisory Panel, 2004). Vendors (employment networks) that participate generally report that even with substantial efforts to avoid serving individuals with high support needs, they are losing money. Many vendors have tried the system and, after determining the unrealistic relationship between ticket revenue and service costs, have decided to drop out. A second fundamental error on the part of the Ticket to Work design is that the payment thresholds were set unrealistically high. SSA beneficiaries who had been determined unable to work at the SGA level are required to work at or above SGA in order for any payments to be made to the vendor.

As emphasized previously, designers of performance-based funding systems must assure that adequate funding is reliably available to maintain the capacity of the system to provide services to its intended customers. In the design of the Ticket to Work and Work Incentives Improvement Act of 1999 (PL 106-170), SSA missed this fundamental point. Payments are so uncertain that employment networks are unable to have any certainty that capital invested in the startup phase could ever be repaid. A core concern regarding the funding design of the Ticket to Work is that employment networks have no mechanism to recoup the dollars expended on supports for individuals who do not achieve the SGA-level earnings outcome criteria. The payments made through the outcome milestones and the outcome payment strategies are based strictly on savings in cash benefit payments generated by SGA-level earnings. These payments do not address the critical adequacy of access issue of employment networks recouping resources expended on individuals for whom performance payments are not received at a level that covers expenses (Adequacy of Incentives Advisory Group, 2003).

CONCLUSION

By making the funding and provision of employment services more outcome oriented, performance-based funding approaches have the potential to increase the cost effectiveness and efficiency in funding employment outcomes. By focusing attention on employment outcomes instead of the monitoring of service processes, performance-based funding provides many possible benefits over fee-for-service arrangements. By emphasizing employment outcomes that are consistent with personal choice and work goals, it can respond to the emerging voice of people with disabilities. Performance-based funding systems that align effectively with individual empowerment through choice and control over employment services will help prepare state VR systems and other funding agencies, program participants, and vendors for the movement to more customer-controlled employment service plans.

Performance-based funding approaches do elicit a number of concerns: Will disincentives to serving people with more significant disabilities be created? Will attention be diverted from creative job matches and creative job development in favor of expediency? Can the most appropriate outcomes be articulated and measured? Can individual cost variations be accommodated? Will career development be impeded? Experience to date with performance-based funding of employment services indicates that many of these concerns can be effectively addressed through a careful review of the successful examples in place *and* the use of a design and implementation process that balances the interests of the key stakeholders.

As discussed in this chapter, there are numerous examples of performance-based funding of employment services in place for which states have reported improved service effectiveness and cost efficiencies. There are many innovative variations on existing approaches being tested. States interested in moving to performance-based funding have a number of examples and resources available to them. The core indicator of the success of inclusive employment services is a valued employment outcome responsive to the job interests and support needs of individuals with the most significant disabilities. By emphasizing outcome criteria that focus specifically on the job stability and job satisfaction of people served, performance-based funding approaches can proactively fund successful employment outcomes.

REFERENCES

Adequacy of Incentives Advisory Group. (2003). *Recommendations for improving implementation of the Ticket to Work and Self-Sufficiency Program.* Champaign: University of Illinois at Urbana-Champaign, College of Applied Life Studies, Disability Research Institute.

Bond, G. (2004). Supported employment: Evidence for an evidence-based practice. *Psychiatric Rehabilitation Journal, 27*(4), 345–359.

Bond, G.B., Becker, D.R., Drake, R.E., Rapp, C.A., Meisler, N., Lehman, A.F., et al. (2001). Implementing supported employment as an evidenced-based practice. *Psychiatric Services, 52,* 313–322.

Collins, M. (2002). *Outcome-based reimbursement, consumer choice and the inclusion of all job seekers: Compatibility issues for state vocational rehabilitation agencies.* Burlington: University of Vermont, Center for Disability and Community Inclusion.

Frumkin, P. (2001). *Managing for outcomes: Milestone contracting in Oklahoma.* Cambridge, MA: The PricewaterhouseCoopers Endowment for the Business of Government. Available online at http://www.endowment.pwcglobal.com

Gates, L., & Klein, S. (2003). *Performance based contracting demonstration: Evaluation findings.* New York: Columbia University School of Social Work, Workplace Center.

Inge, K. (2001). *Paying for success: Results based funding.* Richmond: Virginia Commonwealth University Rehabilitation Research and Training Center on Workplace Supports and Job Retention.

McGrew, J., Johannesen, J., Griss, M., Born, D., & Katuin, C. (2005). Performance-based funding of supported employment: A multi-site controlled trial. *Journal of Vocational Rehabilitation, 23*(2), 81–100.

McHugo, G., Drake, R., & Becker, D. (1998). The durability of supported employment effects. *Psychiatric Rehabilitation Journal, 22*(1), 55–61.

Novak, J., Mank, D., Revell, G., & O'Brien, D. (1999). Paying for success: Results-based approaches to funding supported employment. In G. Revell, J. Inge, D. Mank, & P. Wehman (Eds.), *The impact of supported employment for people with significant disabilities: Preliminary findings of the National Supported Employment Consortium* (pp. 25–42). Richmond: Virginia Commonwealth University Rehabilitation Research and Training Center on Workplace Supports and Job Retention.

O'Brien, D., & Cook, B. (1998). *The Oklahoma Milestone payment system.* Available on-line at http://www.onenet.net/~home/milestone

O'Brien, D., & Revell, G. (2004). Performance-based funding: Developing a successful strategy. *Job Training and Placement Report, 28*(8), 1–5.

O'Brien, D., & Revell, G. (2005). The Milestone system: Results-based funding in vocational rehabilitation. *Journal of Vocational Rehabilitation, 23*(2), 101–114.

O'Brien, D., Revell, G., & West, M. (2003). The impact of the current employment policy environment on self-determination of individuals with disabilities. *Journal of Vocational Rehabilitation, 19*(2), 105–118.

Oklahoma Department of Rehabilitation Services. (2001). *Contract for supported employment services.* Oklahoma City: Author.

Rehabilitation Act Amendments of 1992, PL 102-569, 29 U.S.C. §§ 701 *et seq.*

Revell, G., West, M., & Cheng, Y. (1998). Funding supported employment: Are there better ways? *Journal of Disability Policy Studies, 9*(1), 60–79.

Ticket to Work and Work Incentives Advisory Panel. (2004). *Advice report to Congress and the Commissioner of the Social Security Administration: The crisis in EN participation. A blueprint for action.* Baltimore: Social Security Administration.

Ticket to Work and Work Incentives Improvement Act of 1999, PL 106-170, 42 U.S.C. §§ 1305 *et seq.*

Wehman, P., & Revell, G. (2003). Lessons learned from the provision and funding of employment services for the MR/DD population: Implications for assessing the adequacy of the SSA Ticket to Work. In S. Bell & K. Rupp (Eds.), *Paying for results in vocational rehabilitation: Will provider incentives work?* (pp. 355–393). Washington, DC: The Urban Institute.

Wehman, P., Revell, G., & Kregel. J. (1998). Supported employment: A decade of rapid growth and impact. *American Rehabilitation, 24*(1), 31–43.

West, M., Wehman, P., & Revell, G. (2002). Extended services in supported employment: What are the providers doing? Are customers satisfied? In D. Dean, J. Kregel, & P. Wehman (Eds.), *Achievements and challenges in employment services for people with significant disabilities: A longitudinal impact of workplace supports* (pp. 85–98). Richmond: Virginia Commonwealth University Rehabilitation Research and Training Center on Workplace Supports and Job Retention.

Chapter 17

The Impact of Employment on People with Disabilities Receiving Social Security Administration Benefits

Valerie A. Brooke and Jennifer Todd McDonough

Mapping the historical roots of the Social Security Administration (SSA) and the programs and services that it offers to beneficiaries with disabilities receiving Supplemental Security Income (SSI) and Social Security Disability Insurance (SSDI) is an important step in developing a strong conceptual understanding of these government programs. By tracing the legislative history of the SSA and its early connection with vocational rehabilitation (VR), it becomes clear that work and return to work have been strongly held program values. Since its inception in 1935, the SSA has provided benefits to the retired and to individuals with disabilities and their families. The SSA continues this long tradition by reaching out and providing benefits to approximately 4.9 million Americans receiving SSDI and an additional 3.9 million individuals of working age receiving SSI, for a total expenditure of $60 billion (SSA, 2003). It is projected that one out of every three people receiving SSA benefits has a disability or is a dependent or a survivor of a worker, many of whom also have disabilities.

The Social Security Act of 1935 (PL 74-271) established federal/state VR as a permanent program after 15 years of temporary funding. Congress clearly voiced the intent of this legislation by citing that VR services to individuals with disabilities should not be based on past program criterion of "deservability" but rather on public duty. Yet, it was not until the Social Security Act Amendment of 1965 (PL 89-97) that a permanent and direct relationship with VR was established. This legislation essentially married the SSA and VR by stating that the overall mission of VR was to serve the greatest number of applicants for the SSDI program (Popick, 1967). Congress mandated that SSDI benefits were intended to cover the costs of "selecting disability beneficiaries" through state VR agency services.

In the 20 years that followed the passage of the Social Security Act Amendment, several significant events occurred that altered society's image and perception of people with disabilities. Primary among these events were the multiple demonstrations of people with significant disabilities working in business settings across the country (Bates, Renzaglia, & Clees, 1980; Rusch & Mithaug, 1980; Rusch & Schutz, 1979; Sowers, Thompson, & Connis, 1979; Wehman & Hill, 1980; Wehman, Hill, & Koehler, 1979). These employment results initiated an examination of values governing services to people with disabilities and the beginning of a strong and organized disability movement. Over time, people with disabilities, families, and professionals began to demand high-quality educational programs alongside students without disabilities and real jobs in business settings earning wages and benefits equal to those of co-workers without disabilities. By the end of the 1980s, a national paradigm shift had occurred, and VR programs serving people with significant disabilities began organizing services around a new philosophy with strong convictions regarding an individual's right to employment, despite the severity of disabilities (Brooke, Inge, Armstrong, & Wehman, 1997).

In step with the national disability movement and linkage to VR programs, the SSA began making programmatic changes to reduce the existing disincentives to employment for beneficiaries with disabilities receiving SSI and/or SSDI. Recognizing these disincentives to employment and eager to assist individuals with disabilities, the SSA instituted a series of reforms and incentives to support individuals with disabilities who wanted to test their ability to work without immediately risking their SSA benefits. Yet, despite the SSA's best attempts, many of these new work incentives programs went underutilized for several years by SSI and SSDI beneficiaries for a variety of reasons (O'Mara & Kregel, 1996).

In 1994, the SSA published a report titled *Developing a World-Class Employment Strategy for People with Disabilities* in which it acknowledged some of the most significant barriers to employment inherent to the Social Security system. Topping the list was the SSA's identification of its own ineffective infrastructure in place to steer beneficiaries toward employment through the utilization of work incentives. The SSA projected that the only step it was taking at the time was to refer a small percentage of beneficiaries, approximately 10%, to the public VR at the same time that they were notified of the SSA's disability decision.

The following sections of this chapter describe how times have changed for the SSA beneficiaries with disabilities. New legislation has been enacted by Congress that has the intended purpose of providing employment support provisions to beneficiaries and is designed to provide the critical assistance necessary to support movement further away from benefit dependency and toward independence. Essentially, these employment supports are in place to provide support with entering or reentering the work force by protecting eligibility for cash payments and/or health care until beneficiaries achieve their goal of independence. This chapter describes these changes and provides specific information on 1) the SSA's most recent legislation promoting employment, 2) the existing menu of SSI and SSDI work incentives, and 3) case study illustrations of how SSA work incentives have helped beneficiaries interested in obtaining and maintaining competitive employment.

TICKET TO WORK AND WORK INCENTIVES IMPROVEMENT ACT

The Ticket to Work and Work Incentives Improvement Act (TWWIIA) of 1999 (PL 106-170) was designed to substantially expand work opportunities for people with disabilities. In general, the Ticket to Work program is intended to increase beneficiary choice, remove barriers, and provide greater opportunities for people with disabilities to participate in the work force and lessen their dependency on public benefits. Many of the specific provisions of the act have been rolled out slowly across the country, with individual regions becoming effective at different times. Table 17.1 highlights key provisions of the law and provides a brief description of the various programs that apply to beneficiaries receiving SSI and SSDI.

Table 17.1. Key provisions of the Ticket to Work and Work Incentive Improvement Act of 1999 (PL 106-170)

Legislative provision	Description of provision
Ticket to work and self-sufficiency program	This program provides a ticket to a beneficiary with disabilities who is older than the age of 18 and receives Supplemental Security Income (SSI) and/or Social Security Disability Insurance (SSDI) to take to a certified provider of his or her choice for rehabilitation and employment services.
Expedited benefits	This work incentive is called Expedited Reinstatement (EXR). EXR is a way to easily return to Social Security disability benefits when work is significantly reduced or stopped because of an individual's original disabling condition. EXR also permits individuals to receive provisional payments while the EXR request is being processed.
Expansion of Medicare	This work incentive is called Extended Period of Medicare Coverage (EPMC). EPMC helps working beneficiaries with disabilities by extending the amount of time beneficiaries who lose entitlement because of substantial work may receive premium-free Part A and premium-based Part B Medicare. This new rule applies to anyone who currently has Medicare coverage based on disability benefits, provided that the disabling condition continues, and allows coverage to continue for at least 93 months after the trial work period (TWP) ends.
Expansion of Medicaid	Individual states have the option to expand Medicaid coverage to working SSI and SSDI beneficiaries with disabilities, using income and resource limits set by the state.
Postponed disability	A beneficiary using a ticket will not have to undergo the regularly scheduled Continuing Disability Review (CDR) that may have been triggered by earnings.
Employment support representatives	SSA established a new administrative office known as the Office of Employment Support and has further set up additional employment support representatives across the SSA field office known as area work incentives coordinators (AWICs) and work incentive liaisons (WILs).
Benefits planning and assistance	SSA has established community-based benefits planning and assistance programs called Benefits Planning, Assistance, and Outreach (BPAO) programs. The BPAO programs are designed to provide accurate information on work incentives to SSA beneficiaries. These programs were established through 117 cooperative agreements to every state, territory, and the District of Columbia to provide benefits counseling and assistance and conduct ongoing outreach efforts to inform beneficiaries of available work incentives.
Protection and advocacy	SSA established a network of grant programs for protection and advocacy (P & A) agencies in each state, territory, and the District of Columbia to assist beneficiaries.
Demonstration projects and studies	In this report, the Ticket to Work and Work Incentives Advisory Panel (the Panel) provides advice to the Commissioner of Social Security on the most effective designs for demonstrations and other research associated with a proposal for a $1-for-$2 benefits offset under the SSDI program. The $1-for-$2 benefit offset is intended to eliminate the "cash cliff" associated with the SSDI program, thereby encouraging work and providing savings to the trust fund. A demonstration is authorized in Section 302 of the Ticket to Work and Work Incentives Improvement Act of 1999 (PL 106-170). The act requires the Commissioner to conduct demonstration projects and compile other data to evaluate the $1-for-$2 proposal. It also requires the Commissioner to take into account the advice of the Panel (Title III, Section 302 [b] [1]).

Adapted from Social Security Administration. (2001). *A desktop guide to the Ticket to Work and Work Incentives Improvement Act of 1999.* Baltimore: Author.

The regulations implementing the Ticket to Work program were published in the *Federal Register* on December 28, 2001, and they became effective 30 days after that date. The SSA began to distribute tickets to eligible beneficiaries in the first 13 states in early 2002, once the regulations went into effect, with 20 additional states receiving tickets in November 2002, and the final 17 states rolling out in November 2003. Once the national roll out was completed, most SSDI and SSI recipients with disabilities between the ages of 18 and 64 received a ticket. It is important to understand that this program is voluntary. If recipients choose not to participate in the program, their decision will not affect their SSA benefits. The SSA beneficiaries who choose to use their ticket can receive employment services, VR services, or other support services from organizations called *employment networks*. An employment network can be a private organization or government agency that has agreed to work with the SSA and has formally been approved to provide employment services to ticket holders.

One of the major disincentives to employment that the ticket removed was the need to fill out a new application to reinstate benefits, including Medicare and Medicaid. For the first time, beneficiaries who want to test their ability to work without having to go through the arduous SSA application process if their work attempt fails will be able to easily return to SSA benefits, not only when work stops, but also when work is significantly reduced due to the individuals' original disabling conditions. This Expedited Reinstatement (EXR) incentive will also permit a person to receive provisional payments, as well as Medicare and Medicaid, for up to 6 months while his or her case is being reviewed. If the individual is not found to be "disabled," then these benefits are not considered an overpayment and, therefore, do not have to be repaid to the SSA.

The second disincentive to employment that the ticket has made provision for is the potential loss of medical benefits. The potential risk of losing medical benefits stops individuals with disabilities from pursuing careers of their choice. The ticket addresses this beneficiary concern with a work incentive called the Extended Period of Medicare Coverage (EPMC). This provision helps by extending the amount of time beneficiaries who lose entitlement because of substantial work may receive premium-free Part A and premium-based Part B Medicare. Furthermore, individual states have the option to expand Medicaid coverage to working SSI and SSDI beneficiaries with disabilities using income and resource limits set by the state where the beneficiaries are living.

The SSA recognized that many of its work incentive programs were complex, and in order for large numbers of beneficiaries to gain access to employment, the SSA would have to do a better job of ensuring that accurate work incentive information was getting into the hands of beneficiaries. After years of underutilization of work incentives, the SSA understood that beneficiaries would need detailed information about how work would affect their individual SSA benefits as well as other federal benefit programs such as food stamps, housing, worker's compensation, and veteran's benefits. The Ticket to Work legislation provided for this concern by establishing community-based benefits planning assistance and outreach programs (BPAOs) across the country to fill this needed service. These new BPAOs provide free benefits counseling to all SSA disability beneficiaries, giving accurate information on how work can affect benefits, including information about protection and advocacy, and ultimately giving all beneficiaries greater choice. In addition to this community-based resource, the law also provides for the SSA to establish a core of work incentive specialists within SSA offices to provide timely and accurate information regarding the array of the SSA's employment support programs for beneficiaries with disabilities who want to work.

MAJOR SOCIAL SECURITY ADMINISTRATION EMPLOYMENT SUPPORTS AND THEIR IMPACT ON EMPLOYMENT

When an SSA beneficiary is considering employment, there are multiple questions and concerns that must be addressed prior to actively searching for employment. As stated previously in the chapter, the SSA has had multiple work incentive programs that have remained underutilized for many years. Key to increasing the utilization of these programs is to demonstrate how the application of these employment supports can personally affect a beneficiary. The first step in understanding the SSA employment supports is being able to distinguish between the SSA's two major programs administering to beneficiaries with disabilities. The eligibility criteria for these two programs are highlighted in Table 17.2.

Table 17.2.   Major Social Security Administration (SSA) programs serving beneficiaries with disabilities

---

Title XVI: Supplemental Security Income (SSI)

To be eligible for SSI based on a medical condition, the individual must

- Have limited income and resources
- Be a U.S. citizen or meet the requirements for noncitizens
- Be considered medically disabled or blind
- Be a resident of the 50 states, the District of Columbia, or Northern Mariana Islands
- File an application
- File for any and all other benefits for which he or she is eligible
- Not be working or working but not performing substantial gainful activity (SGA) when he or she applies *if his or her impairment is other than blindness*

Title II: Social Security Disability Insurance (SSDI)

The worker must

- Have worked and paid Social Security taxes for enough years to be covered under Social Security insurance
- Have paid some of the taxes in recent years

The worker, the worker's widow(er), or the worker's disabled adult child (requirements for a disabled adult child include the individual must be unmarried, age 18 or over, and his or her disability must have begun before age 22) must

- File an application
- Meet Social Security's definition of medically disabled
- Not be working or working but not performing SGA

Source: SSA (2004a).

By quickly looking over the information in the table, it becomes apparent that these two programs are very different. The SSI program, sometimes referred to as Title XVI, is a strictly needs-based program, providing people with disabilities with a minimum level of resources. This program stands in stark contrast to SSDI, often called Title II, in which eligibility is based on working and the number of quarters of paying into the SSA system. An individual can be a beneficiary of both programs at the same time. Because of the inherent difference in these two programs, there are unique employment supports that are specific to each program. A list of employment supports is presented in Table 17.3 and is organized based on Title XVI or Title II.

Table 17.3.   Social Security Administration (SSA) employment supports

Supplemental Security Income (SSI) employment supports

1619(a)—Special SSI payments an individual receives when he or she is working and earning more than substantial gainful activity (SGA)

1619(b)—A provision that allows SSI recipients to continue Medicaid coverage, even if their earnings, along with their other income, become too high for an SSI cash payment. There are specific requirements that must be met in order to receive this benefit.

Blind Work Expense (BWE)—The deduction of expenses that an individual has that are necessary in order for the individual to work but do not need to be related to the individual's blindness

Impairment-Related Work Expense (IRWE)—The deduction of expenses that an individual has that are necessary in order to work and due to their disability

Plan for Achieving Self-Support (PASS)—A work incentive available to SSI recipients that allows them to set aside income and/or resources over a reasonable time that will enable them to reach a vocational goal to become financially self-supporting

Student Earned Income Exclusion (SEIE)—A work incentive stating that, if an individual is younger than age 22 and regularly attends school, the Social Security Administration will not count a set amount of earned income per month when determining the individual's SSI payment amount

Social Security Disability Insurance (SSDI) employment supports

Expedited Reinstatement of Benefits (EXR)—The ability to request a reinstatement of benefits within 5 years after benefits have stopped without having to file a new application. Up to 6 months of provisional benefits are available while the Social Security Administration is making a decision on the request.

Extended Period of Eligibility (EPE)—Time period of 36 months following the trial work period (TWP) when an individual may receive cash benefits any time his or her earnings drop below SGA without filing a new application

Impairment Related Work Expense (IRWE)—The deduction of expenses that an individual has that are necessary in order to work and due to his or her disability

Subsidies and special conditions—Supports an individual receives on the job that may result in more pay than the actual value of the work he or she performs

Trial Work Period (TWP)—A time period that allows an individual to test his or her ability to work or run a business for at least 9 months and receive full SSDI benefits no matter how high his or her earnings reach

Unsuccessful Work Attempt (UWA)—An effort to perform substantial work (in employment or self-employment) that was stopped or reduced to below the SGA level after a short time (6 months or less) due to the individual's disability

Adapted from Social Security Administration. (2004a). *2004 red book*. Baltimore: Author.

WORK INCENTIVES AVAILABLE
FOR RECIPIENTS/BENEFICIARIES OF TITLE XVI

In order for beneficiaries and recipients of SSA benefits to go back to work, they need to understand the ramifications of how work will affect those benefits and all of the work incentives that are available to recipients of each program. As stated previously, it is unfortunate that in the past the work incentives that are available to beneficiaries have been highly underutilized. If an individual fully understands the incentives and chooses to return to work with the support of these incentives, then he or she can make the transition to greater independence a much smoother process.

General and Earned Income Exclusions

When the SSA looks at an individual's income to determine the amount of SSI the beneficiary will qualify to receive, it looks at both earned and unearned income. *Earned income* is income that is obtained as a result of wages from a job. *Unearned income* is considered by the SSA as money received, such as private pensions and annuities, periodic public payments, life insurance proceeds, gifts and inheritance, support and alimony, SSA Title II benefits, workers compensation, and unemployment benefits (Sheldon, 1994).

Although the source and amount of all earned income must be determined, not all income counts when determining SSI eligibility and payment amount. The General Income Exclusion allows the first $20 of income an individual receives to be excluded from the equation when determining eligibility and payment amount. This $20 is taken first from any unearned income the individual receives. If the individual has no unearned income, then it is deducted from any earned income. If the individual has earned income, then the beneficiary can exclude the first $65 of that income. This is referred to as the Earned Income Exclusion. When the SSA is determining an individual's benefit amount, it excludes this money first before beginning the calculation. The SSA then takes the remaining amount and divides it in half. The remaining amount is considered to be the individual's countable income. This is commonly referred to by the SSA as the *1 for 2 reduction*. In addition to these two exclusions, there are several work incentives that individuals can utilize to assist them in becoming gainfully employed and slowly reducing their dependence on SSA benefits.

1619(a) and (b)

As an SSI recipient begins working and earning increasingly more money, two other provisions come into play. When the individual begins working at Substantial Gainful Activity (SGA) level ($860 per month in 2006), his or her SSI benefits are protected by 1619(a). The individual will continue to receive a cash benefit when he or she earns more than SGA through 1619(a) until he or she reaches the point at which his or her earnings decrease his or her check to zero. This is known as the *break-even point*. At this point, Medicaid benefits are protected by 1619(b). Although the individual will no longer receive a cash benefit, he or she will still be entitled to Medicaid eligibility, providing the individual still meets all other SSI eligibility requirements such as disability and resource tests. In addition, the individual must demonstrate a need for Medicaid in order to work. The 1619(b) provision will protect the individual's

Medicaid benefits, given he or she continues to meet all the SSI eligibility require-ments up until the recipient's earnings exceed his or her state's threshold amount. Each state's threshold amount varies and can be as low as $14,000 to as high as $45,000 per year (in 2005; Tremblay, Smith, Xie, & Drake, 2004).

Student Earned Income Exclusion

Student Earned Income Exclusion (SEIE) is a work incentive available to SSI recipi-ents who are younger than age 22 and regularly attend school. Individuals who meet these requirements can exclude up to $1,460 per month and a maximum of up to $5,910 per year (in 2006; O'Mara & Ferrell, 2003). Since the passing of the TWWIIA, these figures have been adjusted on an annual basis. This exclusion is ap-plied only to earned income, so it may only be used in months in which the eligible student is actively working and earning a wage. This work incentive can be used up until the annual amount is exhausted or until the student is 22 years of age.

One of the key pieces of information to understand with this incentive is the SSA's definition of *regularly attending school*. According to the SSA, an individual is reg-ularly attending school if he or she meets the following criteria:

- In a college or university for at least 8 hours per week

- In grades 7–12 for at least 12 hours per week

- In a training course to prepare for employment for at least 12 hours per week (15 hours per week if the course involves shop practice)

- In a training program for less time than indicated for reasons beyond the student's control (e.g., illness; Sheldon, 1994)

If the student is being home-schooled because of a disability, then he or she may be considered regularly attending school by

- Studying a course or courses given by a school (grades 7–12), college, university, or government agency

- Having a home visitor or tutor who directs the study

It is important to note that when determining the amount of the student's SSI bene-fit, the SSA will apply the SEIE before the General Income Exclusion or the Earned Income Exclusion, thus producing a greater financial benefit for the beneficiary.

Impairment-Related Work Expense

The SSA deducts the expenses of certain impairment-related services and items that an individual needs in order to work when determining the amount of an individual's countable earnings. These costs are called Impairment-Related Work Expenses (IRWE), and the SSA deducts these expenses when:

- The item or service enables the individual to work

- The individual needs the item or service because of his or her disabling condition

- The individual paid the cost out of his or her own pocket and is not reimbursed by another source (e.g., Medicare, Medicaid, private insurance)

- The cost is "reasonable," meaning it represents the standard charge for the item or service in a given community

- The individual paid the expense during a month in which he or she was working

In addition, SSI beneficiaries must have paid the expense during a month that he or she received earned income or performed work while he or she used the impairment-related item or service (SSA, 2004a).

The purpose of the IRWE provision is to enable recipients of SSI to recover some of the costs of work-related expenses. When determining the monthly SSI payment, the dollar amount of the IRWE is subtracted from the individual's income. By reducing the total countable earnings, the IRWE results in an increase in the SSI benefit. This increase in benefit allows the individual to recover some of the cost of the expense. SSI recipients can generally recover up to half of the cost of the IRWE through an increase in their SSI.

There are many items and services that would qualify as IRWE. It is important to remember that this is a very individualized work incentive. What may be considered an IRWE for one individual may not be allowed for another person. The SSA gives general guidelines for what is allowed and not allowed as IRWEs, but the ultimate decision is left up to the local claims representative.

The SSA's list of allowable expenses under the IRWE work incentive is extensive and includes such things as attendant care services, transportation expenses, medical support devices, work equipment and modifications, and routine drugs and medical services. With regard to attendant care services, deductible services include services performed in the work setting as well as services performed in the process of assisting the person going to and returning from work, such as bathing, dressing, cooking, and eating. Services that incidentally benefit the family, such as cooking a meal that is also eaten by the family, and services that are performed by a family member for a cash fee in which the family member suffers an economic loss by reducing or terminating employment in order to be able to provide the service are allowable. When considering an IRWE for routine drugs and routine medical services, the types of things that would be deductible include regularly prescribed medical treatment or therapy that is necessary for individuals who experience a seizure disorder.

It is important to remember that because of the IRWE criteria, these expenses are not allowable as IRWE in every instance. In some cases, it may be beneficial to go into the local SSA office to meet with the claims representative to clarify why the individual needs an identified support or service to work. It may assist the claims representative in understanding the full scope of the individual's limitations and why the specific item is needed in order to work.

Blind Work Expense

The Blind Work Expense (BWE) may be utilized for SSI recipients who are working and have a primary diagnosis of blindness. This work incentive allows recipients who are blind to exclude all work expenses that are attributable to the earning of income (SSA, 2004b). It is important to understand that items to be deducted as a BWE do not have to be related to the recipient's blindness (SSA, 2004a). This is the primary difference between a BWE and an IRWE. Another distinction between these two work incentives is the manner in which the SSA figures the BWE into its calculation to determine the recipient's SSI benefit. This calculation is done in such a manner that it allows a beneficiary to receive a higher SSI payment by utilizing a BWE rather than an IRWE.

As with IRWEs, BWEs must be approved by the SSA, and the recipient must pay for the item, service, or support with his or her own income and not be reimbursed by anyone else. The cost must be reasonable, and the recipient will need to keep receipts for all expenses (SSA, 2004b). The SSA has an extensive list of allowable items under the BWE provision, including taxes (federal, state, and local); transportation costs to and from work; guide dogs (including dog food, licenses, and veterinary expenses); meals eaten during work hours; mandatory pension contributions; and drugs and medical services that are essential to enable individuals to work (SSA, 2004b).

Some of the BWE expenses can potentially meet the criteria to be considered as an IRWE (SSA, 2004b). In this case, an individual who receives both SSI as well as Title II benefits could use the expense as a BWE for SSI and as an IRWE for SSDI. If the individual only receives SSI, then it would be best to utilize the cost as a BWE. As a BWE with SSI, the individual will be able to exclude the full amount of the expense as opposed to just half of the cost if it was used as an IRWE.

Plan for Achieving Self-Support

One of the most powerful tools an SSI recipient can utilize is the SSA work incentive called the Plan for Achieving Self-Support (PASS). This work incentive allows an individual to set aside income and/or resources to achieve a specific vocational goal (Miller & Brooke, 2002a). In order to write and utilize a PASS, an individual must have a feasible occupational goal and money other than an SSI check to set aside, as well as a list of anticipated expenses (Miller & Brooke, 2002b). When determining an individual's SSI benefit, the SSA completely excludes income and resources set aside in a PASS plan for the duration of the plan.

The SSA has many requirements for a PASS. The plan must be individualized so that it is designed specifically for the individual for whom it is written. It must increase the person's self-sufficiency and ultimately reduce the recipient's dependence on SSA benefits. The plan must have a feasible and reasonable work goal. It must include very specific steps and milestones, and each of these must have an associated time frame for accomplishment. Furthermore, there must be a clear time frame for completion of the plan.

The individual must show specifically the resources and income that will be used for the expenses associated with the steps to achieve the goal. The individual must provide explanation of the expenditures to be covered by the resources and income that is set aside. The SSA requires for the plan to be in writing on form No. SSA-545. The individual must show how the specified income and/or resources will be set aside from other funds. Finally, the plan must be approved by the SSA and periodically reviewed by the SSA to check for compliance (Miller & Brooke, 2002a).

TWWIIA has helped increase the utilization of PASS plans. Prior to the establishment of BPAO projects and benefits planners, few recipients knew of the benefits of PASS plans. Those who had heard of this work incentive typically had a limited knowledge of how to utilize this important benefit. Too often, individuals found out that there was a 14-page form that had to be completed in order to get approval, and that was enough to scare recipients out of attempting to utilize the incentive. Now that there are teams of highly trained benefits planners available across the country to assist in writing and completing the PASS plan form, states are seeing an increase in the utilization of this powerful tool.

WORK INCENTIVES AVAILABLE
FOR RECIPIENTS/BENEFICIARIES OF TITLE II

Trial Work Period

Unless medical recovery is expected, individuals who receive Title II benefits are entitled to a trial work period (TWP). The TWP provides the beneficiary the opportunity to test his or her work skills while maintaining his or her full Title II benefit check regardless of how much he or she earns (O'Mara, 2003). An individual's TWP begins the first month that he or she is entitled to Title II benefits or files an application for benefits, whichever is the later of the two. In order for a month of work to count as a trial work month, the individual must earn more than $620 (in 2006). Due to the recent TWWIIA rules, annual increases will apply to the amount of earnings that can count as a TWP month.

An individual's TWP only ends if he or she has performed 9 months of trial work within a rolling period of 60 consecutive months. This time frame must be closely tracked because, immediately following the ninth month of trial work, the extended period of eligibility (EPE) begins.

Extended Period of Eligibility

Once an individual has completed his or her TWP, his or her EPE begins. During this time frame of 36 consecutive months, the SSA looks at the individual's ability to perform SGA ($860 per month in 2006; O'Mara, 2003). The individual's ability or inability to perform SGA will determine whether he or she receives a cash benefit each month.

The first month of the EPE in which an individual earns more than SGA is his or her *cessation month*. During the cessation month and the next 2 months (known as the *grace period*), the individual will receive a cash benefit no matter how high his or her earnings. Following the cessation month and grace period, for the duration of the EPE, any month in which the individual earns more than SGA, he or she will not receive a cash benefit. Any month in which the individual earns under SGA following the cessation month and grace period during the EPE, he or she will receive a cash benefit. In those months during the EPE that the individual does not receive a cash benefit, his or her case still remains open with the SSA, and he or she is still covered by Medicare benefits (O'Mara, 2003).

After the EPE has ended, the first month an individual earns more than SGA, his or her benefit eligibility ends and his or her case is closed by the SSA. In order to receive further benefits, the individual has to either file a new application or request expedited reinstatement of benefits.

Unsuccessful Work Attempt

An unsuccessful work attempt (UWA) is an attempt by the beneficiary to work at a substantial level that is either stopped or reduced below SGA after only a short period of time (no more than 6 months). In order to qualify for UWA, the reduction or stopping of work must be due to the individual's disability or because special circumstances that are required for the beneficiary to work at a substantial level have ended. For example, if an individual needs a job coach in order to perform the job and no longer has the coach, then this would qualify as a special condition.

Subsidies and Special Conditions

In some situations, a person's disability will result in him or her needing extra assistance, a reduced production rate, frequent breaks, or fewer job duties than are assigned to his or her co-workers performing the same job. When this occurs, the individual's income represents pay for his or her own work as well as direct assistance from his or her supervisor or co-worker or higher pay for lower production. When the SSA is determining an individual's ability to work at SGA, this type of situation needs to be evaluated. Because the SSA is only concerned with the individual's earning potential, the extra assistance or special conditions (i.e., subsidies) related to the individual's work need to be deducted from his or her income (Miller & Brooke, 2002b).

Subsidy, like most of the SSA work incentives, is very individualized. The SSA looks at each case and situation independently to see what assistance and accommodations are being utilized. Some examples of subsidies include assistance from a co-worker to perform required tasks of the job; adjustment of the work schedule to accommodate additional breaks; delayed start time of work schedule; abbreviated work day; reassignment of certain job duties to other staff members; and use of a job coach to assist with learning and performing job duties.

Impairment-Related Work Expenses

When an individual receives Title II benefits, he or she is eligible to use the IRWE work incentive. The difference with Title II benefits and Title XVI benefits is how the SSA considers the IRWE when determining the individual's benefits. With Title II benefits, the SSA deducts the amount of the IRWE from the individual's gross monthly earnings. These costs are called IRWEs. The SSA deducts these expenses when they meet the same five criterion that was presented previously for beneficiaries of SSI: 1) the item or service enables the individual to work; 2) the individual needs the item or service because of a disabling condition; 3) the individual paid the cost out of his or her own pocket and was not reimbursed by another source, 4) the cost is "reasonable," and 5) the individual paid the expense during a month that he or she was working.

It is important to remember that there are many items and services that would qualify as an IRWE because this particular SSA work incentive is highly individualized. In cases in which the beneficiary has any question as what may qualify as a work incentive, it will be helpful to make a visit to the local SSA office to personally meet with a claims representative to clarify why the individual needs an identified support or service to work. It may assist the claims representative in understanding the full scope of the individual's limitations and why the specific item is needed in order to work.

Expedited Reinstatement of Benefits

In January 2001, a new work incentive called EXR of benefits was signed into law. This provision is a way for beneficiaries of Title II to return more easily to SSA benefits when their work is reduced or stopped due to their original disabling condition. In order to qualify for EXR, an individual must meet all of the necessary criteria. Beneficiaries must

- Have been eligible for an SSA disability benefit
- Have lost their disability benefit due to the performance of SGA
- Request reinstatement within 60 months of the last month of entitlement

- Have the same (or related) disability that was the basis for their original claim
- Have a disability that is determined to make them incapable of SGA-level work. (*Note:* A medical review standard that is less stringent than the initial eligibility criteria is applied with EXR)

If the individual meets all of the previous criteria, then his or her benefits will be reinstated. This means that he or she does not have to go through the initial application process again. While he or she is waiting for the EXR request to be processed, he or she may receive up to 6 consecutive months of provisional benefits and health insurance under Medicare. In addition, after the individual has been paid 24 months of reinstated benefits, he or she will receive a new TWP and EPE, as well as another 60-month period to request EXR if his or her benefits are lost due to SGA-level work (O'Mara, 2003).

SARAH

Sarah is 20 years old and not married. She is a student at the local community college and receives a full SSI check in the amount of $603. In January 2006, she began working answering telephones at an area staffing agency. She will be earning $600 per month from her new job. In order to determine her SSI check for this month, the SSA will use the following formula:

$600.00 (gross earnings)
$\underline{- \$600.00}$ (SEIE)
0 (countable earnings)
$603.00 (federal benefit rate for 2006)
$\underline{- \$0}$ (countable earnings)
$603.00 (SSI check)

The first month Sarah works, she will receive $600 in earnings from her job as well as an SSI check for $603. This gives her $1,203 of usable income for this month. If Sarah continues to earn $600 per month, then she will be able to use the SEIE for the next 9 months. By the end of September 2006, she will have used a total of $5,400 in SEIEs. If, in October 2006, she is still working and is still earning $600 per month, then she will only be able to exclude $270 of her earnings because the SSA only allows a beneficiary to exclude up to a certain amount of earnings per year using the SEIE (in 2006, that figure is $5,910). The formula to determine her SSI check for September is as follows:

$600.00 (gross earnings)
$\underline{- 510.00}$ (remaining amount of SEIE)
$90.00
$\underline{- 20.00}$ (general income exclusion)
$70.00
$\underline{- 65.00}$ (earned income exclusion)
$5.00

$5.00/2 = $2.50 (countable income)

$603.00 (federal benefit rate for 2006)
$\underline{- 2.50}$ (total countable income)
$600.50 (adjusted SSI check)

According to the formula, Sarah will receive an SSI check in the amount of $600.50 for September 2006. Here, it is easy to see how powerful the SEIE is to a beneficiary as he or she works to gain economic self-sufficiency.

ALYSSA

Alyssa is 21, a senior in high school, and plans to become a licensed practical nurse someday. To do this, she will need to finish getting her diploma, apply to nursing school, get accepted, go through 2 years of schooling, and earn her associate degree. Alyssa then will have to pass a state test to get certified, get a job as a nurse, and complete the probationary period before becoming a permanent employee. She projects this will all take her about 5 years because she plans to go to school part time and work part time. Alyssa currently receives SSI ($603 per month) and works part time in the hospital cafeteria. She has been using the SEIE, but this will end this summer when she reaches her twenty-second birthday.

Alyssa enrolled with the public VR program and, based on her plan, VR has agreed to help her with her school expenses (after she applies for a PELL grant). Alyssa, however, needs to buy a car to get back and forth to classes, which are 20 miles from her home. A car is her only alternative because there is no public transportation to and from the university.

Alyssa wrote a PASS (with her teacher's help) to use the money from her job at the hospital to pay $300 monthly car payments for the next 3 years. Her SSI check would be determined as follows:

$700.00 (wages from her job)
$-\underline{20.00}$ (general income exclusion)
$680.00 (remainder)
$-\underline{65.00}$ (earned income exclusion)

$615.00/2 = $307.50 (countable income)

$307.50
$-\underline{300.00}$ (PASS amount: car payment)
$7.50 (total countable income)

$603.00 (federal benefit rate for 2006)
$-\underline{7.50}$ (total countable income)
$595.50 (SSI check)

When Alyssa meets her career goal of becoming a permanent employee as a licensed practical nurse, the PASS will end. At that point, she will probably be making more than $24,000 per year if she is working full time. At this earnings level, she would lose her SSI check but may continue to get her Medicaid, depending on which state she resides in (Ferrell, Brooke, Kregel, & Getzel, 2002).

JULIAN

Julian is a Title II beneficiary (SSDI) and has been working for 1 year as a host at a local restaurant. He works full time and earns $6 per hour for a total of $1,008 per month. He has completed his TWP and is being reviewed by the SSA for SGA determination. During the Continuing Disability Review, the SSA requests information as to whether a subsidy might exist for Julian. Julian's employer determined that a subsidy did exist by reviewing Julian's work in terms of time, skills, and job responsibilities when compared with the work of the other hosts he employs. Of the 10 job duties the hosts perform, Julian only performs 7. Therefore, using this calculation, it could be said that Julian is 30% less efficient than his fellow hosts.

To determine how much of Julian's gross income should be considered when determining SGA, the SSA uses the following information and formula:

$1,008.00 (gross monthly earnings before subsidy is applied)
– $302.00 (subsidy, or 30% of gross earnings)
$706.00 (total monthly gross earnings counted toward SGA)

Because Julian's total monthly gross earnings after applying the subsidy are less than SGA ($860 in 2006), the SSA would determine that he is not earning SGA, and he would begin his EPE. It is also important to note that, although the subsidy exists for Julian in terms of SSA regulations, his employer is extremely pleased with his work performance and does not consider it a "subsidy." Julian can be counted on to come to work each day and is always friendly and happy to serve the customers.

STEVEN

Steven is receiving $625 per month in Title II benefits (SSDI). He starts working as a mechanic's helper and earns $950 gross wages per month. Because his earnings are greater than SGA ($860 in 2006), he will lose his SSA benefits when he completes his TWP. If, however, Steven utilizes an IRWE for the specialized transportation that he has hired to take him to and from work for a total of $150 per month, his countable income will fall below SGA. Once the IRWE is implemented, then Steven will be able to keep his SSA benefits. The following shows how Steven's benefit will be calculated:

$950.00 (gross monthly earnings)
– $150.00 (IRWE amount for specialized transportation)
$800.00 (adjusted gross earnings)

CONCLUSION

In reviewing these case studies, it quickly becomes apparent that these individuals are better off working and using the SSA work incentives than they would have been to just stay on benefits and not attempt to work. There are many community professionals who are telling beneficiaries with disabilities to either not attempt work or to keep the number of hours employed at an artificially low level. In all cases, beneficiaries should locate the benefits planner identified for their community and set up a time to sit down with this individual to determine how employment will affect benefits in their particular case. A highly trained benefits planner will consider the vast array of work incentives that are presented in this chapter to help the beneficiary make a thoughtful consideration regarding the impact of employment. Effective use of community benefits planners and SSA work incentives may finally bring down a long-standing barrier to employment success for people with disabilities.

REFERENCES

Bates, P., Renzaglia, A., & Clees, T. (1980). Improving the work performance of severely/profoundly retarded young adults: The use of changing criterion procedure design. *Education and Training of Mentally Retarded, 15*(2), 95–106.

Brooke, V., Inge, K., Armstrong, A., & Wehman, P. (Eds.). (1997). *Supported employment handbook: A customer-driven approach for persons with significant disabilities.* Richmond: Virginia Commonwealth University Rehabilitation Research and Training Center on Workplace Supports and Job Retention.

Ferrell, C., Brooke, V., Kregel, J., & Getzel, E. (Eds.). (2002). *Get a job! How employment affects your supplemental security income and Medicaid benefits.* Richmond: Virginia Commonwealth University, Benefits Assistance Resource Center.

Miller, L., & Brooke, V. (Eds.). (2002a). *Plan for Achieving Self-Support.* Richmond: Virginia Commonwealth University, Benefits Assistance Resource Center.

Miller, L., & Brooke, V. (Eds.). (2002b). *Subsidy and special conditions.* Richmond: Virginia Commonwealth University, Benefits Assistance Resource Center.

O'Mara, S. (2003). *Understanding Social Security disability benefits.* Richmond: Virginia Commonwealth University, Benefits Assistance Resource Center.

O'Mara, S., & Ferrell, C. (2003). *Student earned income exclusion* (Fact sheet). Richmond: Virginia Commonwealth University, Benefits Assistance Resource Center.

O'Mara, S., & Kregel, J. (1996). Social Security. In P. McLaughlin, & P. Wehman (Eds.), *Mental retardation and developmental disabilities* (pp. 371–382). Austin, TX: PRO-ED.

Popick, B. (1967, May/June). Social Security and rehabilitation on the move. *Journal of Rehabilitation,* 10–12.

Rusch, F.R., & Mithaug, D.E. (1980). *Vocational training for mentally retarded adults.* Champaign, IL: Research Press.

Rusch, F.R., & Schutz, R.P. (1979). Nonsheltered employment of the mentally retarded adult: Research to reality? *Journal of Contemporary Business, 8,* 85–98.

Sheldon, J. (1994). *Work incentive for persons with disabilities under the Social Security and SSI programs.* Chicago: Clearinghouse Review.

Social Security Act of 1935, PL 74-271, 42 U.S.C. §§ 301 *et seq.*

Social Security Act Amendments of 1965, PL 89-97, 42 U.S.C. §§ 101 *et seq.*

Social Security Administration. (1994, September). *Developing a world-class employment strategy for people with disabilities.* Washington: DC: Author.

Social Security Administration. (2001). *A desktop guide to the Ticket to Work and Work Incentives Improvement Act of 1999.* Baltimore: Author.

Social Security Administration. (2003, June). *Latest facts and figures publication. Social Security Enews* [Electronic newsletter].

Social Security Administration. (2004a). *2004 red book.* Baltimore: Author.

Social Security Administration. (2004b). *Program operations manual system.* Baltimore: Author.

Sowers, J., Thompson, L., & Connis, R. (1979). The food service vocational training program: A model for training and placement of the mentally retarded. In G.T. Bellamy, G. O'Connor, & O.C. Karan (Eds.), *Vocational rehabilitation of the severely handicapped persons: Contemporary service strategies* (pp. 181–205). Baltimore: University Park Press.

Ticket to Work and Work Incentives Improvement Act (TWWIIA) of 1999, PL 106-170, 42 U.S.C. §§ 1305 *et seq.*

Tremblay, T., Smith, J., Xie, H., & Drake, R. (2004). *Impact of specialty benefits counseling on SSA.* Baltimore: Social Security Administration.

Wehman, P., Hill, J., & Koehler, F. (1979). Helping severely handicapped persons enter competitive employment. *AAESPH Review, 4*(3), 274–290.

Wehman, P., & Hill, M. (1980). Employer and nonhandicapped coworkers' perceptions of moderately and severely retarded workers. *Journal of Contemporary Business, 8*(4) 107–112.

Index

Page numbers followed by *f* indicate figures; those followed by *t* indicate tables.